Raising Freedom's Child

AMERICAN HISTORY AND CULTURE
General Editors: Neil Foley, Kevin Gaines,
Martha Hodes, and Scott Sandage

Raising Freedom's Child

Black Children and Visions of the Future after Slavery

Mary Niall Mitchell

NEW YORK UNIVERSITY PRESS
New York and London

M

NEW YORK UNIVERSITY PRESS
New York and London
www.nyupress.org

Library of Congress Cataloging-in-Publication Data
Mitchell, Mary Niall.
Raising freedom's child : Black children and visions of the future
after slavery / Mary Niall Mitchell.
p. cm. — (American history and culture)
Includes bibliographical references and index.
ISBN-13: 978-0-8147-5719-2 (cl : alk. paper)
ISBN-10: 0-8147-5719-7 (cl : alk. paper)
1. Freedmen—Education—Southern States. 2. African Americans—
Education—Southern States—History—19th century. 3. Education
—Economic aspects—Southern States. 4. Children, Black. I. Title.
LC2802.S9M58 2008
371.829'96073075—dc22   2007044349

New York University Press books are printed on acid-free paper,
and their binding materials are chosen for strength and durability.

Manufactured in the United States of America

10 9 8 7 6 5 4 3 2 1

For my family

Contents

Acknowledgments

Because historians rely on documents, we also depend upon the people who take care of them. I would like to thank archivists and librarians at the following institutions for their caretaking and assistance: Amistad Research Center, Tulane University; Dr. Charles Nolan and the staff at the Archives of the Archdiocese of New Orleans; Elmer Holmes Bobst Library and the Law Library, New York University; the Brooklyn Public Library; Marie Windell, Florence Jumonville, and the staff of Special Collections of Earl K. Long Library at the University of New Orleans; Leslie Rowland and the Freedom and Southern Society Project at the University of Maryland; Hill Memorial Library, Louisiana State University; the Historical Society of Delaware; the Historic New Orleans Collection and the Williams Research Center; Howard Tilton Memorial Library, Special Collections and the Law School Library of Tulane University; the Library of Congress; J. Edgar and Louise S. Monroe Library, Loyola University, New Orleans; the National Archives, Washington, D.C., and its Northeast, Southeast, and Southwest Regional Branches; the New Orleans Public Library and its Louisiana Collection; the New-York Historical Society; the Sisters of the Society of the Sacred Heart and their archives in St. Louis; the Sisters of the Holy Family in New Orleans; the Southern Historical Collection, the University of North Carolina, Chapel Hill; Strozier Library, Florida State University; Special Collections, Temple University Libraries; the Virginia Historical Society; and the Cammie G. Henry Research Center, Watson Memorial Library, Northwestern State University of Louisiana.

The photographs and other images used in this book have been reproduced here with the help of a number of people who assisted with reproductions and permissions. Many thanks to staff members and archivists at the following: the Denver Public Library; the Historic New Orleans Collection; the Historical Society of Delaware; the Library Company of Philadelphia; the Massachusetts Historical Society; the

Metropolitan Museum of Art, New York; the Schomburg Center for Research in Black Culture and the New York Public Library; Penn Center, Inc.; Historical Collections and Labor Archives, Special Collections Library, the Pennsylvania State University; Rare Books and Special Collections, Harvey S. Firestone Library, Princeton University; the Philadelphia Museum of Art; the Southern Historical Collection at the University of North Carolina, Chapel Hill; Christopher Denismore at the Friends Historical Library, Swarthmore College; the Sophia Smith Collection at Smith College; the Virginia Historical Society; Yale University Art Gallery; and the Victoria and Albert Museum, London. Many thanks, as well, to Tony Seideman for sharing his private collection of *cartes-de-visite*. I am also grateful to Ryan Mattingly for his help with securing many of the permissions for this book, and to Sara McNamara, Despina Papazoglou Gimbel, and Martin Tulic for assistance in the manuscript's final stages.

Generous funding for this project, from its beginnings as a dissertation and its expansion into book manuscript, came from the Oscar Handlin Fellowship from the American Council of Learned Societies, the Harry Frank Guggenheim Foundation Dissertation Fellowship, the Littleton-Griswold Grant for Research in U.S. Legal History from the American Historical Association, the Department of History and the College of Liberal Arts at the University of New Orleans, the Department of History and the Graduate School of Arts and Sciences at New York University, and Margaret and William Mitchell.

I am indebted to all those who have read chapters and drafts of this manuscript. For his support, encouragement, and brilliant insight, I owe my friend and adviser Walter Johnson an enormous debt. Also thanks to Ada Ferrer, Martha Hodes, Robin Kelley, Julius Scott, and Rebecca Scott, whose suggestions, critiques, and support made this a far better book than it would have been. Any mistakes herein are mine alone.

This manuscript, while still unfinished, and many file boxes traveled with me during a two-month absence from New Orleans in 2005, following Hurricane Katrina. The book's final stages were not easy, given the vicissitudes of living and teaching for many months in a city full of dark, ruined neighborhoods, half emptied of its people. The strength of the citizens of New Orleans, in the aftermath of such a disaster, has made life here bearable.

Throughout, the support and patience of my editor, Deborah Gershenowitz, helped me to see the end of this project. Special thanks as well to Martha Hodes and Eric Zimmerman for wanting to see this book in print. Also thanks to the editors of this series and anonymous readers for this press; to anonymous readers and to the editors of the *History of Education Quarterly* and the *American Quarterly* (chapters 1 and 2 of this book appeared there, respectively, in earlier form); and to the prize committees for the Henry Barnard Prize from the History of Education Society, the Anita S. Goodwin Award for Junior Scholars in Women's History at Sewanee, and the Constance Rourke Prize from the American Studies Association. Audiences and their questions and comments at the following meetings and conferences greatly improved this manuscript, in particular: the American Historical Association; the Berkshire Conference on the History of Women; the Georgia Workshop in Early American History and Culture; the History of Education Society; the Louisiana Historical Association; the Organization of American Historians; the Society for the History of Childhood and Youth; the Southern Historical Association; the symposium "Society, Slavery, and the Civil War" at the University of Illinois at Springfield; and a joint conference "Haití—Revolución, Independencia, y Emancipación—La lucha contra la esclavitud," sponsored by the Harriet Tubman Resource Centre on the African Diaspora, the Comisión Costarricense de Cooperación de UNESCO, and the Universidad de Costa Rica.

Friends and colleagues have also read chapters and otherwise provided encouragement during the completion of this project, especially Rosanne Adderley, Ida Altman, Connie Atkinson, Kathleen Barry, Warren Billings, Günter Bischof, Joe Louis Caldwell, Raphael Cassimere, Erin Clune, Jean Cohen, John and Anna Ellis, Arnold Hirsch, Joseph Hawes, Daniel Horowitz, Peter Kaufman, Richard Kilbourne, James Marten, Stephen Mihm, Karl Miller, James Mokhiber, Ellen Noonan, John O'Connor, Chris O'Neill, Lynne Palazzi, Madelon Powers, Sherrie Sanders, Elisabeth Settimi, Dawn VanderVloed, Isabelle Wallace, Jeffrey Wilson, Sarah Wood, and Jonathan Zimmerman. For help with the French language, I thank Gayle Marks and Olivier Bourderionnet. Any poor translations are my own. The interest, energy, and determination of my students at the University of New Orleans also helped me to finish this book. Special thanks, as well, to Poul Lange, for designing a lovely cover for an unknown author.

My family has supported me in every way possible. Much love and gratitude go to my parents, Margaret and William Mitchell, on whose encouragement I have always depended; and to my sister, Meg, who has read and listened to more versions than anyone. Also thanks to Walter and Evelyn Mitchell, Mary Lu and Wade Mitchell, Scott Pentzer and the Pentzer Family, the Pult Family, Dick Tyler, Lee Tyler Darter, and Tommie Lil Tyler, born in 1908, who lived nearly one hundred years, almost long enough to see this book in print.

Finally, I am indebted to the little band on Annunciation Street. To my best friend, Poupette, who persevered for so long; to Buster and Dashiel for their companionship; and not least to my dear husband, Jon Pult, who has been so helpful, patient, and willing to cook, and his very close friend Sazerac T. Clowne, who knows the importance of laughter, the ukulele, and a good martini.

Introduction
Portrait of Isaac and Rosa

The boy and girl looked toward the camera. They were just old enough to understand the task assigned them: to stand very still, with arms linked, and direct their gaze to the contraption in front of them. Isaac was eight and Rosa, six. How two former slave children from Louisiana ended up in a Broadway photographer's studio in 1863 requires some explanation. For now, it is enough to know that both children had been the property of slaveholders in New Orleans not long before their image was printed on *cartes-de-visite* (a new format for photography in the mid-nineteenth century, allowing for more than one copy, on individual cards, made cheaply) and offered for sale. The sale of their portrait would fund newly established schools for former slaves in southern Louisiana, a region already occupied by the Union army. In fact, the Civil War still had its hold on the nation, with death tolls and discontent on the rise. The portrait of Isaac and Rosa, at once charming and provocative, said much about the uncertainties that hung in the air that year.

They would have made an uncommon pair, the black-skinned boy and the white-skinned girl. Although there were many racial taboos in nineteenth-century America, a white girl on the arm of a black boy was surely one of the most scandalous. That Rosa was a "colored" girl who only looked white—that she toyed with a person's ability to see blackness at all—only made the pair of them more intriguing. Isaac wore a suit with tie and collar, his cap in hand, and Rosa a dress and cape, full petticoats, and a fancy hat. Despite their young ages, they stood posed like a gentleman and lady making an entrance. But that was much the point of the photograph: to anticipate the adults they would become. The portrait "Isaac and Rosa, Emancipated Slave Children from the Free Schools of Louisiana," was, above all, a picture about the future. Or, rather, about the many futures that seemed possible in 1863.

Isaac and Rosa were emissaries of a message they only partly understood. Both children had been born into slavery in the South, freed by the Union army in 1863, and, with several other freed children and adults, taken on tour in the North. Three of the children, including Rosa, appeared to be white—a testament, their sponsors argued, to the brutal system of slavery that condoned the sexual exploitation of enslaved women by white men and, in turn, produced children as fair-skinned as any "white" child. Through public appearances and the sale of photographs, the group's sponsors proposed to raise money for the education of former slaves recently freed in the South. Yet the timing of this tour suggests that Isaac, Rosa, and the others were part of a larger campaign. On January 1, 1863, President Abraham Lincoln had issued the Emancipation Proclamation, freeing all enslaved people in Confederate-held territory. Although it did not free every enslaved person (some, within Union territory, remained enslaved while many others had already freed themselves by following Federal troops), it made it clear that the abolition of slavery would be a result of the Civil War. Since the proclamation's signing, the war had become increasingly unpopular in the North, where a large urban working class resented the conscription of its men in a war to end slavery, particularly when wealthier men could buy their way out of service. These same workers also dreaded the competition that might come from millions of freed blacks from the South who would work for low wages. Only a few months before Isaac and Rosa had their picture made in New York, draft rioters had taken to the city's streets, burning buildings and assaulting people, often targeting the local black population.[1]

The urban working class was not alone in its anxiety about the end of slavery. Middle-class northerners, too, fretted over the consequences of abolition. The antislavery movement had for some time argued that slavery could be abolished peacefully, with little disruption to the South's plantation economy, an economy on which northern manufacturers depended. Still, many in the North looked warily at the prospect of immediate emancipation. At best, skeptics declared, former slaves would refuse to work or would move north en masse to escape the plantations, leaving the South's cotton fields to lie fallow. At worst, freedpeople would seek revenge against their former masters, fulfilling Thomas Jefferson's dark visions of slave emancipation as a race war.[2]

Abolitionists did what they could to assuage such fears. Lydia Maria Child, for instance, in an antislavery pamphlet published in 1860, recounted tales of earlier, peaceful emancipations in the Caribbean that proved profitable for Atlantic markets. After presenting evidence from Jamaica, Montserrat, even Haiti (the black republic that resulted from a violent slave revolt—because rights had been denied slaves, Child wrote, not because they had been granted them), the author concluded: "History proves that emancipation has *always* been safe. It is an undeniable fact, that not one white person has ever been killed, or wounded, or had life or property endangered by any violence attendant upon immediate emancipation, in any of the many cases where the experiment has been tried. On the contrary, it has always produced a feeling of security in the public mind."[3]

Few images could better foreshadow a peaceful emancipation than Isaac and Rosa's portrait. By some readings, their photograph was an assurance to northern viewers about the future after slavery. The image of neatly dressed "emancipated slave children" who were attending school, preserved in portraiture on photograph cards and posed like their white northern middle-class counterparts, presented education as the means to transform young former slaves into models of discipline and propriety. Schooling children like Isaac and Rosa, guiding them by the light of northern "civilization," would eradicate slavery's effects, producing instead industrious young people with the desires of free market consumers. From the looks of Isaac and Rosa, emancipation *would* be peaceful and prosperous for the nation. This was the vision of the children's sponsors, perhaps—their vision of the transition from slavery to freedom—but there were others.

As a remnant of history—or a "relic of the Civil War," as someone later scrawled down the side of the *carte-de-visite*—Isaac and Rosa's photograph is more prism than portrait. Although it was created as antislavery, pro-emancipation propaganda, in truth, it could be read a number of ways, depending upon the viewer, since like most propaganda, the photograph engaged the arguments of opponents as well as supporters. It evoked not only an orderly emancipation but also its opposite. Common to every possible reading of this photograph, however, from the most hopeful to the most pessimistic, was the notion that such children might be the heralds of slavery's aftermath.

Looking at Isaac and Rosa, for instance, some nineteenth-century viewers may have seen abolition's triumph. Free people of color, in particular, had long begun to doubt the possibility of freedom and equality for people of African descent in the United States. In the 1850s and

1860s many of them began looking to Mexico and Haiti as havens from the repressions of the antebellum South. They looked for a country in which they and their children could prosper, a place where race would no longer be a barrier to citizenship. For free people of color, the image of Isaac and Rosa could have been an assurance that their children would enjoy the benefits of a public education, with the support of the federal government. For former slaves, too, the education of their children was critical to protecting their rights and autonomy after emancipation. As one former slave testified to Union officials in June 1863, the reason freedpeople were so determined to send their children to school was that "the children in the after years will be able to tell us ignorant ones how to do for ourselves."[4] Freedpeople's demands that their children receive regular schooling became central to labor negotiations with planters and federal agents throughout the South after emancipation. To consider Isaac and Rosa from the perspective of former slaves, therefore, is to see black freedom's promise. So young, without the visible scars of bondage, their faces still unlined by grief and sun, their tailored clothes a far remove from the coarse shirts and bare feet of slave children, this generation might be spared the full agony of slavery and establish themselves as free people.

As a representation of both slavery and freedom, however, this photograph would have been as frightening to some as it was hopeful to others. Among white northern viewers, in fact, the portrait of Isaac and Rosa might have raised more eyebrows than it did donations. If their youth and innocence pointed to slavery's cruelties, Rosa's pale skin brought slavery close to home for white northerners. Aimed at white viewers, it was a racial argument in visual terms, advocating slavery's destruction. Here was an institution that could enslave not just black children but children as light-skinned as Rosa. What, then, would keep rogue slaveholders from enslaving white people? Many northerners who had reached the South during the war had noted the large number of enslaved people who seemed to be "white." The racial anxieties Isaac and Rosa may have stirred were not limited to the spread of slavery, however. The black-skinned boy and the white-skinned girl, both of whom were "colored," raised questions about who was "white" and who was not, and how someone could (or could not) tell the difference. What were the consequences of freeing racially ambiguous people like Rosa? Would emancipation encourage further "mixing" between the races? Would it throw *all* "white" people's whiteness into question?

The sight of these educated freedchildren, in suit and starched petticoats, foretold of another transformation as well: the disappearance of a black agricultural labor force in the South. Isaac and Rosa were not dressed for a day's work in the fields. As representatives of the campaign for the education of freedpeople, this pair in middle-class attire bode ill for southern planters as well as northern industrialists. Southern slaveholders had made it a crime to teach slaves to read and write for fear that they would forge their own passes, absorb the radicalism of antislavery tracts, and otherwise plot their way to freedom. But the fears of slaveholders also sprang from their own vulnerability. For all their talk about their slaves' dependence on them, it was they who were dependent on their slaves. In one southern educator's view of slave emancipation, "The cook, that must read the daily newspaper, will spoil your beef and your bread. The sable pickaninny, that has to do his grammar and arithmetic, will leave your boots unblacked and your horse uncurried."[5] From the perspective of southern planters, then, the image of Isaac and Rosa would have foretold the collapse of the plantation economy and a social revolution of frightful proportions. Yet some white southerners predicted that the education of black children would have even more dire consequences, expressing apocalyptic visions tinged with fears about sexual interaction between blacks and whites after slavery. One Louisiana legislator argued in 1864, in the course of debates over the abolition of slavery in the state, that the prospect of educating black children would lead to bloody race riots.

The visions of black freedom that children like Isaac and Rosa conjured are the subject of this book. As members of the first generation of African Americans to grow up in the former slaveholding republic, the black child—freedom's child—represented the possibility of a future dramatically different from the past, a future in which black Americans might have access to the same privileges as whites: landownership, equality, autonomy. The "problem of freedom" (to borrow historian Thomas Holt's phrase), therefore, was not limited to what kind of labor system would replace slavery, whether former slaves would receive land, or even whether they would learn to read and write.[6] Struggles over the meaning of freedom—that is, over what slave emancipation would mean in practice—were attempts to spell out what *should* be. The problem of freedom, in the largest sense, was how to reconcile the conflicting visions of the future that slave emancipation inspired.

In this, the black child became both muse and metaphor. While some views of the black child were infused with hope, others burdened their prophets with frightening images of disorder. Through representations of freedom's child and her future, nineteenth-century Americans anticipated the social, political, and economic consequences of slave emancipation. The meanings attached to the black child in the nineteenth century, in turn, reflected the multiplicity of imagined consequences of black freedom from slavery: the expansion of a transatlantic free black community, threats to white nationalism and white supremacy, the transformation of former slaves into free laborers under the banner of Anglo-Saxon civilization, the assertion of black autonomy and equality, and racial discrimination after slavery.

Visions of the future, competing for space within any historical present, are the very fiber of social struggle.[7] Conflicts over the fate of the freedchild—that is, over the consequences of slavery's abolition—constituted a many-sided debate over the destruction or preservation of a brutal racial hierarchy in the United States. This debate had been, for abolitionists like Frederick Douglass, the ideological crux of the Civil War. Fearing that the true meaning of the Civil War was being erased in favor of romanticized stories of military bravery and national reconciliation, Douglass reminded an audience in 1878 that the sectional conflict had been "a war of ideas, a battle of principles . . . a war between the old and new, slavery and freedom, barbarism and civilization."[8] If the opposing sides in this ideological battle were clear for Douglass, however, the archives have preserved a more complicated struggle. The debate over the meaning of the Civil War that so frustrated Douglass, in fact, had its roots in the aspirations and fears Americans brought to the prospect of slavery's abolition. Free people of color, white northern audiences, freedpeople, former slaveholders, white northern military officials and reformers, politicians north and south—all these groups brought to slave emancipation radically different ideas about black freedom.

To render these competing visions, each of the chapters that follow tells a separate story about the end of slavery and its aftermath. Though distinct, these stories are connected by the struggle they narrate: the fractious debate over racial hierarchy and racial equality at the dawn of slave emancipation in the United States. Through the prism of freedom's child, we see the uncertainty of the nation's future, the untidy sum of projected hopes and fears, as slavery gave way to freedom. We can see that the battle over the future of the nation's racial hierarchy was not just a conflict about political power, civil rights, and wage scales. Rather, as Frederick Douglass reminded his audience, it was also a struggle over worldviews and aspirations. As Douglass also recognized, the social issues raised by emancipation would last for generations. White supremacy, as an ideology and as a legal and social system, flourished for one hundred years following the end of the Reconstruction in the South. With a close eye to the competing visions of the future that the freedchild inspired, we uncover both the ideologies that fed the swell of white supremacy after the Civil War and those that might have stemmed it.

It is to these diverse and competing views, then, that the chapters of this book are dedicated. In roughly chronological order, each chapter presents another view of the transition from slavery to freedom, and each is constructed around a theme that ties those ideas together— emigration, racial classification, civilizing missions, labor, and public schools. Chapter 1 begins with the 1850s, when, under the increasing racial repressions that preceded the war, free people of color encouraged their children to forecast lives for themselves in places outside of the United States, in countries that might offer them freedom and equality. In letters inquiring about and imagining migration to the Caribbean, free children of color acquired the space to script their own futures, free of the repressions of a slave society, as well as a sense of transatlantic ties that bound together people of color and strengthened them in the fight against inequality. Chapter 2 studies northern abolitionists' enlistment of light-skinned, "white"-looking enslaved girls in an ideological campaign against slavery. Light-skinned girls like Rosa conjured the past and future of sexual relations between blacks and whites sanctioned by slavery. And they seemed to foreshadow both the blurring of racial categories (such that "white" people might be enslaved if slavery continued) and the difficulty of classification that would come once "white"-looking slaves became free. Representations and images of light-skinned slave girls, in fact, served to argue that slavery's spread threatened the freedoms of "white" people. Chapter 3 considers the ideas of reformers and missionaries in the wartime and postbellum South. Visions of former slave children, transformed from "ragged" slaves into tidy freedchildren, projected the future for freedpeople in the South as part of a larger Anglo-Saxon civilizing mission—so large, in fact, that the cause of freedpeople and their education eventually fell to the wayside in the effort to spread Anglo-American civilization in the late nineteenth century. Chapter 4 focuses on struggles between freed-people and planters, both of whom saw black children and their labor as instrumental to black self-sufficiency. Freedpeople and former owners used the system of apprenticing freedchildren to a "master" or "mistress" as a means, respectively, to achieve or to thwart the autonomy of former slaves. In struggles over apprenticeship, both sides enacted their definitions of free labor in the postbellum South. Finally, with chapter 5, in debates among politicians and activists, black and white, the issue of the black child's public education—namely, whether she would be segregated from or integrated with white children in public school—became an augur for the future of race relations in the South and the nation. Where white supremacists defended segregation as the only means of maintaining social order in the South, far-seeing proponents of school integration in the nineteenth century predicted the long and tragic consequences of Jim Crow.

Although the history of freedom's child is concerned, for the most part, with adult visions of the black child, the reader will find here the real children who inspired many of those ideas, children such as Armand Nicolas and André Grégoire, Rosa Downs and Isaac White, Elsie and Puss, Ella Washington and Porter Nickols, Clement Dellande and Olivia Edmunds.[9] The first chapter even renders individual children's voices, through the letters of free children of color. Throughout this book—in the records of the Freedmen's Bureau after the war, in court testimonies, photographs, legislative debates, newspaper accounts, and missionary reports—I have tried to emphasize individual children and their stories, whenever possible. And I have chosen to define their social role as "children" not solely by their ages (although most of the "children" you will meet in these pages were under seventeen) but also by their dependence upon adults. It was both their youth and their status as dependents whose futures could be decided by adults that made them the subject of such speculation, debate, and struggle.[10] The terms I have used to refer to some of the subjects herein—"freedpeople," "freedwomen," and "freedchildren"—are ones of both utility and economy. Some recent historians have adopted "freedpeople" as a better descriptor, in place of "freedmen," even though "freedmen" was perhaps the more common term in the nineteenth century. I have adopted "freedwomen" and "freedchildren," as well, because they serve to identify particular social groups, with particular sets of concerns, and groups who were of interest to reformers, former owners, and political leaders in the aftermath of emancipation.

The reader will also notice the use of much visual evidence in the second and third chapters. Only after writing this book to its end did I understand why I was so drawn to photographs. Because they are documentary images (in the sense that they rendered living, breathing people), looking at them we seem to share, or nearly so, the vision of nineteenth-century viewers—that is, we see what they saw, in the most mechanical sense—in a way that no other documents from the period allow. (I am reminded here of critic Roland Barthes's recollections of seeing a photograph of Napoleon's brother, taken in 1852: "And I realized then, with an amazement I have not been able to lessen since: 'I am looking at the eyes that looked at the Emperor.' ")[11] And yet, there is nothing direct about how Isaac and Rosa appeared to their contemporaries. Indeed, what is useful about their portrait is that it tells more than one story: here was a world turned upside down or right side up, depending on who was looking at it. Reading these photographs, finding our way into the place and time that gave them meaning, is quite difficult. But my aim has been to uncover what Americans imagined would happen after slavery's demise. And in the portraits of children like Isaac and Rosa we have a precious window, however obscured.

This book begins and ends in Louisiana, and with the activities of New Orleans's French-speaking free people of color, or Afro-Creoles. This population has been left out of histories of the South, the Civil War, and slave emancipation in the United States because many writers have considered it unrepresentative of the African American population in the South, slave or free. While this group did share a vision of freedom for all people of color that went beyond the U.S. South—a vision that included other points around the Caribbean—in this they were not an aberration but something of a vanguard. By 1861, before the start of the Civil War, even Frederick Douglass, the leading black abolitionist in the United States, had come to think that Haiti might be a place more promising for the equality of blacks than his native country. The Afro-Creoles' intellectual accomplishments (many of them were writers and poets), combined with their long history of political activism, made them, along with Frederick Douglass, the most eloquent and forward-thinking proponents of the rights of freedpeople and formerly free people of color after the Civil War. As we will see, with the end of

Reconstruction and the hardening of the color line in the South, the Afro-Creoles launched numerous legal challenges in efforts to keep the United States from becoming "two peoples" on opposite sides of a racial divide, most famously with the landmark antisegregation case *Plessy v. Ferguson* (1896). Their very public struggle for racial equality was, by their terms, a question not of southern repression but of national citizenship. Its inspiration was a vision of the future in which all Americans would be equal citizens, regardless of race, color, or previous condition. Indeed, the most positive interpretation of the portrait of Isaac and Rosa—that emancipation signaled a future of equal opportunity for blacks as well as whites—would surely have come from the Afro-Creoles of New Orleans. And so it is with them that we begin the story of freedom's child.

1

Emigration
A Good and Delicious Country

It was in the summer of 1857 that William Green began thinking about Veracruz, Mexico. The prospect of travel from New Orleans to the Caribbean, if one had business there, was commonplace in the nineteenth century. But Green had very particular reasons for thinking about the Mexican coast that summer and wrote a letter about Mexico to his friend Léon Dupart in Mobile, Alabama. Having been informed by a mutual acquaintance that Dupart was leaving "on the next vessel bound to that coast," Green wrote, "I thought it my duty to give you several advices on the industry that you ought to follow in that country." Mr. Green urged Dupart to enlist in agricultural pursuits but bid him to be cautious about where to plant his crops. "On first arriving there," he wrote, "you ought to buy a farm, and commence to cultivate the land, and have, if possible, the send of all the vegetables in the market, and some fruit also. Don't buy the place too close to the river for if a flood should come it would destroy your crops of corn and cotton." Green confessed he would like to go along, "but my business will prevent me from doing so now, time being so dull and I hardly make my month's rent. I must stay, as I can't get no person to represent me here." Still, he saw an important role for himself in Dupart's venture: "If you can not get the materials of farming, send out here, and I will send you them and seeds for the garden also, if you can't get any I will send you some. Do not fail to answer this," he urged, "for I will be ready at your request."[1]

Though he aimed to suggest otherwise, William Green had little experience with settlement abroad. Thirteen at the time he wrote his letter about Mexico, William was a free boy of color attending school at the Catholic Institution in New Orleans, and his letter was an assignment written for his English composition class.[2] The gentleman in "Mobile," Léon Dupart, was one of his classmates in New Orleans. The destination of his letter, and of his friend, were imagined ones, just as all destinations are, in some way, imagined. The letter was not posted to Mobile, and Léon, it seems, did not go to Mexico. William's scheme was crafted, nonetheless, from the actual goings-on around him.

Throughout the United States in the 1850s, free people of color were debating the prospect of migration to other countries to protest their treatment in the United States and fulfill their destiny as a people. Amid heated sectional debate over slavery, state and federal laws increasingly limited the small freedoms of free people of color in the United States. As their status became closer to that of slaves than of free men, their dreams of full equality in their native country began to dim. Some free men of color advocated going to Africa, others to Latin America and the Caribbean. From New Orleans, as William wrote his letter, a real migration was under way to Mexico. Hoping to find a better life outside of the United States, many free people of color from Louisiana made plans to settle in the state of Veracruz, near the Caribbean coast.

William's own plans for settlement were no less important for being somewhat imaginary. The assigned task of writing about migration to Mexico carried within it pointed lessons about geography, racial identity, and the market. At a time when the small liberties of free people of color were swiftly evaporating, William's teacher had asked him to design his own freedom. The assignment reflected, in part, the radical politics of the Catholic Institution's leaders, who were French-speaking, intellectual free men of color inspired by the ideals of both the French and the Haitian revolution. With their letters, William Green and his schoolmates revealed the aspirations of the Afro-Creoles of New Orleans—transatlantic dreams of freedom drawn from political desire, racial identity, and economic ambition, as well as their sense of belonging to a broad Atlantic and Caribbean community of which the American South was only a part. In the free colored child's map of the Atlantic World—a network of places and place-names linked by ties of trade, family, and race—we see, perhaps, most clearly the kind of future free people of color in the South envisioned on the eve of the Civil War.

Two places, in particular, played a part in the writings of William and his classmates: the state of Veracruz in the Republic of Mexico, and the black republic of Haiti. Each was, for a time, a space of opportunity upon which many free people of color projected their hopes for freedom from the slaveholding republic of their birth. Though we lack any comprehensive figures on migration to either Mexico or Haiti, one estimate suggests that between 1820 and 1862 some ten thousand free people of color left the United States bound for Haiti.[3] Whereas the Haitian migration drew people from the North and the South, emigration to Mexico seems to have been limited largely to free blacks along the Gulf Coast. Yet as the children's letters reveal, antebellum migrations were ideologically and politically significant both for the few who emigrated and for the many who did not.

Although most free people of color did not emigrate to Africa or the Caribbean, and most of their leaders did not advocate migration, free blacks in the 1850s and 1860s shared a common goal in their striving for political equality and freedom. The letters of the students at the Catholic Institution, such as William's letter to Léon Dupart, narrated that search in both practical and ideological terms. In their concern for economic opportunity and survival, the students documented the political realities of the nineteenth-century Atlantic World. But in their hopefulness and enthusiasm, they reflected the aspirations of free people of color determined to find a place where they could be prosperous, equal citizens. The space that existed *between* nations was perhaps the most important part of their imagined journeys: that distance offered the chance to cross the sea in any direction, to chart their own course, to find (in the words of one of the writers) "a good and delicious country."[4] It was in the search for such a country that freedom's child was born.

Despite the "failure" of the colonies established in Mexico and Haiti, both countries became well-worn places on the students' imagined map of the Atlantic World. Reading their letters, we find that the Civil War did not mark the first time that these young free people of color anticipated racial equality and freedom. For in the late 1850s and early 1860s, on the pages of their letterbooks, these children had already begun to search for a country where they might be free from constraints—economic and political—placed upon them because of their race. Freedom was a notion the students learned to define for themselves, and its contours shifted over time as events unfolded at home and abroad. In the course of their political awakening, they learned that freedom was not a simple or a fixed notion but, rather, an idea shaped by circumstance. The students' thinking about freedom developed both from consideration of emigration's possibilities and from their experience as free people of color in the late antebellum South. In their letters about emigration, repression, and war the notion of freedom appears reduced to its purest, if never complete, form: an ideal to be reached through optimism and struggle.

Living in the port city of New Orleans, as William did, brought with it the anticipation of goods arriving from the North and around the Caribbean. But the ships that docked each day, on their way to the next port, also presented the possibility of departure, particularly for boys. All the surviving letters from the students at the Catholic Institution were the work of boys between the ages of twelve and seventeen, on the edge of seeking their fortune.[5] Although this leaves us to wonder about the girls who attended the school, the boys were no doubt the focus of their teacher's encouragement in terms of thinking about migration. Consider Léon Dupart's very adult letter about Mexico to William Green in "Vicksburg, Miss." "I have heard that you are about setting off for Mexico in three weeks," he wrote. "If you want any clothes or some money, I will send them to you before your departure. I will send my boy with you, for him to learn a trade whatever that can give him some money."[6] Migration to Mexico might help a boy like himself earn his way in the world. He could become one of the future planters, artisans, and merchants required of any successful colony. Although most free people of color who left the United States in this period did so as part of a family, the importance of women's labor was overshadowed, oftentimes, by the conviction of most free black leaders that the work of men would determine the fate of all those who emigrated.[7] And, indeed, the boys wrote in the voices of future businessmen and patriarchs, often assuming in their imagined travels the burden of protecting and supporting their families. The boys considered other nations, searching for countries where they (as men of color) would be both free and powerful enough to care for their dependents.

From their perch in New Orleans, at the mouth of the Mississippi and the gateway to the Caribbean, these boys had already gained a certain perspective on the Atlantic World. They watched heavy steamers full of passengers and cargo docking from Ohio or bound for the West Indies. The shipping news, announcing ship arrivals and departures, ran daily in the *New Orleans Daily Picayune*. Léon concluded his letter, in fact, with a note about a shipment of produce from Cuba. "There is about six months that I am expecting one of my friends who has been in Havanna," he wrote. "He told me that when he will arrive he will bring a great deal of fruit for me, if he bring all what he promised me, I will be very glad with him."[8] But Léon and his schoolfellows also witnessed the dark underside of the bustling economy in the South's largest port: the trade in human beings. Although the Atlantic slave trade no longer brought Africans into U.S. ports (the *legal* transatlantic slave trade to the United States ended in 1807, though illicit trading continued), the domestic slave trade still flourished, fueling the spread of cotton cultivation in the West. The New Orleans slave market, the South's largest, was westward expansion's greatest engine.[9] From what the students could see, it was commerce and cultivation—the movement of goods and the labor of people—that produced wealth and augmented power.

Although they rarely wrote about slavery or slaves (a topic most likely discouraged by their teachers to avoid the suspicions of white authorities that free people of color might collude with slaves), the students seem to have understood the importance of plantation slavery to the Atlantic economy, and the southern economy in particular. In fact, the only two references to slavery in the students' writings before the Civil War pertained to an episode in the illicit Atlantic slave trade between Africa and the United States, a trade that was monitored and policed by British vessels.[10] Léon Dupart wrote to his classmate "A. Frilot" about an item he had read in the New Orleans newspaper:

> I have read last week in the newspapers that the British and the Americans fought upon the sea some weeks ago, because the Americans go to Africa, and take some negroes thence, whom they carry here to be sold to planters, but the British wait for [them] in the Gulf of Mexico, and the Spaniards too, because they do not want to see that. The British met them, they destroy them all, they searched their vessels, but (they) did not find anything in them. Now they cannot do that anymore, because the Spaniards and the British are watching them all around. They say before a long time, the British will declare them war here, because I heard a man, who lives by my house, saying that the men of war of both countries are fighting upon the sea.[11]

Frilot replied with his own account of "American merchant men stealing negroes from Africa." He, too, had read the papers and related that when the English boarded the vessel, "they found many Africans in the hold. That is the reason, for what the English want to declare war to the Americans. The former do not want slaves at all." In his postscript he wrote: "That is all I can relate to you my dear friend, because that is all I saw in the papers. For my part I would not care if they would come here."[12] Given the plight of free people of color in 1858, Frilot might have welcomed an English invasion. But it is not clear, at the close of the letter, whether "they" referred to a British occupation or the importation of Africans.

Either way, these letters betray an awareness of the role that slavery played both in the American economy and in international relations. These letters, and those of their classmates, make clear that they knowingly shared the land and seascapes of slaves and capitalists. And yet the boys' letter writing was radical in its subversion of that slave-based system of Atlantic commerce. In their imaginations, the students effectively reversed the arrows of the slave trade using the same shafts—the lines marking the movement of people and goods—to tie communities of African Americans together, rather than to break them apart. Writing all these letters from within the confines of a racially divided slave society, and ultimately a nation in civil war, the students at the Catholic Institution constructed their own moral geography: that is, they mapped their prospects for freedom, testing ideas about a future in other nations outside of their own. Through place-names and correspondences, they constructed a world that was navigable not only in terms of travel and communication but also in terms of capital flows and political power. The teachers at the Catholic Institution clearly understood the importance of such an exercise. Drawing transatlantic lines of communication and trade in their letters, the free children of color at the Catholic Institution envisioned a black Atlantic community that transcended the boundaries of individual nations and, in the minds of the students, perhaps, transcended racial oppression as well.[13]

Free people of color were, in many ways, African America's first emissaries for black freedom and its future. Their aim was to find or to build a nation where blacks could prosper, while also working to defeat the system of Atlantic slavery that kept full freedom beyond the reach of all people of African descent. Though there were slaveholding free blacks in the United States (a complicated social equation some historians have tried to explain), they were far outnumbered by those who did not own slaves.[14] The majority of free blacks desired a nation without slavery. Such a plan, by its very nature, was farsighted, whether that nation was an adopted country in the Caribbean or their native United

States. While they designed their political future in the context of adversity and oppression, it was a future rooted in a positive view of black people's destiny in the world.[15] In many instances, this destiny was explained in Old Testament terms, as the struggle of Africa's sons in the deserts of oppression; in other cases, it came from a racial consciousness rooted in geography, history, and politics. In the writings of some, like black nationalist Martin Delany (to whom we shall return), it was a combination of both.[16] In whatever language it was expressed, however, this dream of a better nation relied heavily upon the next generation. The aspirations of free people of color were most clearly articulated through the education of their children, free children of color whose future, like the future of the nation as a whole, was bound to the fate of chattel slavery in the United States.

The official name of the school William Green and Léon Dupart attended in New Orleans was the Société Catholique pour l'instruction des orphelins dans l'indigence (Catholic Society for the Education of Indigent Orphans), but among English speakers it was also known as the Catholic Institution. It had been founded at the bequest of the widow Justine Fervin Bernard Couvent, a wealthy free woman of color who, by some accounts, had been born in Africa and brought to Louisiana as a slave.[17] Madame Couvent wanted to provide a school for free black orphans in the Faubourg Marigny, a neighborhood in the downtown section of the city. Though a public school system had been in place since 1841, it was open only to white children.[18] Couvent's bequest lay dormant for several years, but in 1848 free black philanthropist and slaveholder François Lacroix, with the help of several other prominent French-speaking free men of color, pressed to have Couvent's school opened. Boys and girls traveled from every section of the city to attend the school, and by 1852, 165 students were enrolled, the number of boys and girls being nearly equal. The next year, the enrollment climbed to 240, a number that amounted to nearly one-fourth of the free children of color attending school in New Orleans.[19] The school was ostensibly under the guidance of the Catholic Church, following the terms of Couvent's will, but the institution admitted children of any religious denomination and remained largely a secular institution. Orphans and the destitute attended free of charge, and other children paid a small monthly tuition.[20] Not all those who attended were French-speaking Creoles. William Green, for instance, agreed to correspond with his classmate Armand Nicolas "provided that my correspondence be in French, and yours in English, for that will give you a chance to learn English and I, French."[21]

In the legacy of Madame Couvent, the free people of color in New Orleans seized an opportunity to educate the children of their own race.[22] They had paid taxes each year to support schools their children could not attend, an iniquity that many free blacks experienced, north and south, before the Civil War.[23] Though many of the wealthiest people of color previously hired private tutors or sent their children abroad for their education, poor families had never before been able to provide what the school's directors termed "une éducation libérale" for their children until the Catholic Institution opened its doors.[24] The school's directors resolved that the poorest orphans would always be admitted ahead of other children who were presented for admission.[25] According to a former student and teacher at the Catholic Institution, "most of [the] students came from poor families."[26] In his history of blacks in New Orleans, John Blassingame wrote that the Catholic Institution catered mostly to "the upper-class of free Negroes," and that it was "the most famous Negro private school."[27] But evidence suggests that poor children did attend and that the directors and the free colored community considered the school a public one. Donations sent to the Catholic Institution from societies and other charitable organizations were often addressed to the president and directors of l'Ecole Publique des Orphelins indigents du Troisième district (the Public School for Indigent Orphans of the Third District). The school received funds from the state for several years, and the school's board agreed that the Catholic Institution should follow the disciplinary rules of the public schools.[28]

The school's teachers and directors were some of the leading French-speaking free black intellectuals and writers in Louisiana. With ideas inspired by the eighteenth-century revolutions in France and Haiti, as well as the work of contemporary French writers, the Afro-Creoles of Louisiana developed a radical agenda aimed at attaining civil and political rights for people of color in the Americas.[29] The Catholic Institution was the cornerstone of the Afro-Creoles' political work. One pair of historians even dubbed it "the nursery for revolution in Louisiana."[30] At the Catholic Institution the students received an education both practical and political. Their teachers instructed them in mathematics and oratory, and emphasized the importance of learning a trade and making business connections. Most of the children were expected to enter an apprenticeship with an artisan or tradesman at the end of their schooling. Trades such as tailor, grocer, or shoemaker had long been the monopoly of free people of color in New Orleans.[31] According to the school's prospectus, every student would receive "une éducation pratique, morale, et religieuse" regardless of his or her economic status or future profession. The directors believed the students would be able to apply what they learned "to industrial enterprises, to commerce, and to the arts." The curriculum was designed to offer "invaluable advantage to the students who are only able to give a limited time to their instruction," particularly children of the poorest classes who might only be able to devote a year or a few months to their education.[32]

The greatest appeal of the Catholic Institution for many families, however, was that their children would be educated by men and women of color. Former student Rudolphe Desdunes recalled that "all the teachers [at the Catholic Institution] were of the black race; thus they were able to develop sympathetic relationships with the children in their care."[33] Desdunes's term "sympathetic relationships," however, takes on far deeper meaning in light of the surviving letters written by the students. This sympathy translated into a concern among the leaders and teachers of the school that their students develop a political awareness and a sense of allegiance to other free people of color in the Atlantic World. Indeed, while the composition assignments given to the children trained them in the art of letter writing and in the proper maintenance of business relations, they also required the students to think about the possibility of living in a nation without racial oppression, where people of color could enjoy full political and economic freedom.

At desks, with pen and paper, the students at the Catholic Institution countered much of the history that had produced them. Free black communities in the United States and throughout the Americas were the result of an Atlantic slave trade that brought millions of Africans to the New World from the sixteenth into the nineteenth century. In the earliest years of European colonial settlement in the Americas, some enslaved Africans earned enough money to buy their freedom or were manumitted by individual owners. In the eighteenth century, many gained their freedom as a result of the War of Independence, when thousands of slaves enlisted with the Americans or the British in exchange for their manumission. After the American Revolution—fought on the principle that men should be free from tyranny—many northern states began emancipating their enslaved populations, either immediately or gradually with the emancipation of children born to slaves. Following the same ideals of freedom and equality, and in some cases evangelical Christian charity, a number of individual slaveholders in every region manumitted their enslaved workers.[34] The Haitian Revolution in 1791 —the only successful slave revolt in the Atlantic World—further increased the free colored population of the United States, particularly in Louisiana. In 1802, thousands of whites and free people of color who supported the rebellion fled Haiti (or were deported) in advance of Napoleon's military campaign to reclaim the island that had once been France's richest colonial possession. The refugees went first to Cuba, only to be expelled in 1809 and forced once again to seek asylum. Free black Haitian refugees who left Cuba for New Orleans nearly doubled the city's free black population, from 1,566 in 1805 to 3,102 by 1810.[35] By 1820, the free black population in the southern states had reached some 130,000 and in the North nearly 100,000. But in terms of their respective enslaved populations, the map of the United States had begun to foreshadow the sectional division over slavery, with only the southern half of the nation holding onto the "peculiar institution." Throughout the nineteenth century southern states wrote laws making it increasingly difficult for masters to manumit their slaves and requiring free blacks to leave the state once they had gained their freedom or face reenslavement. By the 1850s, most southern states had outlawed manumission outright.[36]

The decade before the Civil War was a turning point for free blacks throughout the United States. In a dismal era, free people of color found their already limited freedoms in a slaveholding nation increasingly circumscribed as the sectional struggle over slavery's spread to the West crept closer to civil war. Free people of color in New Orleans had enjoyed a form of quasi citizenship since the colonial period. They could testify against a white person in court, sell and hold property in their own names, enter into contracts, and initiate legal disputes. But throughout the 1850s, the state legislature and the city of New Orleans steadily erased the legal distinctions between slaves and free blacks. New laws forbade free people of color to own coffeehouses and billiard halls where liquor was sold, and a city ordinance outlawed the assembly of people of color, free or slave. Noting the exodus of free black families to Haiti in 1859, the *New Orleans Daily Delta* suggested that though free passage and tracts of land induced many to emigrate, "stringent laws" recently passed by the state legislature regarding free persons of color also played a large part in the group's decision to leave Louisiana.[37]

In the 1850s, throughout the United States, what had been an unstable social category—free and black—became a dangerous, perhaps untenable one. This crisis was brought forth, primarily, by acute legal repressions spun from the sectional contest over slavery's expansion, most notably, the Fugitive Slave Act of 1850 and the *Dred Scott* decision in 1857. The fugitive slave law was drafted in Congress as part of the Compromise of 1850, the last such compromise to stave off civil war over slavery's spread to the West. The Fugitive Slave Act facilitated the recapture of fugitive slaves who had escaped to the free states. Under the law, those who harbored fugitive slaves could be criminally prosecuted. It also allowed for the forcible enlistment of northerners to aid in the recapture of fugitives. Once before the court, should the judge decide in favor of the alleged fugitive, he received five dollars as compensation, but a ruling in favor of the slaveholder brought him ten. The most onerous aspect of the law for free blacks, however, was that although the burden of proof rested with the alleged fugitive, the law gave them no legal means of defense. Because of this provision, slave catchers could be indiscriminate about who they captured, and kidnappers could more easily spirit free blacks to the South on the premise of returning fugitives to their owners. Free blacks in the North formed vigilance committees to protect their communities, so real was the possibility of enslavement by slave catchers.[38]

The response to the act among free blacks and abolitionists in the North was fervent. From the Fugitive Slave Act, the abolitionist movement acquired its most famous treatise with Harriet Beecher Stowe's *Uncle Tom's Cabin*, written largely in response to the law's passage. For Stowe, as with many northern abolitionists, the law implicated the whole nation in the preservation of slavery. It also reinforced ties between blackness and slavery, threatening to place free black people, whatever their history, into the same predicament as those enslaved.[39] Martin Delany, a free black leader and black nationalist who argued in favor of emigration, was one of the most eloquent critics of the law. He condemned the Fugitive Slave Act not only as an unconstitutional means to degrade free blacks "beneath the level of the whites" but also as a way to hold them in a kind of slavery:

> We are slaves in the midst of freedom, waiting patiently and uncon-cernedly—indifferently and stupidly, for masters to come and lay claim to us, trusting to their generosity, whether or not they will own us and carry us into endless bondage. The slave is more secure than we; he knows who holds the heel upon his bosom—we know not the wretch who may grasp us by the throat.[40]

Delany was not alone in his dire estimation of the law, and the emigra-tion movement he championed in the 1850s was built, in part, on free black opposition to the Fugitive Slave Act. As with several of the char-acters in Stowe's novel, in the last three months of 1850, thousands of free blacks and fugitives fled to Canada, the nearest haven outside of the United States.[41]

Arguably the most significant attempt to uphold slavery and induce the submission of both the free black population and the antislavery movement, however, was the *Dred Scott* decision, handed down from the U.S. Supreme Court in 1857. In *Scott v. Sanford*, an enslaved man named Dred Scott sued for his freedom after his master had taken him for several years into the free state of Illinois and to a nearby territory. The nation's highest court, in a decision penned by Chief Justice Roger Taney, ruled that Scott was not free by virtue of having lived on free soil. In addition, he argued that the Missouri Compromise of 1820 (which ruled that there could be no slavery in the nation's territories north of the 36°30' latitude) was unconstitutional—that is, that the Congress could not legislate which states were slave states and which ones free. To ban slavery from any territory, in this Court's view, was to deprive citizens of their property. Further still, the Court (with a bench that had a southern majority) ruled that people of African de-scent in the United States were not citizens and the framers of the Con-stitution never intended them to be. *Dred Scott* made clear the strength of proslavery forces not just in the South but also in the nation as a whole.[42]

Together the Fugitive Slave Act and the *Dred Scott* decision worked to encourage debate over free black migration. For some, like ex-slave and minister William Wells Brown, in the face of these injustices, free blacks ought to demand and defend their right to remain. "The colored people in the free States are in a distracted and unsettled condition," he said.

> The Fugitive Slave Law, the Dred Scott decision, and other inroads
> made upon the colored man's rights, make it necessary that they should
> come together that they may compare notes, talk over the cause of their
> sufferings, and see if anything can be done to better our condition. We
> must take a manly stand, bid defiance to the Fugitive Slave Law, Dred
> Scott decision, and every thing that shall attempt to fasten fetters upon
> us. We will let our white fellow-citizens see that we know our rights,
> and, knowing, will maintain them.[43]

For others, the increasing repression of free people of color in the United States was a clear signal that black Americans' future lay elsewhere. Martin Delany, in his address "The Political Destiny of the Colored Race," delivered in 1854 (even before the *Dred Scott* decision was handed down), declared that emigration was the only remedy for "the great political disease" that afflicted black people in America. The time had come, he said, for all of Africa's descendants to confront "the politician, the civil engineer, and skilful [*sic*] economist, who direct and control the machinery which moves forward, with mighty impulse, the nations and powers of the earth" and "to meet them on vantage ground, or, at least, with adequate means for the conflict."[44] It was time, in Delany's view, for people of color to build an economically and politically powerful nation of their own.

The possibility of emigration out of the United States had been present among free blacks since the late eighteenth century. Colonial documents show that a group of Africans petitioned to return to Africa as early as 1773. Even earlier efforts arose in the form of slave rebellions and mutinies in the eighteenth-century Atlantic slave trade to the Americas, uprisings through which enslaved Africans, bound and thrust into a new world they did not recognize, struggled to free themselves and return home.[45] The first formally organized effort by free blacks from the United States to settle in Africa, however, arose in 1783 when groups in Boston and Newport, Rhode Island, sought to energize their fellow free blacks toward settlement on the west coast of Africa. They aimed to take back to Africa the political ideals and Christian teachings of their native New England. Such early emigrationist circles formed in busy port cities, where free blacks were daily reminded of the Atlantic trade in African peoples. The steady arrival of ships carrying enslaved Africans into Boston and Newport profoundly shaped the political agenda of free black communities there. They looked to settlement in Africa not only as an opportunity for evangelism but also as a means to curb the slave trade between Africa, the United States, and the West Indies. These early plans for settlement in Africa, however, never came to fruition. Although emigration as an idea never entirely disappeared, by the turn of the nineteenth century it became clear that free black communities lacked the funds to organize transport and maintain settlements in Africa.[46]

The 1820s saw a revival of the free black emigration movement, though it was no longer limited to Africa. The republic of Haiti, under the leadership of President Jean-Pierre Boyer, welcomed free blacks from the United States as a means to bring money and skilled artisans to the struggling nation. Many free blacks answered President Boyer's appeals, and antislavery leaders estimated that by 1840 between 7,000 and 10,000 free blacks had migrated to Haiti from the United States. Historians point to a decline in the numbers of migrants to Haiti sometime in the 1830s, however, due to a growing biracial antislavery movement in the United States. With the steep decline in the condition of free blacks in the late 1850s, however, free black interest in migration to the Caribbean rose once again.[47]

While colonization did attract the interest of some free blacks, most had remained opposed to the schemes of groups such as the American Colonization Society (ACS), founded by Quakers and slaveholders in 1817, in the interest of removing free blacks from the United States and "returning" them to Africa. (It was under the auspices of the ACS that the colony of Liberia was founded in West Africa in 1824.) In fact, free black communities organized politically for the first time in large numbers in 1817, forming state and national conventions to corral opposition to the ACS.[48] Among those free blacks in favor of and those opposed to emigration, there remained a marked difference between free black people's deliberate search for liberty and equality beyond their native soil and white people's desire to rid the United States of black people by forcibly removing them. At many conventions, at the state and national level, free black leaders formed committees to study the issue of emigration and consider its merits. In those same meetings, however, delegates largely denounced the schemes of the ACS. As the black state convention of New England declared in 1859, since the founding of the

ACS, "the colored people of the United States have never ceased to de-
nounce and protest against it, repelling from the idea, come from whatever quarter it might, that colored Americans are under any more obligations to emigrate to Africa than white Americans to return to the
lands of their ancestors."[49]

In his treatise *The Condition, Elevation, Emigration, and Destiny of
the Colored People of the United States* (1852), Martin Delany distinguished between "emigration" and "colonization" as two very different
movements. "When we speak of colonization," he wrote, "we wish distinctly to be understood, as speaking of the 'American Colonization Society'—or that which is under its influence," an organization of southern slaveholders "having for their express object, as their speeches and
doings all justify us in asserting in good faith, the removal of the free
colored people from the land of their birth, for the security of the
slaves, as property to the slave propagandists." Liberia, in his view, was
"a mere dependency of Southern slaveholders and American Coloniza-
tionists, and unworthy of any respectful consideration from us." Free
black emigration to South and Central America and the Caribbean, on
the other hand, was worthy of their efforts and worth the sacrifice of
leaving their native country: "We do not go, without counting the cost,
cost what it may; all that it may cost, it is worth to be free."[50]

Emigration for free blacks would prove more important as an idea,
and a point of debate, than as an event. The largest numbers, some ten
thousand in the nineteenth century, went to Haiti, with smaller numbers
of free blacks going to Africa and elsewhere in the Caribbean. As some
historians have argued, this may have been because leaders who favored
migration, like Delany, failed to reach the majority of working-class free
blacks. Another obstacle to emigration, however, was the lack of resources to launch and sustain successful colonies outside of the United
States. But perhaps the most significant reason for the unpopularity of
migration was that most free blacks, like William Wells Brown and the
delegates at the New England Convention, thought of themselves as
Americans.[51] In his condemnation of colonization schemes like that of
the ACS, Frederick Douglass conveyed his reluctance to support free
black emigration. In his newspaper the *North Star* in 1849, he declared
"for two hundred and twenty-eight years has the colored man toiled
over the soil of America" so that "white men might roll in ease." Just as
the antislavery movement in the United States was gaining steam, declaring slavery immoral and against the principles on which the nation

had been founded, "the mean and cowardly oppressor is mediating plans to expel the colored man from the country." His condemnation of colonization pointed to both the painful labors of his ancestors and his birthright as a native of the United States. "Shame on the guilty wretches that dare propose, and all that countenance such a proposition," Douglass wrote. "We live here—have lived here—have a right to live here, and mean to live here."[52]

Free black emigration, then, did not inspire a mass exodus—not even among the French-speaking Afro-Creole community in New Orleans, a group who saw themselves as a people culturally distinct from the Americans, black and white, who had populated Louisiana after the Louisiana Purchase in 1803. But from the particular experience of the students at the Catholic Institution—the uncommon view their writings present into the strategies of free people of color—we learn that emigration did two very important things. First, it strengthened the ideological and historical ties that existed between free blacks in the United States and other settlements of free blacks within the Diaspora. Second, the prospect of emigration created an ideological and geographic space in which free blacks could envision and articulate the kind of freedom they hoped to achieve in a society without slavery.

The value of emigration as an idea is clear in the boys' letters. Through letter writing they learned to make connections between New Orleans and other ports on the Atlantic and the Caribbean—Veracruz, Port-au-Prince, Boston, Mobile—intertwining commerce with transatlantic relationships. They built their "imagined community" with the materials at hand: dry goods, produce, tools, maps, schooners, pen, and paper. In creating and relaying stories about migration, and making fictive business deals in their compositions, the students developed a political consciousness using a pointedly economic narrative upon which they themselves elaborated. In letters with commercial and agricultural narratives, the boys scripted futures for themselves as merchants and planters at a time when opportunities for free people of color in the American South were increasingly uncertain. And using the language of speculation and trade, they charted their own links between their lives in Louisiana and the lives of free people of color in the North and across the Atlantic and Caribbean. Always, they were in search of a better place, a better "country" in which to establish themselves.

Because we know far less about the politics of free people of color in the antebellum South than of those in the North, the boys' letters are particularly revealing in terms of southern free blacks' strategies of survival and advancement. The emphasis on trade and production in the children's writings suggest that the teachers and leaders at the Catholic Institution may have been familiar with the writings of Martin Delany. At the very least, they would have been in strong agreement with him. In his treatise on emigration and the destiny of people of color, Delany had set down an economic strategy that the boys at the Catholic Institution seem to have been following:

> In going, let us have but one object—to become elevated men and women, worthy of freedom—the worthy citizens of an adopted country. What to us will be adopted—to our children will be legitimate. Go not with an anxiety of political aspirations; but go with the fixed intention—as Europeans come to the United States—of cultivating the soil, entering into the mechanical operations, keeping of shops, carrying on merchandise, trading on land and water, improving property—in a word, to become the producers of the country, instead of the consumers.[53]

Delany (as one also suspects of the teachers at the Catholic Institution) emphasized the ability of the next generation to secure the freedom of people of color. But he emphasized, as well, the political energy produced not in the electoral arena but in the Atlantic marketplace. The boys at the Catholic Institution seem to have been acting out Delany's vision of freedom. Their attentions, however, were not limited to "merchandise" and "cultivation" in an "adopted country," but included trading letters to port cities in the North, as well. Still, all the letters about trading and about Mexico emphasized the creation of imagined economic ties over great distances. The trade letters, mixed in as they were with letters about Mexico, suggest that the students were learning to be, first and foremost, "producers."

The typical trade letter concerned a specific commercial deal, describing the exchange of specie for dry goods and containing promissory notes. The writer detailed the goods involved—for example, "3 boxes of calico, 1000 yds @ 6c, 5 boxes of gloves, 60 pairs @ $1 a pair"—and copied the notes stating the balance outstanding on the exchange.[54] The students were thinking about these business relations in terms of a network of trade that linked people in cities at great distances from one another. Writing to "P. Dufour, Esq." in Marseilles, France, for instance,

Alfred Claiborne explained that he had received money "from a dealer in Boston, and also some goods," and informed Dufour that he would send to him in France "four Hundred dollars ($400) in species, and two hundred in grain." He then figured the number of sacks of corn, wheat, and "Rio Coffee," with the market price of each sack. In his postscript, he expressed hope for continuing business relations with Dufour: "In your next letter you will let me know if you have received your money and goods and also if you will continue to deal with me."[55] Though creating this web of financial relationships might seem appropriate for boys hoping to become merchants, not every student would enter the dry goods or grocery business. Many of them would pursue other careers, like bricklaying, joining, or tailoring, professions that perhaps would not require the same connections. But even these students would be following Delany's prescription, learning a trade that would be useful either at home or in an "adopted country."

Some students sought advice from friends and associates in other "countries" about the best trade to enter and what place might prove the most advantageous for their endeavors. These letters, which several of the boys wrote, were based on the premise that the writer had recently come into a large sum of money and was faced with the problem of how to invest it. André Grégoire, who was "in possession of six thousand dollars," wrote: "I wish very much to undertake a trade, but I do not know if I shall keep a grocery store or not. Do you believe that I shall succeed in that enterprise?" He then inquired of his friend, who was in "Hartford New Haven," whether it was a good place for a grocery trade. "Is not your country better for that undertaking?" he asked. There were a few letters like these written to places in the South. Alfred Claiborne, writing to a friend in "Vicksburg, Mississippi," informed him that he was in possession of "fifteen thousand dollars ($15,000) with which I do not know wether [sic] I shall buy a little dry good store or a grocery." Like André, Alfred inquired whether or not that "country" would be better for such a venture than New Orleans. William Green asked a similar question of Armand Nicolas (a classmate) in "Galveston, Texas."[56] Though Alfred and William were not looking beyond the southern states, they may have been, like André, experimenting with cities, weighing them against one another: Would Galveston be more lucrative than New Orleans? Was Vicksburg a possibility? Were other cities in the South any better than their own? Indeed, writing to Galveston or Vicksburg may have come from the boys' curiosity about what was happening to free people of color in other parts of the South, outside of New Orleans. Choosing a destination for their letters—selecting a city from all possible cities and inquiring about the possibilities there—they began to consider the relationship between opportunity and geography.

Race was a quiet current that ran through the lines of the students' letters as they investigated the possibility of setting themselves up in business in another city. William Green, for instance, believed he was "about to enter the commercial line." "My intention," he wrote, "is not to inhabit forever a country that offers so little advantage as this. And I am about to prepare seriously to leave by studying, to bid an eternal adieu to my native home."[57] "So little advantage"—racial discrimination, the children knew, was what pushed them to consider discarding their "native home" in favor of a nation that afforded them economic opportunity and freedom from a repressive racial order. Indeed, at the same time that the boys began to write letters to "Galveston" and "Hartford" seeking a new "country," they were starting to explore the possibilities of migrating to Mexico. To a friend in "Boston," Armand Nicolas revealed that he had "lately won ten thousand dollars" (again, the fictive premise of the assignment) and that he planned to keep "either a dry goods line or a Grocery store, but I do not know to which of these lines I shall give the preference." His brother had also acquired "a good sum," but according to Armand "he says he does not like to have a thing in this country. Tell me if I shall not do better to come to the country where you are now [Boston] or go to Mexico? For I do not think I shall do well to stay here, and be in business."[58]

The racial repression behind the Mexican migration would have been clear to the students. The decision to establish a colony in Mexico, in fact, seems to have sprung from violent incidents against free people of color in the rural parishes outside of New Orleans. In 1855, a wealthy Afro-Creole named Lucien Mansion helped to fund the migration of free people of color from Attakapas, an area west of New Orleans, after they had been threatened by "vigilance committees." It was not until two years later, however, that an official agreement was signed between the Mexican republic, the proprietors of a large hacienda in the state of Veracruz, and Louis Nelson Fouché, a supporter of the Catholic Institution, to establish a colony named Eureka outside of Tampico.[59] The Mexican republic may have attracted free blacks from Louisiana, in large part, because of the racial equality that Mexico's leaders promised its colonists. With the founding of Eureka in 1857, Mexico's president

Ignacio Comonfort welcomed Louisiana's free people of color, insisting that they would have "the same rights and equality enjoyed by the other inhabitants [of Mexico] without at any time having to feel ashamed of their origin." Free black people from New Orleans also may have chosen to migrate to Veracruz because it was a part of Mexico with a relatively large population of African descent since the country's colonial period.[60] But the lucrative commercial traffic between Veracruz and New Orleans must also have been of interest to free black merchants, grocers, and dry goods men, as well as to those who went (as William Green had advised Léon Dupart) to farm.

The students began to write letters about Mexico in 1856. Most of these letters were addressed to friends or acquaintances in the port city of Veracruz or to nearby Tampico, although Eureka also appeared as a destination. Many of these Mexico letters were addressed to family members, and it is possible that some of the students' relatives had departed for Veracruz and that these letters reached them. But most appear to have been the same letter in several variations, suggesting that these, like the business letters, were fictive. Mexico first enters their compositions, for instance, as part of a story about Nicaragua. In it, the letter writers are addressing their brothers about the prospects in Nicaragua versus those in Mexico. "You inform me after you have settled in Mexico," William Green wrote, "(where you are making a good deal of business) that you have the intention to leave for Nicaragua, where you expect to succeed." William advised him against going to Nicaragua, since "something might happen to you, or else you will be taken as a soldier by Walker who wants some. You had better stay where you are."[61]

This mention of William Walker and his filibustering activities in Nicaragua suggest that the boys were keeping up on political events in Latin America. They may have overheard the talk of adults on the subject, or may have read about Walker themselves in the papers. (The *New Orleans Daily Picayune* had its own correspondent covering Walker's campaign.)[62] Walker, with the enthusiastic backing of southern slaveholders, hoped to expand the American empire into Latin America and open up more land for slavery, a campaign that eventually ended in failure, and Walker's demise.[63] While Walker's men were struggling to take Nicaragua, however, the students contrasted that country in their letters to Mexico, warning friends not to go to Nicaragua but to stay in Veracruz. The danger in Nicaragua, however, was not represented by the students as the threat of slavery per se; rather, they feared that in Nicaragua, their friends would be taken up by Walker's army (as William Green suggested) or that they would not be successful there. Alfred Claiborne, for instance, urged his brother not to leave Mexico.

> You also tell me that your intention is to go to Nicaragua, where you think you will gain a great deal of money. By leaving Mexico, all will be lost for you. If I am permitted to give you an advice, it is not to do what you intend, for there is no money at all in Nicaragua. One of my friends set off last month for that place. He wrote me a letter, and says that he is in the greatest misery that may be imagined and resents very much to have left his country to go in another, where there is nearly any food for the inhabitants. Do not go there, do not go, my dear brother! You will never succeed; follow my advice, it will be better for you.[64]

Nicaragua, potentially a slave society should Walker have his way, promised financial ruin—"all will be lost." Mexico, however, was a haven. Armand Nicolas, in his letter, insisted that his "brother" remain in Mexico instead of seeking his fortune in Nicaragua "because you will succeed better [in Mexico] than in any other place."[65]

Although Mexico may have seemed to promise success, thinking about life there also required that the students picture a different kind of future for themselves than they would have in New Orleans. If many of the boys at first proposed setting themselves up in Mexico as dry goods men or grocers, they soon learned by word of mouth that most of the work available in Mexico would be in the cultivation of land rather than in trades or skilled artisanship. André Grégoire, when writing about Mexico, explained that he had heard that there was "no work in that country" (perhaps meaning dry goods or tailoring), but it was "a very good place for agriculture."[66] This posed a creative problem for the students, given their ideas on the importance of learning a trade in order to be successful. In other letters, the students had expressed great interest in learning a trade, since in their view to learn a profitable trade was the only route of a promising young man. Armand Nicolas, for instance, in a letter to his classmate Léon Dupart, chastised him for sleeping late and ignoring his lessons and in general being "very lazy in your habits." He warned his friend, "If you become a man with such ways you will be forced to work in the fields to get your living and if you have any children, you will not be able to sustain them." Another boy at his school, Armand explained, had been "so idle that they were obliged to let him do as he wished and he has not learned a trade. When he got married he was obliged to work in the fields."[67] Field work was the destiny of those who did not work hard enough in obtaining a trade, and it was a sign of social and economic failure.

Students reformed these ideas about agriculture, however, when they considered life in Mexico. Indeed, in Veracruz or Tampico, the students speculated, agrarian living might offer them the chance to be landholders and live like the wealthiest men in the South: planters. They based this interpretation of a landed life in Mexico on what they heard from those who had gone there and returned to New Orleans with news. In a letter addressed to his brother in "Veracruz," William Green inquired what he thought of Mexico, asking him to "please tell me if the sugar-cane, corn, and other products grow there; and do you think the ground will be good enough to raise some." He added: "I would like better to be a farmer than carry on any other profession, for I can make money by it in the markets." He also inquired about rumors that the Mexican government was granting land "to any one who settles there" and stories he had heard "that the sugar-cane grows there to the height of twelve feet."[68]

William's idea of "farming" certainly seems to have been more akin to large-scale production for "the markets" than homesteading. Indeed, the life he and his fellow students imagined in Veracruz often reads more like a Mexican version of the rural South, with haciendas instead of plantations. Armand Nicolas, for instance, wrote a letter to a friend "to let you know that I desire to leave this country." He told him that he had received word from another friend in Mexico that "he had bought two haciendas and says if I come, I shall have one for sixty dollars."[69] Armand also explained that the nature of labor in Mexico was different than in New Orleans. "The manner of working in Tampico is not the same as here, they work in yards and you would not see anybody working in the streets. You can cultivate your land because the earth is fertile and every field is tilled there." Those who settled in Tampico, it seems, no longer had to ply their trade in city quarters and could assume the life of the landed class. As for labor, Armand explained, "you can get some Mexicans to work for you for five dollars a month and some others for four. The inhabitants of that country are simple and good natured fellows."[70]

The boys were not re-creating the antebellum South on Mexican soil.

Instead, while imagining life free from the oppressions of the southern racial system in the United States, they also explored the idea of an agrarian system based on free labor. They were speculating not only on the freedoms of Mexican society but also on a plantation system without slavery.[71] Consider the letters the boys wrote after André Grégoire's father, along with his associate Louis Duhart, returned from a trip to Mexico. (Both men appear in the passenger log of the *Sarah Bartlett* on the ship's return from Vera Cruz to New Orleans in May 1857.)[72] Although some of the students reported that Grégoire decided not to settle in Mexico "because there is no work there," André and the other boys relayed a favorable report on Mexico's agricultural possibilities:

> My father has arrived from Vera Cruz in this city with his friend Mr. Duhart, last Saturday. They say that it is a very good country for the production of corn, oats, &, &. They have visited all the plantations. There is nothing more beautiful to be seen, Mr. Mortimer has a great plantation, which he has just bought, there are some boys about fourteen years old, who make one or two thousand bricks a day. They are constructing many buildings on his plantation. He is going to have a very fine house built, he has spent already fourteen thousand dollars, and he has not done yet, he has three thousand banana trees, and many in lemon trees.[73]

André described the making of a plantation system with the labor of free workers. The "very fine house" Mr. Mortimer built and his thousands of fruit trees were the signs of his status as a great landholder. Distinctly unlike slaveholders in the South, however, Mortimer's wealth would not be measured by the number of slaves he owned but, rather, by the extent of his production and the numbers of buildings his laborers constructed. And these workers, to accept Armand's assessment, were "simple and good natured fellows," which seemed to make them, in his eyes, a suitable peasant class.

Not every student planned to own large plantations. Some wrote of renting or buying houses and creating, as Léon Dupart described, "a large garden, [it] will consist in some eggplants, cabbages, tomattoes [*sic*], onions, potatoes, some peaches, figs, apples and oranges and many other things."[74] Still, it seems that this produce would be destined for "the markets," where one could make large sums of money. André Grégoire wrote a letter addressed to a friend in "Paris" who, according to

André, was about to set off for Mexico. "There is one of my good friends who lives in that country," he wrote. "Last year he made a crop of corn, oats, and melons, of three thousand dollars cash. And he says that it is a very good country for agriculture. The land is very cheap there; my friend has bought his plantation for four thousand dollars. So, if you go in that country, to be a gardener, I think that you will succeed."[75]

Given the uncertain political situation in the South, writing letters of advice like André's offered the students the chance, on paper, to assume positions of wealth and authority. They could take on the role, for instance, of advisers to friends who planned to migrate or as agents to those who settled in Mexico. In the latter role, students pretended to be merchants writing to associates in Veracruz who had recently emigrated and were in need of supplies. Armand Nicolas wrote his friend: "I have found the implements and garden seed that you told me to buy for you," and he proceeded to list the items he would send—shovels, reaping hooks, bundles of carrot seed—along with their number and cost. Armand concluded his letter stating that "perhaps next week I shall send you the rest, and I believe I shall come myself."[76] Recall that William Green told Léon Dupart, "If you can not get the materials of farming, send out here, and I will send you them and seeds for the garden also, if you can't get any I will send you some."[77] And André Grégoire advised his friend to take $3,000 dollars with him to Mexico, that his passage would cost him $40, adding: "When you will be in that country if you find yourself troubled, just call upon me, I will render you any service that you will ask of me."[78] In addition to what the boys may have learned about how to write a business letter or how to trade with associates in other ports, then, they also succeeded in finding their own use for their "merchant" letters. Using the language of commerce, and pen and paper, they participated in the activity of emigration, though they never sailed to Veracruz themselves.

The fate of those who settled at Eureka and other places near Veracruz is unclear. The threat of Mexican civil war (what the students called "revolution"), as well as the death of two "Creole ladies" at Tlacotalpán (possibly of smallpox or yellow fever), seemed to dampen the boys' enthusiasm for life in Veracruz.[79] Yet migrations to Mexico apparently continued into 1860, since in January of that year the *New Orleans Daily Delta* reported that "scarcely a week passes but a large number of free persons of color leave this port for Mexico or Hayti."[80] By 1863, however, a report by the Mexican government had declared

Eureka a failure. After several months, according to the report, most of the colonists "se marcharon"—they left. Though the report was not explicit as to why Eureka's inhabitants moved away, it suggested that many colonies established in Mexico in the 1850s failed after the outbreak of civil war in 1858, which destroyed lines of communication between the coastal colonies and the government in Mexico City.[81]

Although the students did not write many letters about emigration between 1857 and 1859, when emigrants began leaving for Haiti, their letters suggest that they had begun to rethink the idea of colonization. They realized with the failure of Eureka that successful colonization depended upon a stable political situation, and they seemed to interpret the instability in Mexico in racial terms. Léon Dupart, for instance, began expressing his doubts about going to Mexico in 1857 "because I have heard it said that there will be a war between the Mexicans and the Spaniards," and he had been told that "it would be very bad if there would be a revolution in that country."[82] Interestingly, Léon linked these unstable conditions to his understanding of Mexico as a still unfamiliar country. This unfamiliarity seems to have been rooted in his sense of connection to other Caribbean nations where people of color were in the majority. Léon inquired of his friend whether "it would be better for us to go to Jamaica or Martinico [Martinique]." "I believe it will be better than to go to a country we don't know," he wrote, "for we can't do what we please there as you would in any other place but this."[83] In other words, places populated mostly by people of color—like Jamaica and Martinique—seemed to offer more freedom than either Mexico or the United States. A few days later, André Grégoire also directed a letter to a friend in Tampico, explaining that he had been "on the point to leave for that place." But André, too, had changed his mind. "I don't believe I shall go there," he wrote. "I have a mind to go to another place."[84]

As the racial repression in the United States became more acute, in fact, the students placed less emphasis on the economic prospects of migration and more on settlement in places where black people were in the majority. Their political consciousness shifted from a self-interested one rooted in a kind of free-market liberalism, to one concerned with the collective fate of "colored" people in New Orleans. This shift is difficult to trace because relatively few of the students' letters focus on emigration to Haiti—a silence perhaps related to the increasingly volatile political situation in the South, which would have prevented free children of color from writing much about the black republic. But their thinking about Haiti was clearly influenced by the political situation in New Orleans at the time and the lessons learned from the migration to Mexico.

By the time of the Haitian migration, the students had come to understand that free black people's freedom would not be as simple as a plot of ground or a merchant's ledger. In the intervening years between migrations to Mexico and Haiti, for instance, the students learned first-hand about racial discrimination—something that had not received direct comment in any of their letters about Mexico. In 1858, the Catholic Institution was forced to raise its tuition because the Louisiana state legislature denied the school its usual funds, and this slight did not escape the attention of the students. A. Frilot noted "the prejudice against the colored population is very strong in this part of the country." He explained that "the white people have an Institution [a public school] in every district and they are all protected very well. But we, who have but a single one, cannot be protected at all." In his postscript Frilot wrote: "I wish you could send [this] letter to my friend Léon, so he could see how the prejudice is very bad at this moment."[85] Léon Dupart, in turn, wrote that the school's directors had raised the cost of tuition, and that "the colored people do not want that." Dupart wrote: "I assure you, my dear friend, that now the price of the pupils is very dear. I know many boys whose mothers say that they are going to take them out of school."[86] The worsening injustices against free people of color in the South, brought home by the favoritism shown to white children at black children's expense, may have helped to convince the students that they needed a place belonging to the people of their own race.

The students soon discovered, as well, that the significance of Haitian colonization for the free black population of Louisiana was markedly different from that of Mexican emigration two years earlier. Though the goal of creating economically powerful settlements was shared by the two waves of emigration, the racial and symbolic undertones of free black migration to Haiti were far stronger than they had been during the settlement of Eureka. After the success of the Haitian Revolution, the island had become a powerful symbol—for slaves, free blacks, and slaveholders throughout the Atlantic—of the potential of enslaved blacks to overthrow slavery and white rule, and to establish a nation for people of African descent.[87] Indeed, despite white supremacist attempts to blame Haiti's tumultuous political situation after the revolution on the inability of African people to rule themselves, slaves and free blacks throughout the Americas made Haiti, in the words of one historian, "a symbol of African regeneration and of racial equality."[88] In addition, the Afro-Creole leaders of the Catholic Institution also had a particularly strong historical and intellectual affinity for Haiti. Working in the French Romantic tradition, they along with black writers in Haiti, Guadeloupe, and Martinique upheld the ideals of the French and Haitian revolutions, ideals that condemned slavery and promoted democratic revolution, brotherhood, and equality. And many free colored people in New Orleans had ancestral ties to the island of Saint Domingue.[89] Although we have no record of what the students at the Catholic Institution learned from their teachers about Haiti, the students seem to have understood Haiti as a place where "colored" people were in charge.

The government of Haiti began recruiting emigrants from among the free black population of Louisiana in 1858, when an agent of then-emperor Soulouque I offered them free transportation and Haitian citizenship. Following Soulouque's overthrow and the creation of a new republic, Haiti's president Fabre Geffrard again appealed to Louisiana's free people of color, as well as to free blacks from other parts of the United States, North and South.[90] In 1859 the *Daily Picayune* noted the departure of two hundred emigrants from New Orleans bound for Haiti. The group was composed mostly of families headed by men who had been "brought up to a trade or have followed commercial pursuits." This group sailed to Haiti carrying with them, in a velvet case, "a massive gold medal" inscribed "à Fabre Geffrard, temoinage de sympathie et d'admiration des compatriots de la Louisiane" ("in testament to their sympathy and admiration from his compatriots in Louisiana"). With the medal, they demonstrated their support for the recent overthrow of Soulouque and the new republic under Geffrard, which opened up new possibilities for free black republicans like those from Louisiana. On the other side of the medal were the words "Union et Fraternité."[91] This migration, in contrast to the movement to Mexico, strongly emphasized racial identity and served to reinforce—with the departure of migrants and the sailing of ships—the "imagined" community that joined free blacks in the South with the leaders of Haiti.

The migration to Haiti continued to gain support among many free blacks in the United States until the start of the Civil War, helped along by the Haitian government's recruitment campaign. In 1861, President Geffrard published an "Invitation" to free people of color in the United

States printed on the frontispiece of white abolitionist James Redpath's *Guide to Hayti*. Redpath had been appointed by Geffrard as the agent for procuring black American settlers. He established the Haytian Bureau of Emigration in Boston and hired agents to recruit migrants in the Midwest and Canada and several agents to work in Port-au-Prince. He also received money for the publication and distribution of ten thousand copies of his *Guide*.[92]

Both Geffrard and Redpath made strong pleas for the emigration to Haiti in the name of the social and economic advancement of all African-descended people. Geffrard called upon "our black and yellow brethren, scattered through the Antilles and North and South America," to help cultivate "this marvelous soil that our fathers, blessed by God, conquered for us." The work of "regeneration" would allow Haiti to retake "her ancient sceptre as Queen of the Antilles" and would serve as a "formal denial" to those who believed descendants of Africa incapable of attaining "a high degree of civilization." "Listen, then, all ye negroes and mulattoes who, in the vast Continent of America, suffer from the prejudices of caste," Geffrard wrote. "The Republic calls you."[93]

Redpath, though a white man, was an ardent black nationalist, in the vein of Martin Delany. (Despite their ideological affinity, however, Delany did not support Redpath's appointment as agent, or his campaign. Delany argued that a black nation ought to be founded by black people. James Theodore Holly, an African American who had been advocating Haitian migration for several years, had been passed over in favor of Redpath.)[94] In his earlier writings, Redpath had advocated the creation of "a great Negro Nation." With the *Guide*, he detailed the creation of an economically viable black republic based on free labor, a nation of black people that would bring an end to slavery by defeating it in the Atlantic marketplace. In the *Guide to Hayti*, he presented Haiti as a beacon of hope for oppressed people of color. In Haiti, black Americans would have "a home, a nationality, a future."[95] The *Guide* also made clear the importance of New Orleans as a point of departure for free people of color leaving the South: "Vessels will sail as frequently as a sufficient number of passengers are procured from Boston and New Orleans." Should they face resistance, an "Agent of the Govt will be stationed at New Orleans to protect the interests of emigrants."[96]

The geography of the migration effort is evident in the writings of the students at the Catholic Institution. In a number of letters, they interpreted both Boston and Haiti as good places for people like themselves.

As with the letters about Mexico, in fact, letters about Boston often referred to commerce. A boy named Armand Cloud wrote the following to a friend in "Boston" in October 1859: "I think that a man can catch lobsters (there), and send them to another country, right fresh; if you would send me some, I would be very glad, for I like them very much. I suppose that you are kind enough to send me two or three dozen boxes of them in pickle, and have some fresh ones put in the ice. On my return, if I can send you some bundles of sugar-canes or money, as you (will) desire it."[97] Instead of looking at a northern city as part of a region in conflict with their own, or even as a haven from slavery (as fugitive slaves described it), the boys used goods—the familiar regional goods of sugarcane and lobster—as a way to link the two regions, this with the idea, perhaps, of strengthening the ties of free people of color, North and South, to the island of Haiti.

Haitian emigration drew far more attention from the New Orleans press than had Mexican emigration. This is not surprising, considering the significance of the black republic to slaveholding societies like the South, and the increasingly heated debate over slaveholding itself. When emigrants first set sail in 1859, the *Daily Picayune* acknowledged that the migration of free blacks from New Orleans would be a loss for the city. "Some of our best mechanics and artisans are to be found among the free colored men," the *Picayune* noted. "They form the great majority of our regular settled masons, bricklayers, builders, carpenters, tailors, shoemakers, &c. whose sudden emigration from this community would certainly be attended with some degree of annoyance."[98] In August 1859, the *Picayune* began to change its view of the Haitian migration, reporting that some "well informed persons who have recently gone to Hayti" had returned to New Orleans briefly in order to buy farming implements and machinery to take with them for the cultivation of plots. The paper also noted that due to the scarcity of labor in that country, "those who emigrate in families or associations have . . . the best chances of success." The *Picayune*'s source suggested that "the class of emigrants to whom most inducements are held out are those who will follow agricultural pursuits," but that "carpenters, builders, tailors, and shoemakers" could "readily find employment in the cities and towns."[99]

Over time, however, the response of the local press to emigration became largely a racial one: free blacks were an unwelcome and potentially disruptive element in an otherwise "contented" South. "Contact with fanatics and Abolitionists," wrote the *Picayune* in 1860, "has not been beneficial to blacks; it has improved neither their morals nor their social condition. . . . As for us in New Orleans, we say let them go and God speed them; we can get along quietly enough with our contented and faithful slaves."[100] And according to the *Daily Delta,* free black emigration would mean "less wrangling and disagreement between our slaves and free colored persons." The paper also assured its readers that Louisiana's slaves enjoyed "more comfortable accommodations" than free blacks could hope to find in Haiti.[101]

Despite (or because of) the attention Haitian migration garnered in the New Orleans press, and the printed information available about colonization, the students' letters written to Haiti were brief, with little detail about activities there. Unlike the letters to Mexico, in which the writers had been very explicit about the logistics of colonization and the prospects for success there, the students used vague terms in their few queries about life in Haiti—"you have promised to give me some information on this country," one wrote, while another simply asked for "a full account."[102] Most of the handful of letters they wrote seeking information about Haiti were addressed to "A. Grégoire," and it seems that André had been taken out of school in New Orleans and was living in Port-au-Prince.[103] Though we cannot be certain that André received these letters, the teacher seems to have encouraged his pupils to write their classmate asking for a report of life in Haiti. As John Blandin explained in his letter: "As we have heard from our English master, Mr. Constant, that you are employed at the English consul's office, I wish to know if you are glad to live there." "As to ourselves," Blandin revealed, "our situation is growing worse every day." About Haiti, he had heard conflicting stories: "I have often heard it said from people who came from there, that it is a good [country], and others say it is not. We would be very glad to hear something from you on that subject. Do tell us the right truth and let it be very soon."[104] The urgency in Blandin's tone is plain. Haiti might prove a salvation from the repressive conditions of the late antebellum South, but he needed more information, some sort of assurance. Nonetheless, Haiti represented the possibility of escape.

The students' most frequent question about Haiti, in fact, concerned military duties.[105] Arthur Denis asked Grégoire: "Are the creole young-men who go there obliged to do military service? For I have been told that they make soldiers with them and that the city of Port-au-Prince is not good at all." Despite his misgivings, however, Arthur also wrote: "I hope that the emigration will soon begin again."[106] Isidore Toussaint wrote: "Dear Grégoire, will you [tell] me if the Creoles from here are obliged to become soldiers in arriving in Hayti."[107] And John Blandin, who took a more enthusiastic view of the idea of military service, asked: "Are the Creoles of New Orleans required to do military service and are they glad in that beautiful country?"[108] Only in their queries about military service did they begin to use the term "Creole," a word that continues to appear in their letters through the early years of the Civil War. Despite an enthusiasm for the "beautiful country" of Haiti, they seem to have used the term, most often, to distinguish themselves from other groups, be they Haitians or Americans. This distinction becomes even more necessary for them with the start of the Civil War. Indeed, even as they hoped to distinguish themselves from Haitians to avoid military enlistment, they recognized the role of military service in defining and securing citizenship.

Because Haiti seems to have represented for the students a nation for people of color rather than a business venture, the students' optimism toward Haiti never disappeared, not even when they learned of the attempted assassination of President Geffrard, resulting in the accidental death of his daughter, which sparked further political turmoil. (A letter signed "les amis de *Geffrard*" arrived at the Catholic Institution with eighteen dollars enclosed, money raised for the school at the Church of Saint Anne in memory of young Cora Geffrard.)[109] After hearing the news of the girl's death, student Arthur Denis explained that "there are too many murderers, thieves, etc" in Haiti and that "war will soon sprang up [*sic*]. After this, you will see that it will be a good and delicious country. All the people who went there and return[ed] will be obliged to go back."[110]

Such was the hope, at least, of Redpath and his supporters, who found their cause adversely affected by news of revolution, assassination, and general disorder. Yet by the start of 1861, even Frederick Douglass, the most prominent black abolitionist and former slave in the United States, was willing to consider emigration an option, though he had opposed it publicly for a decade. The cumulative effects of the events of the late 1850s—particularly *Dred Scott* and the execution of abolitionist and guerrilla fighter John Brown—combined with President Lincoln's seeming willingness to compromise with slaveholding interests in order to preserve the Union, led Douglass to rethink his earlier opposition to emigration. In his newspaper in January 1861 he wrote, "Whatever the future may have in store for us, it seems plain that inducements offered to the colored man to remain here are few, feeble, and very uncertain . . . .We can raise no objection to the present movement towards Hayti. . . . We can no longer throw our little influence against a measure which may prove highly advantageous to many families, and of much service to the Haytian Republic." Douglass even accepted an invitation for an exploratory visit to Haiti in the spring of 1861. When the Civil War commenced the following month, Douglass canceled his trip and affirmed his commitment to remaining in the United States: "The last ten days have made a tremendous revolution in all things pertaining to the possible future of the colored people of the United States. We shall stay here and watch the current of events, and serve the cause of freedom and mankind."[111]

The boys at the Catholic Institution, however, were less quick to abandon thoughts of Haiti. When war at last broke out in the United States in April 1861, Haiti did not leave the pages of the letterbook. Instead, it became intertwined with mentions of battles, rights, and freedom from racial discrimination. They placed the Civil War on a map of their own drafting, a map greater than the battlefields of the South, that included Haiti, Cuba, even Africa. The war was a hardship and an unpredictable local event.[112] But it also inspired in them a transatlantic exploration of freedom, citizenship, and race at a time when all three were the subject of violent debate in the United States. On May 29, 1861, for instance, John Blandin, age seventeen, wrote an enthusiastic letter in favor of the Confederacy and addressed it to Haiti. In his composition, Blandin recounted a recent battle at Hampton, Virginia:

It was a battle which had taken place in the forenamed city, in which six hundred of the Lincolnites were slain, and only fifty of our brave Southerners were killed. It was also rumored yesterday that our Louisiana soldiers had a hand in the conflict and not one of them got hurt. Hurrah! for our brave Louisianans and may God bless them and [the] whole "Southern Confederate" army, that they might lick the "Northerners" every time they have an engagement and make them see that we Southern men are not to be played with. . . .

For we Southerners can stand any army they may send, from a hundred to five hundred thousand troops. So the best thing they must do is to acknowledge our rights, for we, we will give them the best licking they ever had since they know themselves.

Receive my dear friend this from the heart of a Creole, and who is proud to be [a] Southern man.

Your obedient and faithful servant.
John Blandin[113]

In the letterbook, the words "Confederate" and "Northerners" in Blandin's letter were crossed out by another hand and reversed, perhaps by a teacher, so that it read "may God bless them and the whole army, that they might lick the Confederacy." Blandin's enthusiasm for the Confederacy and the corrections to his composition reflect the shifting allegiances of free people of color in the first years of the war. In November 1861, fifteen hundred free black men enlisted in the Confederate army, forming the First Louisiana Native Guard. Some six months later, however, after Federal troops occupied New Orleans, a delegation of Afro-Creoles volunteered their services to the Union. The reasons for Afro-Creole support of the Confederacy at the start of the war remain unclear. Some may have been protecting their property interests, particularly the more prosperous members of the free colored community. But testimony taken after the Union occupation suggests that Confederates had threatened the lives of free blacks if they did not cooperate.[114]

Many men of color attributed their participation on the southern side to a strong sense of ethnic identity. John Blandin also wrote about a recruitment speech given by his schoolmaster, Armand Lanusse, who evoked the history of free black military service much earlier in the nineteenth century, when free men of color helped the Americans fight off the British in the War of 1812. "After A[rmand Lanusse] had made his speech he called on our brave creoles to sign their names, which they did with the utmost celerity and the true heart of a soldier. Mr. L. also spoke of our forefathers that struggled with General Andrew Jackson for the cause of liberty at New Orleans; by their brave spirit they repulsed the enemy after a struggle of sixteen days." As Creoles, it was their duty to defend—as did their fathers before them—their native soil.[115] John Blandin conveyed this sort of devotion to Louisiana, and the South, in his composition on the battle at Hampton, writing "from the heart of a Creole."[116]

Yet Blandin's response to the speech also made a link between "rights" and military participation. The deeds of their "forefathers" were to be repeated but this time for a different cause. "It is not for liberty," Blandin wrote, "that we are about to spill our blood in struggling; but our right"—and then here he seems to quote someone, perhaps Lanusse—"our right we shall have or die on the fields of battle."[117] At the close of his first composition, Blandin had predicted the way that Southerners like himself would win the war—"the best thing they must do is to acknowledge our rights, for we, we will give them the best licking they ever had."[118] Yet in a society that increasingly put limits on the freedom of his people, this young Afro-Creole had a complicated notion of what "rights" were and why he wanted to fight for them. It was his belief in the military defense of "rights" that explains, perhaps, his choice of Haiti as the destination for one of his letters. It may have been no accident, in other words, that Blandin chose to address his letter about battlefields and rights to Haiti, where people of color had attained their independence through military struggle.

Not every student was as enthusiastic about the war as John Blandin. Others found travel away from New Orleans to be a more prudent choice. Indeed, despite their enthusiasm for watching soldiers "make their exercises" in New Orleans, the students seldom wrote about battles. Instead, they focused on the ways in which the war divided them from their correspondents (real and imagined) in other countries. Armand Cloud, for instance, wrote of the war with a sense of dread and apprehension. He noted that Lincoln "menaces to burn up the city of New Orleans." He believed that the southerners "cannot whip the North, it is just the same as a son trying to whip his father." But Cloud decided to close with the following: "You said that you wished to come here, but I advise you to remain where you are; I am going away, as soon as possible."[119]

Again, Haiti seemed like a possibility. Two months past the start of the war, several of the students noted the departure of their friend Joseph Lavigne on a schooner bound for Haiti.[120] Lavigne's friend J. Bordenave, who went to the docks to see him off, regretted that he could not join Lavigne in Haiti. Reflecting on his friend's departure, he wrote: "I believe he will be better than us for he will be *in the country of our color*."[121] And the fall after Lavigne left for Haiti, T. Richard wrote to him that he, too, had gone to a new "country," one called "Texas." In what appears to have been an attempt to match Lavigne's good fortune, Richard explained that Texas "is a good city for colored people."[122]

Nonetheless, by 1861, Richard and Bordenave both understood the appeal of Haiti in racial rather than economic terms, that is, as a good place "for colored people."

In many of their letters, the war is less a sectional conflict than an impediment to be overcome on their travels. This is particularly true after the Union navy blockaded Confederate ports following President Lincoln's orders in April 1861. The impossibility of leaving—the loss of the freedom to travel that had belonged to free people of color migrating to Mexico and Haiti—seems to be part of the reason for writing such letters. In some of the boys' letters from this period, the steamships on which they traveled even get a furious chase on their return voyage from Lincoln's navy. John Bordenave, after recounting a voyage to Portugal, wrote, "If you remember, I started from New Orleans before the blockade, and I was coming back in the steamship *John Blandin* when we were near the Balize, we saw the men of war of the Black Lincoln who were coming to chase us. I was obliged to pass by Maine, New Hampshire, and some other states to come to my native one."[123] Bordenave and his schoolfellows must have been reading in the papers about the expeditions of blockade runners supplying the Confederacy with ammunition and supplies and ferrying cotton out of the South.[124] Suddenly, their map of the Atlantic World was filled with the instruments of war and the politics of secession. As H. Relf revealed in his letter, the war was beginning to wear on the city's inhabitants. "I wish to tell you something of the hope I have upon the war between the United States and the Confederate States," he wrote in December 1861. He projected that the war "will not last four months more" because from what he had read in the papers, Lincoln "does not wish to continue the war," and in the Confederate states "every body desires peace, for they are in great distress."[125]

Henry Relf also took a wartime tour, but he focused on important architectural sites in the United States and Europe. He journeyed on a steamship, he wrote, "for the doctor told me that only a journey on the sea would cure me." He chose to visit Fort Sumter in Charleston (where the Civil War began), the Royal Exchange in London, the state houses in Philadelphia and in New Haven, and the Capitol building in Washington. "In returning," he added, "I stopped at Richmond now the Capital of the Confederate States. I was at Manassas when the battle took place, and as I didn't want to fight, I came right back home."[126] Henry also wrote another letter a few months later in which he imagined himself encountering the Union navy on his return from a trip to England. He told his friend that he had started for New Orleans before the blockade and was returning by the steamship *Israel*. "When we were near Balize we saw three men of war of Lincoln who were coming to chase us," he explained, "and I was obliged to pass by New York, Pennsylvania, and the other States to come to my country."[127]

The blockades of southern ports tightened in the first months of 1862, as the Union navy closed in on the South's largest cities. Soon after, John Bordenave wrote of a voyage even more daring than his trip to Portugal. In his letter to "L. Lamanière," Bordenave told a story about sailing to Africa and taking a boy back to Louisiana:

New Orleans, January 15th 1862

To L. Lamanière Esq
Sienna H'and

Dear friend,
Last year I went on the board of the steamboat Louisa to make a voyage to Africa. In arriving there I met with a negroe whose name is Francis and he was so well with me that in coming back home, his family was obliged to let him come with me but on arriving here, I took him by the arm and told him that he was my servant and that he had nothing to do, but he replied that he was a good boy and that he was much satisfied with his sort. Three weeks after I sold him on the plantation of Mr. Morgan, who is a great cotton maker, he was very well there, but trying to kill one of the negroe, he was hung.

Yours,
J. Bordenave[128]

Bordenave not only flouted the Union blockade but did so for the purpose of acquiring a servant from Africa and selling him to a cotton planter. Perhaps he was writing his letter in protest of the Union blockade, but in tricking an African and selling him into slavery, he also reinforced a line of difference between himself and enslaved Africans, a difference that had been fading in the decade before the war. With his story, in turn, he could participate in the political economy of slavery by assuming the role of slave trader, creating a social distance between himself and plantation slaves. With his account of the slave Francis's death, he also displayed an awareness of the violence that maintained slavery as an institution in the South. Like the students writing to Mexico who empowered themselves by assuming the role of planter, Bordenave appropriated a level of power for himself by engaging in the trade in Africans, at a time when slavery—the seat of power in the antebellum South—was under threat by northern troops. Bordenave searched the Atlantic not for a new country but as a means to empower himself in his own. In this, his broad view of the Atlantic was useful. He defined his own sense of freedom and power within the Atlantic World of which New Orleans was only a part.

This wider view of the war also appeared in the students' response to local conditions, especially to the poverty that had descended upon the city after 1861. The daily circumstances of war had encouraged the boys to think about places outside of the South. In a letter he addressed to one of his classmates in "Madrid, Spain," Henry Relf wrote that he had "learned that the State of Missouri fell into the Confederate States," for which he was glad, since "when the United States will see that the South is of the same numbers as they, they will give up." Like most of the students, Relf wanted to see an end to the war that had put such a strain on life in New Orleans. "Here everybody is in great misery and every thing is out of price; the dearest of all is soap, we used to pay $5 for a box weighing 40 pounds, but now it is $19."[129] These dire circumstances led Henry Vasserot to think of escaping the states as soon as possible. "After the war I am going to put myself a sailor," he declared, "till I reach a good country for the misery is too hard every body is in tears there is no work to give the poor men and women nor bread enough to give the soldiers."[130]

Though the boys' attitudes toward the Union had been ambivalent at best in the first year of the war, with the turn of events in 1862, they landed squarely on the side of the Union. Soon after Federal troops occupied the city on May 1, a delegation of free black officers paid a visit to Union general Benjamin Butler. They reported the location of their arms to Butler and stated their desire to fight for the Union. The officers had stored the guns belonging to their regiments in three places for safekeeping, one of which was the Catholic Institution.[131] After some reluctance on the part of Butler, by the end of August 1862, a regiment of a thousand free black men had been mustered to fight for the Union.[132] Once a recruitment site and exercise yard for the Confederate First Native Guard in 1861, the Catholic Institution became an arsenal for the weapons of free black men fighting to defend the Union and defeat the slaveholding South.[133]

After the Union occupation began, the boys began writing a bit more optimistically about life in the city. In a letter addressed to "New York City," Ernest Brunet wrote to his friend, "I tell you if the Yankees would not come here we would be starving to death. About two weeks before the Yankees came in, you could not get a loaf of bread without fighting for it, and after fighting for it you would after pay $40 a loaf." Still, Ernest noted that finding work was still difficult, with the only skills in demand "shoemaker barber shop segar maker and tailor." Because these did not suit him, he explained, he would remain in school.[134] Lucien Lamanière noted that "the town is in great distress that we cannot distinguish the rich and the poor. The only difference that there is now between the rich and poor is that the latter is not so well dressed as the former, but for money neither the poor nor rich cannot have any, for it is too rare."[135]

Most of the optimism in the students' letters written under occupation concerned the presence of black soldiers in the city, after the Union army took the city of New Orleans in April 1862, when the leaders of the Louisiana Native Guard (many of them also leaders of the Catholic Institution) presented themselves to Union officials, offering their services in the war against the Confederacy.[136] The boys also noted with great interest the large numbers of colored troops amassing in the city to fight for the Union that year. Etienne Pérault, in a letter to a friend addressed to "Haiti," with no small amount of pride, remarked: "Dear friend, I had forgotten to tell you that there are about three or four thousand colored soldiers here. They had one regiment that has already been to the camp and that is at the camp now."[137] Troops of black soldiers signaled a new order within southern society. One student reported that when a colored regiment left town, "some amongst them were singing, some that were saying that they would bring the four limbs of old Jeff Davis and some [of] the other ones the head of Beauregard."[138]

If large regiments of colored soldiers were an indication of the changes brought by the war, so were the actions of enslaved people on nearby plantations. After noting that anyone who sang the "Bonnie Blue Flag" in the city was "severely punished" by Union officials, Ernest Brunet reported that he also knew of "a great many Negroes who are running away from their masters and go away with the Yankees."[139] The students rarely referred to slavery in their letters, but they did take note of the political implications of emancipation for enslaved people, as well as for free people of color. They understood the arrival of freedom within the context not only of their own country, however, but also in relation to other slave societies. Lucien Lamanière, for instance, noted the relationship between free people of color and the system of slavery and was aware, too, of emancipation as an event that reached beyond the southern states. He wrote:

> I am very glad since the Federals are here, they are telling that Gen. Butler is going to make the colored men of this city who were born free vote, if he do that the colored men will be very glad to see equality reign here and if he is ever to be elected President of the United States I am sure that he will be President because the colored men will vote for him, and I must tell you another thing. The [white slaveholding] Creoles of this city will die when they will see the Negroes vote as well as them, those Negroes whom they were always whipping in the plantations [will] take their tickets and put it in the box, I do not think that [the Creoles] will stay here, they are all going to Havana, and there, they are dieing like flies with the country's disease, a letter which we received from a friend told us that [the Creoles] are very bad there, the Negroes of that country are cursing them when they pass by them.[140]

The end of slavery in the South, like the war itself, was a political event that could not be contained within the boundaries of the United States. Rather, as Lucien noted, it affected other slave societies like Cuba, throwing into question what remained of slavery in the Caribbean.[141] It was an event, too, that might give former slaves and former free men of color the same political power as white men.[142]

The Civil War, in Lucien's interpretation, turned these slaveholding societies on their heads: giving political power to free men of color and "Negroes" in the United States and causing slaveholders to die "like flies" in Cuba. Etienne Pérault, too, had an impression of the southern social order turned upside down by the war. He wrote a letter within a letter, addressed to Haiti using the voice of a Confederate soldier writing to his sister. Etienne may have written this himself, or he might have copied it from another source, perhaps a newspaper printing letters from the battlefront. Nonetheless, he chose to include this particular story, a story that speaks to the revolution taking place as he wrote. The soldier declared that he would rather "endure all the privations and perils of the service than to die the thousand deaths of the cowardly miscreants of Louisiana of French extraction." Deriding the (white) Confederate soldiers of Louisiana (in words that ring more with Etienne's playfulness, perhaps, than the thoughts of a Confederate), the soldier hoped that Union general Benjamin Butler "will conscript them, and work them in cleaning the streets, *with collars on their necks.*"[143]

Writing about the war, then, was not just an imaginative exercise for the students; it was an exploration into the nature, indeed the *possibility*, of power. In this upended society, the Union general fighting to end slavery—and to whose armies enslaved people were fleeing daily—would put in shackles white southerners who had fought in the name of slavery's preservation.[144] Etienne also addressed this particular letter to Haiti, the only example of slavery successfully deposed by enslaved people themselves, thus placing masters at the mercy of their former slaves.

The Civil War was never separate in the minds of the students from their thinking about other points in the Atlantic World. Just before writing about the Creoles going to Cuba, Lucien had penned another letter. There would be nearly two more years of war, though Lucien could not know this. This letter appears, as does his writing on Cuba, toward the end of the last surviving letterbook. There would be only a few more of the students' letters recorded before they ceased in the fall of 1863. In this letter, Lucien recalled a visit to his aunt and cousin in Paris and told his friend: "I am going next year and I invite you to come. We will go to Paris together and before coming back to New Orleans, we will go and visit that fine country called Hayti and if you are not satisfied of those two countries, we will go and visit Mexico the finest country after Paris."[145] Charged and bright as his plans were, they were dimmed somewhat by the words he had written at the foot of his letter. "Since the blockade," Lucien wrote in his postscript, "I have not heard any news from you."[146] Captive in his own land, Lucien wrote of finding a good country. In the face of a crippling civil war, he planned an ocean voyage. Yet if we consider Lucien's two letters side by side, his plans do not seem so fantastic. It was his belief in the existence of "fine countries" like Paris, Mexico, and Haiti, perhaps, that encouraged his faith in the rapidly changing society in which he lived. His love of these places gave him cause to believe that after the war in the United States "free colored men" and "Negroes" would be able to vote—to "take their tickets and put it in the box"—and that his own country might one day be as "fine" as the rest.

2

Reading Race
Rosebloom and Pure White,
Or So It Seemed

If Lucien Lamanière's imagined voyage around the Atlantic narrated the search for a nation free of racial prejudice, the portrait of Rosa Downs conjured the nation's long history of racial slavery. In a photograph taken in a New York studio in 1864, Rosa appeared to be a little girl born into the Victorian middle class. Such a photograph might have held a treasured spot in any urban, middle-class parlor (figure 1).

It was a portrait very similar, in fact, to that of another girl child photographed in Philadelphia the same year (figure 2). Both girls appeared in vignette, a style popular at the time that left only the head of the sitter visible, surrounded by soft white space—a style that made young children look like angels.[1] But with their portraits the similarity between the two girls ended. Their faces had been photographed for very different reasons. Their prospects would not be the same. And those viewers who, at first glance, took Rosa for a white child would have seen her otherwise once they read the words printed beneath her portrait: "Rosa" (her name in lovely script), "A Slave Girl from New Orleans."

Rosina (alias Rosa) Downs, age "not quite seven," was one of five children and three adults freed in occupied New Orleans by the Union army's Major General Nathaniel P. Banks in 1863. As it turned out, the capture of New Orleans was not just excellent military strategy. Indeed, the occupation of the South's largest port was a boon for wartime propaganda in the North. Like the Sea Islands of South Carolina (taken by Federal troops in 1861), New Orleans was an early experiment in federal governance in the South. A flurry of reports in magazines, antislavery journals, and newspapers reached northern readers by 1863. Rosa and her companions were part of the campaign to inform northern

Figure 1. *Left*: "Rosa: A Slave Girl from New Orleans," *carte-de-visite,* photograph, Charles Paxton, New York, ca. 1864. Slavery/Antislavery Collection, Sophia Smith Collection, Smith College. Figure 2. *Right*: Unknown child, *carte-de-visite,* handprinted, Philadelphia, ca. 1864. William Culp Darrah Collection, Courtesy of Historical Collections and Labor Archives, Special Collections Library, The Pennsylvania State University.

audiences about people and conditions in the South. Colonel George Hanks, serving on a commission under General Banks responsible for the education and labor of freedpeople, took the group north with the help of representatives from the American Missionary Association and the National Freedman's Relief Association.[2] Their tour involved both public appearances and visits to photographers' studios, all to raise money for newly established schools for freedpeople in Louisiana.[3] A photographic portrait of the group from Louisiana (figure 3) was made into an illustration and printed on a full page of *Harper's Weekly,* the most popular magazine of its day. The illustration appeared, along with a letter to the editor from one of the missionary sponsors, under the provocative headline "White and Colored Slaves."[4] Nearly all the portraits made featured the children—Isaac, Augusta, Rosina (or Rosa), Charles, and Rebecca. Of these, most seem to have included only the whitest-looking children: Rosa, Rebecca, and Charles.[5]

The decision to display white-looking children was due, in part, to the success of a girl child named Fanny Lawrence (to whom we shall return) who had been "redeemed" in Virginia (figure 4).[6] But Fanny, too, had her predecessors, as we will see, in girls such as Mary Mildred

EMANCIPATED SLAVES.

Brought from Louisiana by Col. Geo. H. Hanks. The Children are from the Schools established by order of Maj. Gen. Banks.

WILSON CHINN.   MARY JOHNSON.   ROBERT WHITEHEAD.
CHAS. TAYLOR.   AUGUSTA BROUJEY.   ISAAC WHITE.   REBECCA HUGER.   ROSINA DOWNS.

Entered according to Act of Congress, in the year 1863, by PHILIP BACON, in the Clerk's Office of the United States for the Southern District of New-York.
Photographed by M. H. Kimball, 477 Broadway, N.Y.

FANNIE VIRGINIA CASSEOPIA LAWRENCE,

A Redeemed SLAVE CHILD, 5 years of age. Redeemed in Virginia, by Catharine S. Lawrence; baptized in Brooklyn, at Plymouth Church, by Henry Ward Beecher, May, 1863.

Entered according to Act of Congress, in the year 1863, by C. S. Lawrence, in the Clerk's Office of the District Court of the United States, for the Southern District of New York.

Figure 3. *Above*: "Emancipated Slaves," photograph, M. H. Kimball, New York, 1863. Courtesy of the Library Company of Philadelphia.

Figure 4. *Left*: "Fannie Virginia Casseopia Lawrence," *carte-de-visite*, New York, 1863. Library of Congress.

Botts and Sally Maria Deiggs (or "Pink"). As Fanny, Mary, and Sally had done, the three very light-skinned children from New Orleans captivated the white northern audiences who saw them. In an account of the group's appearance in New York, these children were singled out: "three of the children," said the *Evening Post,* "were perfectly white."[7] Isaac and Augusta, both darker-skinned than the others, along with the adults, received less attention. When the sponsors opted to take the children on to Philadelphia for more appearances and sittings in photography studios, in fact, Isaac and Augusta may have been left behind.[8]

For white northern audiences, the portraits of white-looking slave children, rather than black-looking children, conveyed perhaps the most compelling antislavery message for boosting support of the Union campaign in the South.[9] When the *Harper's Weekly* illustration was "recycled" in the *Youth's Companion* in 1865 (a common practice in the nineteenth century), the editors pictured only the three "white slaves," with extra pains taken by an illustrator to draw Charley's head on Isaac's body so that the three could stand together.[10] "Let our friends not be surprised that these girls are white," the editors wrote, with pointed interest in Rosa and Rebecca. "They are in fact as light colored, and we dare say, as good looking as most of our young readers of their sex. And so it often is at the South. Large numbers of the slaves are white. This indicates one of the evils, and the great wickedness of slavery." The editors did not spare their young readers the hard realities of slavery in the South, explaining that such white children "are not unfrequently [*sic*] the children of their masters"; the editors lamented that "the poor white children of the slave mother are sold like brutes to the highest bidder."[11]

As the note in the *Youth's Companion* indicates, white-skinned slave girls generally received the most attention. There appear to be more surviving photographs of them, suggesting that perhaps more people bought pictures of them. And unlike photographs of Charles, the portraits of Rosa and Rebecca seem especially tailored to pique the viewer's interest. In the letter to *Harper's Weekly,* Rosina Downs was described as "a fair child with blonde complexion and silky hair." ("Rosina" was shortened to the simpler name "Rosa" for the portraits.) Rebecca Huger, age eleven, was a little older, and photographers often dressed and posed her to seem more a young lady than a child. Of Rebecca, the missionary wrote to *Harper's*: "To all appearance, she is perfectly white.

Her complexion, hair, and features show not the slightest trace of negro blood."[12] These white-looking girls, in sweet, innocent form, troubled notions of racial difference and fostered an unease laced with fascination among white northern viewers. Indeed, what made Rosa, Rebecca, and the girls who preceded them so beguiling for nineteenth-century audiences was that these lovely white girls were not "white."

As we will see, photographs and public presentations of white-looking slave girls were spectacles with multiple meanings, inviting a combination of sympathy, speculation, voyeurism, and moral outrage.[13] In search of images that would garner support for the antislavery cause, abolitionists and military officials (once the Civil War had begun) found powerful representatives in white-skinned slave girls. The usefulness of white-looking slave girls as living metaphors for slavery's evils sprung from stories about race and slavery already familiar to northern audiences: harrowing tales of white people enslaved in the South, popular representations of white and black children in the nineteenth century, and tragic antislavery stories about light-skinned slave girls and women forced to sacrifice their virtue. And for those girls who appeared in portraiture, their effectiveness was tied, as well, to the new "truth-telling" medium of photography.

All these stories, and the photographs and presentations that seemed to confirm them, were conceived in the labyrinth of racial ideology that both guided and confused white northern sympathies. Because the girls looked white, their images appealed to Victorian sentiments of white audiences toward white girlhood, rather than the girlhood of black or "colored" children. Indeed, while they pressed for the abolition that would free white-skinned children like Rosa, they left the black child and her plight in the shadows. At the same time, images of Rosa and Rebecca also tapped into audiences' fascination with the light-skinned "fancy girls" sold in the slave markets, the largest and most notorious of which was in New Orleans. (Rosa and Rebecca's unhappy fate, as light-skinned slave girls from that city, would have been clear.) Ironically, in the invitation to scrutiny and in their sale price (the money to buy the freedom of some of Rosa's predecessors came from public "auctions"), their orchestrated appearances and photographs for purchase mirrored the activities of hawkers and buyers in the slave market itself. Further, girls such as Rosa also raised the specter of the interracial sex that had produced seemingly "white" but nonetheless "colored" people. Rosa and girls like her appeared destined to become the possession of white men and to produce ever-lighter-skinned people of African descent.

In fact, representations of white-skinned slave girls broached the future in a very pointed way. As Lucien and his classmates at the Catholic Institution were aware, the Civil War brought with it profound uncertainty. So, too, did the face of Rosa Downs. Perhaps more than any other images of the period, photographs and presentations of light-skinned slave girls reflected the racial fears that surrounded the question of slavery and its demise. There were, in fact, two visions of the future to be read in Rosa's portrait, both of which exposed concerns about the preservation of white supremacy once slavery no longer divided white from black. In the first interpretation, (the one intended by abolitionists) light-skinned, white-looking, girl children foreshadowed the racial consequences for the nation if slavery was allowed to spread. Their images played upon fears that white people could become enslaved in the South, should slavery continue, fears that had become more prominent in the 1850s, as the sectional debate deepened. (The staging of Rosa's and other girls' portraits, placing a light-skinned slave girl in the pose of white middle-class girl, engaged these fears directly.) This vision of the future, then—produced in an effort to defeat slavery and promote black freedom—may have stoked the fires of Union sentiment, but it did so by promoting the idea that slavery was a threat to white people.

Rosa's portrait also conjured another possible future, however. Read as an augur of the racial implications of emancipation, her photograph also hinted at the uncertain future of the "Anglo-Saxon" race in the United States once people who looked like Rosa became free. A population of people like Rosa, who looked "white" but were not, would cast doubt on the alleged racial purity of all "white" people. If, in her photograph, Rosa appeared to be a white middle-class child, then would the naked eye be any better at discerning her African ancestry? Either vision of the future read through Rosa's portrait—the expansion of slavery or its abolition—exposed the racial anxieties on the part of whites that often lay at the center of the debate over slave emancipation. As the image of Rosa so cleverly points out, the prospect of black freedom was inextricable from threats to white supremacy in the aftermath of slavery. Rosa's viewers could scarcely view one without seeing the other.

These tangled notions were most plainly expressed, perhaps, in the portrait of Isaac and Rosa, arm in arm (figure 5). Both children, as we

Figure 5. "Isaac and Rosa, Emancipated Slave
Children from the Free Schools of Louisiana,"
carte-de-visite, Kimball, New York, 1863.
Photographs and Prints Division, Schomburg
Center for Research in Black Culture, The New
York Public Library, Astor, Lenox, and Tilden
Foundations.

have already seen, were dressed fancily, with Isaac in pressed suit and
Rosa in petticoats, a cloak, and flowered hat. From first glance, the contrast in skin color between the two is striking, and this was, no doubt,
the point. Isaac's skin served to accentuate Rosa's paleness. Next to
her dark-skinned companion, Rosa appeared unmistakably "white."
But placing Isaac and Rosa together had the opposite effect, as well. It

assured viewers that their own eyes deceived them, that Rosa could not have been "white," since a white girl never would have appeared in public on the arm of a black boy.[14] For playing upon uncertainty, Rosa's image may have been the perfect metaphor, one that signified blackness and whiteness, "miscegenation" and racial purity, sexual innocence and sexual promise, slavery and freedom.[15] In the ambiguous, vulnerable body of a white-looking slave girl, white northern audiences could see the precarious future of their divided nation—a nation many of them still considered to be a "white" one.[16]

The actual numbers of people who saw Rosa and other girls like her is difficult to gauge.[17] Certainly, the coverage they received in northern newspapers and periodicals could have reached a large number of middle-class readers. The appearance of Sally Deiggs, or "Pink," in Brooklyn's Plymouth Church in 1860 was covered in both the *Brooklyn Daily Eagle* and the *New York Times* and even merited headline coverage and photos in both papers in 1927, when she attended the eightieth anniversary of Plymouth Church.[18] And although it is difficult to know who saw the photographs of Rosa and Rebecca, their production at a time when many white working-class people openly opposed the Civil War— most notably with the New York Draft Riots of 1863—suggests that they may have been aimed at a broad northern audience not limited to the middle class. The riots were sparked by white workers' opposition to the draft and to what they perceived as a war to end slavery, fought on behalf of the wealthy (who could buy their way out of service) at the expense of the poor, hence the phrase "rich man's war, poor man's fight."[19] Indeed, the girls' portraits seem to have been an effort on the part of abolitionists and military officials to circumvent issues of class by pressing the argument that southern slavery threatened the freedoms and privileges of all white people.[20]

Abolitionist leader and editor William Lloyd Garrison anticipated the effects of stories about white people enslaved in a speech to the American Colonization Society in 1827: "Suppose that, by a miracle, the slaves should suddenly become white," he wrote. "Would you shut your eyes upon their sufferings, and calmly talk of Constitutional limitations? No; your voice would peal in the ears of the taskmasters like deep thunder; you would carry the Constitution by force, if it could not be taken by treaty; patriotic assemblies would congregate at the corners of every street."[21] Garrison and his colleagues also expressed the belief that the kidnapping and enslavement of white people were becoming commonplace, referring to stories of white children whose skin was blackened with charcoal or soot by their captors to make them appear to be "mulatto" so that they might be sold, undetected. In 1834, for instance, abolitionist writer and editor Lydia Maria Child published a story about two girls, Mary and Susan, one white and one black, who were kidnapped by a slave trader. The trader cut off Mary's hair and crimped it with an iron, and after covering her with soot and grease, he declared: "There! Now you are almost as good-looking a *nigger* as t'other one." Mary's parents eventually recovered their child after the trader's sham had been discovered, but Sally, a free black child, was lost to the slave trade.[22] Former slaves and abolitionists William Craft and William Wells Brown both cited incidents of white people—again, most often children—darkened with soot and sold into slavery. One in particular, that of Sally Miller, a young German girl alleged to have been sold into slavery in New Orleans, launched a court case in Louisiana that received national attention.[23] The concern with kidnapping was further heightened with the passage of the Fugitive Slave Act in 1850. Just as free people of color feared kidnapping and enslavement after the act's passage, white abolitionists argued that this compromise with the slave states might also lead to white slavery.[24] Their fears were supported, as well, by the proslavery fanaticism of people such as the writer George Fitzhugh, who defended southern slavery as a legitimate labor system that was not necessarily racial by definition, and an institution superior to northern capitalists' degradation of the white working class. "In the absence of negro slavery," Fitzhugh wrote, "there must be white slavery, else the white laboring class are remitted to slavery to capital, which is more cruel and exacting than domestic slavery."[25]

By the 1850s and 1860s, white slaves had become some of the peculiar institution's most "vile" specters, and accounts of white people enslaved in the South proliferated in northern newspapers and antislavery journals.[26] These reports sprang from fears that if slavery went unchecked—if the southern slave power had its way—it would soon deny the liberties of white Americans.[27] In one such story, a correspondent from the *New York Tribune* reported in 1863 that a white woman, "through whose veins courses the Anglo-Saxon blood, and who has no negro taint about her," had been sold into slavery near Beaufort, South Carolina, apparently by her own husband, with whom she had had a dispute. Poor white southerners were often implicated in abolitionists' reports of white slavery, in which they were accused of selling their wives and children. "The selling of wives is not uncommon in South Carolina," the writer explained, "especially when their health is broken down and they are unable to do hard work." Mrs. Cribb, the woman in question, even produced a bill of sale for herself for the suspiciously meager sum of five dollars.[28] In Mary Hayden Green Pike's popular anti-slavery novel *Ida May: A Story of Things Actual and Possible* (1854), a southern "gentleman" had a similarly disparaging view of the poor whites of the South. Suspecting (rightly) that Ida May was a white child who had been sold into slavery, he said: "She may be one of the poor whites, and in that case she would be much better off to be a servant here than to live at home. It may be, too that she was sold instead of stolen. I have frequently seen white children who were thus thrown into the market. These miserable 'clay eaters' often sell their children, and I suppose Virginia 'crackers' do the same, and in my opinion it is the best thing they can do for their children."[29]

Other stories pointed to the domestic relations of southern slavery. The *Tribune*, for instance, printed an account involving the son of a white woman. The white woman, the paper explained, had been the product of a planter's daughter's "seduction" and was raised by a slave woman. The girl grew up to be a planter's mistress, and the children she had by him were treated as his slaves. One of her children, Charles Grayson, was sold away from her but not before the truth about his parentage was revealed to him by his mother. According to the *Tribune*, Grayson had "straight, light hair, fair, blue eyes, a sandy beard, and evidently is a white man, with no drop of black blood in his veins." Perhaps even more frightening to white readers was the writer's description of Grayson's demeanor: "He is totally ignorant. He scarcely knows what freedom is." Though "a negro slave has a subdued, and yet, at times a gay air," the writer remarked, "Charles Grayson is continually abject and gloomy." In 1862 Grayson managed to escape into Union lines, where he was aided by members of the Third Michigan Cavalry.[30] A story like Grayson's proved quite useful to the Union military and to abolitionists. Given the increasing unpopularity of the Civil War in the North, abolitionists and Union officials hoped to divert northern eyes from the largely black slave population for whom the war was, arguably, fought. Instead of black freedom, these stories implied, it was the white man's freedom that needed to be defended against the inevitable encroachments of southern slavery.

Tales of "white slavery" had more dramatic appeal, however, when they concerned beautiful white girls, for whom not just freedom but virtue was at stake. The *National Antislavery Standard,* for instance, ran a story in 1863 (which seems to have been fictional) entitled "Sold at Savannah," about an Irish girl named Ellen Neale who while in the South had lost all her kin to the cholera.[31] Though taken in by kindly Quakers, Ellen soon was seized as a fugitive slave under orders from the "yellow-eyed" Elder Mathewson, who had been propositioning Ellen without success for several months. Ellen's face, the narrator explained, was "more than pretty, for it was downright beautiful, with its rose-bloom and pure white and the dark, lustrous eyes and well-shaped mouth." Ellen eventually found herself on the auction block, subjected to the scrutiny of the "chivalry" (white male spectators who attended her sale.) "They did not come to buy," the narrator observes, "but for the most part to look on, scrutinize, and exercise their critical powers." The auctioneer informed his audience, "High bids are expected, for it isn't every day such angeliferous loveliness comes to the hammer." He proclaimed her "a very white mulatto . . . but I have never heard a fair skin objected to in a slave. A housekeeper, gentlemen, governess, *or* companion." Ellen was rescued at the last moment when her Quaker friends brought forward proof of her British citizenship, but her story was a harrowing one meant to show white readers how little distance remained between white women's purity and the abominations of slavery.[32]

Accounts of white-*looking* people who had been born into slavery—that is, those of African descent who appeared to be "perfectly" white —were effective in ways both similar to and different from stories of white people enslaved. William H. De Camp, for instance, working among black regiments in Tennessee, wrote home to the *Grand Rapids Eagle* that he had discovered a number of soldiers in the "negro enlistment" who appeared to be white men: "When one sees standing before him a man of mature years, who possesses not the slightest trace of negro blood in a single feature or complexion, and hair straighter than you can generally find in the pure Anglo-Saxon race and he tells you that his father is Col. Higgins, now of the rebel army," then the "ruling passion in the South" became quite clear. Encountering white-looking former slaves seemed to further convince De Camp of the righteousness of his duty: "I never was an Abolitionist," he wrote, "but I am not in favor of white slaves in a white country, and that where we call our nation a white one."[33]

In one sense, then, De Camp viewed the soldier as a white man, and his outrage stemmed from the thought of white men enslaved. By the same token, audiences were horrified to imagine white-looking children like Rosa as the chattel of southern slaveholders. Yet because of their African ancestry, the furor that white-looking enslaved people inspired was more complex than reactions to accounts of "Anglo-Saxon" people enslaved. Both the soldiers De Camp encountered and the "white slaves" brought North by abolitionists did more than demonstrate white people's vulnerability to enslavement. White-looking people were the embodiment of racial transgression, living proof of the "ruling passion of the South." Although relations between white male slaveholders and their black female slaves were not illicit in the antebellum South, the "mulatto" children resulting from those encounters were nonetheless public manifestations of the relations between master and slave.[34] One need only recall southern diarist Mary Chesnut's famous quip: "Every lady tells you who is the father of all the mulatto children in everybody's household, but those in her own she seems to think drop from the clouds, or so pretends to think."[35] But very light-skinned slaves were, for whites, the most troubling group, since they were capable of claiming to be white even though they were of "mixed" race.

Photographic images of white-looking slaves—a medium that seemed to allow viewers to see for themselves—simultaneously fascinated and tormented viewers because of both the girls' "invisible" ancestry and the sexual history that produced them.[36] Much of the appeal of the white-skinned slave girl, in fact, derived from the medium in which she often appeared. The daguerreotype and the *carte-de-visite* photograph were visual technologies new to the mid-nineteenth century. In the eyes of Victorian Americans, the power of photographs and daguerreotypes lay in their ability to "speak" truths otherwise inaudible. Every photographic image was a testimonial with the capacity to turn "the narrative status of its subject from fiction to fact."[37] (There was even a nineteenth-century serial, unrelated to photography, entitled *The Daguerreotype,* devoted to "The Truth.")[38] Before the invention and spread of photography, the most compelling evidence of the cruelties of slavery were to be found in eyewitness accounts of slavery's atrocities, both written and oral—accounts that carried even more weight when delivered to audiences aloud, by former slaves.[39] Yet there was a vast difference between *reading* about slavery and *seeing* its effects for oneself. The surgeon who examined the fugitive slave named Gordon, for in-

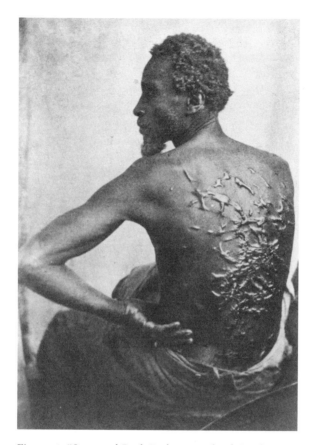

Figure 6. "Scourged Back," photograph of Gordon, an escaped slave, ca. 1863. Photographs and Prints Division, Schomburg Center for Research in Black Culture, The New York Public Library, Astor, Lenox, and Tilden Foundations.

stance—the subject of the widely reproduced photograph "Scourged Back"—observed that "few sensation writers ever depicted worse punishments than this man must have received" (figure 6).[40] Indeed, a photograph allowed northern viewers to see Gordon's mutilated body for themselves, witnessing "firsthand" the evil effects of slavery. Images like "Scourged Back" testified to slavery's atrocities in a way that written ex-slave narratives could not, since the cruel effects of slavery had been inscribed on the ex-slave's person by the slaveholder himself, rather than onto a page by a former slave. On seeing "Scourged Back" in 1863, an editor at the *New York Independent* remarked that the photograph "tells the story in a way that even Mrs. Stowe cannot approach, because it tells the story to the eye."[41] This was clearly the thinking of the sponsors of white-looking slave children, hoping to reveal what might otherwise sound unbelievable to white northern viewers.

The "reality" introduced by the photograph, in turn, opened up new avenues of sympathy and, further still, of imagined pain and suffering. The sight of Gordon's back, covered with hundreds of thickened scars, forced viewers not only to see the effects of slavery but also to imagine the scene of the slave's punishment, the very laying on of the lash. Indeed, the image even placed them in the position of the punisher. Photographs of these white-looking slave girls, no less than the picture of Gordon, exposed the evils of southern slavery. Yet the fantasy they inspired was a quite different one. In the images of Rosa, Rebecca, and Fanny, the slaveholder's violence was read by viewers on the unmarked surfaces of their light-skinned bodies rather than, as with Gordon, stated in firm welts on the skin. The girls' portraits invited viewers— particularly male viewers—to imagine them as the light-skinned "fancy girls" for sale in the New Orleans slave market, young women highly valued for their service as concubines to the white men of the South.

These photographs presented a female body that existed for the viewer somewhere between the real and the imagined, in this respect much like pornographic photography of the nineteenth century. With the invention of photography, pornographers could use the bodies and the direct gazes of *real* women returning the stares of the male spectator rather than fictionalized or painted ones. Like pornographic photographs, images of white-looking slave girls did not replace fantasies of beautiful mulatto and octoroon women enslaved and violated but, rather, further encouraged them.[42] Seeing the portrait of Rebecca kneeling in prayer, for instance, a white northern audience read in her white skin a history of "miscegenation," generations of it, resulting from the sexual interaction of white masters with their female slaves (figure 7).[43] And Rebecca's girlish form raised the possibility of future violations (whereas the image of a woman might have represented virtue already lost) and further invited the exercise of viewers' imaginations as they looked at her photograph.

If viewers read a sexual future in the photographs of these girls, however, they were also doing their utmost to read their race. We can imag-

REBECCA,
An Emancipated Slave from New Orleans.
PHOTOGRAPHED BY KIMBALL, 477 BROADWAY, N. Y.
Entered according to act of Congress, in the year 1863, by P.
Bacon, in the Clerk's Office of the United States, for the
Southern District of New York.

Figure 7. "Rebecca, an Emancipated Slave from
New Orleans," *carte-de-visite*, 1863. Photo-
graphs and Prints Division, Schomburg Center
for Research in Black Culture, The New York
Public Library, Astor, Lenox, and Tilden
Foundations.

ine that viewers studied the portraits carefully, searching each photograph for the curve of the nose or the shape of the head that might in-
dicate the child's African ancestry. Nineteenth-century scholars and scientists valued the "mute testimony" that photography provided as a
means to scrutinize human subjects for physical signs of intelligence,
potential for criminality, or evidence of a deranged mind.[44] A physician

writing in 1859 insisted that one could uncover the physical and psychological essences of a person with photography because only in photographs could one rely on the "silent but telling language of nature."[45] The medium of photography also developed in tandem with theories concerning the separate origin of the races and the biology of racial difference proffered by adherents to the "American school" of anthropology (Louis Agassiz and Samuel Morton the most prominent among them) in the 1850s and 1860s.[46] With the popularity of the easily reproducible *carte-de-visite*, photographic images had just begun to provide a new way of gathering anthropological knowledge—a new way of presenting and seeing race—using the body as evidence.[47] Louis Agassiz himself had several daguerreotype portraits of slaves taken in South Carolina in 1850, presumably to provide visual "proof" of the written observations he made during his visit, particularly those concerning the purported differences in limb size and muscle structure between African-born slaves and whites.[48] As a means of discovering an underlying "truth" not directly visible to the eye, in turn, photography in the nineteenth century enhanced the act of looking itself.[49]

For white northern viewers, reading the images of white-looking slave girls was further complicated by their ideas about white childhood, which had become increasingly sentimentalized in the nineteenth century as middle-class children became separated from both the world of adults and the world of work. Instead of contributing to the family income, they became "priceless" members of the middle-class family: innocent, unproductive, and the focus of nurture and attention.[50] Their images—idealized in fiction, advertisements, and illustrations—reflected the supposed "innocence" and "vulnerability" of white children. These sentiments were manifest, as well, in family portraiture of the middle and late nineteenth century. The soft vignettes in which both Rosa and Rebecca appeared and the image of Fanny holding a toy hoop (figure 8) were the sorts of children's pictures that would have been familiar to most northerners.[51] By 1860, the widespread production of *cartes-de-visite* made portraits affordable to middle-class people, and pictures of one's children, surrounded by all the trappings of middle-class domesticity, were an increasingly common sight in the homes of many Americans.[52] Using the genre of the child's portrait, then, the producers of these images sent a pointedly political message. With each child framed in the vignettes and parlor scenes associated with white northern middle-class girlhood, these images of "slave girls" brought anti-slavery into the homes, perhaps even the family photograph albums, of many white northerners.[53]

The language and ideals of middle-class domesticity had often been employed by abolitionists to condemn southern slavery. The domestic disorder slavery produced—slave-owning fathers who sold their own children, slave women forever subject to the sexual desires of their owners, and slave families torn apart by the market in human beings—made enslavement terrifying, both for enslaved people themselves and in the eyes of northern abolitionists. Both former slaves and abolitionists highlighted stories of outraged motherhood and torn families to bring enslaved people into the realm of Victorian sentiment.[54] And yet the supposed distance (both geographic and racial) that separated northerners from southern slavery's evils must have shrunk considerably at the sight of little Rosa.[55] Though abolitionist writers often fantasized about their own enslavement as well as the enslavement of their children as a means of sympathizing and empathizing with slaves, Rosa's photograph

Figure 8. "Fannie Virginia Casseopia Lawrence," *carte-de-visite*, New York, 1863. Private Collection, Courtesy of Tony Seideman.

introduced something quite new.[56] Fixing visions of seemingly white slave children through photography was for northern viewers a step away from fantasy, closer to "truth," and ultimately more frightening. The effect of these photographs—both despite and because of their Victorian veneer—was that they asked white northern viewers to look upon the enslavement of their own children.

Pure sentimentality is perhaps not the only light in which these images of white girls can be understood, however. The reform literature of the nineteenth century, for instance, introduced another facet of the figure of the white child. In the idealized American home of nineteenth-century reform literature and child-rearing manuals, love and affection replaced punishment as the "proper" means of disciplining children.[57] Yet domestic order achieved through affection rather than harsh reprimand involved a reciprocal role on the part of the child. Children, and girl children in particular, appeared often in temperance literature "not only as objects of discipline but also . . . as its agents."[58] In narratives verging on the incestuous, for instance, drunken fathers found salvation in the tender embraces of their young daughters. (He swore never to drink again; she showered him with forgiving kisses.) The perceived purity, innocence, and vulnerability of young white children made them powerful disciplinary agents of reform, able to subdue their fathers despite the child's inherently weak position. Likewise, in the images of Rosa and Rebecca, notions about young white girls as pure and precious things may have been employed to redeem those viewers who had yet to rally around the antislavery cause and encourage them to act on the girls' behalf.

Images of innocent white children in the nineteenth century, however, whether sentimental or moralistic, developed largely in relation to their imagined opposite.[59] Popular images of black children in the same period often rendered them not as virtuous ideals of feminine beauty but rather as tricksters of untamed and immoral stripe. Representations of black and white children in popular culture, like the real lives of children themselves, therefore, were shaped by notions of prejudice and privilege, one condition dependent upon the other.[60] The characters Little Eva and Topsy, in Harriet Beecher Stowe's influential antislavery novel, *Uncle Tom's Cabin* (1852), were undoubtedly the most familiar symbols of young, white feminine purity versus young, unschooled black devilishness. In one scene, the author explicitly compared her two characters with one another:

Eva stood looking at Topsy . . . the two children, representatives of the two extremes of society. The fair, high-bred child, with her golden head, her deep eyes, her spiritual, noble brow, and prince-like movements; and her black, keen, subtle, cringing, yet acute neighbor. They stood the representatives of their races. The Saxon, born of ages of cultivation, command, education, physical and moral eminence; the Afric, born of ages of oppression, submission, ignorance, toil, and vice![61]

The two little "representatives of their races" in Stowe's narrative existed in light of one another, like good and evil. Through the details of their features and their behavior—Eva's "prince-like movements" and Topsy as her "black, keen, subtle, cringing" counterpart—the author aimed to reveal the true nature of the difference between them. Stowe even explained that Eva was fond of Topsy and her antics "as a dove is sometimes charmed by a glittering serpent."[62]

The invidious distinctions that Stowe drew between Eva and Topsy were drawn in real life as well. In the letters of northern missionaries, black children often were described with less affection than white ones. Strangely, such prejudices become clearer when the "white" child in question looked white, but was not. A northern missionary woman in New Orleans during the war, for instance, was shocked to learn that an orphaned child named Clara Wilbur was the property of a man who lived on the Red River. "Oh! The thought that that child had been a slave!" she wrote. "It was almost naked, but its little rosy cheeks and dimpled chin, all told too plainly that Saxon blood was in those veins."[63] Of a freedchild named Bess, on the other hand, a missionary teacher wrote: "She is very black, and in outward appearance stupid and unprepossessing," even though the woman admitted that Bess was one of her best students.[64]

Even when black children were depicted as good but unfortunate (rather than "devilish" or "stupid"), the tragic stories of their lives still served to shore up an idealized white childhood. This opposing, mutually defining relationship between white childhood and black childhood came most directly from antislavery appeals to white children. For instance, the writers of the "Children's Department" column of the *American Missionary* magazine (the official organ of the American Missionary Association) were particularly keen to link the lives of white and black children; yet inevitably white childhood's preciousness and separation from the evils of the world were affirmed through the telling of

these stories, whereas slave children's lives remained wretched and forlorn. "Don't you pity the poor slave children?" read one column. "Will
you do all you can, as you grow up, to put away slavery from the land?
O, be thankful that you are not slaves." The writer then asked each
young reader to say aloud, thankfully:

> I was not born a little slave,
> To labor in the sun,
> And wish I was but in my grave,
> And all my labor done.
> My God, I thank Thee, who hast planned
> A better lot for me;
> And placed me in this favored land
> Where I may hear of Thee.
> Placed me in the *free* States! O, how thankful I am and how kind I shall be
>   to all who are not so well off as me.[65]

Even while persuading white children to identify with the plight of
their black counterparts—thus disciplining the conscience of the white
child by pointing to the misfortunes of the slave child—antislavery writers continued to draw lines of difference between the two groups. In
a column from the *American Missionary,* the writer explained to his
young readers that enslaved children lived a life of sadness and fear at
being torn from their parents, and that though they (as white children)
might empathize with the black child, they would never be subject to
the ravages of the slave trade. "We should remember that parents and
children are separated every day by the cruelties of slavery, never more
to meet on earth. And such separations are just as wicked and cruel as it
would be for the same men to come and separate *you* and *your parents,*
and sell you into all the horrors of bondage!"[66] The sentiment aroused
by sympathy for the black child's plight not only privileged white childhood but also placed the young white reader in a position of power by
asking them to "remember" enslaved children in their prayers.[67] White
children also read of "a poor little heathen girl" in Africa whose father sold his own children. "Dear children," the magazine asked, "are
you not thankful that you have Christian parents, who love you, and
teach you what is right and good. . . . Will you not then remember
the poor little heathen children who have not the priceless blessings you
enjoy?"[68]

In *Uncle Tom's Cabin,* the most familiar of all antislavery narratives, Harriet Beecher Stowe seemed to bestow intact families and sugared sentiment upon only the white and light-skinned children in the story. Wealthy and white Little Eva was the precious child of loving (if decadent and neurasthenic) parents. Harry—"a small quadroon boy . . . beautiful and engaging" with "glossy curls about his round, dimpled face"—avoids being sold from his mother, Eliza, when she bravely runs away with him; Harry is later reunited with his father, too, and grows up in freedom.[69] Uncle Tom's children, however, lose their father to slave traders early in the story. And the infamous Topsy was altogether parentless. After Miss Ophelia (a northern white woman with abolitionist sympathies living in the home of her slaveholding brother) was given charge of Topsy, she asked the child where her mother was. Topsy explained that she had never had one. "Never was born," she said. "Never had father nor mother, nor nothin.' I was raised by a speculator, with lots of others. Old Aunt Sue used to take car [*sic*] on us."[70] Through such renderings of black slave children, the white (and near-white) child was re-created again and again as precious, protected, and fortunate, while the black child remained woeful and alone.

In fact, the sympathy elicited from *Harper's Weekly* readers concerning the three "white" slave children was gleaned, in part, from their status as members of families. Rebecca "was a slave in her father's house, the special attendant of a girl little older than herself." Rebecca had been in school a few months and "has learned to read well, and writes as neatly as most children her age." Her mother and grandmother (to whom the writer had spoken) "live in New Orleans, where they support themselves comfortably by their own labor." "The grandmother, an intelligent mulatto, told Mr. Bacon that she had 'raised' a large family of children but these are all that are left to her." Rosa had a father "in the rebel army." She had "one sister as white as herself, and three brothers who are darker." Rosa's mother "a bright mulatto, lives in New Orleans in a poor hut and has hard work to support her family." And of Charles readers learned: "Three out of five boys in any school in New York are darker than he. Yet this white boy has been twice sold as a slave. First by his father and 'owner,' Alexander Wethers, of Lewis County, Virginia, to a slavetrader named Harrison, who sold [him and his mother] to Mr. Thornhill of New Orleans."[71] By providing detailed information about these three children and their origin, the writer was intent to prove that they had indeed been enslaved, should anyone in the North doubt the veracity of their former status or their nonwhiteness.[72] Still, readers learned almost nothing of Augusta and Isaac, of how they lived and with whom. Of Augusta (the lighter-skinned of the two) the reader knew that she was nine years old and that her "almost white" mother still had two children in bondage. And Isaac's parents were never mentioned. He was "a black boy of eight years; but none the less intelligent than his whiter companions," and had made admirable progress in school. Despite praise of Isaac's schoolwork, the personal histories the others received—histories that were denied Isaac and Augusta—may have served to distance the two darker-skinned children and their childhoods from the conscience and sympathies of white northern audiences.

By the eve of the Civil War, abolitionists recognized the potential of white-looking children for stirring up antislavery sentiment. They could evoke the precious sentiments that surrounded white children (rather than the indifference that black ones often received), yet they were real (not fictional) children who had been born into the clutches of slavery. The photographs of Rosa, Rebecca, and Fanny, then, were more than a visual trick, a tromp l'oeil to play on the emotions of white viewers. The lines of sympathy had already been drawn in the antislavery rhetoric of the day. Yet these lines held the white child in a cherished and protected light and the black child in a tearful, motherless place. Empathy for white-looking slave children, therefore, instead of dissolving racial differences, only reaffirmed the viewers' sense of themselves as privileged and white.[73] Although it was the image of a raggedy, motherless Topsy that viewers might have expected to see in a photograph of a slave girl, it was the "innocent," "pure," and "well-loved" white child who appeared, a child who needed the protection of the northern white public.

The sponsors of seven-year-old Mary Mildred Botts, a freedchild from Virginia, may have been the first to capitalize on these ideas, as early as 1855. Her story also marks the beginning of efforts to use photography (in Mary Botts's case, the daguerreotype, as the *carte-de-visite* format was not yet available) in the service of raising sentiment and support for the abolitionist cause (figure 9). According to the *Boston Telegraph,* Mary's father had escaped slavery on the plantation of a Judge Neal in Virginia and fled to Boston. After earning enough to buy his own freedom, he enlisted the help of abolitionists to assist with the purchase of his wife and three children. He also received the aid and at-

Figure 9. Unidentified girl (probably Mary Botts), daguerreotype, Julian Vannerson, ca. 1855. Photo 1.256.
Massachusetts Historical Society.

tention of Massachusetts senator Charles Sumner, who served as agent
in the purchase of the man's wife and children. Mary and her family visited the offices of the *New York Daily Times* on their way to Boston, after which the newspaper reported: "The child was exhibited yesterday
to many prominent individuals in this City, and the general sentiment,
in which we fully concur, was one of astonishment that she should ever
have been a slave. She was one of the fairest and most indisputable
white children that we have ever seen."[74]

In his own characterization of Mary Botts, Sumner set a pattern that
other abolitionists would follow. In a letter printed in both the *Boston
Telegraph* and the *New York Daily Times,* he compared Mary Botts to
a fictional white girl who had been kidnapped and enslaved, the protag-
onist in Mary Hayden Pike's antislavery novel *Ida May*: "She is bright
and intelligent—another Ida May. I think her presence among us (in

Boston) will be more effective than any speech I can make."[75] By invoking Ida May, Sumner dared those who saw Mary Botts to distinguish her from a white child. He was also referencing a story of redemption. In Pike's novel, Ida May's real identity—her whiteness—is discovered, and by the close of the novel she is reunited with her father.[76] Mary's new nickname must have served her sponsors well, drawing on the popularity of the fictional Ida May while transforming that fictional child into flesh. When a Quaker woman named Hannah Marsh Inman saw Mary at a meetinghouse in Worcester, Massachusetts, for instance, she recorded in her diary of March 1, 1855: "Evening all went to the soiree at the Hall. *Little Ida May the white slave* was there from Boston."[77]

As proof that Mary was worthy of her title, Sumner also offered a daguerreotype of her for viewing, insisting that the power of the image would draw the sympathy of those who saw it. He wanted members of the state legislature to see it "as an illustration of Slavery" and challenged them to consider their own views on the slavery question. "Let a hardhearted Hunker look at it," Sumner wrote, "and be softened." (The image reproduced here is most likely a second copy, "in a different attitude," that he sent to John A. Andrews, the governor of Massachusetts.)[78] Editors at both newspapers saw the image. The Boston editors described the photograph as that of "a most beautiful white girl, with high forehead, straight hair, intellectual appearance, and decidedly attractive features." Readers were informed that it could be "seen for a few days at the State House, in the hands of the Clerk of the House of Representatives."[79] The *New York Daily Times* seconded Sumner's assessment of Mary's image as the portrait of a "real 'Ida May' ": "a young female slave, so white as to defy the acutest judge to detect in her features, complexion, hair, or general appearance, the slightest trace of negro blood."[80] Governor Andrews also had in his possession another image with a darker-skinned boy who had been enslaved, possibly Mary's brother (figure 10). Like the portrait of Isaac and Rosa taken during the war, the daguerreotype of Mary with a dark-skinned boy confirmed that she was not white even as it challenged the viewer to detect in her traces of "negro blood."

White-looking slave girls like Mary would bring forth a new level of outrage among slavery's opponents. As the original recipient of Sumner's reprinted letter, Dr. James W. Stone, declared in a postscript: "Such is slavery! There it is! Should such things be allowed to continue in Washington, under the shadow of the Capitol?"[81] By her photograph,

Figure 10. Two slave children (Mary Botts and brother?), ambrotype, Cutting & Bowdoin, Boston, ca. 1855–1856. Photo 2.218. Massachusetts Historical Society.

public presentation, and the fictional story to which her nickname referred, Mary successfully combined the figure of the unprotected white-looking child with that of the white female slave, inspiring the fears white audiences associated with both.

Since the 1840s, nineteenth-century viewers, north and south, also had become quite familiar with the figure of the white female slave in sculpture, in the form of *The Greek Slave* (1844), by the American Hiram Powers, a work that attracted crowds of museumgoers and spawned reams of commentary in the American press (figure 11). Though Powers did not set out to make an abolitionist symbol, one historian has argued that the sculptor borrowed the image of the naked

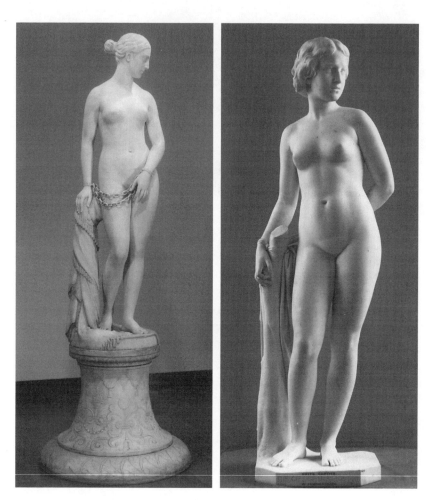

Figure 11. *Left*: Hiram Powers, *The Greek Slave* (after original of 1844), marble, 1851. Yale University Art Gallery. Olive Louise Dann Fund.
Figure 12. *Right*: Erastus Dow Palmer, *The White Captive,* marble, 1858–1859. The Metropolitan Museum of Art. Bequest of Hamilton Fish, 1894 (94.9.3).

female in chains from antislavery emblems.[82] Yet public reception of the sculpture, which toured in the 1840s and 1850s from the Northeast to as far south as New Orleans, suggests that audiences read Powers's slave (meant to represent a Greek woman enslaved by Turks) as an emblem of ideal feminine purity, submissiveness, and Christian faith. Among abolitionists, feminists, even antiabolitionists, however, the sculpture became a point of reference to the enslavement of African Americans in the South and to the enchained status of all women in American society. Indeed, many antislavery feminists were outraged by the depiction of the "ideal" woman as submissive and resigned to her terrible fate.[83]

Though less popular than Powers's sculpture, Erastus Dow Palmer's *The White Captive* (1859) also made the marble body of a white woman enslaved a point of reflection (figure 12). Palmer, also American, was responding to the popularity of Powers's earlier work but brought his sculpture closer to his audience by providing an American setting for his female figure. Instead of a Greek woman, Palmer sculpted a young white woman (indeed, almost girl-like in expression if not form) captured by Indians. Palmer himself described her as "the young daughter of a pioneer," suggesting that she was not yet mature and was still living with her parents when captured. The parallels between *The Greek Slave* and *The White Captive* were deliberate and striking. The figures were similarly posed, bound by the hands to a post and gazing resignedly over their shoulder. They were victims in desperate need of saving, but beyond reach. Yet they also seemed, by their very powerlessness, to have a hold over the viewer. As an article in *Harper's Weekly* observed of *The White Captive*, "No: it is not she, it is we who are captive."[84]

Nineteenth-century audiences, with clues from the works' creators, read in these marble sculptures a narrative about the impending violation of the white woman enslaved. Given the information that *The Greek Slave* was a young, white Christian woman in a Turkish slave mart, stripped of her clothing and all her possessions but for her cross, viewers imagined for themselves the fate that awaited her at the hands of lecherous men.[85] Similarly, the white girl captured by "savage" Indians and tied tightly to a stake would soon lose her girlish innocence in the wilderness, where no white man could save her. Nineteenth-century writers mused in just this way about these sculptures, embellishing the stories with their own commentary about the girls' posture and expressions betraying "the sudden thought of coming trial."[86]

Although the visual clues given in the photographs of Mary, Rosa, and Rebecca were quite different from those belonging to *The Greek Slave* and *The White Captive*, a narrative of lust was common to all of them. If the sculpted women were poised at the threshold of a horrifying scene, the white-looking slave girls stood on the slim ground of girlhood—their youth, their skin, and the knowledge that they had been

Figure 13. Engraving of John Everett Millais's *Cherry Ripe*, 1879. V&A Images/Victoria and Albert Museum.

enslaved combining to suggest a harrowing future. Also, by their perceived powerlessness, both the sculptures and the white-looking girls seemed to hold viewers in sway. Yet though audiences had no control over the fate of *The Greek Slave* or *The White Captive*, abolitionists made the point that for little slave girls in the South, it was not too late. Where the sculptures could only inspire agony, the images, as propaganda, could inspire action. The endangered virtue of white and white-looking little girls, in turn, made appeals for their protection all the more urgent and made the thought of *not* helping them a scandalous one.

Within the context of white, middle-class Victorian culture, white little girls (perhaps even more so than white women) embodied the "Victorian ideal" of femininity—childlike, dependent, and sexually pure. Yet they nevertheless exuded, in the eyes of mostly male artists and photographers, a budding sexuality. The association of white girls with innocence and purity gave their images the allure of the forbidden, thus making them all the more enticing and seemingly sexually vulnerable.[87] The eroticism inherent in pictures of "innocent" white girls—pure yet alluring—seems to have contributed to the appeal of white girlhood as the subject of paintings and mass-reproduced prints that sold by the thousands in the middle and late nineteenth century.[88]

Renderings of young white girls such as John Everett Millais's mass-reproduced *Cherry Ripe* (1879) captured at once little girls' innocence, their sexual allure, and their popular appeal (figure 13).[89] This theme is especially clear in Seymour Joseph Guy's *Making a Train* (1867), in which the young girl slips her dress from her shoulders in order to make the train of a grown woman's gown (figure 14). Lewis Carroll's pictures

Figure 14. Seymour Joseph Guy, *Making a Train*, 1867. Philadelphia Museum of Art, The George W. Elkins Collection, 1924. E1924-4-14.

Figure 15. Charles Dodgson [Lewis Carroll], Alice Liddell as "The Beggar-Maid," photograph, ca. 1859. Morris L. Parrish Collection, Department of Rare Books and Special Collections, Princeton University Library.

of young Alice Liddell also play on the idea of the "incipient woman" within the child. In his photograph of Alice Liddell as "The Beggar-Maid" (ca. 1859), Carroll cleverly made the suggestion of the fallen woman using the bared limbs and shabby dress of an unfallen upper-class child (figure 15).[90]

The idea of the woman within the child, however, was even more easily projected onto the bodies of white-looking slave girls from the South, since their sexuality, or at the very least their anticipated fertility, would have been part of their purchase price. Allusion to the sexuality of Mary and her successors did not require pointed visual or verbal clues like those attached to Guy's *Making a Train*. Because they looked white, but had been slaves, and because they were female, their portraits no doubt summoned the familiar figure of the "tragic mulatto," a woman noted for her beauty, her near whiteness, and her unspeakable violation by the white men of the South. From the mid-nineteenth century, in fact, abolitionist propaganda and rhetoric reflected an increasing preoccupation among middle-class white northerners, with sexuality and the unrestrained sexuality of southern slaveholders in particular.[91]

Fictional portrayals of "mulatto" slaves became a familiar trope of nineteenth-century sentimental fiction, their popularity stemming from the notion that white, often female readers would more readily identify with the plight of white-looking women.[92] It was this trope that the Reverend Henry Ward Beecher invoked when he first presented an enslaved woman before the congregation in Plymouth Church in 1856. Although the *New York Daily Times* described her as "a slave girl," Sarah Scheffer was twenty-two or twenty-three at the time of her appearance in Brooklyn. Beecher told his congregation that he had been enlisted to help Sarah, the daughter of a Virginia slave owner and an enslaved woman, whose father intended to sell her "in the far South, for purposes such as you may imagine when you see her." A slave trader who had known Sarah took pity on her and bought her "to give her a chance to save herself by purchasing her freedom." Beecher said that he could help raise money for the woman and her friends in Washington (where she had raised some money toward her freedom already) only if she were to appear in person before his church. When he asked the woman to stand before the people, according to the *New York Daily Times*, "the slave rose in her seat, a tall fine looking woman, with barely enough of tinge in her complexion and wave in her hair to betray her colored blood, and hardly an eye in the immense audience but was wet with sympathetic tears, as she, trembling, and completely with emotion, stumbled up the pulpit stairs." The newspaper reported some three thousand people in the audience. "I wish you all to see her," Beecher reportedly said, "that you may know who they are that are sold as slaves—that are put into the scales and silver heaped up as an equivalent to them."[93]

Beecher may have believed he was bringing the "tragic mulatto" of nineteenth-century fiction to life before his congregation. An engraving of the incident depicts Sarah as a delicate woman in white, with brown hair tumbling to her waist, her head bowed.[94] Yet he did not reveal to his congregation that Sarah was already a "fallen" woman. According to the *Daily Times*: "After Sarah had left the church, and while the money was being counted, Mr. Beecher said that there was one portion of the story which he had not thought best to mention at the time, lest they might not be able to bear it." A physician in Baltimore who "taking advantage of her servile condition and her wish for freedom had become the father of a child by her." The child, too, had been bought by the sympathetic slave trader, and because the amount of money collected at Plymouth Church was large enough, the child, too, would be purchased. Beecher also revealed that Sarah was the daughter of "a white citizen of Virginia, a man of wealth and influence," who had not wanted to sell her but, rather, "endeavored to establish" an "outrageous relationship" with his own daughter. Though Sarah had pleaded with him to sell her away from the torments of his legitimate children (and, no doubt, his advances) it was only after Sarah had escaped to Baltimore that he agreed to do so.[95]

Perhaps Beecher feared that alluding to the impending ruin of the young woman would draw more sympathy and money from the congregation than would telling, in full, the nature of Sarah's past. In any event, soon after Sarah's appearance, Beecher seems to have found more advantage in presenting white-looking girls, rather than women, before his congregation. The delicate issue of a slave woman's ruinous past did not have to be skirted if the slave before the congregation was still a child. Whereas white northerners might have imagined the mournful life of a light-skinned woman from lines of fiction or the accounts of former slaves, he could point to the imperiled *future* of a white-looking girl child. The first girl that Beecher freed before his Plymouth congregation was Sally Maria Deiggs (or Diggs), also known as "Pink." With Sally, Beecher staged a more elaborate presentation than the one Sarah had received. According to the *Brooklyn Daily Eagle*, Sally was nine years old at the time and "nearly white, having only one sixteenth of negro blood, or half an octoroon, a gradation of amalgamation not specifically designated."[96] She had been brought from Washington, where she was living with her grandmother, a freedwoman, after having been separated from her mother. Sally's owner had promised the grandmother that the child would never be taken from her, but the owner did not keep his promise, and slave dealers went to the grandmother's house and took the child. According to a letter written to the *New York Times*, the child had made a valiant effort to resist: she ran "to the garret, barricaded the door with old furniture and trunks, and declared she would die rather than come out to be sold."[97] The *Times,* in a veiled reference to Sally's future as a "fancy girl," reported that although the child was to be sold for $800, "it was thought that when she grew up to womanhood she would be worth $3,000."[98] A clergyman in Washington took up the girl's cause and petitioned Beecher and his church for help.

In a scene that foreshadowed Fanny Lawrence's presentation to his congregation a few years later, the Reverend Henry Ward Beecher brought Sally before his church. Her story also appeared in the "Children's Department" of the *American Missionary.* Children learned that an unnamed little girl who had been under the protection of her grandmother had tried to hide from slave traders, but that they "burst in the door and dragged her away." ("How would you feel, children, if the slave traders should come and tear you away from your home and friends?" the writer asked. "And why should they do so to this little girl any more than to you?") As Beecher recounted the girl's story to the congregation she stood quietly beside him, a representative of the kind of innocent, near-white girlhood toward which his audience already felt such tender sentiment and sympathy:

> She was very pretty, of a light complexion, with brown, wavy hair. There was in her face an expression of innocence and gentleness, and a look of sadness too. As she stood there, in her brown frock and little red sack, and Mr. Beecher with his arm thrown protectingly around her, it made a pretty tableau. Tears came into the people's eyes as they gazed at this child, and thought of the thousands of little slave girls in our land, held in a cruel and hopeless bondage. While we looked at her, we seemed to see them all.[99]

Beecher's intent was for the audience to see the "little slave girl" as a child very like their own children, and he drew pointed parallels between the enslaved girl and the children of his parishioners. "Mothers," said Beecher, "how would you feel if your little daughters were to be sold away from you? I know you will not let this child go back to slavery." With the presentation of the light-skinned "little slave girl," then, the black child was replaced in the minds of sympathetic white northerners with visions of their own (white) children enslaved. The collection plates were passed around Plymouth Church for the "little slave girl" until enough money had been raised to buy her from the slave traders. When Beecher at last exclaimed, "The *child is free!*" the audience "clapped their hands for joy."[100] After her "sale," Beecher placed on Sally's finger a woman's ring from the collection plate, declaring it her "freedom ring."[101]

As an adult, Sally Deiggs Hunt could recall clearly only one detail from her presentation in Beecher's church. Upon her return to Plymouth Church for its eightieth anniversary in 1927 (after having been "found" in Washington, D.C., where she lived with her husband, a successful lawyer), she told the congregation, "My hair was combed back from my face and held in place with a long curved rubber comb, such as children wore at the time. Evidently Mr. Beecher had not noticed this before I was put upon the platform, but when he did see it he came quietly to me, removed the comb, and said, 'never wear anything in your hair except what God put there.'"[102] Given his reputation as a showman, however, Beecher may have had other motives. Taking the comb out of the child's hair might have loosed the "wavy" hair that made her seem closer to "white." Her long hair, let down, might also have evoked the tragic womanhood that awaited her.

The accounts of Fanny Lawrence's presentation and baptism at Plymouth Church in 1863 suggest that Beecher pressed this argument still further. Every account of Fanny's appearance reads much like the following, penned in the dramatic tones of sentimental fiction:

> When the audience supposed that the ceremony was ended, Mr. Beecher carried up into the pulpit a little girl about five years of age, of sweet face, large eyes, light hair, and fair as a lily. Pausing a moment to conquer his emotion, he sent a shiver of horror through the congregation by saying "This child was born a slave, and is just redeemed from slavery!" It is impossible to describe the effect of this announcement. The fact seemed so incredible and so atrocious that at first, the spectators held their breath in their amazement, and were then melted to tears.[103]

Beecher then addressed his audience, explaining that the child, baptized Fanny Virginia Casseopia Lawrence, had been discovered "sore and tattered and unclean" by a nurse tending Union soldiers in Fairfax, Virginia, who adopted Fanny as her own. "Look upon this child," said Beecher, "tell me if you ever saw a fairer, sweeter face?" Beecher then made explicit the fate that awaited little girls like Fanny. "This is a sam-ple of the slavery which clutches for itself everything fair and attractive," he explained. "The loveliness of this face, the beauty of this figure, would only make her so much more valuable for lust." Like Ellen, who had been saved from "yellow-eyed" Elder Mathewson, Fanny was presented as a white-looking female rescued from the grips of a lecherous slaveholder. Beecher's rhetoric (as it had with the "little slave girl" before her) also placed Fanny alongside the children of his own congregation, bemoaning slavery's trespasses not upon black children but on "fair and attractive" white ones. While their children were sheltered from the ravages of slavery, he intoned, Fanny (until "redeemed") had been left exposed.

Ironically, we cannot even be certain that Fanny was *not* a free white child. In the autobiography of Catherine Lawrence, Fanny's benefactor, the author consistently evades the question of whether the child had, in fact, ever been enslaved or the possibility that both of her parents may have been white.[104] Beecher himself seems to have understood that the presentation of white-looking slaves was also in danger of doing the job too well. While Beecher, like Sumner, had sought to prove the existence of these children and invited viewers to see for themselves that they were indistinguishable from white children, the girls also opened their sponsors up for accusations of fakery. In the case of Mary Botts, at least one newspaper alluded to her as a " 'bogus' slave" (in opposition to the paper's competitor, which had declared her "white"). And Sally "Pink" Deiggs was referred to in the *Brooklyn Daily Eagle* as "the alleged slave girl in Rev. Mr. Beecher's Church." The same Brooklyn paper ran a clip from the *New York News* that accused Sally of being "no more black than [the white actress] Agnes Robertson, the Scotch Octoroon—that she was a pure white who was sent North on speculation, and that Beecher and his audience were confoundedly hoaxed."[105] Anticipating such arguments, perhaps, Beecher had possession of Sally's bill of sale from her owner, as well as the "liberation document" that granted the child her freedom.[106]

Fanny's ambiguous past, however, makes all the more clear that by 1863 Beecher, and perhaps Catherine Lawrence herself, saw benefit (or, in the case of Lawrence, perhaps an income) in the presentation of a white-looking slave girl such as Fanny. "While your children are brought up to fear and serve the Lord," Beecher declared, "this little one, just as beautiful, would be made, through slavery, a child of damnation."[107] The lines of sentimentality and sexuality crossed at the point of sympathy, thereby deepening the audience members' response to each girl's possibly "tragic" end and spurring them to act in order to preserve her from it.[108] Winning the war, in turn, was the only way to protect the virtue of white-looking little girls like Fanny: "let your soul burn with fiery indignation against the horrible system which turns into chattels such fair children of God! May God strike for our armies and the right that this accursed thing may be utterly destroyed!"[109] Instead of a battle for black freedom, the war to end slavery, in Beecher's words, became a means to preserve the freedom and purity of the white race, both of which seemed to be threatened by slavery. The future of the Union— embodied in a young, unspoiled "white" girl rather than a black one— was at stake.

It is chilling to consider, however, how closely Beecher's description of Fanny follows that of an auctioneer in a slave market.[110] As with the antislavery story about Ellen, "Sold at Savannah" (recall the auction- eer's words that "it isn't every day such angeliferous loveliness comes to the hammer"), Beecher made his appeal by pointing to Fanny's "fair, sweet face," and thus to the price she could have commanded. White northern viewers, in turn, valued each girl's presentation for much the same qualities that would have brought her owner a considerable sum in the slave market: her gender and the whiteness of her skin.[111] The kind of looking encouraged by the public presentation of Fanny and the others, in turn, was unmistakably akin to the very acts of "reading" bodies that occurred in the slave market. Like white-looking girls and women on the auction block, Fanny, Rosa, and Rebecca were subject to scrutiny by northern audiences and viewers. If their semblance to white girls made them more valuable in the market, it also may have made them seem more worthy of urgent rescue than a black child. And with the help of their well-meaning sponsors, the girls once again had a price attached to them—along with the words "slave girl"—though this time their image was for sale, rather than their bodies.

The desire to scrutinize a person's body to determine his or her "true" racial identity surfaces throughout northerners' accounts of their visits to the South during the Civil War. What confounded them was that one could not always observe traces of "African blood" in a per- son. A Boston "traveler" who visited a New Orleans jail reported, for instance, that among those people of color imprisoned for not having a pass were "several women that in New York or Boston would pass for white women, without the slightest difficulty or suspicion," and a

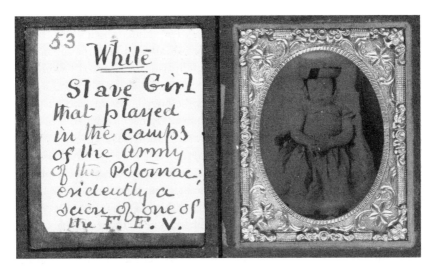

Figure 16. White slave girl, ambrotype by unknown photographer, ca. 1861–1865. Photo 2.129. Massachusetts Historical Society.

young girl "with a beautiful face . . . whose complexion was that of a pretty Boston brunette."[112] And a correspondent for the *New York Times* encountered a "colored soldier" in the Louisiana Native Guards whom he took for a white man, only to be corrected by the commanding officer. "And do you really think him white?" the colonel asked. "Well you may, Sir: but that man is a 'negro'—one who carries the so-called curse of African blood in his veins." And yet the writer concluded after studying the "fine-looking young man, not unlike General McClellan in mould of features," that he "would have defied the most consummate expert in Niggerology, by the aid of the most powerful microscope, to discover the one drop of African blood in the man's veins."[113] A daguerreotype of an unidentified girl child who had been found among the Army of the Potomac speaks to a similarly noteworthy discovery of a white-looking person—in this case a white-looking girl child, like Rosa (figure 16). The inscription opposite the child's image (in the ornate case typical of daguerreotypes) reads: "*White* Slave Girl that played in the camps of the Army of the Potomac; evidently a scion of one of the F.E.V. [Forces of Eastern Virginia?]" (with the word "white" twice underscored). The unnamed girl, the caption suggested, was the child of a Confederate soldier or officer and had come into the possession of the Union troops in the eastern theater of the Civil War. Like Rosa and the others, she wore a dress and bonnet. Behind her seems to be a man in a suit. She was very small, and perhaps she had to be kept still in her chair, as small children usually required holding or metal braces to keep them from moving during long exposure times. It is not clear to whom this daguerreotype belonged, nor to whom the inscription was directed. But the child was clearly deemed worthy of photographing, on account of her identity as a "*white* slave girl."

The ways in which the children from Louisiana were described, photographed, and publicly presented as freed slaves, therefore, suggest that while audiences were scandalized by the children's whiteness, they were also troubled by the inability to see their blackness. If the end of slavery is what the children's sponsors sought, their careful presentations of white-looking slave girls also must have had another unintended effect —that is, they hinted at the dangers of emancipation. Though slavery was inscribed in the experiences of the adults in the group (figure 3)— Wilson Chinn had the initials of his former master branded on his forehead, Mary Johnson bore on her left arm "scars of three cuts given her by her mistress with a rawhide" and on her back "scars of more than fifty cuts given her by her master," and Robert Whitehead's history was marked by the dollar amounts at which he had been bought and sold— the unscarred, racially ambiguous bodies of the children made it clear that old ways of "reading" slavery and race were insufficient.[114] Images such as these, in fact, may have further endorsed the determination of a person's blackness through blood and descent, since they rendered any direct reading of race unreliable.[115] If the words "slave child" beneath the portraits kept the girls from walking out into the world as white, then viewers may have wondered how they would be able to discern nonwhiteness when slavery no longer held such people in check.

Further still, what would this state of affairs mean for those who considered themselves white? If even photographs could not detect "African" blood, then was the race of every white person soon to be in question? Consider the story that accompanied the picture of "white and colored slaves" in *Harper's Weekly*. With indignation, the writer recounted the ejection of the three whitest-looking children, Rebecca, Charles, and Rosa, from the St. Lawrence Hotel in Philadelphia while they were on tour there. The hotel's proprietor insisted that since the children had been slaves, they "must therefore be colored persons" and

Figure 17. "Our Protection" and "'Oh! How I Love the Old Flag.'" Portraits of Rosa Downs, Charles Taylor, and Rebecca Huger, *cartes-de-visite*, 1863. Slavery/Antislavery Collection, Sophia Smith Collection, Smith College.

emphasized that he kept a hotel for "white people."[116] Beneath a photographic portrait of the three children taken in Philadelphia after the incident, this story served as part of the caption: "These children were turned out of the St. Lawrence Hotel, Chestnut St, Philadelphia, on account of Color." The story was a critique of northern white supremacy and prejudice against "colored" people, but for viewers already unsettled by the appearances of the children, it would also confirm their fears. If white-looking children could be denied entrance to a public establishment on the suspicion that they had been ("colored") slaves, then any white person's race might be open to question.

It was to counter such fears, perhaps, that the children's sponsors staged a few photographs that were far less subtle than the vignette portraits of Rosa and Rebecca, and which made explicit the threat slavery, and not emancipation, posed to the liberties of white people. In one, Rebecca is by herself, seated and gazing up at the American flag (figure 17). The caption beneath her reads: "'Oh! How I Love the Old Flag,'" representing the Union as a refuge for white-looking children from the evils of slavery. Another portrait shows the three children, Rosa, Charley, and Rebecca, each wrapped in his or her own flag, with the words "Our Protection" printed beneath them (figure 17).

One interpretation might be that these patriotic photographs critiqued the system of slavery, which denied white-looking children the protections enjoyed by free white children and threatened the safety of any who looked like them. But another reading of these images finds a young white face on emancipation—rather than a young black one—and suggests, in hopeful terms, that the postbellum United States would remain a white nation.[117]

3

Civilizing Missions
Miss Harriet W. Murray, Elsie, and Puss

If appeals for slavery's demise took the form of white-looking slave girls, the work of northern "civilization" in the South after
emancipation was embodied in a black child. The photographic portrait
of a woman named Harriet Murray with two of her students, taken in
South Carolina in 1866, was a tableau meant to express the good that
would come from emancipation in the South: two former slave girls
gathered round a book held by a white woman (figure 18). Puss, the
larger of the two, stood very straight, while Elsie appeared more pliant
in Miss Murray's kindly yet firm embrace.[1] This image makes a telling
comparison with the portraits of Rosa and Rebecca, in which both girls
had taken up the role of the Victorian middle-class white child, adopt-
ing the off-camera gaze or sentimental pose they had been given by the
photographer. Instead of the velvet-trimmed frocks in which Rosa and
Rebecca had appeared, Elsie and Puss stood plainly before the viewer in
boots without laces and hand-me-down dresses. The backdrop—the
"setting" provided for Elsie and Puss—was not a Victorian parlor but a
cultivated field. And unlike the photographs of Rosa and Rebecca, this
picture did not ask white northern viewers to imagine Elsie and Puss as
their own. These freedgirls were not destined for the parlors of the
white northern middle class except perhaps, by some people's endeavors, as maids.

The disparities between Rosa's portrait and the photograph of Elsie
and Puss reflect, in part, the passage of time—from the height of the
Civil War to the years immediately following slavery's defeat. Onto the
bodies of white-looking slave girls, abolitionists had hoped that white
northerners could project their hatred and fear of slavery, even their fascination with it. After emancipation, though, reformers and missionaries sought to quiet anxieties about the responses of millions of black
freedpeople to freedom (that they would migrate to the North, or kill

Figure 18. "Miss Harriet W. Murray, Elsie, Puss," 1866.
From the Penn School Collection. Permission granted
by Penn Center, Inc., St. Helena, S.C. Photo 820b.

their former masters, or refuse to work, letting cotton and sugarcane
rot in the fields)[2] with images of black freedgirls in a rural landscape
under the civilizing influence of a white female teacher. Although the
picture of a white-looking slave girl may have fueled northern indignation toward the South during the war, Rosa's image would not have
been a welcome one once slavery (and the caption "slave child") no
longer kept her from "passing" as the "white" child she appeared to
be. Rather, what most white northerners seemed to imagine about the

South after emancipation was just what they saw in the picture of Elsie and Puss with their teacher: dutiful black children (so "black" that they could not pass for "white") ready to receive the order and discipline of a victorious northern white "civilization."

Like Rosa's portrait, the portrait of Harriet Murray with Elsie and Puss was staged carefully—the white woman in broad skirts with her young black charges, the painted backdrop, and the open book. And as with Rosa's portrait, in the staging of the photograph lay the grammar of its argument—the choice, for instance, to stress the freed girls' need for "civilization" (Murray's arm training Elsie toward the book) rather than their innocence or vulnerability (Rosa Down's doleful gaze). And while both pictures pled the necessity of emancipation, they posed separate questions about the future. Rosa's fair skin may have broached emancipation's consequences, but the most immediate message her face conveyed was, What if slavery continues? The portrait of Elsie and Puss, though, raised and answered a new question, one about slavery's aftermath. In the words of New England antislavery reformer Samuel Gridley Howe in 1864, "What shall be done with the negroes?"[3]

Harriet Murray was one of a small but determined group of northerners seeking to answer Howe's question. She was among those working for a collection of freedmen's aid societies at Port Royal and the Sea Islands of South Carolina after the region's occupation by Union troops in 1861.[4] The coast of South Carolina, like the southern part of Louisiana, fell under Union control early in the war. The Port Royal experiment, endorsed by President Lincoln and funded and arranged through freedmen's aid societies from New York, Boston, and Philadelphia, was to be a model postslavery plantation society dedicated to a peaceful, orderly, and prosperous transition from slavery to freedom. The Port Royal Relief Committee declared in 1862 that it would teach freedpeople "the rudimentary arts of civilized life."[5] Those assigned to posts as plantation superintendents would organize and oversee the labor of former slaves while teachers addressed the educational needs of the islands' freedpeople. After a year's effort, nearly two thousand students, most between eight and twelve years old, were under instruction on Sea Island, the largest of the South Carolina islands.[6] Much was at stake, however, since the supporters of the Port Royal experiment were determined that theirs be the example for the nation. As one Port Royal advocate wrote in 1862, "The success of a productive colony there would serve as a womb for the emancipation at large."[7]

While education was central to the campaign at Port Royal (as it was the governing theme in the portrait of Harriet Murray, Elsie, and Puss), it was education in the service of creating a "civilized" black working class in the South. With the help of Miss Murray, the portrait of Elsie and Puss suggested, the girls would learn their letters. Yet Murray's presence—her motherly embrace, her finger directing Elsie to the book —said something, too, about the civilizing northern presence in the postslavery South. Murray played the part of the white, middle-class female who often mediated, indeed domesticated, the boundaries between "civilization" and the "uncivilized" in the nineteenth century, whether through missionary work or colonization or in allegorical illustrations and advertisements.[8] Her presence suggested to northern viewers that while freedchildren learned to read and write, they would also learn the value of discipline and industry—the very fundamentals of Anglo-Saxon civilization (this despite the fact that former slave children already knew something about hard work).[9] In fact, reformers such as Harriet Murray had a rather complicated relationship to the future of freedpeople and their place within the nation's racial hierarchy. While they promoted slave emancipation and the idea that former slaves would be hardworking free laborers, they often did so using the racialized language of Anglo-Saxonism and civilization. In both written and visual form, it was a language that would proliferate throughout the nineteenth century.

Northern benevolent and missionary societies in the South during and just after the Civil War had begun to answer Samuel Howe's question with a parable. It was a story of discovery, transformation, and civilization told in print and in photographs, one that often began with ragged slaves and ended with neat, disciplined freedchildren. The ragged child was a figure already present in antebellum urban reform efforts in the United States and Britain. But the ragged slave child redeemed (a notion implicit in the portrait of Elsie and Puss), reflected a new concern with the civilization of nonwhite peoples that would only grow throughout the nineteenth century, as Europe (particularly in Africa) and the United States (in the western territories, Latin America, and the Pacific) pressed to expand their empires. Told in the form of "before and after" narratives—the ragged slave child alongside the tidy freedchild—these appeals were akin to those of nineteenth-century advertisers, political campaigners, social reformers, and even medical doctors. Such stories evoked both present and future in the newly free South. Readers and viewers could see for themselves, ostensibly, both what *was* happening and what *would* happen. Indeed, as an early illustration of civilization as a spectacle to be consumed, this narrative allowed viewers and readers to witness the event of the ragged child's reform. To a large extent, then, the selling of emancipation as a civilizing mission, to a wary northern public—the proffered answer to Howe's question—took the form of an educable, employable black freedchild. With freedchildren, missionary and benevolent societies executed a process, on paper, using lens and light and shadow, through which a former slave population became scrubbed of history, relatives, and the indelible marks of slavery. Here, they said, was a generation capable of rescue, receptive to reform. Here was the tidy, disciplined future of freed black labor in the South.

Renderings of the freedchild's rapid advance under the supervision of white northern reformers would prove a faint match for the social realities of the postbellum South: the opposing demands of freedpeople and former slaveholders, the violence, the politics, and the poverty. The images created in the name of aid and benevolence were, in the end, both grand, even global visions of civilization's triumph and cardboard fantasies acted out in front of a painted landscape in a photographer's studio. Still, these appeals drew upon shared ideals—a familiar system of symbols and arguments—in order to persuade their audience. And in that sense, perhaps they were successful. These clever acts of persuasion aimed at the northern public may have convinced some reticent souls that black children deserved the aid of the North, and that emancipation would benefit the nation as a whole.[10]

In some cases, such arguments may have been too convincing. The marketing of the black child as the future of freed black labor went beyond metaphor when zealous northern reformers in the South tried to "place out" individual freedchildren and their services to the homes of northern employers. Placing out poor orphans to work in households was an accepted alternative to orphanages in the North by the 1860s. But most freedpeople needed the labor of children to support their families and did not see the advantage of sending away nieces and nephews, grandchildren, and their own children to help in someone else's household. Indeed, the irony of sending former slave children hundreds of miles away to fill the needs of northern employers for dishwashers and house servants—in the aftermath of a system of slavery that had divided black families for generations and a sectional conflict that had ended the interstate trade in human beings—seems to have escaped some of their sponsors almost entirely.

To recognize the portrait of Elsie and Puss as a response to Howe's question about the fate of "the negroes," we must recall, first, the urgency with which abolitionists had tried to predict what would happen after emancipation. Abolitionists hoped to persuade Congress and the public that emancipation would not tip off a bloody, ex-slave rebellion by promoting the idea that enslaved people were, by nature, peaceful and industrious. Many prominent abolitionists, such as Senator Charles Sumner of Massachusetts, romanticized the "African" race, insisting that "this whole objection [to immediate emancipation] proceeds on a mistaken idea of the African slave. . . . The African is not cruel, vindictive, or harsh, but gentle, forgiving, and kind."[11] Others sought to offer *proof* of the industriousness of former slaves by turning to earlier emancipations in the West Indies to assuage concerns about black freedom in the South. Perhaps the most well known treatise in this vein was a pamphlet by Lydia Maria Child entitled *The Right Way, the Safe Way, Proved by Emancipation in the British West Indies, and Elsewhere* (1860). Child gathered testimonies from officials and observers in Antigua, Barbados, Jamaica, and smaller islands in the British West Indies to argue for immediate emancipation (rather than the gradual process of emancipation that some proposed) for slaves in the United States.[12]

The picture Child rendered of the British West Indies after slavery was one of rapid improvement meant to foreshadow conditions in the South after full-scale emancipation, and the responses of freedpeople in the United States to freedom. For instance, she quoted a Moravian missionary's account of former slaves' response on the day of emancipation:

> Planters and missionaries, in every part of the island, told us there was not a single dance, by night or day; not every so much as a fiddle played. There were no drunken carousals, no riotous assemblies. The emancipated were as far from dissipation and debauchery as they were from violence and carnage. Gratitude was the absorbing emotion. From the hill-tops and the valleys, the cry of a disenthralled people went upward, like the sound of many waters: "Glory to God! Glory to God!"[13]

The end of slavery in the American South, Child suggested, could be just as peaceful. Instead of retaliating against their former masters with violence, former slaves would praise God for their release. Child cited other examples of freedpeople's easy adaptation to the system of free labor and adoption of the consumer desires of "civilized" peoples. Manners, dress, home decoration all improved among the freed population in the West Indies, according to Child's informants. Emancipation in the British colonies, then, swiftly brought to the plantation regions all the necessities of "civilization": domesticity, orderly Christianity, and conspicuous consumption. Child predicted this same constellation of behavior, in short order, for freedpeople in the South.

Armed with examples from the West Indies, Child also predicted the compliance of freedpeople to northern ideals of order and "safety" and the least amount of disruption to the plantation system of production. Freedpeople would remain on the plantation and happily work for a wage. Drawing from the account of an estate manager in Antigua, Child reported that "the love of home was such a passion with negroes, that nothing but bad treatment could force them away."[14] A visitor to Dominica encountered freedpeople "working cheerfully, and cheaply to their employers, as compared with slavery." Having visited all the islands in the British West Indies in 1840, the same man noted: "The change for the better, in the dress, demeanor, and welfare of the people, is prodigious." And according to an observer on Montserrat, "Schools were springing up in all parts of the island. Marriages were occurring every week. The planters now encouraged missionaries to labor among their people, and were ready to give land for chapels, which were fast multiplying."[15] In Jamaica, once full emancipation had replaced a system of apprenticeship, all the signs of "civilization" appeared. The "thatched hovels, with mud walls, thrown together without any order or arrangement," vanished from the landscape. Instead, freedpeople living in whitewashed houses "now have looking-glasses, chairs, and sideboards decorated with pretty articles of glass and crockery. Each dwelling has its little plot of vegetables, generally neatly kept, and many of them have flower-gardens in front, glowing with all the bright hues of the tropics."[16]

Early witnesses to the Port Royal experiment had similar aspirations. In 1863, journalist Charles Nordhoff published the story of his visit to Port Royal, *The Freedmen of South-Carolina: Some Account of Their Appearance, Character, Condition, and Peculiar Customs.* Nordhoff was particularly interested in the opportunity for creating consumer desires among former slaves. He predicted that the former slave men enlisted in the Union army "will bring back with them improved ideas and new wants, and will work a change both in dress and furniture." Nordhoff's hope was that such new habits of taste would soon be readily apparent in the simple cottages of freedpeople: "I noticed that on some walls were hung pictures from the illustrated journals; and I have no doubt cheap colored prints would find a ready sale." Behind the Union troops, another kind of army would advance the cause of progress in the South: "The day which sees the introduction on these islands of the itinerant Yankee peddler will be an important one. If he is only moderately honest, and quick-witted, he will be a valuable helper in advancing civilization here."[17] Edward Philbrick, who had worked as a plantation superintendent near Port Royal, with the ambition to prove that free labor was more profitable than slave, had just that idea. He opened a store there and reported that freedpeople quickly bought up his dry goods, hardware, and other provisions. "It may readily be seen that a considerable demand may arise for the articles above-named and others of kindred nature, when a population of some millions shall be in a position to apply their earnings to the supply of their rapidly increasing wants. Should not the manufacturing interests of the North be awake to this?"[18]

Talk of freedpeople's "increasing wants," of printed pictures tacked to bare walls, was of a piece with the educational efforts of northern benevolent societies in the South. Together they told a story of advancing civilization and expanding markets.[19] This vision was carried into the South Carolina Sea Islands with the arrival of the first missionaries and reformers. Edward Pierce, one of the leaders of the Port Royal experiment, engaged schoolchildren there in a "dialogue" in 1863 that reflected this concern for the spread of self-reliance, a Protestant work ethic, and consumerism.

"Children, what are you going to do when you grow up?"
"Going to work, Sir."
"On what?"
"Cotton and corn, Sir."
"What are you going to do with the corn?"
"Eat it."
"What are you going to do with the cotton?"

"Sell it."

"What are you going to do with the money you get for it?"

One boy answered in advance of the rest,—

"Put it in my pocket, Sir."

"That won't do. What's better than that?"

"Buy clothes, Sir."

"What else will you buy?"

"Shoes, Sir."[20]

The children also promised to send *their* children to church and school, when the time came, and promised to pay for the parson and the teacher themselves, rather than relying on the government. In conclusion, Pierce wrote: "One who listens to such answers can hardly think that there is any natural incapacity in these children to acquire with maturity of years the ideas and habits of good citizens." These "ideas" and "habits" would become a point of dispute between freed laborers and plantation owners in postbellum South Carolina, as elsewhere in the South after slavery. Nonetheless, Pierce and other reformers clearly had high hopes for the creation of a freed black working class that participated in (and enriched) the nation's markets.[21]

As Child's treatise suggested, however, the ambitions of those concerned with the fate of freedpeople were in many ways larger than the national crisis they struggled to address. Abolitionists, reformers, and missionaries alike viewed their work as part of the transatlantic movement bringing "civilization" to the "uncivilized" peoples of the world. For missionaries, in particular, the inclusion of the black population of the South in this larger civilizing movement had begun before the Civil War. Writing in 1858, in the "Children's Department" of the *American Missionary* magazine, the editors told young readers of the shared desires of children abroad and at home to become Christian: "Ten thousand little children, from the shores of Africa, India, and China, are turning to you, and stretching out their little hands, earnestly pleading for the Gospel." And there were children in the United States with the same desires. "From the poor slave in our own land, groaning under the lash of a cruel master comes the same earnest plea, 'Oh! Send us the Gospel.'"[22] The *American Missionary* often ran stories about the daily lives of African children at the association's mission in West Africa alongside reports from missionary teachers working with freedpeople in the South.[23]

This global view of reform, in turn, shaped abolitionists' and missionaries' consideration of black freedom and black people's prospects for civilization. Two months after the start of the Civil War, the *American Missionary* ran an excerpt from the writings of the Reverend J. Leighton Wilson, a missionary working in Africa, under the heading "Capacity of the Negro for Improvement"—a pointed lesson for readers concerned with the prospect of a newly freed "Negro" population in the United States. Wilson explained: "Looking at the African race, as we have done in their native country, we have seen no obstacle to their elevation which would not apply equally to all other uncultivated races of men." Wilson compared Africans with South Sea Islanders, "the Indian tribes of our own country," and "even with the great masses of ignorant poor who throng all the great cities of the civilized world." In sum, they (Africans, Negroes) "do not appear to any disadvantage whatever."[24] The soon-to-be emancipated slave population of the South, as the headline suggests, would be included in this worldwide civilizing campaign. As Edward Pierce, former Union officer and chief promoter of the experiment at Port Royal, advised a leading pastor in Boston the next year: "You must see that the heathen to whom we owe a special duty . . . are nearer to us than the Ganges."[25]

The particular aims and expectations of those bringing "civilization" to freedpeople in the South had their roots in the early nineteenth century, when a notion of "civilization" developed, according to anthropologist George Stocking, "in the shadow of other broad forces of historical change," namely, the Industrial Revolution, evangelical Christian revivalism, and radical protest in France. All these developments contributed to a proactive nineteenth-century definition of "civilization" that encompassed not just evangelical Christianity and the celebration of European (and Anglo-American) superiority but also the desire to promote human progress generally, by working directly with the "uncivilized" peoples of the world.[26] When a collection of leading abolitionists and missionaries founded the National Freedmen's Relief Association in New York in 1862 to immediately address the situation at Port Royal, they did so in the name of "civilization and Christianity."[27]

Women played a particularly important role in the spread of Anglo-Saxon civilization. Female missionaries and teachers, in particular, often served as intermediaries in the civilizing process.[28] From the earliest phase of European exploration, female figures served in symbolic ways to mark the "threshold" between European civilization and the New

World.[29] But by the first half of the nineteenth century, in the context of massive evangelical revivals that attracted a largely female following, women had begun to engage directly in civilizing activities, from carefully plotted "rescues" in efforts to end prostitution in the streets of New York to attending abolitionist meetings and supporting a flourishing industry in antislavery literature. As missionary efforts gathered speed in the second half of the nineteenth century, British and American women traveled widely in support of their cause, from Africa and India to the Pacific Islands and the American West.[30] At the close of the Civil War, the work of northern evangelical women in the South became a further extension of this work. Yet by the 1860s, ideas about the civilizing effects of an idealized middle-class domesticity had become as important to reform efforts as the spread of Protestantism. This is evident in Lydia Maria Child's treatise, as well as the writings of other Protestant reformers. Even missionary Austa French, who traveled early to Port Royal, explained her calling there, in one passage of her memoir, in terms not of Christianity but of domestic order: "Still some would have us sit in northern parlors, with hands folded, to entertain some caller, or even slaveholder," while freedwomen continued to raise children in cabins French found squalid, without the fundamentals of "domestic knowledge."[31]

The experiment at Port Royal, which drew both Austa French and Harriet Murray out of their parlors, was the first of many such efforts in the South during and after the Civil War. Northern benevolent societies had begun sending teachers south as early as 1861, to Fortress Monroe in Virginia, and 1862, to the island of Port Royal on the South Carolina coast.[32] Some of them represented missionary societies, the largest of them being the American Missionary Association (AMA), an organization that prior to the Civil War had been working among freed populations in Jamaica, Canada, and the northern United States, as well as with the native inhabitants of West Africa.[33] Other northerners, most though not all of whom came from an evangelical, abolitionist tradition, represented organizations formed expressly for the purpose of freedpeople's aid: among them the National Freedmen's Relief Association, the Boston Educational Commission, the American Freedmen's Aid Commission, and the Pennsylvania Freedmen's Relief Association, the latter formed with the help of the Quakers. Other Quaker societies also developed, including the Friends Association of Philadelphia and its Vicinity for the Relief of Colored Freedmen. The Friends also took in orphaned freedchildren at their Home for Colored Orphans in Phila-delphia.[34]

Government-administered schools for freedpeople after the war typi-cally were staffed by teachers from northern benevolent societies, as well as local southerners, black and white, and supervised by the Bureau of Refugees, Freedmen, and Abandoned Lands, or Freedmen's Bureau—the federal agency started in 1865 and charged with the management of abandoned lands, the facilitation of labor contracts, the distribution of food and clothing, and the establishment of schools for freedpeople, among other duties.[35] At the peak of the educational effort administered by the bureau, there were reportedly 3,300 teachers educating freedpeo-ple in the former Confederacy, although the actual number must have been larger, since many schools, particularly those not supported by the bureau, did not send in reports. Despite the many regional and denomi-national affiliations of northern reformers and missionaries, this group as a whole was mostly white and middle-class. Some African American missionaries arrived from the northern states, but the majority of those sent from groups like the AMA were white.[36] The majority of *northern* teachers in freedpeople's schools were, in fact, single white women. By 1868, however, the bureau's superintendent for education reported that black teachers slightly outnumbered white teachers.[37] Given the large number of black teachers reported that year (some 4,000—a number, again, that does not include the many schools that did not submit re-ports), it appears that many of them were local.[38] Further research has also discovered a large portion of the white teachers were southerners. The motivations of the latter were mixed. While some simply needed work, others signed up out of genuine desire to educate former slaves.[39]

But it was the white northern female teacher, the "Yankee school-marm" so derided by hostile southern sympathizers (some historians among them) well into the twentieth century, that most often appeared in literature on schools for freedpeople (both in promotional material and in news reports), and it was through this figure that most north-ern readers understood the educational efforts ongoing in the South. Though generally unpopular among whites in the South, white female teachers were a welcome sight for freedpeople. Black scholar and activ-ist W. E. B. Du Bois, writing in 1903, declared these northern women heroes, who had taught the black *and* white people of the South: "Be-hind the mists of ruin and rapine waved the calico dresses of women who dared, and after the hoarse mouthings of the field guns rang the rhythm of the alphabet."[40] Northern women's activism on behalf of freedpeople, in fact, extended well beyond the schoolroom—they engaged in debates on labor reform, bought and sold land for cultivation by freedpeople, and lobbied the federal government.[41] But in the marketing of the freedchild as the future of the black population in the South, the white, female figure that most often appeared was a teacher.

Northern visitors throughout the South after the Civil War were impressed by freedpeople's desire for education. (Most southern states before the war prohibited the education of blacks, and in 1860, more than 90 percent of the South's adult black population was illiterate.)[42] One northern teacher, for instance, testified to the American Freedmen's Inquiry Commission that "without exception I never saw such greedy people for study. Then there is the great ambition to be able to read the Bible for themselves. I have not seen an indifferent child or an indolent one—dull ones, I have seen of course; they are all zealous." Some freedpeople insisted that schooling for their children be provided as part of labor contracts.[43] When queried about their demand for schooling for their children, freedpeople explained it in practical terms. Testifying before the American Freedmen's Inquiry Commission in South Carolina in 1863, for instance, freedman Harry McMillan was asked: "Did your masters ever see you learning to read?" to which he responded: "No, sir; you could not let your masters see you read; but now the colored people are fond of sending their children to school." When asked why this was, McMillan replied: "Because the children in after years will be able to tell us ignorant ones how to do for ourselves." McMillan also had a vision of a time when freedpeople would govern themselves entirely, without the help of whites. "Probably with the children that are coming up now white men will not be needed," he said. Learning to read and write, and training to be doctors, ministers, and lawyers, the young people would free their race from dependence on whites. "After five years," McMillan said, "they will take care of themselves; this [older] generation cannot do it."[44]

The resources for freedpeople's education would never be sufficient to meet the demands of the nearly four million freedpeople—adults and children—reformers hoped to educate. They could not even reach all of the nearly two-and-a-quarter million freedchildren in the South after emancipation.[45] In the state of Georgia, for instance, only 5 percent of freedpeople attended school in any one year.[46] In 1870, the superintendent of education for the Freedmen's Bureau bemoaned the inability to provide instruction for most freedpeople: "The mass of these freedmen are, after all, still ignorant. Nearly a million and a half of their children have never as yet been under any instruction."[47] Without sufficient government and charitable support, most often, freedpeople had to rely on their own meager resources to fund schools and teachers.[48]

But in the immediate aftermath of the Civil War, benevolent societies and representatives of the Freedmen's Bureau had great expectations for their campaign to educate former slaves. Education for freedpeople, like education for northern children, was fundamentally about the instruction of discipline and industry. Indeed, the education of the freed population was a necessity akin to the education of all working classes. As an editor of the *American Missionary* wrote, "It is the duty of every government to provide against crime, pauperism, and wretchedness, by providing against ignorance."[49] The textbooks for freedpeople's schools, given the financial straits of benevolent societies, were more often than not used textbooks from northern schools. And while Lydia Maria Child's new *Freedman's Book* (1865) instructed freedpeople on the history of such radical figures as Toussaint L'Ouverture and William Lloyd Garrison, its primary message was still one of self-reliance, uplift, and hard work—betraying the idea that reformers feared freedpeople, without civilizing instruction, would not work for themselves.[50] As the western secretary of the AMA declared in 1866—the year Elsie and Puss stood in the portrait studio—the teachers and missionaries descending on the South were the greatest "Army of Civilization" the nation had ever mustered.[51] The portrait of Harriet Murray, Elsie, and Puss, as a piece of propaganda, was at once a reenactment of that "army's" success and a projection of the future for freedpeople in the South, carefully arranged around a theme that nineteenth-century viewers readily understood: the ragged child redeemed.

The first organized efforts directed at the nineteenth century's growing numbers of so-called ragged children began in the 1840s with the Ragged School movement in London, born of concern for the working-class children who filled the industrial city's streets. Founded largely by evangelical groups, Ragged Schools recruited street children, often giving them food and shelter and providing free instruction. By the 1850s, however, other reformers in the United States and Britain, less focused on religious conversion and more concerned with rescue and reform, began to introduce their own strategies to address the problem of the ragged child. Guided by their conviction that "goodness could be concealed beneath rags," these new efforts sentimentalized the street child. At midcentury, reformers had yet to fully engage the system of industrialism that encouraged child labor and instead placed emphasis on the inadequacies of the working-class family to raise poor children.[52] Such children, they argued, needed to be rescued by society and educated in the ways of civilization and honest labor.

Ragged children, as reformers rendered them, were either without parents or living with parents whose alcoholism and "slovenly" habits destroyed their ability to care for their children. (Evidence suggests, however, that many of the children who became the focus of reform efforts were not orphans, and that often families *chose* to send their children to missionary institutions on the grounds that they could not care for them themselves.)[53] It was in the interest of ragged children, or "street orphans," that Charles Loring Brace founded the Children's Aid Society (CAS) in 1853 in New York City. The CAS sent "home visitors" into the dwellings of poor families to monitor the conditions of the "tenement classes," a group that in the view of reformers had, by the 1850s, become a dire threat to the social order. The growth of street trading in cities like New York drew children into public commerce in increasing numbers. According to Brace, they lived "by begging, by petty pilfering, by bold robbery," while others "earn an honest support by peddling matches, or apples, or newspapers." But left to their own devices, "without mother or friends," these children "if unreclaimed" would "help to form the great multitude of robbers, thieves, vagrants, and prostitutes who are now such a burden upon the law-respecting community."[54]

Although reformers like Brace often lamented the perceived absence of parental control, nineteenth-century missionaries and reformers working in Europe, Africa, and the United States generally viewed parents and other relatives as a hindrance to the civilizing of ragged children. In his first *Plea for Ragged Schools* (1849), Scottish missionary Thomas Guthrie wrote on behalf of the many "unhappy children who are suffering from the crimes of their parents and neglect of society." "Suppose a man already indolent, improvident, and dissipated, to have four children," Guthrie wrote, "without this institution [the Ragged School] these grow up in their father's image."[55] Although Guthrie did not propose to remove children from their homes, his plan for schooling would keep them well away from their parents, in school from dawn until after supper. In Africa, too, missionaries took up the strategy of rescue and strove to remove children from the immediate influence of their "heathen" parents. The readers of the "Children's Department" of the *American Missionary* in 1862 learned that African "mission children" were "boys and girls whom the missionaries have taken—with the consent of their fathers and mothers—to live with them in the mission till they grow to maturity," and that the children were learning to sew and "work on the farm." Missionaries believed that by removing the children from the influences of their parents and relatives, they could create a more "industrious" African population.[56] African children who learned "American ways" would be useful in teaching civilization to their people. But this task was made difficult because "temptations are all about them. Their fathers, mothers, brothers, sisters, and all their relatives and friends, except those in the mission, do differently from what missionaries require them to do. They cook, eat, dress, and work in a different way from what the children are taught to do. . . . We teach them to be industrious, but as their country people spend much time in idleness, is it strange that labor at times seems a burden and occasions discontent."[57]

In the United States, two significant efforts in the middle and late nineteenth century removed large numbers of children from the influence of their families. The first came from the Children's Aid Society, which began "placing out" poor and orphaned children in the 1850s to homes in the country. In its literature, the CAS declared that the charge of its agents was "to get these children of unhappy fortune utterly out of their surroundings, and to send them away to kind Christian *homes in the country.* No influence, we believe is like the influence of *Home.*"[58] Soon the CAS was sponsoring "orphan trains," aimed at improving the lot of thousands of poor urban children (many of whom were not orphans but simply poor boys seeking to improve their lot) by sending them to the Midwest and West to live with farm families.[59] The second was directed at Native American children after the Civil War. In the interest of assimilation, thousands of Indian children boarded trains in the opposite direction, headed east to learn their letters and become schooled in the ways of "civilized" society. One agent for the Bureau of Indian Affairs, writing in 1878, saw such boarding schools as the only means of assimilation: "It must be manifest to all practical minds that to place these wild children under the teacher's care but four or five hours a day, and permit them to spend the other nineteen in the filth and degradation of the village, makes the attempt to educate and civi-

lize them a mere farce."[60] Also by the 1870s and into the twentieth century, many reformers advocated sending older African American and
Native American children to industrial schools in Virginia and the
Northeast, both to teach them skills and to remove them from the influences of family and the small-town South.[61]

Despite the fact that there were large numbers of children orphaned
or separated from their parents by the slave trade and then by the chaos
of the Civil War, an organized system of removal never developed for
the freedchildren of the South.[62] Before the Civil War, antislavery activists had centered their appeals on the cruel separation of families encouraged by the slave system, decrying the brutality of slaveholders who
placed profit over the bonds of family. It would have been difficult for
them, in turn, to endorse family separation after emancipation. In addition, many orphaned freedchildren were absorbed into their extended
families and the fictive kin groups that had been formed under slavery
as a means to combat the emotional and material effects of family separation by the slave trade.[63]

Still, the desire to remove freedchildren from the influences of their
families did surface from time to time in the correspondence of teachers
and reformers in the South. A teacher for the AMA suggested that a
normal school be established "where boys and girls can be sent from
their home for a year or two then return to set a proper example among
their own people. . . . It is very little use of teachers doing a faithful
part for pupils to be laid aside as soon as the children return home
which is frequent."[64] (Such schools would come to fruition by the early
1870s, for older students.)[65] Elizabeth Botume, reflecting on the question "How far can the negroes go in education?" resolved that the family life of her students was a hindrance to them: "The children learn
readily and memorize quickly. Then the lack of habits of application
bars the way. What is learned in school is repeated at home, and so the
whole is leavened. In this way the family is instructed and advanced,
while the progress of the child is retarded. He hears only the plantation
dialect, and becomes familiar with the plantation superstitions."[66]

After the war, it seems, white northern abolitionists took on what they
considered to be a new enemy. Antislavery campaigns had decried the
brutality of slaveholders, and antislavery activists had employed the
language of sentimental fiction to voice their outrage against the system that tore babies away from their mothers.[67] But that campaign

had been waged from a distance. Once white northern abolitionists reached the South, their work was no longer antislavery but, rather, civilizing.

After the agony of children and parents lost to the slave trade, however, freedpeople fought any attempts to deprive parents of their children and their children's labor, often to the chagrin of northern reformers and officials.[68] Indeed, the overarching reason that there was no campaign to export freedchildren from the South was that they were valuable as workers—both to their families and to former slaveholders and other employers. An organized effort to place freedchildren elsewhere would have met resistance from all sides. Still, freedchildren proved central to reformers' campaigns to "rescue" the freed population from an uncivilized existence and transform it into a "disciplined" black working class.

Common to all efforts to rescue the ragged child in the nineteenth century were the stories of discovery told by reformers, stories that drew upon the writings of missionaries in Africa as well as upon popular sentimental novels of the period.[69] The discovery stories about street children and freedchildren were akin to what Mary Louise Pratt terms narratives of "anti-conquest," that is, stories of chance discovery told by missionaries or other representatives of an imperial or civilizing power, that allowed them to employ "strategies of innocence," strategies that might conceal their trespasses and efforts at "conquest."[70] Such discovery narratives surfaced in the accounts of reformers such as Henry Mayhew, Charles Loring Brace, and Lydia Maria Child, when they made their forays into the streets and tenements of New York and London (in the case of Mayhew). It was in the streets, for instance, that Child encountered, "a ragged little urchin" whose "sweet voice of childhood was prematurely cracked into shrillness" from selling newspapers. Such children lived in tenement houses, according to reformers, that contained "dark narrow stairways, decayed with age, reeking with filth, overrun with vermin."[71] Similar passages appear in the fiction of Charles Dickens and his contemporaries. The ragged little crossing sweeper, Jo, in Dickens's *Bleak House* (1853), for instance, who had "no father, no mother, no friends" and knew nothing of a "home," lived "in a ruinous place . . . a black, dilapidated street, avoided by all decent people." Dickens also takes his reader down that street: "Now, these tumbling tenements contain, by night, a swarm of misery. As, on the ruined human wretch, vermin parasites appear, so, these ruined shelters have bred a crowd of foul existence that crawls in and out of gaps in walls and boards; and coils itself to sleep in maggot numbers, where the rain drips in."[72] In addition to describing Jo's surroundings, Dickens mused about the story he was spinning, one that would bring together a child like Jo and the wealthy Lady Dedlock and Sir Leicester: "What connexion can there have been between many people in the innumerable histories of this world, who, from opposite sides of great gulfs, have, nevertheless, been very curiously brought together!"[73] Although the author himself joined the life of the street urchin and the lady together, his narrator declared it a "curious" accident.

Using similar stories of discovery in their own writings, reformers could direct benevolence toward ragged children while at the same time asserting control over them and directing their future.[74] Accounts of freedchildren must be seen in this light, as well. They were part of this genre of discovery writing and benevolence, a genre that encompassed both street children and former slave children. Just after her trip to Port Royal in 1862, for instance, Austa French told the story of a freedwoman to whom French and a group of women paid a visit. She introduced the story (told at the start of a chapter entitled "Cruelty Reigns") by explaining, in sympathetic terms, the "heartless" condition of freedwomen: "No time, strength, patience, or heart, for sympathy have the poor 'field hand' women. They all have little feeling at the death of [a child] because all want to die who would, by grace, have the tenderness to feel."[75] In telling the story of the freedwoman, French began with the notion that slavery had stripped its victims of all capacity for feeling. Only the intervention of French and her female companions would set the household aright and would chance to save the life of the ragged child on the floor. The boy "lying upon a few rags on the hearth, too weak to cry, is a child of six years, in a dying state, from consumption or neglect." The missionary women intervened with soap and clean clothes, explaining,

"You must take it up and bathe it, using some of this nice healing soap. We have brought all clean clothes and a bed" (a large clothes-basket filled with nice straw, and covered with soft cloths).

"Can't wash him; mus' go fo' rations."

"You must wash him; he is suffering so."

"I'll do it when I come home."

"You must do it now; we cannot leave until you do."[76]

According to French, the woman told them that the child was her sister's, and that she had her own baby to attend to and could not "hold that big nigger" while her child cried. Shedding tears herself, she said she would be "glad" if the child died, like five of her children, " 'cause so much trouble.' " When the freedwoman explained that the boy's head was suffering from "maggits," French wrote, "our sister, with uplifted hands, ran out and home to get remedies," while French and the others remained, "enforcing and superintending the washing." After cleaning the child, French and her colleagues expressed empathy for the woman, not blaming her but pitying her for being "so destitute of domestic knowledge": "We do not have to work in the field as you always have to do. Still, you want to learn to do things right, don't you?" French admitted, however, that "her rags were all as clean as possible without soap, as so many of them had none to wash with."[77] The child, despite the intervention of French and her "sisters," died two days later. As for the freedwoman, French explained that she would be "attended to."[78]

Like Dickens, French exposed the living conditions of poor children, and their alleged abandonment or neglect by parents or guardians, to point out the distance between the ragged child and civilization, a distance that reformers hoped to bridge. In other representations of ragged children in the nineteenth century, however, reformers used racial categories as a means to highlight the difference between civilization and savagery in which the ragged child lived. Thomas Guthrie described street children as "Arabs of the city" and "as wild as desert savages." Reformer Thomas Beggs, in *An Inquiry into the Extent and Causes of Juvenile Depravity* (1849), reported that the "predatory hordes of the street" in London might "almost belong to a separate race." British children new to the Ragged Schools "behaved more like savages than civilized human beings." Charles Loring Brace, too, seems to have adopted the term "street Arab," but also compared New York's poor "houseless" boys to Native Americans, in that they bore "something of the same relation which Indians bear to the civilized Western settlers" who existed as "a happy race of little heathens and barbarians."[79] Not incidentally, perhaps, many of these children described as "barbarians" were the offspring of Irish immigrants, nearly two million of whom arrived in the 1850s and settled in eastern cities like New York and Boston.[80]

In relating the child to the savage, missionaries working in the 1840s and 1850s were ahead of social science. It was not until the 1860s and 1870s that social scientists proposed the theory of *recapitulation*—that is, that both children and colonized people were at the beginning stages of human development. Whereas the "savage" represented an early stage in mankind's evolution, so the theory went, the child's growth *recapitulated* the developmental stages of the human race, from savagery to civilization.[81] Recapitulation eventually collapsed under the weight of science, but while in vogue it served to reinforce the work of missionaries and other reformers promoting the development and dispersal of Victorian civilization among the nineteenth century's poor children.

Unlike London's young "street Arabs," African American children were seldom linked to "savage" parts other than sub-Saharan Africa, where the American Missionary Association, in particular, had made inroads before the Civil War.[82] The antebellum missionary work under way in West Africa seems to have inspired missionaries hoping to start their own schools among African Americans in the United States. By the 1860s, Africa was quickly becoming a source of fascination with American readers, a fascination that would continue to grow with the publication of European and American explorers' accounts.[83] Indeed, enthusiasm for an imagined Africa is evident in the reports and letters of aspiring missionaries in the United States. A teacher writing to the American Missionary Association in 1864, petitioning for a teaching position in the South, clearly hoped to impress the reader of his petition by proving his sense for missionary duty. He explained that while living in the free state of Ohio, he had stumbled upon "a collection of negro huts, occupied by free blacks." When he saw the children, he knew "that I found this, my first *missionary* field. I had longed for it a great while, and when I saw it, I *knew* it. The woods were swarming with little woolly-headed, half-dressed children, and my heart warmed to them in a minute." He then turned and spoke to the mother of some of the children but made no observations about her to the reader. Instead, he focused on the children as if they (unlike the mother) were not African Americans living in Ohio but little Africans: "I said to the mother of six of the young savages, for really small Hottentots would not have looked any more like real live heathen to me than they did: 'Don't your children go to Sunday-school?' "[84] When he discovered that white children harassed the black children and kept them from attending school, he resolved to start his own class. He explained, "I went there next Sunday and sat down under a tree, with a great log in front of me, whereon sat thirty-four half-naked children, their little black legs hanging down, too short to touch the ground, and had a Sunday school." An observer in Illinois described a similar scene. He watched a young man "teaching a group of little darkies" under a "magnificent oak," noting that "twenty or thirty negro children were sitting around him in a circle on the ground, as the heathens do in the missionary picture books."[85]

Those who recorded or recounted their first visit to the South during the Civil War described their missionary endeavors in similar fashion. The freedchild often inspired in missionary teachers an enthusiasm that grown freedpeople did not. If they were little "savages," they were savages who could be civilized. In a letter that appeared in the *American Missionary* in 1864, teacher Caroline Jocelyn explained: "I can never meet the peculiarly mournful gaze of the mute, overawed negro," she wrote, "but a fountain of tears is stirred within me. There is, however, in Young Africa, a jubilant hopefulness which sweeps over all barriers, and will bear their possessors on to success and prosperity."[86] Northern benevolent societies printed accounts like these because they served as dramatic tales of discovery. In such writings and in photographs, in turn, the black freedchild represents both the beginning and the end of Pratt's "anti-conquest": the discovery of former slaves in "ragged" or "degraded" form and their transformation into tidy, disciplined freedpeople. Freedchildren were instrumental to the white northern "anti-conquest" of the South because they—like Africa itself—were to the eyes of white northern reformers new territory for the spread of "civilization" and discipline, each child an untouched, if untamed, field ready for cultivation.[87]

The portrait of Harriet Murray, Elsie, and Puss, therefore, was more than just an image of a white female teacher with her black charges. In the figures of freedchildren, white northerners read stories of discovery and rescue that contained within them ideas about both geography and phylogeny—that is, of national progress and racial progress. Seen under the instruction of their white female teacher, Elsie and Puss embodied the transformation of the South under the direction of the North, a region to be cultivated by "disciplined" free laborers. At the same time, given their capacity to develop, freedchildren like Elsie and Puss also represented for white northern audiences the black race's historical coming-of-age. In the narratives of missionaries and officials, freedchildren illustrated the race's swift passage from slavery to freedom, from "savagery" to "civilization," under the influence of northern reformers.

New arrivals to the South often began with descriptions of the land-scape and its freed inhabitants, as if both were completely foreign.[88] Writing in 1893, Elizabeth Botume, a northern teacher and missionary to freedpeople in South Carolina, introduced her memoir with a passage about the "discovery" of freedpeople in the Low Country at the start of the war. Northerners, according to Botume, "knew but little of slavery" in the South, for them it was *"terra incognita"*: "When brought face to face with the slaves, as they were during the war, it was like the discov-ery of a new race. . . . What was known of the slaves themselves? Had they any individuality? Were they, as we were often told, only animals with certain brute force, but no capacity for self-government? Or were they reasoning beings?"[89] Though she had been warned that slaves on rice plantations were "the most degraded of the race" and perhaps "the connecting link" between humans and "the brute creation," Botume in-sisted that they were the people with whom she wanted to work. She had hoped to labor in what she considered uncharted territory, her enthusiasm for *"terra incognita"* being the principle motivation.[90] Al-though Botume wrote this in 1893, when U.S. imperialism was reaching new heights, it is still striking that her words were not unlike those that appeared in accounts from the 1860s. Sounding like the missionary who found his calling among the "Hottentots" of Ohio, Botume declared: "As this was purely missionary work, these were the people I wished to come in contact with."[91]

Edward Philbrick and Austa French, both writing from Port Royal, seemed captivated by the wildness of their surroundings. Both writers used the landscape and its black inhabitants to argue that its white in-habitants, by their decadence and cruelty, must forfeit it to more compe-tent managers.[92] French, the wife of the Reverend Mansfield French, a leader of the Port Royal experiment, explained that in South Carolina, "vegetation, too, is singular. Even that seems to partake of the spirit of slavery. Trees luxuriant, but misshapen, gnarly, ill-tempered. . . . Every splendid thing seems to overtop something which dwindles under its influence."[93] Philbrick, who would become a plantation superinten-dent, wrote upon his arrival in 1862: "Dilapidated fences, tumble-down buildings, untrimmed trees with lots of dead branches, weedy walks and gardens and a general appearance of *un*thrift attendant upon the best of slaveholding towns, was aggravated here by the desolated houses, sur-rounded by heaps of broken furniture and broken wine and beer bottles which the army had left about after their pillage." Freedchildren, in

Figure 19. "Feeding the Negro Children under the Charge of the Military Authorities at Hilton Head, South Carolina," *Harper's Weekly,* June 14, 1862.

Philbrick's description, were a natural part of this careless, untended place. As he made his way through the town of Beaufort, "Quantities of negro children lay basking in the morning sun, grinning at us as we passed."[94]

Like the southern landscape and its inhabitants, northern observers presented the freedchild as mostly untouched and unsocialized, except by the inhuman cruelties of slavery. With an image that appeared in *Harper's Weekly* in 1862, entitled "Feeding the Negro Children under the Charge of Military Authorities at Hilton Head, South Carolina" (figure 19), the editors suggested that freedchildren remained in a savage state, one that could be remedied only by northern instruction: "Our picture shows the feeding of these negro pickaninnies. Poor little creatures! they are realizing for the first time that they are human beings, and not of the same class in animated nature as dogs and hogs."[95] But the picture itself shows the children sitting on the ground in a yard —"under the charge of military authorities"—eating with chickens, ducks, and dogs. There is even a dog sitting upright, begging, alongside the children. Plenty of former slaves angrily recalled having to eat out of one large pan placed in the yard as children.[96] Still, this image, as one of emancipation, implied that freedboys and freedgirls were not much more advanced than the barnyard animals around them and urgently needed the enlightenment that only northern civilization would bring. In contrast to the children, the adults in the picture stand or sit to the side of the image, making the children appear completely unsocialized by their elders, unaware (unlike the adults around them) that they were not, in fact, in the same class as the chickens.[97] Further still, viewers had a standing perspective on the child figures seated on the ground, thus allowing them to look down upon the children feeding with animals. The children appeared in a helpless state of "savagery" and in need of white northerners' help.[98]

As we saw in the last chapter, the National Freedmen's Relief Association's presentation of girls like Rosa and Rebecca, and Henry Ward Beecher's appeals from the pulpit of Plymouth Church, were rescue stories. The white-looking girls (and others like them), so the story went,

Figure 20. "Fannie Virginia Casseopia Lawrence," *carte-de-visite*, 1863. Private collection. Courtesy of Tony Seideman.

Fannie Virginia Casseopia Lawrence.
A Redeemed Slave Child, 5 years of age. Redeemed in Virginia, by Catharine S. Lawrence; baptized in Brooklyn, at Plymouth Church, by Henry Ward Beecher, May, 1863.
Entered according to Act of Congress in the year 1863, by C. S. Lawrence, in the Clerk's Office of the District Court of the United States, for the Southern District of New York.

needed the help of the northern public to spare them a future of slavery and sin. Fanny Lawrence, too, was discovered "sore and tattered and unclean" by Catherine Lawrence when Lawrence was working as a nurse in Virginia. Fanny's sponsor even staged a "ragged" *carte-de-visite* of her as part of a series of photographs to raise money to support Fanny and herself (figure 20). Very different from the other portraits of Fanny, and the individual portraits of Rebecca and Rosa, this photograph was taken from a distance, with a faint landscape painted on canvas in the background. Fanny looks forlorn, standing with her head bowed and her feet bare.[99] Like the drawing of the freedchildren eating on the ground, this picture invited northern intervention and, like the illustration, put viewers in the position of the discoverer, as if they had just come upon her standing there, a slave child unprotected.

Reformers' descriptions of freedchildren's development had many precursors in fictional stories about ragged children in the nineteenth century. There were the popular tales of street children in the fiction of Charles Dickens, for instance, narrating the rescue and reform of the youngest, most vulnerable members of society. The work of Dickens and his contemporaries often reflected the nineteenth-century fascination with growth and transformation, and with an individual's evolution. (It has even been suggested that Charles Darwin's discussions of transformation and metamorphosis owed much to the writings of Dickens.)[100] The most familiar ragged child, transformed into an upright, hardworking young man, would be the one portrayed in Horatio Alger's *Ragged Dick,* first serialized in 1867. Dick first appears to the reader in a sorry state. His pants are tattered, his shirt "looked as if it had been worn a month," and Dick "had no particular dislike of dirt, and did not think it necessary to remove several dark streaks on his face and hands." Still, "in spite of his dirt and rags, there was something about Dick that was attractive. It was easy to see that if he had been clean and well dressed he would have been decidedly good-looking."[101] The rags and the dirt (by Alger's design) were a way of measuring distance, marking Dick's passage from street urchin to a well-dressed, hardworking young man. That Dick "would have been decidedly good-looking" if cleaned up foreshadows his ultimate reform.

The literature of antislavery had its own familiar ragged child (one who preceded Ragged Dick by more than a decade) in Harriet Beecher Stowe's Topsy, in whom (like Dick) there was goodness beneath the rags. Topsy is introduced in *Uncle Tom's Cabin* (1852) as the true test of northern civilization, a civilization embodied by the Yankee spinster Miss Ophelia. When Topsy first appears in the story, she is a model of the unschooled, devilish "pickaninny": her "woolly hair" in braids that "stuck out in every direction," her expression a mix of "shrewdness and cunning" veiled in "the most doleful gravity," her clothes ragged and dirty. As Stowe's narrator declares, "altogether, there was something odd and goblin-like about her appearance—something, as Miss Ophelia afterwards said, 'so heathenish' as to inspire that good lady with utter dismay."[102]

Miss Ophelia is a white northern woman recently arrived in Louisiana living in the household of her slave-owning cousin, Augustine St. Clare. Since Ophelia so often preached the importance of education among the "heathen," St. Clare presents her with Topsy, whom he declares to be "a fresh-caught specimen" on which to test her ideals. Though at first opposed to the idea, Ophelia decides that it might, indeed, "be a real missionary work" and so "applied her mind to her heathen with the best diligence she could command." Topsy is scrubbed down and "shorn of all the little braided tails wherein her heart had delighted, arrayed in a clean gown, with well-starched apron," thus making the child, in the eyes of Ophelia, at least a bit "more Christian-like."[103]

Though Topsy is shorn of her braids, she is never transformed into a pliant, angelic child despite Ophelia's efforts. She steals gloves and bits of ribbon, and takes revenge on any of the other slaves in the household who cross her. Only Eva, St. Clare's saintly white daughter, can discipline Topsy and inspire kindness in her. As Eva begins to die, Topsy finally manifests signs of "goodness." But in popular culture, Topsy remained the picture of devilishness. Her signature phrase, recognized well into the early twentieth century, was "I'se so wicked."[104] Ironically, Topsy's intransigence made her all the more useful to northerners describing their first encounters with freedchildren in the South. She remained, in popular memory, the uncivilized child born of slavery, with no mother or father to care for her, and only "speculators" to raise her. As such, she was the perfect symbol for northern civilizing efforts. Northerners could use Topsy, incorrigible as ever, both to justify their presence in the South and to explain away freedchildren's resistance to their efforts to civilize them.

The frequent comparison of freedgirls to Topsy, in fact, was testament to the extent to which Stowe's popular characters shaped northerners' experience of the South.[105] One observer at a southern hospital (possibly in Mississippi) in 1863, for instance, wrote of her encounters with slave children there: "People have often laughingly wondered if 'Topsy' was not a creature of Mrs. Stowe's prolific fancy. Could they have enjoyed a brief season in Corinth, I think they would scarcely have questioned the truthfulness of the character. Topsies might be found here by the hundred."[106] A teacher working for the American Missionary Association in Savannah confessed in a letter to her sister in the North: "I could tell you many amusing incidents of school life: we have so many *Topsys*."[107] And after relaying in her letter that she planned to take in Puss (the child in the photograph with Harriet Murray) to "bring up," Laura Towne described the child as "about the worst little monkey that ever was. Topsy has nothing to her."[108]

The teacher who insisted that Topsys could be found "by the hundred" said that she even "had one" in her room. She described Nell, the child in question, as "a bright, quiet little creature with a tiny round face as black as the ace of spades." The woman "dressed her up and kept her about" to do errands for her, but she served as entertainment as well. "She would dance, sing and act quite as comically as Topsy ever did." Nell ran into trouble, however, with one of the hospital clerks who declared her "a perfect little imp!" The clerk and his friends enjoyed teasing Nell (in coercive ways, given his admission that they "often got her into the store downstairs to hear her make droll remarks"). The clerk explained that he had "got in the habit of tapping her upon the head, pretending to be vexed, just to see her roll up her eyes at me in her comically-deprecating way." "Her wool is pretty thick," he said, "and I guess I tapped her pretty hard sometimes, relying on its softness to protect her." Tired of such abuse, Nell got the better of him by sticking pins beneath her kerchief with the points up, and the clerk got a dozen of them through his hand, soon covered in blood. When the woman (who found it all very funny) questioned Nell about why she stowed the pins in her hair, the child replied, "Why, miss, he was allus a spattin' o' me."[109]

Topsy's influence, as trickster and minstrel, extended to other "first impressions" of freedchildren, even when Topsy herself was not directly invoked. Teacher Elizabeth Botume recalled that when she first approached her new schoolhouse in South Carolina, "the piazza was crowded with children, all screaming and chattering like a flock of jays and blackbirds in a quarrel. But as soon as they saw me they all gave a whoop and bound and disappeared."[110] And Laura Towne remarked upon the children she encountered when she first arrived in St. Helena, South Carolina. She noted that they were "all very civil" despite their "mischief." Yet they were still the stuff of minstrel shows: "The number of little darkies tumbling about at all hours is marvellous. They swarm on the front porch and in the front hall. If a carriage stops it is instantly surrounded by a dozen or more wooly heads."[111] When a special correspondent for the *New York Times* visited Port Royal in 1862, he found "curly-headed picaninnies whose large rows of white, glistening teeth, were only exceeded in whiteness by their rolling eyes, swarmed on every doorstep, and could be seen piled tier above tier in every room." The writer could not resist using Mrs. Stowe's character for inspiration, too, when he saw "a swarm of happy Topseys [*sic*]" sitting together in church.[112]

Such descriptions also implied that freedchildren were unsocialized by adults. Indeed, Topsy's devilishness, in large part, was attributed to her lack of a mother and father to raise and love her. She had "just grow'd" with other slave children under the supervision of an old woman and a slave trader. Topsy's life story was part of Stowe's many-sided attack on the system of chattel slavery that destroyed families and orphaned children. But it also made Topsy a useful character in the aftermath of slavery because it served to place her in the company of the mid-nineteenth century's ragged children.

Reformers soon recognized the utility of visual representations of the ragged child and her redemption. In doing so, they also drew upon other examples of "before-and-after" imagery. The idea for "metamorphic" or mechanical cards, on which an image could be changed by folding and unfolding the card, dates back as far as the sixteenth century. But the ability to mass-produce such images arrived in the nineteenth century. Political campaigns, haberdasheries (changing a "tramp" in ragged clothes into a gentleman), and manufacturers of hair dye all employed "before-and-after" tricks to sell their products.[113] The makers of patent medicines and even hospitals began to use before-and-after illustrated advertisements to argue that an elixir or a particular kind of treatment or surgery could change a person's life. The most elaborate, four-color before-and-after trade cards did not become widely available until the late 1870s. The National Surgical Institute of Philadelphia, for instance, produced a trade card (a popular medium using three-by-five-inch colored illustrations) featuring one child on crutches and another child a few paces ahead casting away her crutches and standing on her own.[114] Soap advertisements in this period, too, conveyed the before-and-after scenario with one illustration—"black" adults or children with part of their face or arms scrubbed "white" with the advertiser's product.[115] The mass marketing of radical transformation, then—the notion that ailments, household chores, frailties, and defects could be instantly alleviated or completely eradicated—was already well established by the middle of the nineteenth century. Like the written accounts of missionaries and fictional tales of rescued street urchins, graphic artists, too, played upon the theme of transformation.

It is not clear who first employed the camera to produce "before-and-after" images. In the 1860s, medical doctors used photography to document the effects of amputation as well as reconstructive surgeries to treat birth defects.[116] Such photographs were useful given the camera's ability both to document medical conditions objectively, or scientifically, and to record and promote (among doctors and patients) the successful outcome of those operations. Reformers seem to have begun to use the before-and-after photograph as a fund-raising tool around the same time. The creator of the most well known series of photographs of ragged street children changed into tidy workers was the British missionary Dr. Thomas Barnardo, a leader in the Ragged School movement in London. But Barnardo may have gotten the idea for his "contrast" photos after meeting with a then relatively obscure missionary from Chicago, Dwight Morris, who had taken a set of "before" and "after" photographs of street children at his mission in 1862.[117] Both men used these serial images to raise money and awareness for their work with poor children. What made them so effective, as propaganda, was their apparent realism, rendered through the use of photography. As documents, they were marked by a particular kind of doubleness: the perceived reality of the children's improved appearance and the rhetoric of progress inherent in the spectacle of transformation. Viewers could see the difference for themselves.[118]

Yet the use of "contrast" photographs also raised the issue of authenticity or, rather, duplicity. The propaganda methods of Thomas Barnardo were famously discredited in 1877, when he was accused in court of having staged his before-and-after photographs. The mothers of some of his subjects came forward to object to images of their children in tattered clothes (one mother insisted that she had sent her children to the mission in *decent* clothes) or the image of a girl selling newspapers, a job the girl had never done. Children testified that their clothes had been torn to shreds before Barnardo photographed them. The court arbitrators lamented that Barnardo had made "fictitious representations of destitution" for the "purposes of obtaining money." After the cases were resolved in 1877 with Barnardo still running his mission, if less triumphantly, he ceased taking propaganda photographs, only recording children for the purposes of identification in case they ran away.[119]

Barnardo's defense, in the face of all the evidence against him, was that his "contrast" photos, if not literally true, contained a deeper truth about the conditions of ragged children, much like the truth conveyed in painting or literature. Barnardo was right, although perhaps in a way he did not intend. The "contrast" pictures of ragged children *were* in the tradition of popular fiction, particularly the work of writers like Dickens and Stowe. Scholars have also written about Barnardo's images as reflective of evangelical, rather than literal, truths—truths based not on fact but on inner feeling, expressing a faith in the radical transformation of the individual.[120] Yet as we have seen, evangelicalism was intertwined with the sorts of images that Barnardo did not, and would not have, named—advertisements for magic elixirs, patent medicines, cosmetics, and cure-alls. Indeed, as Jackson Lears has noted about American advertising in this period, the preacher and the peddler were not so far apart. Those who sold snake oil and those who praised Jesus both conveyed messages of self-transformation and the possibility of a changed future.[121]

This very same message proved central to the efforts of antislavery reformers on behalf of former slaves. Perhaps the earliest example of before-and-after photography to promote slave emancipation in the South and raise money was a set of *cartes-de-visite* sponsored by the Society of Friends in 1864 (figures 21 and 22). Emphasizing that the children photographed had been discovered *and* rescued, their portraits appeared over the titles "As We Found Them" and "As They Are Now." A captain in the Sixth U.S. Colored Infantry named Riley rescued two children, a brother and sister, eight and six years of age, in Virginia. He had been sent to rescue some Union families in Matthews County. On his return, he came upon the two children living with an elderly slaveholder named White and five other children "in a most destitute

AS WE FOUND THEM

These children were owned by Thomas White, of Mathews Co., Va., until Feb. 20th, when Capt. Riley, 6th U. S. C. I., took them and gave them to the Society of Friends to educate at the Orphan's Shelter, "Philadelphia.

Profits from sale, for the benefit of the children.

AS THEY ARE NOW

The Mother of these children was beaten, branded and sold at auction because she was kind to Union Soldiers. As she left for Richmond, Va., Feb. 13th, 1864, bound down in a cart, she prayed "O! God send the Yankees to take my children away."

Profits from sale, for the benefit of the children.

Figure 21. *Left*: "Virginia Slave Children Rescued by Colored Troops—As We Found Them," *carte-de-visite*, ca. 1864. Virginia Historical Society, Richmond, Virginia (2001.10.1-2). Figure 22. *Right*: "Virginia Slave Children Rescued by Colored Troops—As They Are Now," *carte-de-visite*, ca. 1864. Virginia Historical Society, Richmond, Virginia (2001.10.1-2).

condition." The slaveholder pled poverty and begged the soldiers not to take his chickens. The mother of the brother and sister, he claimed, was dead. White left the slaveholder with the warning to "take care of the little colored children, they will be free some day." But he soon learned from a "contraband" slave that the mother of the boy and girl had been sold the day before and that White was a cruel master. Riley returned, taking both the children and the chickens after admonishing him and quoting scripture. (No mention was made of the other five children living with White.) Riley found clothes and bedding for the brother and sister and took them to a Quaker woman, Eliza Yates, who sent them to the Friends Shelter for Colored Orphans in Philadelphia, something of an American counterpart to the Ragged Schools of London.[122] At the time the children's picture was made in Philadelphia, the Friends were still searching for their mother.[123]

In the first photograph, "As We Found Them," the children stood in tattered clothes, the boy a bit slouched and leaning on the banister that served as the photographer's prop. The boy's shirt was held round his neck by just a button at his collar. The girl wore a torn jumper that hung loosely. Both children had bare feet. In the second, "As They Are Now," the children were neatly dressed. The boy appeared in a jacket, with a hat (on the banister), and whole, clean trousers. His sister wore a starched polka-dot dress. They both wore shoes. The Union army had rescued these children, but the intervention of the Society of Friends transformed them—with soap and starch and clean linen. This kind of before-and-after photograph of freedchildren seemed to document the total success that Miss Ophelia never enjoyed with Topsy, rendering a metamorphosis, a transition from past to present, slavery to freedom. With the two pictures side by side, the transformation seemed instantaneous, turning the ragged little slave, the savage, into a tidy, obedient child.[124] Here was proof, in flesh and blood, shadow and substance—"As We Found Them" and "As They Are Now"—of the potential of freedpeople to become civilized.

The text beneath the portrait of the brother and sister authenticated their past lives as slaves and endorsed the intervention of the Society of Friends, using the words of the children's mother. The text beneath "As We Found Them" states the name of their owner, "Thomas White of Mathew Co, Va." and explains their rescue at the hands of Captain Riley and with the help of the Society of Friends. Beneath the title "As They Are Now" (the portrait of the children clean and well clad) was printed an endorsement from the children's mother, a woman who had been "beaten, branded, and sold at auction because she was kind to Union soldiers." As she was carried away, "bound down in a cart, she prayed 'O! God send the Yankees to take my children away.'" Not only were the children in need of help, but also their mother (according to this story) pled directly to northerners to take her children under their care. The pair of portraits, therefore, delivered to viewers the past, present, and future of the children rescued by the Society of Friends, a story made "real" through the photographic medium, allowing the eye to see the children's transformation, in elapsed time, from ragged to tidy.

But were the children rescued by Captain Riley and the Society of Friends really "As We Found Them"? Did someone take them straight from the slaveholder's yard to the photographer's studio? Their tattered clothes do look somewhat picturesque, as if they have been torn in even shreds, with the little girl wearing a ripped smock over a skirt and shirt. Did their value as subjects of propaganda really trump their need for proper clothing? Or is it more helpful to recognize that the Society of Friends used a bold argument of radical transformation—the spectacle of the ragged child redeemed—to convince northern viewers that the need for their help was urgent?

Perhaps we should take something, too, from Barnardo's argument about the constructed representation of a certain kind of "truth." Thousands of freedpeople, in 1864, were destitute and in need of clothes, food, and medicine.[125] Freedwomen with children who followed Federal troops in the South were particularly vulnerable to disease and displacement, since most had no official work with the Union army and were often considered a hindrance to operations. Teachers and missionaries in Virginia and South Carolina, in particular, where Union forces were established by 1863, reported on the ragged and destitute conditions of freedpeople there. In cities like Washington, D.C., shantytowns and overcrowded tenements prompted the government and benevolent agencies to look for employment for freedwomen and children elsewhere, in northern cities.[126] The war and the crowded conditions that ensued also created thousands of orphans. According to a letter posted from Wilmington, North Carolina, in 1866, printed in the *American Missionary,* General Sherman's march through the South had sent twelve thousand refugee freedpeople into the city, of whom one-third died by summer's end, leaving behind "crowds of young orphan children" without family, yet the Freedmen's Bureau had no homes for them. Evoking the notion of ragged child directly, the letter writer explained: "Some have found refuge in Freedmen's families, some are staying with parties who cannot feed them—most of them are knocking about, starving and naked— *becoming street children.* You in New York know full well what that means."[127]

Another way of getting freedchildren off the streets, though it was an avenue open only to boys, was through military service. The before-and-after portrait of "Drummer Jackson," a boy enlisted into the Union army at Port Hudson, Louisiana, combined the idea of the ragged child's reform and the potential of male slaves to serve the nation in war (figures 23 and 24). Before-and-after portraits of slave men appeared in *Harper's Weekly* in 1864 to promote the recent enlistment in the Union

Figure 23. *Left*: Unidentified boy ("Drummer Jackson"), ca. 1864. Courtesy The Historic New Orleans Collection, Museum/Research Center.
Figure 24. *Right*: "Drummer Jackson," *carte-de-visite*, ca. 1864. Courtesy The Historic New Orleans Collection, Museum/Research Center.

army and to argue that, indeed, slaves could look and fight like men. One such series featured an anonymous "escaped" slave, before his en-listment (taken of him sitting down, artlessly looking straight ahead) and after (standing in uniform, with backpack and canteen, leaning on his rifle and gazing off into the distance). When the photographic por-trait of Gordon's "Scourged Back" was made into an illustration for *Harper's Weekly* in 1863, his before-and-after portraits (very similar in pose to those of the unknown "escaped slave") appeared on either side of the picture of his heavily scarred back.[128] The portrait of "Drummer Jackson" also played upon the theme of male slave-turned-soldier. In the first image, Jackson was dressed in a shirt so tattered it barely clung to his frame, and he stood before the camera, hands at his side, in bare feet. This was Jackson as a slave (or as he was found) working for the

Confederate army. Time seems to have elapsed for the second photograph, in which Jackson (whose hair had grown longer and his face fuller) appears in uniform as a drummer for the U.S. Colored Troops.[129] Yet Drummer Jackson's portraits also drew upon the idea of the ragged child redeemed. While suggesting that slave boys and men could be disciplined and productive if given proper work, it also made appeals for the rescue of vulnerable slave children in tattered clothes. This argument was furthered by the pride Jackson seemed to show through his good posture, his uniform, and his drum.

The story of the ragged slave child rescued through the intervention of the northern army may have had some utility for individual northerners who viewed themselves as rescuers. For instance, there are two surviving photographs of a child named Paul Leveau, who appears to have been adopted by a man named Charles Rumford, a lieutenant in the Union army from Delaware (figures 25 and 26).[130]

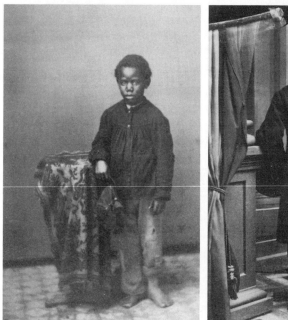

Figure 25. *Left*: Portrait of Paul Leveau, A. J. White, photographer, DeVall's Bluff, Arkansas, 1865. Courtesy of the Historical Society of Delaware.
Figure 26. *Right*: Charles Rumford and Paul Leveau, Garrett, photographer, Wilmington, Delaware, ca. 1870. Courtesy of the Historical Society of Delaware.

There is no evidence that Rumford had Paul Leveau's portrait taken for any public sale or display, and the circumstances of Paul's redemption have not survived. What remain are simply two portraits of him, the first taken in DeVall's Bluff, Arkansas, in November 1865, when Paul was six years old. He stood barefoot, with pants worn through with holes. One pant leg was rolled up above the ankle, making him look especially ragamuffin. He held his cap in his hand. His jacket was in fair shape, if a bit long in the sleeves, looking borrowed. He stood alone before the camera, as had the boy and girl from Virginia. The second portrait was taken in 1870 in Wilmington, Delaware, Rumford's home. Rumford stood with his back to the camera, looking toward a painted horizon in a landscape of sky and distant palm trees. Paul Leveau, age eleven, was kneeling on the floor, looking directly into the camera. Was Rumford looking back to his days of military service in the South and to the redemption of the freedboy he had brought to Delaware? Did the portrait reflect his mastery over the boy he had redeemed? Whatever meaning we might take from these portraits, it is clear that Paul Leveau was part of a story Rumford told after the Civil War, one that was not complete without the image of the boy he had rescued from slavery, fed, and clothed—the child he himself had changed from ragged to tidy.

The teachers at Port Royal in South Carolina produced their own "contrast" portraits of freedboys (figures 27 and 28). In the first of the images, two young boys appear in tattered clothes, the youngest of them nibbling on a piece of what looks like hardtack. Handwritten beneath their portrait is the word "Slaves."[131] But on closer inspection, it appears that this photograph of ragged "slaves" was part of a series of photographs of freedchildren, one of which (by way of contrast to "Slaves") was labeled "School Boys—Freed." The freedboys pictured stood at almost regimental attention before the camera, dressed in suits. The portrait of "Slaves" was taken in the same studio as "School Boys" and the portrait of Elsie and Puss. The backdrop behind the "slaves" is the same canvas that hung behind the freedchildren and their teachers, though the "slaves" stood in front of a different section of it. Instead of the neat furrows of farmland in Elsie's picture, behind the "slaves" hung a muted, watery landscape dotted with palmettos. The rough plank floor on which the "slaves" stood was, in the other images, covered over by a carpet. Whereas these two "slave" boys appeared in ragged overalls and with bare feet, the freedboys were posed standing

Slaves   School boys — freed

Figure 27. *Left*: "Slaves," South Carolina, ca. 1866. From the Penn School Collection. Permission granted by Penn Center, Inc., St. Helena, S.C. Photo 832a. Figure 28. *Right*: "School Boys—Freed," South Carolina, ca. 1866. From the Penn School Collection. Permission granted by Penn Center, Inc., St. Helena, S.C. Photo 832b.

erect, in suits of clothes and shoes—clothes that suggested not physical labor but book learning. The freedboys standing close together, some with hats in hand, and all of them wearing suits, suggested the orderly, gentlemanly behavior in which the boys were being trained. (On the backdrop, to the right, there may be a regiment of soldiers, but it is unclear.) Within one space, then, with clothing and studio props, the photographer had created dutiful schoolchildren from "slaves."

The two images, "Slaves" and "School Boys," demonstrated for propaganda purposes the results of the Penn School's educational mission among freedpeople. And it is in this context that most reformers' narratives of slave children transformed, appeared—that is, in the context of schooling. As teachers, they placed particular emphasis on the relationship between education, civilization, and racial progress among the former slave population. In the writings and photographs of benevolent societies in the South after the Civil War, the themes of education and discipline are inextricable. As in the North, in addition to reading and figuring, schools taught morality, hard work, and self-control, the fundamentals of Victorian-era Protestantism.[132] When in 1864 Major General Nathaniel Banks created a system of Sunday schools within the Department of the Gulf, he did so "for the purpose of giving greater care, industry, and intelligence to the laboring classes of freedmen, and inspiring them with a higher sense of their obligations to society, to their race, *and to all rightful authority.*"[133] As E. M. Wheelock, one of the leaders of the AMA in Louisiana, remarked, "Our military expeditions do the pioneer work of blasting the rock and felling the forest. Education follows to sow the grain and raise the golden harvest." It was also a means to instill the self-control and self-possession desired of workers in a free-labor economy. Wheelock put the matter bluntly: as the "small pacific army of teachers and civilizers" advances upon the South "the school-house takes the place of the whipping post and scourge."[134]

The role of schools as civilizing institutions was common enough in the nineteenth century, although many northern teachers feared at times that they had met their match with the freedchildren in their charge. In the end, however, they would always see progress.[135] A missionary teacher named Josiah Beardsley, working in Baton Rouge, for instance, reported that when he began his labors among the freedchildren there, "most of them were ignorant of any restraint and the order and discipline of the school-room were entirely new. In fact, we could obtain nothing like order except by means of a severe and rigid discipline. The dress, habits, and appearance of the scholars were far from neat and attractive. Not a day passed without two or three fights among the pupils when at their plays, and these were often severe and bloody." Yet the swift intervention of white northern teachers like himself, Beardsley argued, had nearly erased the brutal effects of slavery. "We are now fully convinced that colored children can learn," Beardsley proclaimed. "In some ten years experience in the schools of my native state, I have never seen greater advancement in the same time."[136]

Indeed, the most difficult tasks, in the view of missionaries, were not intellectual but rather disciplinary and moral. "It must be admitted," Beardsley added, "[the children] are prone to deceive and pilfer, but perhaps no more so than any people would be after such a manner of life.

To deceive and to pilfer have been a part of their education. By means of the one they have often escaped the lash of a cruel master, and by the other they have sometimes been able to satisfy the pang of hunger."[137] Another missionary teaching in New Orleans remarked of the freedchildren in his charge that "most of them are quite as smart as white children, but perhaps [one] cannot judge on so short a trial." There were some "exceptions," however, and "a few seem nearly as degraded as the brute creation . . . .Stealing prevails to an alarming extent. I feel that nothing but the interposition of Omnipotence can check it. It is beyond all human control." By the end of the month, however, the children had advanced so well in their studies that the same teacher was "puzzled, not knowing how much of their apparent progress to attribute to my having become accustomed to their oddities. I can see decided improvement not only in prompt obedience and order, but also intellectually and morally."[138]

Proof of success, however, was closely tied to the improved physical appearance of students. Nineteenth-century accounts of charitable cases depended upon descriptions of the body and its poor appearance to lend authenticity both to the objects of their charity and to the stories they told about them.[139] In the case of street children and freedchildren, description of their ragged appearance and its subsequent improvement lent authenticity to benevolent societies' civilizing mission. In an article reprinted in the *American Missionary* the writer recounted a visit to Beaufort, South Carolina, for a Sunday school meeting. " 'One year ago,' said a high military officer to the writer, 'they were all in rags, that is to say those that had rags.' Now they were all neatly dressed, walked in regular procession, sat with perfect decorum."[140] A visitor to a freedmen's school in Vicksburg writing to *Harper's Weekly* in 1866, was impressed, as well, by the tidy appearance of the pupils. "One of the most noticeable features of these schools for freedmen is the cleanliness and good clothing of a majority of the scholars. Of course, there are ragged and rough specimens, but these are not the rule." The neat appearance of the pupils ("from the grandma down to the infant") convinced him of the eminent success of emancipation. "It is one of the many evidences I have found in Mississippi of the general well-being of the negroes, and their capacity to take care of themselves."[141]

This change in appearance probably had more to do with freedpeople's newfound autonomy and their desire to wear (and to dress their children in) what they wanted, clothes paid for with the wages they had earned.[142] But reformers nonetheless read the change in appearance of their pupils as a sign of both moral progress and their own success as educators. Northern observers also chose to see improved dress and overall appearance as evidence of former slaves' potential as human beings, and proof of their lack of inferiority based on race. An AMA teacher in Florida summed up the sentiments of many: "I could not help thinking it is not the color of their skin that makes any one degraded, but their habits. If people are crushed down all their lives by the heel of oppression, can we expect them to rise all of a sudden & be a bright intelligent class of community, without even the dust of their past conditions clinging to them? A great many of them do shake it off & get up brighter than would be expected. The jewels are here, & we have an interesting work to polish them up for this world, & I hope, for the world to come."[143]

The teacher's choice of metaphors is telling—the "dust of their past conditions" and the earnest work required in order to "polish them up" —because they are metaphors of domesticity and cleanliness, metaphors that will become ever more prominent over the second half of the nineteenth century in the writings of reformers and advertisers alike. By the late nineteenth century, following slave emancipation in the U.S. South and the spread of European and U.S. imperialism, civilization's progress became a consumer spectacle, told through images of domestic cleanliness—most prominently with soap advertisements. In representations of domestic rituals, according to Anne McClintock, "animals, women, and colonized people," and, I would add, in particular, children, were transformed in spectacles of Victorians' devising. By the late nineteenth century, the mass marketing of late Victorian imperialism, according to McClintock, would "distribute evolutionary racism on a hitherto unimagined scale."[144]

Such "evolutionary racism"—where black skin, scrubbed white in advertisements, was a symbol of the imperial mission—was not prevalent in post–Civil War accounts. Most appeals for benevolence toward the freed population were appeals for the "progress" of the black race. Indeed, most teachers failed to find any connection between skin color and intellectual ability. Teachers making observations about skin color and intellect usually admitted that they could find nothing to suggest that black children were less intelligent than white children or nonwhite children of lighter skin. The American Missionary Association, on a standard report form, asked its teachers whether they could detect any difference between "mulatto" children and black children in terms of ability. Many respondents who wrote of their earliest experiences with freedchildren in the classroom found that skin color was not an indicator of a child's intellectual ability. A teacher in Norfolk, Virginia, wrote that among the children in his charge "very few are pure blacks, but color is no criterion of excellence. The boy of the ebony face learns just as well as his classmate with a complexion nearly as light as the little ones I used to see in [northern] Industrial Schools."[145] In the reports from teachers working for the AMA in Louisiana, in answer to the question of whether mulattoes excelled, many respondents wrote simply, "No." For most who worked with freedchildren and those who promoted benevolent work in the South, the shades of skin color soon became largely irrelevant.[146] Progress was measured not biologically, on a scale from African to Anglo-Saxon, but in the effectiveness of the education brought to the freed population, as it had been brought to Africa and the streets of London and would be taken, as well, to the Native Americans in the West.

Rather than a progression toward Anglo-Saxonism read on the skin, reformers saw the education of freedchildren as the march of the black race as a whole toward civilization. Consider, for instance, the observations of a representative of the American Missionary Association in Louisiana. The Reverend E. H. Alden claimed to have witnessed the evolution of freedchildren from savage to civilized. It was not a natural process, however, but rather a transformation driven by the arrival of northern benevolence. After visiting a school for freedchildren in New Orleans, Alden described the freedchildren as moving through the stages of mankind. "I feel more and more interested in these poor colored people and am daily forgetting that they are black," he wrote. Looking over his classroom, he saw "children in all stages of progress from those taken from the cotton press where the officers of the Red River expedition left them in all their savage wildness and ignorance which a barbaric master has produced, to those who have learned to read and write and understand the rudiments of Geography and Arithmetic, and Grammar and are daily manifesting deep wells of affection and love, good taste and judgment and a keen intellect."[147]

Alden's letter bears the stamp of nineteenth-century recapitulation theory, that is, that the child in its development reenacts the evolution of the species. The evolutionary transformation of the children from "savage wildness" to "good taste and judgment" seems to have been, in Alden's view, also an evolution away from blackness (or at least toward his "forgetting" about their blackness) and toward civilization. Yet it was education, in Alden's telling, that rescued freedchildren from "savage wildness" and even from blackness. Through the study of geography, arithmetic, and grammar, Alden claimed, they were transformed into humans (rather than black people or savages) with taste and judgment.[148] Another missionary in Louisiana saw a similar progression away from savagery in freedchildren's rapid advancement from simple letters to arithmetic. "The country schools are prosperous and thronged," he reported, "and although they have been in being but a few months, they are rapidly demonstrating the capacity of the African to receive our civilization. Children who eight weeks ago were beginning the alphabet, are now reading in First Readers, and solving with facility problems in the primary rules of arithmetic."[149]

Because of their capacity for rapid progress, many reformers pinned hopes upon freedchildren most of all. Edward Philbrick wrote from South Carolina in 1862 that he did not have much faith in changing adult freedpeople into free laborers, and only through the help of the schools would there be a new black working class. "I do not believe much can be made out of this generation by free labor, nor out of the next without teaching them to read, and am sorry so little has been done in the teaching department."[150] A schoolteacher in Florida, too, looked to the next generation. Most of the freedpeople near her school in Jacksonville were "so filthy in their habits, have always been driven almost to death with work and all the time they had from work, which was very little, they took for rest; and can we expect them to go suddenly from that manner of life and become neat thrifty housekeepers? It will take time; perhaps till the next generation. I think they do as well —perhaps better—than any other class of people under the same circumstances."[151]

There was also another kind of before-and-after narrative, told visually, with which we are already somewhat familiar. In the portrait of Elsie and Puss with Harriet Murray, viewers could watch civilization arrive as the children and their teacher focused on the book at the center of the image. The presence of the book in Murray's lap suggested, in a more subtle way than "As We Found Them" and "As They Are Now," the transformation of freedchildren from ragged to civilized. Along with Miss Harriet Murray, other teachers at the Penn School posed for portraits with their students. Laura Towne, who directed the Penn School, appeared in a portrait with her students Amoretta, Dick, and Maria (figure 29). Towne sent a letter to a friend in March 1866, beginning with: "I send the enclosed picture of me with three of my pets."[152] The girls in the photograph, Maria Wyne and Amoretta, Towne described as "bright"; Amoretta was "as sharp as a needle," and Maria was good at math, although she was "very dull and slow" in reading. Amoretta, wearing a white head kerchief, was a candidate for baptism, what the Gullah people on the South Carolina coast called a "seeker."[153] Towne described Dick, however, as her "right hand man, who is full of importance, but has traveled and feels as if he had seen the world. He is incorrigibly slow and stupid about learning, but reads bunglingly in the Testament, does multiplication sums on the slate, and can write a letter after a fashion."[154] Dick, in Towne's representation, was more a trusted

Figure 29. *Left*: Portrait of Laura M. Towne with students Dick, Maria, and Amoretta, South Carolina, ca. 1866. From the Penn School Collection. Permission granted by Penn Center, Inc., St. Helena, S.C. Photo 819.
Figure 30. *Right*: Portrait of freedchildren with teacher, ca. 1864. Friends Historical Library of Swarthmore College.

servant struggling to learn his letters than a young scholar. Whereas the girls were considered clever and promising, in her characterization of Dick, Towne seemed to have already placed him in her service.

Despite Towne's doubts about Dick as a student, it was the book that held the group together. Towne seems almost aggressive in her insistence that the children pay attention to the book in her hand. Her pose is suggestive not just of learning but of submission, of discipline. Another group portrait, produced by the Society of Friends, makes Towne's point even more emphatically (figure 30). Instead of a pair of "contrast" portraits or a single group portrait, this image was constructed as a tableau, a scene that all at once, from beginning to end, told the story of the redeemed slave child. A schoolteacher with great, long skirts sat holding a book open in her lap, directly in front of a kneeling black child in bare feet and a plain dress. The ragged child was facing civilization in the form of a book and a white woman. On either side of the woman stand two girls in polka-dot print dresses. These girls have already learned to read the book, have already been welcomed into civilization. While the smaller of the two holds the teacher's hand, the taller girl points to the book with one hand while propping a basket on her head with the other. Learning to read and cipher, her pointed finger seems to argue, will make you like me: a clean, competent worker. In this story of civilization, as with the others, written and visual, clean, proper clothes and good posture were evidence of an inner transformation. This image, though, is both the most explicit and the most succinct about northern reformers' visions for the future of freedpeople in the South. With the civilizing mission, the bourgeois ideals of industrial society could be imposed upon the young bodies of black children, thus demonstrating for northern audiences their pliability and promise as free laborers rather than slaves.

There were other, rather disturbing manifestations of this desire to transform young slaves into free laborers. There is evidence that white northerners in the North applied to the Freedmen's Bureau in Louisiana and to missionaries in South Carolina to have black children sent to them. It was not unusual in the nineteenth century for working-class children and poor orphans to be "apprenticed" to employers in exchange for food and shelter. Although ripe for abuse, such apprenticeship was designed to keep children off the streets.[155] The system, administered by local courts, had a sinister underside (as we will see in the next chapter) for people of color, free and freed, in the antebellum and postbellum South. But in many cases where northerners sought black child labor after the Civil War, the arrangements were not proposed as formal apprenticeships but, rather, as a means of employment for freed-children from the South (only *some* of them orphans or children already separated from their families). Indeed, the evidence from northern missionaries and reformers, of black children being placed with white families in the North, suggests that southerners were not the only ones who knew cheap labor when they saw it. It is unclear how many freedchildren might have gone to the North through such arrangements. Most, of course, did not. Yet given what we know of reformers' campaigns to market the civilizing of the freed black child, their efforts to secure individual children for northern employers seem a logical, if extreme, edge of their philosophy.

In addition to her duties as schoolteacher in South Carolina, for instance, Laura Towne also took on the task of finding black children to send to her friends in the North. To one friend she wrote: "I wish you could have the comfort the Heacocks have in the little darkies they sent North. The two young girls are strong and able to do pretty much all the work of the house." She explained that the girls worked without wages "but are to have the privilege of schooling" (a privilege they had in South Carolina, too). Even more revealing, Towne declared that "the experiment" (referring to the Heacocks' young workers) "has been a perfect success, and every few weeks some one sends to them for another girl or boy, and all have given satisfaction so far."[156] A boy named Pompey Jenkins, about nine years old, whom Towne referred to as "my little oaf," was swept up in her plans as well. Pompey had suffered mistreatment at the hands of a man who had taken him from the orphan asylum in Charleston to "mind child," and Towne had considered sending him back to the asylum but feared he would suffer a similar fate again. In a letter to a friend, she wrote, "Doesn't Mr. Thompson want such a little boy? Tell him this boy is about ten, is black as coal, hearty and strong." Towne recounted that Mrs. Thompson had spoken to her "about bringing a child North" and hoped that she would consider Pompey. "I will bring him North when I come, without expense to her."[157] In another letter sent north, Towne again seemed to be filling orders for children. But the aunt of the child in question was unwilling to send him to the North to work. "About your boy, I can't get my choice—Evans," Towne wrote to a friend. "His aunt won't let him come for even ten dollars a year. I am in some doubt about Solomon being useful. I fear he has been a pet; but there is no hurry, and I am looking round, and, as Solomon is in school every day, I am judging of his capacity by little trials."[158]

Towne was not the only white northerner endeavoring to place freedchildren in northern households as workers. Like Towne, an AMA teacher in Georgia named Rebecca Craighead, enthusiastically sought to accommodate her friends in Ohio who "want[ed] girls." Craighead had been appointed the matron of the AMA orphanage in Atlanta and did her best to keep freedpeople from interfering with her placement of freedchildren in white homes, in essence, making orphans of them despite protests from their kin. "My idea is that *they* have no further claim upon them, and that we have a right to find homes for such, just as much as though they had no relatives."[159] Craighead placed out as many children as she could—by one count, as many as eighty-five children at one time—and was eventually censured by her superiors at the AMA.[160]

Some in the North, however, appealed directly to the Freedmen's Bureau for freedchildren. A Mr. John F. Maxfield of New York wrote to Louisiana's superintendent of freedmen, Reverend T. W. Conway, requesting that a "col'd girl" be sent to him, for whom he would furnish the transportation costs. At the bottom of his letter (signed "Your Bro in Christ") he included a postscript, a description not unlike that of a slaveholder in search of a new servant: "I want a col'd girl say 10 years old if possible one that is smart-looking and large enough to wash dishes." Maxfield was not only specifying a particular kind of worker; he also went further to request that her appearance be to his liking.[161] Another man from New York, apparently a personal friend of Conway's, also made application on Maxfield's behalf, stating that Maxfield "is desirous of obtaining a colored girl to take into his family as we have Mary," suggesting that he, too, had been able to secure custody of a freedgirl. He even suggested a girl named Cecilia, whom he apparently encountered on a visit to Conway's house in Louisiana.[162] He assured Conway that the child "would have a good home in Mr. Maxfield's family," though he failed to mention the duties of dishwasher. Such proposals illuminate the extent to which black children after emancipation were still vulnerable to being valued and even marketed according to their capacity to labor. Northerners' descriptions of freedchildren, in words terribly close to the language of the slave market—Pompey as "black as coal, hearty and strong," or a girl "smart-looking and large enough to wash dishes"—reinforced the idea that their bodies were being acquired as well as their labor.

According to *Harper's Weekly,* there was a demand for the labor of freedchildren, or at least an enthusiasm for placing out black "orphans." The magazine ran a story titled "Southern Emigrants" in 1867, featuring the Freedmen's Bureau's "Employment Agency" (a unit established under General Otis Howard in Washington, D.C., intended to lessen the crowded conditions among freedpeople who had migrated into the city from the South).[163] The government agency collaborated with private agencies and societies so that "the negroes are induced to come North as house-servants and field laborers." In the same article, the writer announced that the colored orphan asylum at Charleston was full of children and that "Miss Chloe Merrick of Syracuse, New York," had opened a similar asylum in the former home of the rebel General Finnigan, at Fernandina, Florida. "Each of these ladies furnish Northern people with these young colored children as servants upon application, and our citizens in want of such, or anxious to find worthy objects of sympathy and charity, are advised to apply direct to these ladies."[164] The writer thus left open the possibility that while some might seek a cheap source of labor among orphaned freedchildren, others might reach out to former slave children out of "sympathy and charity."

Orphaned freedchildren or children who had been left in orphan asylums until their families could care for them were the primary objects of northern reformers' attentions in campaigns for sending freedchildren to the North. Laura Haviland, working for the Freedmen's Aid Commission, passed through Missouri in 1865, gathering orphaned and destitute children, along with a few mothers and grandmothers, all to be taken to an orphanage in Michigan. According to Haviland, while waiting with her group at a train depot, "various remarks were made as to what I was going to do with all this company." She overheard one man speculate that she had "a big plantation to stock with a picked set of young niggers, she's going to train to her own liking." When asked of her purpose, she replied with a story of discovery and rescue, explaining that she was taking orphan children "who have been picked up on the streets, and out of freedmen's homes," to an orphanage in Michigan. "They will be sent to school until good homes can be secured for them, where they will be taught habits of industry, as well as to improve their intellects. We of the North think they can learn, if an opportunity is provided."[165] Another bystander, "who had a large number of slaves," told her they would be better off with her, going north, since it "would be a right smart of a while before it'll be settled here to have schools for 'em."[166]

If some northern reformers thought they were helping freedchildren by sending them north, the outcome of these experiments was often uncertain. Catherine Lawrence, for instance, who had "discovered" and adopted Fanny Lawrence, placed Fanny's two sisters in northern households with the understanding that the girls would be well cared for and educated. When Lawrence returned later to see the girls, however, she found to her dismay that both had been put to work as domestic servants for the families who had agreed to adopt them and had not received the promised schooling.[167] Towne, in her letters at least, did not pretend to send children north for any other purpose, mainly, than to fill the labor needs of her friends. If the freedchild represented, for northerners, the future of the South—the ragged child redeemed—she also represented the working-class future of black people. As we will see in the next chapter, children who were sent to the North with the aid of reformers were sometimes sent without the permission of parents or guardians, who then filed fervent complaints with the government to have their children returned.

It was not long, however, before benevolent societies would turn their attentions away from the freedchildren in the South. As early as 1867, societies that needed private funding to continue their work were already aware of the northern public's waning enthusiasm for charitable contributions to benefit freedpeople. That year, a leader of the Friends Freedmen's Association requested their teachers in the South to enlist the help of the freedmen themselves to raise money, as "the zeal of the Northern people is beginning to flag perceptively."[168] Public support of government aid, too, was declining. In his final report as the Freedmen's Bureau's superintendent for education, in 1870, John W. Alvord, predicted: "Education associations, unaided by Government, will of necessity largely fall off. The states South, as a whole, awake but slowly to the elevation of their lower classes. No one of them is fully prepared with funds, buildings, teachers, and actual organizations to sustain these schools." Without support for their education, Alvord foresaw the *creation* of ragged children in the South. With reports of hundreds of schools closing for lack of funds, they were "sending thousands of children, who beg for continued instruction, to the streets, or what is far worse, to squalid degraded homes, to grow up not as props and pillars of society, but its pests."[169]

A letter from Quaker reformer Lucretia Mott begins to explain the shift in attention away from the plight of the South's freedpeople, even among those engaged in benevolent and missionary activities. Expressing frustration with fund-raising efforts, she wrote in 1869: "The claims of the Indians—so long injured & cheated & wronged in so many ways, seem now, with many of our Friends, to take the place of the Freedmen, so that we can hardly collect money eno' to pay our 8 or 10 teachers [in the] South." Mott would later report, too, that donations for freedpeople in the South were slow in coming because people thought the government would pay the bills if private money did not.[170]

Mott's fears about the shifting attentions of her fellow reformers, and those of her government, were not unfounded. In 1877, the political compromise that put a Republican in the White House also withdrew Federal troops from the South, leaving the freed black population to fend for itself against a swell of white supremacy. Meanwhile, in the twenty years following the Civil War (and as a result of the last Indian wars), the destitute Native American population had been confined to reservations in the West. Reformers and missionaries, concerned that reservations only reinforced the old "Indian ways," began to focus renewed energy on civilizing the Native American population and aiding its assimilation into American society, with particular attention and resources devoted to the education of Native American children. Reformers were not the only ones directing resources toward the assimilation of Native Americans. With the Dawes Act in 1887, the federal government had begun to break up the reservation system in favor of private property in the form of individual landholdings, in an effort to teach the Indians the fundamentals of capitalism. And by 1891, attendance at government-sponsored reservation schools was mandatory.[171]

In their propaganda campaign for the assimilation of the American Indian, however, reformers seem to have drawn upon earlier campaigns for inspiration, particularly regarding representations of the Native American child. The children attending the Indian Industrial Training School in Carlisle, Pennsylvania, established in 1879 by Richard Henry Pratt, were the subjects of some of the most familiar images of Native Americans in the nineteenth century.[172] The Carlisle photographs appeared in sets of two, such as the portraits of Chiricahua Apaches taken upon their arrival at Carlisle from Fort Marion, Florida, in 1886 (figures 31 and 32). (After the surrender of the Chiricahua Apaches fighting with Geronimo that year, the rest of the Chiricahua tribe had been sent

Figure 31. *Top,* "Chiricahua Apaches as They Arrived," 1886, J. N.
Choate, photographer. Denver Public Library, Western History Collection, no. 32903. Figure 32. *Bottom,* "Chiricahua Apaches as four
months later," 1886, J. N. Choate, photographer. Denver Public Library,
Western History Collection, no. 32904.

by train to Florida and housed in a decrepit military fort.) The children in the photographs had been sent to Pennsylvania, where they were to learn "civilized" American ways, at a far remove from the supposedly uncivilized, un-Christian practices of their people. Pratt used the photographs, taken by photographer John Nicholas Choate, as proof of his successes at the Carlisle Institute.[173] The viewer first sees the children on their arrival, dirty and disheveled, some in traditional dress, others in rumpled, secondhand jackets and pants, several of them barefoot. In the second frame, the same children appeared again, a few months later, in a portrait studio, posed standing and seated. The boys had dressed in tailored suits, and the girls wore neat blouses and trim skirts with pleats along the bottom.

There were many other such portraits made, and reproduced, of Native American children in the late nineteenth century, often accompanied by the same convictions about the civilizing of a "savage" race that accompanied the northern reform efforts in the postbellum South. (For Native Americans, one reformer declared, "We need to *awaken in him wants.*" It was necessary "to get the Indian out of the blanket and into trousers—and trousers with a pocket in them, and with a *pocket that aches to be filled with dollars!*") Pratt himself argued that savagery was a product of cultural learning, not a condition natural to Native Americans as a race, and that the habits of industry and discipline could be taught to Indian children, just as to white children.[174] The rhetorical and visual similarities between efforts to reform freedchildren and assimilate Native American children (like those between street children, African children, and freedchildren) are striking. But perhaps most important, they help to explain reformers' visions of freedom for the South as part of a longer and wider story of "savagery" and "civilization" in the nineteenth century, a story that the portrait of Harriet Murray, Elsie, and Puss begins to tell.

4

Labor

Tillie Bell's Song

"I am the mother of a woman Dina who is now dead. My Daughter Dina had a child by the name of Porter." This is how Cyntha Nickols began her appeal, in 1867, to the assistant commissioner of the Freedmen's Bureau in Louisiana, hoping that he might help her retrieve her grandson from the man who had once owned her. "I am a Colored woman former slave of a Mr Sandy Spears of the parish of East Feliciana La.," she explained. Porter, "now about Eleven years of age," had been bound to Spears under an apprenticeship, a labor contract that would leave the boy under Spears's control until he became an adult, without her consent. Apparently unable to convince the local bureau agent to help her, she directed her plea to his superiors, choosing her words carefully. "I do not wish to wrongfully interfere with the arrangement of those who are endeavoring to properly control us black people," Nickols explained with pointed deference to the bureau's authority. "I feel confident that they are doing the best they can for us and our present condition—but I am the Grandmother of Porter—his father Andrew is now and has been for sometime a soldier in the army of the U.S. he is I am told some where in California I do not know only that he is not here to see to the interest of his child I am not by any means satisfied with the present arrangement made for my Grand Child Porter." She had known Mr. Spears "for many years" and would write "nothing of his faults but I have the means of educating my Grand Child of doing good part by him." Porter's uncle "lately discharged from the army of the U.S." would be able to help care for Porter. "We want him we do not think Mr. Spears a suitable person to control this boy."

Nickols placed before the bureau every available qualification for her guardianship of Porter: her blood kinship, her ability to provide for his education, and the military service of his father and uncle. She also argued that Spears was unfit: Spears was "very old and infirm," and "for many years addicted to the use of ardent spirits. This fact I do not like to mention but truth requires me to speak now is there no chance to get my little boy the agent of this place will not listen to me," she explained, "and I am required to call [on] you or I must let my Grand-Child go, which greatly grieves me." Nickols closed with another plea, signing her letter: "Truly yours a poor old black woman."[1]

An apprenticeship contract would have placed a child such as Porter in service to a master usually until the age of eighteen (or fifteen, if the child were a girl) with stipulations that the child learn a trade or skill, be fed and clothed, and receive some schooling.[2] (The latter part of such agreements made it imperative for freedpeople like Nickols, contesting such arrangements, to prove that they could provide for the children's education.) Although apprenticeship had been in practice before the Civil War, often used as a means to secure shelter and support for orphaned children, it was seized upon by former slaveholders like Spears just after the Civil War as a way to hold on to the children of their freed slaves, often regardless of whether the parents were living or dead, and with little consideration for extended family members like Cyntha Nickols. Bureau agents, too, favored apprenticeship as a way to shelter and feed destitute freedchildren whose parents were not present to care for them. Freedpeople could voluntarily apprentice their children, and some did. But more often than not, even in cases of parental or familial consent, the meaning and purpose of contracts like these were subject to considerable, sometimes violent debate between freedpeople, former owners, and bureau agents.

The local agent, James DeGrey, offering his opinion of the case in an endorsement to Nickols's letter, reported that Sandy Spears was indeed "Old.—but not infirm" and "addicted to ardent Spirits, but not more so than the most of men in the Parish." "The boy Porter is ten (10) years of age," DeGrey wrote, putting a finer point on the age Porter's grandmother had given, seeming to undermine her claim to the boy. "He (Spears) raised him from a child. My belief is that the old lady wants the boy because he is now able to do Some work." While DeGrey accused Porter's grandmother of pure economic interest in the boy, he painted Spears—the former slaveholder—as the parental figure in Porter's life. It was Spears, he wrote, who had "raised" Porter, a point Spears must have made to DeGrey when the agent investigated the case. The characterization of Spears as the boy's true guardian and caretaker was not only in the interest of the former slaveholder, but of the bureau as well, since leaving the boy with Spears would keep him in a labor contract for the next eight years. Despite his support of Spears, however, DeGrey also understood, almost despite himself, the strength of freedpeople's suspicions regarding apprenticeship and the active role of extended family in the lives of freedchildren. At the close of his endorsement to the letter he wrote: "The binding out of children Seems to the freedmen like putting them back into Slavery—In every case where I have bound out children thus far Some Grandmother or fortieth cousin has come to have them released."[3]

The most pressing economic problem in the South after emancipation, as many historians have noted, was what kind of labor system would replace chattel slavery. The process of slave emancipation throughout the Americas in the nineteenth century was fueled by arguments, both ideological and material, about who would define the "free" in free labor and how that would translate into profit and loss, wages and shares, or sustenance and want. Planters in the southern United States, in fact, would not be alone in trying to use the children of their slaves, or former slaves, to avoid disruptions to the plantation labor system. In 1834, the British parliament freed all children under six in Britain's Caribbean colonies while keeping their parents in an interim "apprenticeship" system until 1838 (in the British context, apprenticeship was a transitional system between slave labor and wage labor), with the expectation that parents would choose to apprentice their children to work on the same plantation. In many cases, however, parents chose to send their children away from the plantation to live with other relatives, or at least to keep them free from the toil of plantation labor and engaged in household gardening, attending school, or learning a trade.[4] And in 1870 and 1871, authorities in Cuba and Brazil, respectively, made emancipation a gradual process through laws that freed children but not their parents. Few slaves were truly *freed* by such laws, since freeborn children in both places (classed as *libertos* in Cuba and *ingênuos* in Brazil) remained with and continued to labor on plantations alongside their slave parents, as if their status had not changed.[5] As a result of the Civil War, however, slave emancipation in the United States was immediate rather than gradual, leaving slaveholders to develop their own impromptu means of slowing the dissolution of their labor force. Seizing on the most vulnerable members of the former slave population, planters in the U.S. South did the reverse of their counterparts in Jamaica, Cuba, and Brazil: unable to slow the emancipation of adult slaves, they legally bound freedchildren through apprenticeship contracts in an effort to guarantee themselves several more years of labor that was not free.

If struggles over control of freedchildren and their labor after the Civil War became debates over the future of labor in the South, however, they were also disputes about the autonomy of black households and the authority of black adults to control their own offspring. Under slavery, black parents and relatives often had to watch as slaveholders directed, punished, and otherwise controlled the fate of their children. The awful recollection of Caroline Hunter, a former slave interviewed in 1937, is often quoted regarding this aspect of slavery because she so plainly expressed her mother's agony: "During slavery it seemed lak yo' chillun b'long to ev'ybody but you. Many a day my old mamma has stood by an' watched massa beat her chillun 'till dey bled an' she couldn' open her mouth."[6] After emancipation, freedpeople demanded the legal right to raise their own children and, in so doing, also demanded the right to sustain their own households. Deprived of the labor of children, freed black households suffered.[7] As a white Unionist in Maryland named Joseph Hall observed in a letter to the bureau, freedpeople "can and would do very well if they Can have what they ought to have. that is to get there children un bound. or restored to them and have the privilege of hireing them or working them themselves. in order that they can help now to surport there parents in order that they may not be come a burthen upon the government."[8] Former slaveholders, however, were not so ready to relinquish power over the raising of freedchildren precisely because it meant the erosion of the households they once controlled—households that, until the war, had structured the lives and labors of blacks as well as whites.[9]

In addition to facing down her former owner over the right to raise her grandchild, however, Cyntha Nickols also had to appeal to the federal government, in the form of the Freedmen's Bureau, which was charged with promoting the successful transition to free labor in the South. In practice, as James DeGrey's position between Cyntha Nickols and Mr. Spears illustrates, often the bureau's most contentious role was as an intermediary between former slaveholders and freedpeople. The bureau's overarching concern in governing these disputes was to keep agricultural production in the South from faltering by encouraging the signing of labor contracts. But as many a bureau agent discovered, the signing of a labor contract in the postbellum South was not a purely economic transaction.

Negotiations and disputes over contracts—particularly disputes over the apprenticeship of freedchildren—were not just about "the meaning of freedom," a phrase that perhaps does not go far enough to convey what was at stake in the often bitter struggles between freedpeople and former slaveholders after slavery. Rather, they were disputes over power in the postbellum South, as expressed in the reconfiguration of black and white households after slavery, disputes that could take violent form.[10] The labor and apprenticeship of freedchildren, however, in the brief period that marked the end of slavery and the beginnings of a free labor system in the South, sparked particularly explicit debates over power and autonomy because they straddled the most fundamental institutions of southern society: the household and the market. The boundaries of each had to be renegotiated after slavery, as freedpeople tried to void the claims of former slaveholders over their families and their labor, and many former slaveholders tried to retain what control they could over their former slaves. Because of freedchildren's necessary attachment to a household (*someone* had to raise them) combined with their immediate and anticipated value as workers, contests over freedchildren became very explicit debates about the social and economic future of blacks in the South, debates that fused the language of family and contract, of domestic relations and the marketplace.

The organizing principle of the antebellum South—in social, legal, and political terms—was the white patriarchal household, a domestic and economic arrangement that derived its power from the dependency and labor of women and slaves.[11] It is not surprising, then, that former slaveholders' arguments to retain control over freedchildren were often voiced in the seemingly intimate but easily appropriated language of family. The ideology of slaveholder paternalism—based on the notion that southern slaveholders were good to their slaves because their slaves depended upon them, as children upon a father—became part of a testimonial to their concern for the freedchild's best interest. Indeed, very often the justification offered by former slaveholders for retaining freedchildren was that they had "raised" the children from infancy. Just as before the war, however, this was an ideology that failed to conceal their economic interest in the people they once owned. Mr. Spears "raised" the child Porter, but he *contracted* for his labor until he was grown. In fact, Spears seems to have bound Porter to him in 1867, when he was ten or eleven, not in 1865, at the close of the war. He opted to legally support the child, through contract, only after he reached a more productive working age.

DeGrey's criticism of Cyntha Nickols for wanting Porter's labor, however, also had truth in it. Children's economic value as workers was an understood part of their role as members of freed households. As contributors to the family economy, children often made it possible for freed families to separate themselves from the claims of former owners and sustain independent households. After emancipation, most freed-people remained in rural areas of the South, working parcels of planta-tion land for a share of the crop or for wages and rations. But they also grew their own food for sustenance and marketing. The labor of freed-children, both for the plantation owner and for their families, was criti-cal to the survival of most freedpeople's households. In addition to bringing in earnings as field hands or house servants (labor contracts frequently carried the names of children), they fed the family's livestock, sold produce at the market, tended younger children, hunted game, sewed clothes, and cleaned house.[12]

It is not clear where Porter lived before Nickols approached the bu-reau, but DeGrey's assessment that "the old lady wants the boy because he is now able to do Some work" suggests that Porter may have been living with Spears. If so, then Porter's predicament also may document a strategy used by many freedpeople, particularly freedwomen: they left their children in the household of former owners (where they would re-ceive food and shelter in exchange for small household duties) until the women could support themselves and their children. In Porter's case, Nickols might have been able to support her grandson only once he was able to contribute economically to the household. At the very least, Nickols did not want Porter to be bound over to Spears until he was grown—an arrangement that would deprive her of her grandson and his labor for years. She would not be able to take him from Spears's place, nor would she be able to hire him out, as the white Unionist from Maryland astutely pointed out. Despite this sort of dependence on freedchildren's labor, however, the economic value of a child like Porter does not seem to have canceled their emotional value, and may have even strengthened bonds between family members.[13] Indeed, the words of Cyntha Nickols suggest that her relationship with Porter was far from detached. "I am the Grandmother of Porter," she wrote. And "I am required to call [on] you or I must let my Grand-Child go, which greatly grieves me."

Porter's case, and those of other freedchildren at the center of such disputes, was further complicated by ideas about the welfare of poor children that governed the thinking of many bureau agents, ideas that combined poor children's domestic arrangements with the expectation that they would be put to work. This link between labor and shelter with individual families, for poor orphans, was increasingly common in the plans of northern reformers, as an alternative to orphanages.[14] Recall, for instance, reformer Laura Haviland's explanation of why she was taking orphaned freedchildren North: "They will be sent to school until good homes can be secured for them, where they will be taught habits of industry, as well as to improve their intellects."[15] The idea behind such arrangements was not just to find shelter for poor children but also to place them in an environment that would teach them hard work and mental discipline. This attitude toward the welfare of poor children could work against freed families (and in favor of former slaveholders) as often as it aided freedpeople in the retrieval of their children. DeGrey, for instance, was clearly making the assumption that Porter would be better off working under Spears as an apprentice than for Nickols, his grandmother.

Thousands of freedchildren like Porter became caught in this tangle of emotional, economic, and bureaucratic demands. Efforts to free them started a fierce pull and tug—backward to the dependencies and false kinship of the slaveholder (although some masters had fathered their slaves) or forward toward a wage system and the rights of black families. Complaints and hearings before agents of the Freedmen's Bureau about the custody of freedchildren seem to appear in nearly every monthly report from local agents to their superiors between 1865 and 1867, in addition to longer correspondences related to the custody of freedchildren. (This fails to include, of course, the incidents that never appeared before the bureau at all.) Just as the freedchild was the subject of northern reformers' visions for a "civilized" and productive postbellum South, freedchildren also appeared at the center of daily debates over the future of southern society. In the simplest terms, battles over the custody of freedchildren were negotiations (often uneven ones) between bureau agents, freedpeople, and former slaveholders. But the question of *who* would raise freedom's child was fundamentally a question about who would determine the economic future of black people after slavery.[16]

The greatest point of conflict regarding freedchildren's labor after the Civil War was the apprenticeship system, a form of labor contract written into state laws since the colonial period, which was reinforced by planter-controlled legislatures across the South in 1865 as part of the infamous Black Codes. Until the mid-nineteenth century, apprenticeship as it was practiced in the United States in areas outside the rural South was a system of labor by which a male apprentice lived in a master's household and trained in a trade or skill until he came of age and established himself in business. (Recall that many of the boys at the Catholic Institution in New Orleans in the 1850s had plans to apprentice themselves and learn a trade.) Apprenticeships also served as a means of supervising and training potentially wayward working-class boys by teaching them to earn a livelihood and keeping them off the streets. But with the rise of factories in the 1830s, apprenticeship arrangements increasingly resembled those of wage labor. Although the apprentice still trained with a master, he earned a wage and no longer lived in the master's household. Eventually, particularly in urban areas of the North, apprenticeship was replaced entirely by wage labor among boys from twelve to fourteen.[17]

In the South, too, apprenticeship had been an early form of social welfare particularly for orphaned or "half-orphaned" children and had served to train boys in a skill or trade. But in the slaveholding South, apprenticeship also became a means of social and racial control. Southern judges apprenticed the illegitimate children of poor white women and free women of color, typically on the grounds that such arrangements would keep them from becoming public charges. As in the northern states, mothers of illegitimate children in the South had common-law right to custody of the child. But apprenticeship laws in the antebellum South increasingly served as punishment for unmarried poor or working women who lived outside the white patriarchal frame of southern society, or behaved in ways that challenged it, and made it especially difficult for these women to establish independent households. Mulatto children born to unwed white women and the children of unmarried free women of color were particularly vulnerable to forced apprenticeship.[18] As one judge in North Carolina decreed, the county court had the "power to bind out *all* free base-born children of color, without reference to the occupation or condition of the mother."[19] Such a system served to police the sexuality of poor women, white and free black, and aimed to punish those who transgressed racial boundaries.

It was into this history of apprenticeship in the South that former slaveholders tapped at the close of the Civil War. Southern courts and legislatures continued to use apprenticeship as a form of racial control and forced labor, but in the service of postbellum realities, using it to extend unfree labor and black people's dependence upon the planter class after emancipation. In Maryland, which already had a state law on the books regarding the apprenticeship of "free negroes" before the Civil War, former slaveholders were quick to bind the children of their freed slaves to them in the state orphan's courts.[20] The prewar Maryland code allowed the orphan's court to "summon before them the child of any free negro, and if it shall appear upon examination before such court that it would be better for the habits and comfort of such child that it should be bound as an apprentice to some white person to learn to labor," then the court could bind the child "as an apprentice to some white person, if a male till he is the age of twenty-one years, or if a female, till she is of the age of eighteen years."[21]

The race to apprentice freedchildren was described by the provost marshal in one Maryland district, Captain Andrew Stafford. After the governor announced the adoption of the new state constitution barring slavery, Stafford wrote, "a rush was made on the Orphan's Court of this County, for the purpose of having all children under twenty one years of age, bound to their former owners, under the apprentice law of the State." These former owners clearly relied on antebellum arguments in favor of apprenticeship to press these contracts through the court. Stafford explained, "In many instances, boys of 12 and 14 years are taken from their parents, under the pretence that they (the parents) are incapable of supporting them, while the younger children are left to be maintained by the parents. This is done without obtaining the parents consent, and in direct violation of the provisions of the Act of Assembly, and almost in every instance by disloyal parties." In the month following the Maryland legislature's passage of an act for slave emancipation, these courts had apprenticed some 2,500 children and young adults to former slaveholders.[22]

Other former slaveholders, like the man who owned Millie Randall in Louisiana, took less successful extralegal measures in efforts to maintain custody over freedchildren. Randall, only six when the war ended, remembered what happened when her former owner realized he had lost control of his adult slaves.

> Atter freedom ol' marster wouln't low my maw to hab us chillen. He tuk me an' my brudder Benny in a wagon an' drove us 'roun an' 'roun so dey couln' fin' us. My maw hatter git de Jestice of de Peace to go mek him t'un us a-loose. De man brung me an' my brudder to Big Cane [Louisiana] to us maw. Was we glad to see her cause we figger we ain' gwineter see her no mo'.[23]

Jane Kamper in Maryland testified to a similar experience with her children in her statement to military authorities in 1864. She recounted how her former master, William Townsend, refused to relinquish her children and her bedclothes. "He told me that I was free," she said, "but that my Children Should be bound to [him]. He locked my Children up so that I could not find them. I afterwards got my children by stealth and brought them to Baltimore." Townsend had pursued Kamper, but she managed to hide her children and make her escape by boat.[24]

Both women, in the war's aftermath, had authorities to whom they could appeal to enforce the return of their children, or at least to report wrongdoing on the part of a former owner. (Jane Kamper, after all, got her children "by stealth.") So to help desperadoes like Townsend and Millie Randall's former owner, southern legislatures issued new apprenticeship clauses aimed at the freed population at the close of the war, through the Black Codes. Under presidential Reconstruction in 1865, before Congress derailed President Andrew Johnson's lenient policies toward the South, southern legislatures passed codes that set forth the legal rights and limitations of the freed population. The codes varied from state to state but generally made provision for former slaves to marry, to enter into contracts, to sue and be sued in courts, and to testify in cases that did not involve whites. For former slaveholders, however, the codes primarily were a legal means to limit the mobility of freedpeople and to compel them to contract with planters. Vagrancy laws in some states required that freedpeople carry proof of employment at all times or face arrest. Florida's law allowed for whipping or forced labor for those who broke labor contracts. South Carolina applied its vagrancy statutes to "persons who led idle or disorderly lives."[25]

The apprenticeship system, however, was perhaps the most egregious of the codes. Most apprenticeship clauses allowed for the indenture of "orphaned" children or those whose parents did not have the means to provide for them. Apprenticeship had the effect not only of depriving freedpeople of their children and the labor they could contribute to the household but also of limiting the mobility of both freedchildren and their parents and relatives, who wanted to remain near their bound children.[26] Mississippi's Black Codes were some of the South's most notorious, but they conveyed the sentiments of most southern legislatures in 1865. The Mississippi code allowed for the apprenticeship of "all freedmen, free Negroes, and mulattoes under the age of eighteen within their respective counties . . . who are orphans, *or whose parent or parents have not the means,* or who refuse to provide for and support said minors." Also, "the former owner of said minors shall have the preference" to bind orphans when the court determined that he or she was "a Suitable person for that purpose." Under the Mississippi law, males were to be bound until the age of twenty-one and females to eighteen. If an apprentice left a master or mistress without their consent, the master or mistress "may pursue and recapture said apprentice," and if the apprentice refused to return, the justice of the peace could put the child in jail until the case could be investigated. If the apprentice "had good cause to quit his said master or mistress," the child would be released from indenture and the master or mistress fined, with the money going to the apprentice. But if the court judged that the apprentice left "without good cause," then the court could order the apprentice "punished, as provided for the punishment of hired freedmen, as may be from time to time provided for by law, for desertion," until the apprentice agreed to fulfill the apprenticeship contract. It was also a crime for any one to "entice away any apprentice from his master or mistress," a clause clearly designed to hinder parents or relatives from retrieving their children.[27]

In 1867, Congress demanded that all southern states rewrite their constitutions, ratifying the Fourteenth Amendment on civil rights and establishing voting rights for all male citizens. In the process, the Black Codes met their demise, although apprenticeship remained a legal avenue of child welfare, so long as it made no distinction between black and white children.[28] In 1865, however, neither freedpeople nor former slaveholders knew that apprenticeship would fail as a system of compulsory free labor. (As one bureau agent very crudely observed about southern planters after the war, "They *hate* to give up the *little niggers* in hopes that something will turn up. If Mac [George McClellan] had been elected [instead of Abraham Lincoln] they expected the little nigs would be good property and now they hope for something else to happen.")[29] Freedpeople made it clear, however, as agent James DeGrey found out, that they viewed apprenticeship as it was practiced during and after the war, "like putting them back into slavery." A freedwoman in Maryland whose child was bound as an apprentice against her wishes told the Freedmen's Bureau: "We were delighted when we heard that the Constitution set us all free, but God help us, our condition is bettered but little; free ourselves, but deprived of our children. . . . It was on their account we desired to be free." And an angry freedman from Alabama wrote: "I think very hard of the former oners for Trying to keep My blood when I kno that Slavery is dead."[30]

Black children could be bound to employers as apprentices through the state district courts, but the Freedmen's Bureau also governed and administered apprenticeships. According to bureau regulations, agents could not bind out children if their parents opposed the apprenticeship. Under the bureau, girls, typically, were apprenticed to the age of fifteen and boys to eighteen, with their contracts stipulating they should receive clothing, medical attention, and "a reasonable amount of schooling" in return for their labor.[31] The "trade" or "skill" usually listed on the forms of indenture were those of "housekeeping" (most often for girls) and "planter" or "farmer" (for boys). Some children, girls and boys, were contracted to receive "training" in both. In 1866, for instance, ten-year-old Thomas Boultt Johnson was bound to William Payne until the age of eighteen, "to learn the occupation of farming and also that of House Servant."[32]

Apprenticeship arrangements were, first and foremost, contracts. And as such, they were pieces of paper invested with conflicting economic and social meanings by former slaveholders, former slaves, and bureau agents. In the nineteenth century, labor contracts in general were documents through which groups voiced different visions of slavery and freedom. Abolitionists, northern workers, slaveholders, and freedpeople all defined free labor and slavery in light of one another, and they often did so while debating the positive and negative aspects of the wage contract. Although antislavery advocates framed the labor contract as the very negation of slavery and the demonstration of self-ownership, for instance, freedpeople and other wage workers often viewed contracts more ambivalently. Though apprenticeship agreements took the *form* of contracts—agreements between free laborers and employers—freedpeople recognized the ambiguities within such arrangements, proliferating as they did on the still slippery ground between slavery and freedom.[33] In the eyes of many freedpeople, the conditions of apprenticeship left black children in a relation of servitude to their former owners.

Freedchildren's status as dependents, however, also meant that arrangements for their labor would give way to discussions of proper guardianship and adult responsibility. Conflicts over black children's labor, in fact, often turned into critiques of black women as caregivers. Black women seeking custody of children, particularly single mothers, moved through a tangle of planter paternalism and government-directed notions of child welfare that, entwined together, threatened to pull their children away from them. These ideologies reinforced one another against the image of a "loose" or "unfit" mother. In the interest of child welfare (an idea that increasingly governed legal disputes in northern and southern courts in matters of child custody), the image of the unfit black mother or caregiver could allow planters and bureau agents to discount the claims of black women to their children.[34] For freedwomen, in particular, the South after emancipation defied the antebellum idealism of abolitionists and reformers. Arguing against slavery, abolitionists had contrasted the slave family torn apart by the market in human beings, to the free family, a domestic circle inviolate, protected from the demands of the marketplace.[35] Rather than being sheltered from the demands of the market after slavery, however, black women and their children stood at the very center of the postbellum southern economy. But in freedom, at least, these women could be far more active participants in the market than they could as slaves, using their newfound mobility, the wages they earned, the power to contract for their labor and the labor of their children, and even the anxious desires of former slaveholders to retain freedchildren, all to move closer toward independence from the economic and domestic constraints of slavery.[36]

One of the first tasks facing local bureau agents after the Confederate surrender was to situate freedchildren who appeared to them to be orphans, or, as one agent put it, "the disposal of children practically orphans."[37] Another agent asked cautiously whether he might apprentice children who seemed to him to be "without proper protection" in his parish. Several planters had petitioned him either to bind children to them or to remove them from their property. "In worse instances," the agent explained to his superior, "the fathers of such children are dead and the mothers have left them on plantations without making provisions for them." He was concerned that the children's parents were still living and might object but was told abruptly by headquarters to "bind these children out," that the parents could claim the children later if necessary.[38]

The bureau's desire to bind children out often worked to the disadvantage of freedpeople whose families had been separated by slavery or the war. When parents or extended family did come to retrieve children, they found them bound to former slave owners unwilling to relinquish their claims.[39] But even when relatives were present and able to care for children, former slaveholders and others wishing to apprentice children lied to the bureau, often representing the children as orphans. In some cases, the former slaveholders may not have known the whereabouts of the children's parents. In others, they seem to have been purposefully dishonest. An agent in Madisonville, Louisiana, explained to his superiors, for instance, that he had indentured "the two Grandchildren of Simon Bookster to Thos Zachary last September, Zachary misrepresented the case by stating the children, Edward and Eliza, were total orphans, and were living with him, and had no friends or relatives to care or provide for them." But upon investigation, the agent discovered that Zachary had "abducted the children in the absence of the Grandparents." Zachary had also lied about the ages of the children, stating that Edward was eight and Eliza five, when Edward was, in fact, ten and his sister eight. (Lying about the ages of children was a tactic used to prolong the period of indenture. According to a chaplain serving as a local bureau agent in Mississippi, "children are almost invariably bound out from two to 12 years younger than they are.")[40] The agent investigating Edward and Eliza's case also learned that their grandfather had "supported and schooled them since their Freedom and is willing and able to do so."[41] Another freedman, Edward Johnson, went to the bureau to complain that his granddaughter was living with him when an agent of the bureau bound the child to a Miss Mary Lasier. Lasier was informed by the new agent in charge that the child had been illegally bound and that Lasier "must give her up to her Grand father."[42]

Some freed families were jeopardized not by the schemes of former slaveholders but by the bureau's idea of child welfare. With ideas similar to those of reformers like Laura Towne, some agents sought to find places for freedchildren in the North. But unlike Towne, placements through the bureau often occurred without the consent of parents or other relatives. Many such cases, for instance, transpired under the auspices of the Employment Agency established by the bureau in Washington, D.C., in 1865. The agency was created in an effort to disperse the large numbers of destitute freedpeople moving into increasingly overcrowded sections of the city. Its aim was to settle freed families on farms and find placement as domestics for single women with children, all in the interest of making them self-sufficient.[43] The agency initially focused on outlying areas near the city, but with the cooperation of northern freedmen's aid societies also sent freedpeople to cities and towns in the North with transportation paid for by the federal government. But the agency received complaints from freedpeople whose children had been sent to orphan asylums without their consent, or had been sent so far away that when parents or relatives tracked them down, they had to be retrieved by agents of the bureau.[44] In July 1867, the assistant commissioner of the bureau in Washington, D.C., wrote to the local superintendent there that "numerous complaints have been made at this Office to the effect that minor freedchildren have been sent from this city on Government transportation, without the knowledge of their parents," directing the superintendent to "issue such instructions to the Employment Agents under your charge as will prevent a recurrence of this evil."[45]

The bureau had hired a number of women, black and white, as employment agents, or "intelligence agents," working to place freedpeople outside of the city, among them Josephine Griffing and well-known abolitionist Sojourner Truth.[46] While often these women had a more generous notion of relief than did the bureau officials, many also had overly enthusiastic ideas about the placement of freedwomen and children in work situations. Josephine Griffing, for instance, proposed that single women with children might be better off placing their children in an orphan asylum until the mothers were self-sufficient enough to support them. (This was not so far off from the strategies of some freedpeople who found temporary shelter for their children with orphanages or former slaveholders. But as government policy, it would have overstepped the line between benevolence and force.) Griffing's superiors also asked her to explain a number of cases involving freedchildren sent north without the consent of their parents or relatives.[47] In once instance, Mrs. Ann Earle, writing on behalf of a freedwoman named Annie Brooks, did battle with Griffing and a black female agent named Sarah Tilmon. Annie Brooks's six-year-old daughter, Kitty, had been sent north without her mother's consent. Brooks learned that Griffing had taken Kitty to New York and left her with Tilmon, who then sent Kitty to a man named Charles Baker in Fordham, New Jersey. Baker had subsequently moved and disappeared, along with Kitty. The bureau sent an agent to New Jersey to investigate and hopefully retrieve Kitty, but he was unable to track Baker or the girl, declaring in his last recorded correspondence that he would "not relinquish efforts to find the girl as long as any probability of success remains." After a year and a half of trying to get assistance from Griffing and Tilmon, Earle wrote to General Oliver Otis Howard at bureau headquarters, "I feel sure that Mrs. Tillman [*sic*] can find her, if she can be made to do it." She also had some choice words for Josephine Griffing: "I refrain from expressing my feeling in regard to Mrs. Griffing, who it seems to me as clearly kidnapped little Kitty as if she had been a slave trader."[48]

Sadly, it is not clear if Kitty and her mother were ever reunited. What is apparent from these and other stories is that although the official policy of the bureau prohibited the sending away of freedchildren without their parents' consent, the inclination of individual agents was often to secure shelter and employment for freedchildren, without careful concern for the needs and demands of their families, by farming them out (like Kitty) or binding them to planters through apprenticeship contracts.[49] This agenda, however ill suited to the circumstances of freedpeople in the postemancipation South, clearly had its roots in the child welfare movement in the North that preceded the war. By the 1850s, the Children's Aid Society had already begun to send destitute and orphaned city children on the orphan trains to live with western rural families.[50] Sending freedchildren like Kitty to New Jersey or binding them to a planter were solutions (if often poorly judged) to the problem of child welfare at a time when many freedchildren had been separated from their parents by the war or the interstate slave trade.

On occasion, the bureau's desire to bind out children went beyond the necessity of finding shelter for them. Indeed, agents and their superiors sometimes favored making orphans out of freedchildren, or declaring them illegitimate (hence, without a father's legal guardianship) even when parents had appealed for custody. In some cases, agents even refused help to former slaves seeking custody of their children from former slaveholders because the freedpeople had no documentation of their marriage to prove their offspring legitimate. One agent, for example, determined that by law the indenture he had approved was legal and binding even though it was against the parents' wishes, "the parents not being legally married."[51] The characterization of black children as "practically orphans" also reflected agents' frequent refusal to acknowledge other relatives and freedpeople who wanted to take children under their care. When a freedwoman sought custody of her godchild from the child's former owner, for instance, the bureau agent declared that she had no right to the child "being the child's Godmother which establishes no legal claims whatever."[52]

Evidence of grandparents, godmothers, and other relatives appealing to the bureau makes it clear, however, that mothers and fathers did not leave their children behind "without making any provision for them." Grandmothers, grandfathers, godparents, aunts, and uncles all appealed to the Freedmen's Bureau for assistance in obtaining custody of children. Enslaved people throughout the Americas had developed systems of kinship that involved both blood relations and "fictive" or "quasi kin" (relations often referred to as "aunt" or "uncle"). These familial ties were a means of both caring for children separated from their parents and creating channels through which subsequent generations could learn the culture and values of their African and African American forebears.[53]

In 1867, for instance, Adam Woods, a freedman from Leavenworth, Kansas, appealed to the bureau in Louisville, Kentucky, in hopes of securing custody of his dead brother's children—"Milton about fourteen years old. John about ten years old and Pleasant about eight years"— who had been left with their owner when their father enlisted in the Union army in 1864. Their mother had died sometime before. Woods had been sold away from his brother to Missouri in 1850 and had settled in Kansas after the war. He had approached the former owner of his brother's children, Franklin Ditto, in Mead County, but Ditto would not release them from their apprenticeship contract unless Woods "had legal right to them." Woods also revealed the extent of his family ties still in Kentucky. According to the agent, "He says he has four sisters living and they are all doing well. Two of them are in this City and one in the County nearby and the other at the mouth of Salt River in Hardin County He also has two Brothers one in this City and one at the mouth of Salt River and are doing well and each and all of them are able and willing to assist in raising and educating these children."[54] Another man, Martin Lee, who had been sold away from his family in Georgia and was living in Alabama, met resistance when he tried to take his nephew back to Alabama with him. He explained that he had

"Got My daughter And hear childern but I could not Get My Sisters Son She is live and well there is a Man by the name of Sebe—Burson that ust to one [own] them and he will not let me or his Mother have the boy." Sebe "says he has the boy bound to him and the law in our State is that a childe cannot be bounde when the[y] have Mother father brother sistter uncl or Aunt that can take care of them." The agent in Georgia told Lee that the boy was not bound to Sebe but still demanded twenty-five dollars to help Lee retrieve him.[55] The letter of Martin Lee and the affidavit of Adam Woods reveal both the great labor required to reconstitute freed families and the desire of extended family to raise the children of their relatives. They also point to the obstacles that stood in the way.

While some agents recognized the importance of extended families among freedpeople, however, they could choose not to allow such relationships to override apprenticeship contracts. When Philip Holliday appeared before his local bureau agent in Louisiana seeking custody of his grandson, the agent observed: "The Child properly belongs to Philip as he is the nearest 'kind.'" But the agent decided that Holliday could have the boy only if the child had not already contracted elsewhere.[56] Federal officials even intervened directly on behalf of employers in order to keep determined family members from "interfering" with the work of their employees. A provost marshal for New Orleans, for instance, drafted a notice stating that a girl named Charlotte was in the employ of a Mr. W. M. Culloch and that while she worked for him, she was "to be free from molestation by any parties representing themselves as her relatives." The city police were under orders to arrest any "parties" who persisted in "troubling" her.[57] And a local agent in Vermillionville noted a charge brought by a former slaveholder against the uncle of a child named Adam. Adam had been apprenticed to a Mr. Broussard but "had been violently and without the consent of his master [?] taken from him by his uncle," who carried Adam with him to the nearby parish of New Iberia. The agent had sent word to his colleague there "in order to take the necessary steps against the uncle."[58]

Even when local agents were wary of former slaveholders' motives in applying for custody of freedchildren, their superiors sometimes chose to accept the word of planters if it served the interest of labor. A freedwoman in Vermillionville named Eveline, for instance, encountered great resistance from Coralie Broussard when she tried to take custody of her young daughter. Eveline had been ill when she agreed to let Broussard take the girl, but she had since recovered and wanted to have her daughter back again. The child had apparently been bound to Broussard until she was twenty-two years of age, well past the legal end of apprenticeship for female minors, something to which Eveline would have been unlikely to agree voluntarily. (The Broussard family, also featured in the previous example, had a reputation for bad dealings and was, according to the local agent, "ever foremost and always in the front rank when there is any injury or outrage to be committed on *Freedpeople*.") The assistant commissioner of the bureau nevertheless requested that the agent take no action in the case "unless the interests of the child suffer by the present arrangement," since by the bureau's logic, removing the child might discourage other planters from agreeing to "provide" for other "indigent" children. The agent in this case, however, had greater insight into Coralie Broussard's motives. He ordered Broussard to give up the child and in an explanation to headquarters wrote: "Our planters and their wives take no other interest [in] raising freedchildren than to have the same and hold them, when grown up as a kind of house servants."[59]

Although disputes over the custody and apprenticeship of freedchildren involved children of all ages, those perhaps most often at the center of custody complaints brought before the bureau were at least ten years old. Pointing to struggles between freedpeople and former owners, a bureau agent in Virginia wrote snidely: "Blood don't seem to thicken until children get to be about ten years of age."[60] Yet most slaveholders, before the war, recognized the age of ten as the point at which a child became valuable as a worker and less in need of caretaking by an adult. An antebellum law in Alabama, for instance, prohibited the sale of children under the age of ten.[61] It seems that in agricultural labor, children aged ten or older were the most able to contribute to the daily workload. When Diana Jackson lodged a complaint against her husband, Joseph Jackson, for abandonment and lack of support for his child, the agent initially ordered Joseph to pay eight dollars per month to support the child. But on the advice of a superior, he "modified this decision to $4.00 per month until the child is ten years old at that age she will be able to take care of herself."[62] Northern employment agents working for the Freedmen's Bureau found that an employable child in the North was somewhere between ten and twelve. The agents reported having trouble finding homes for families with younger children, since employers did not want them until they were at least twelve. In the words of Josephine Griffing, "[It was] as though Black Babes were 12 yrs old when they were born."[63]

A child's labor and the money he or she could bring in were a necessity in freed families, just as they were among working-class families in the urban North and agricultural families in the West. Strictly in terms of labor, the rural childhoods of most freedchildren were comparable to those of poor children in other rural areas of the United States, especially white children on the western frontier and Chicano children in California. They often labored within a family, under the direction of parents or relatives, and attended school for a few months out of the year. Whether the family was sharecropping, working the task system (predominant in coastal plantation areas of Georgia and South Carolina), or cultivating their own land, the agricultural labor of children was critical to the household's survival. Freedchildren also performed domestic labor and like most working-class children in the nineteenth century (black, white, and Hispanic, urban and rural), many were "hired out" by their parents for periods of time, to work in other households.[64]

The hiring of freedchildren, from the point of view of their relatives, was much preferred over apprenticeship. Freedpeople could negotiate the contracts of their children and could file complaints when employers failed to pay them. Indeed, freed parents and relatives made hundreds of complaints to the Freedmen's Bureau concerning wages that had not been paid to their children.[65] Freedchildren themselves also made complaint when they had not received the pay that was due to them. (In 1865, the going rate for boys under fourteen was three dollars per month and for girls, two dollars.)[66] Other children made complaint to the bureau against employers for abuse or for refusing to let them board with their parents.[67] But the dependent status of the freedchild made the contract between freedpeople and employers always a matter of interpretation. A boy named William, for instance, charged that a Mrs. Crawford had refused to pay him for one month and two weeks labor at three dollars a month. Crawford protested that William was "not worth anything more than his rations" and had sent word to that effect to his mother. Crawford did not see William as a wage laborer. Rather, she wanted to have him as a child-servant, fed but not paid, "raised" but not otherwise compensated for his work. The agent in the case decided in favor of William and awarded him a month's wages.[68]

In interviews with former slaves conducted by the Federal Writers' Project in the 1930s and 1940s (most of whom were children at the time of emancipation), the speakers narrated their childhoods in freedom by explaining the arrangement of their families (who lived with whom, who had died, who had left to work some other place) and the kind of work that they themselves did.[69] If schooling was mentioned, it was usually to say that they did not have much. (Albert Patterson, raised on a sugar plantation in Louisiana and fifteen years old at emancipation, told an interviewer: "We had no schools, they wouldn't let a nigger look at a school.")[70] Particularly in single-parent families, children had to contribute to the household income as soon as they could. Ex-slave John Moore explained that after his father died of cholera, "my mudder hire me 'n' some 'r' d' uder chillen out t' wuk 'n' she draw us money." After Millie Randall's mother retrieved her children from their former owner—the man who drove them " 'roun an' 'roun" in a wagon to keep them from her—she had the job of supporting herself and her children. Randall recalled, "Maw tuk ober de care of de chillen an' done de bes' she could. Dey put me in a fiel' of co'n to hoe."[71] And when Ella Washington's parents decided to part after emancipation, her mother and aunt took her to Galveston, Texas. "When we got here," Washington said, "my mother hired out [to] some white folks an' when I got big 'nough I did, too."

It is clear that emancipation certainly did not lessen most freedchildren's workloads and probably increased the loads of some. Ex-slave Calvin Kennard recalled, "I neber had no time to study books, I had to work. Didn't play too much 'cause it was allus 'Cal run here, Cal run dere.' " Children, particularly those from large families, were expected to become part of the work team. As Ellen Broomfield explained in an interview, "There were 19 chil'ren in our family an' we had to work as soon as we were big enough. I use to plow, it was hard, but it may be that's what made me so so strong." And former slave La San Mire, who was fourteen years old at emancipation, described his experience even more matter-of-factly: "We were freed on July 4th. After the war I remained with my old master. I worked in the house, cooked in the kitchen."[72]

The accounts of Ellen Broomfield and La San Mire suggest that the work assigned to freedchildren was not strictly determined by gender, but rather by the situation of parents or guardians or the labor needs of white employers. (Before emancipation, in fact, most slaves in rural areas had performed labor on the plantation that was not defined by gender, whereas urban slaves performed more gender-specific tasks, such as laundry work, for women, and stevedore, for men. Most of the ex-slaves interviewed by the Federal Writers' Project had spent time on rural plantations as slaves.)[73] Ellen used the plow, and La San Mire worked in the house and in the kitchen. Ex-slave Carlyle Stewart, a girl of seven at the time of emancipation, worked carrying sugarcane. She recalled, "I could only tote five stalks at a time."[74] Janie Sienette, an ex-slave from Louisiana, was born in slavery but was likely about fourteen or fifteen at emancipation. She told an interviewer, "The most work I done during slavery was to pick cotton and work around the house for the mistress," for which she received cakes. She also had to tend to her younger siblings. Her mother died in childbirth, after working in the cotton field, when Janie was eleven. After the war, when her aunt left the plantation for New Orleans, "my master wanted me to stay on but I cried so until he sent me to Algiers [La.] with my aunt. Then she puts me to washing and ironing for de white folks dim big hoop skirts with all dat cloth in dim and waist we tucks and if I did not do it right she whipped the blood out of me." Sienette also told her interviewer: "I never did go to school in my life if us had of picked up a piece of paper the Boss would have tore us up good."[75]

Freedpeople's complaints before local bureau agents, too, reveal the importance of children's labor to the survival of the household. A freedman named Alphonse appeared before the agent in Vermillionville, Louisiana, to complain that "his son, aged 15 has run away from him and refuses to return." According to the agent, the freedman "asked if he could not force him to return as he needs him to pick cotton." When the agent told him that he had "the right" to compel the boy to go home, without interference, Alphonse "went on his way rejoicing."[76] When freedman John Baptiste appealed to the bureau for his son Cazio, who was fourteen, he explained that Cazio had been bound to a Mr. Bernard without the consent of his mother, but also that the mother "now wishes him to come home and help his stepfather who have [sic] rented land."[77] The agent declared the contract with Bernard void, it having been made without the parents' consent.

The importance of freedchildren to freed households is perhaps clearest when the children were at the center of struggles between freedpeople. Agents of the Freedmen's Bureau recorded many such disputes, fueled by economic need and the complicated nature of family relations after slavery. Freedwoman Lilly Leath, for instance, complained to the Freedmen's Bureau that her former husband, Luke Jackson, carried off her son, a child of four or five years. Neighbors testified that they saw Jackson enter Leath's house "by force" and that the child "screamed and refused to go but Luke Jackson dragged him off." The agent decided in favor of the mother, since she had taken care of the child since birth.[78] Other freed families, however, managed to compromise. There were seven children between Lucy and Cambridge Smith, and Lucy testified that she was unable to get them from their father. The agent to whom she complained decided that they belonged with the mother, since the Smiths were not married, and he told Lucy Smith she could "have as many as she wants." Lucy decided to take four of the children, leaving Cambridge with three.[79] Whatever the motivation behind the division of the children between the parents, it is likely that the children's labor was also being divided.

In many cases, bureau agents made explicit the economic role of the freedchild in these disputes. But the arguments still hinged on the best interests of the child. When Henry Powell's parents both sought custody of him after their separation, the agent described his father, William, as "an industrious hard working Freedman" who "wishes to establish upon the boy's mind the necessity of knowing how to work while he is young." Henry's mother, Maria Jackson, on the other hand, was living "in idleness," and "while the boy was young, and could not work she did not care anything about him but now he is old enough to make a good living (if with someone that has some control over him, which she has not any) she wants him and for nothing more than to wait on her."[80] The core of the argument the agent (and presumably the father) made was that William Jackson would teach Henry "the necessity of knowing how to work," whereas the mother would use the child's labor to her own ends. The claim of a freedwoman named Ermine Mouton also addressed the issue of children's labor directly. Mouton was the aunt of three orphans and entered into a dispute with the children's uncle and grandfather over who should have custody of the children. They had been raised by Mouton to the ages of ten, twelve, and fourteen. In what appears to be Mouton's account, the bureau agent explained in his report that "now after the children are able to go to work in some manner," the uncle and grandfather hoped "to avail themselves of the opportunity to let them go to work they having done nothing for their education." What was unjust, in the eyes of Mouton, it seems, was not that the children would go to work, since she recognized that they had reached working age. Rather, she objected to the claims of the men on the grounds that they had not raised the children or tended to their education—activities that established her claim to the children, and quite possibly to their labor.[81]

Though many freedpeople fought apprenticeship arrangements that held their children hostage, others used such contracts as a means of protecting their children and assuring them of food and clothing. To remove their children from the households of their former owners, when possible, freedpeople bound out their children to relatives or other freedpeople, often relying on the extended familial networks they had constructed in slavery. Such ties proved important after emancipation as well, particularly with respect to the protection of freedchildren from forced apprenticeships and to the independence of freedpeople's households. A freedwoman named Mary, for instance, bound her child Lizzie to Lizzie's godmother, a woman named Kitty. Kitty agreed to "clothe, feed, and protect" Lizzie until she became "of age."[82] The binding of children to relatives, in fact, was a common strategy among poor people in the colonial and antebellum South, in some cases because parents could not afford to send all their children to school.[83] But in the context of the postbellum South, such arrangements also better ensured that the child would be raised by family members.

Freedpeople also appealed to the bureau expressly to have their younger relatives bound to them. Sallie Harris wanted to bind her cousin Wilson to her rather than have him remain with a white man named Jefferson "because he is not treated well and as he is my Cousin I think it my duty to see to him." Harris explained in her letter, "I have a house for him and will take care of him and do all I can for him."[84] Wister Miller also wrote to the same bureau agent requesting that his wife's seven-year-old brother, Charles, be bound to him, since Charles's mother was dead. Miller assured the agent that if he agreed to bind the child to Miller, "at the proper time he shall have all that he is entitle [*sic*] to."[85]

Freedpeople binding their young relatives to themselves accomplished three things. It protected the child from forced apprenticeship with a former owner, it satisfied the bureau agent by creating another labor contract, and it kept the child's labor and earnings within the circle of his or her family. The bureau agent handling the cases of Sallie Harris and Wister Miller seemed to come to that realization, if slowly. It seems that both boys involved, Wilson and Charles, had been bound to Jefferson, who, according to the agent, "has the name of a hard master, but I do not know of his being cruel." There was rumor, too, that Jefferson had whipped Wilson, though the agent intended to "enquire into it." In his report to his superior, though, the agent seemed to have realized that perhaps the boys were better off with their families. "I sent the boys there with the understanding that I would apprentice [*sic*] them if agreeable to [Jefferson], against the protest of all their relations, thinking it would be a good home." As it turned out, the agent had been misled by another man, Rowlett, who claimed that he had owned the boys and that he had custody of them, but wanted the agent to bind them out. In fact, Wilson had been living with an uncle, who was sending him to school. (It is unclear if the same circumstances applied to Charles.) Jefferson threatened the uncle if he protested the boy's indenture to him. The agent reported that "there is a decided opposition to binding these children to col'd people" in his district but explained that his "object is to get good homes for these children. Wealth, power, or influence does not make a good home always." He requested further direction on the matter—whether or not the freedpeople petitioning him were "ready to undertake these obligations"—but wrote, "I have no doubt in my [mind] that they will do all they promise to do."[86]

For their part, when former slaveholders argued against freedpeople's claims to custody of children—and in favor of the preservation of an apprenticeship contract—they often did so with a vocabulary of concern for the interest of the child. Recycling antebellum rhetoric, planters often expressed their entitlement to black children's labor in familial, paternalist terms. In most of the South (unlike much of the North by midcentury), the antebellum household had been a working household, and slaveholders' defense of slavery before the Civil War centered on their paternalism toward their slaves and offered up the slaveholding fantasy that posed exploitation in the garb of domesticity, put most succinctly when they referred to "my family, white and black."[87] But freedpeople had shattered many former owners' paternalist fantasies about the emotional ties that bound their "property" to them. Many "loyal" slaves walked off plantations and out of kitchens. They talked back, ignored orders, and "deserted" the people who had "raised" them.[88] And yet many a former slaveholder tried to stitch the fragile pieces of that worn-out paternalism back together. With the language of parental entitlement, they hoped to lessen the damage done and reassert their ownership rights over the "good property" that freedchildren used to represent. Their most common refrain in this regard was one that Lieutenant James DeGrey seemed to accept without critique in the case of Porter, that is, that they had "raised" the children themselves. Mary Golbert, demanding the return of a "servant girl" named Sarah, was typical in her pleading with federal authorities. In 1863, Sarah had sought refuge from her mistress in a New Orleans hospital, and in efforts to have her returned, Golbert declared: "She is a girl I have raised and I am good to my servants."[89]

Planters aimed to extend slavery through the lives of freedchildren, but to do this they had to make them into orphans whom they had "raised" from birth. To render the parents and relatives of freedchildren ineligible as custodians of their children, then, former slaveholders often presented themselves to the Freedmen's Bureau as freedchildren's only guardians. Planters sought to rewrite their history of ownership (holding children as chattel with cash value) as a history of guardianship (taking them into their care, with the children's best interests in mind) and erasing the role of parents and relatives in the raising of freedchildren. Exploiting the dependency of children, then, and laying claim to the child's upbringing—indeed, the child's life history—planters tried to create for themselves a pool of unfree labor. This postbellum narrative also served to patch together the story many slaveholders had long told themselves about the benefits of slavery for those they held in bondage, that is, that binding a freedchild to them was, in fact, the best thing for the children.[90]

In one way, this new paternalism turned the old paternalism on its head. Before the war, many slaveholding paternalists prided themselves on keeping slave families together or buying the relatives of their slaves and reuniting families. In trying to keep freedchildren under their control, however, some also fought to keep freed families apart. Former slaveholder Louis Préjean, seeking custody of Alexandriene and Mary against the wishes of their grandmother, argued that the children ought to remain with him on account of "his daughter having reared them and treated kindly as her own from their birth up to this time." Further still, Préjean, a true paternalist, declared one of the girls to be his daughter while the other was "born on the place."[91] Not every former slaveholder made claims of paternity, and such claims were difficult to substantiate, particularly when the child's mother was no longer living. Nevertheless, former slaveholders like Préjean aimed to present the arrangements of slavery (white ownership and exploitation of black people and their labor) as the most stable, nurturing environment for freed black children.[92] Three judges in Maryland, for instance, making ample use of the state's antebellum apprenticeship laws, informed an agent of the bureau that his court was processing "a large number of *Orphan* children" between ten and twelve years old who "require some immediate action in their behalf." (He did not mention orphan children younger than ten, who would not have been as useful in terms of work.) According to the judges, "When their previous owners are known to the court to be proper persons to care for & bring them up to the habits of industry &c, we invariably bind to them." But the judges also received requests from "former masters to have negro children that they have raised bound to them," children who clearly had parents, particularly mothers, who objected. When satisfied that the parents could provide for the children, according to one judge, the court did not interfere. However,

> we think it very probably our course has been misrepresented by some mothers. who think they can support themselves & family, their previous antecedents being enquired into by the court it is made too apparent their utter inability to properly provide & teach habits of industry &c in such cases the court regards it as an act of humanity when proper employers can be selected for them.[93]

Relying on antebellum rules about the binding of children of free women of color, the judges intervened at the behest of former slaveholders to keep freedchildren in their possession and beyond the control of their mothers.

The danger of this child-directed paternalism, for freedpeople, was twofold: one, that it represented former slaveholders as the most suitable guardians for black children—indeed, as the persons who had *raised* them—and the persons best able to provide for the children; and two, that the bureau's overriding concern of encouraging freedpeople to sign labor contracts might lead them to eagerly accept the sentiment of former slaveholders. When challenged by the children's relatives, agents could justify their decisions in favor of former owners as decisions made in the best interest of the child.[94]

The familial arguments made by some former slaveholders were made more powerful still by their sincerity. As manipulative as their pleas may seem under a historian's scrutiny, it would be wrong to suggest that at least some of these former slaveholders did not believe what they said. When several freedpeople complained to the bureau, for instance, that a woman named Woodward "has repeatedly abused a child in her possession," Woodward responded that the child's parents were dead and "that she had raised the child from infancy and was anxious to keep him and do well by him." The agent investigated and decided that the complaints were "unfounded." "The boy (?) Lincoln was therefore apprenticed to Mrs. Woodward until he shall arrive at the age of eighteen." So, Woodward not only got to keep the boy named Lincoln, but also got a contract for him—the child she had raised "from infancy"—until he was grown.[95] Considering the complicated webs they had spun, as masters and mistresses, between their paternalistic feelings for their slaves and their economic interest in them, many former slaveholders surely felt that they had "raised" the black children on their plantations and that this entitled them to possession of those children, and their labor.

This sort of paternalism did not always come from former owners but, rather, from whites who claimed orphaned freedchildren, even if those children had been left in the custody of freedpeople. A freedman named Henry Elin and his wife brought a case before the Freedmen's Bureau in Algiers, Louisiana, against Mary Wood (a white woman) in 1867, for refusing to return the boy William to them. William was "about eleven years of age," and his father had served with Henry Elin's regiment during the war. The father died three days before his regiment was mustered out and had asked Elin to take care of his two sons, William and an older brother. Of the two boys, Henry Elin testified, "the oldest one is about fifteen years old and I have given him to my brother and kept William myself." Henry Elin and his wife both testified that they had left William with a "colored woman" when Henry Elin found work elsewhere. According to Mrs. Elin,

> Last summer my husband was working up the river and I went after him in the month of June and left the boy in charge of another colored woman. In my absence, he became attached to Mrs. Wood and went to her sick. The boy came home and went away again. After my husband returned I went to Mrs. Wood for the boy, but she would not allow him to come stating that the boy would not come back to me, or words to

that effect, but the boy has been put up to say that by Mrs. Wood or her family. I think I am willing and able to take care of the boy.

The court then heard from William himself, who argued strongly against the Elins, describing his life with them as one of depravation and abuse. (Mrs. Elin, anticipating such testimony, had already warned the court that William "had been put up" to it by Mrs. Wood or others.) William testified that while living with the Elins "he never got half enough to eat and was beaten badly, that he ran away from them twice, and went to New Orleans." He also said that "last summer Henry and his wife went up the coast and left him with a colored woman by the name of Nancy who never took care of him and he left and went to Mrs. Wood." The court reported that William declared himself "unwilling to go back to Henry and his wife, but wishes to remain with Mrs. Wood."

For her part, Wood insisted that she took William in only out of charity:

The first I saw of the boy was last May. I asked him to carry in some wood for me. He did so and I paid him for the same. He then asked me for something to eat. I gave him some and about two days after he came back again and asked me to give him some food. I did so and after that he came most every morning for something to eat. One evening he came to my house when I was going to bed and asked me if he could not stay. I told him he had better go home. He replied that he could and would not go home that he would run away from Henry and his wife for they had treated him badly. Shortly after Henry's wife went away and left the boy in charge of a colored woman Nancy who is a worthless woman, who took no notice of the boy whatever.

Wood insisted that William wanted to stay with her and made the case that she should be the child's guardian. "I am willing to raise him and my son-in-law will learn him a trade. When he becomes large enough," she said. The Elins, she insisted, could not be proper guardians for William. "I find William to be a good boy and will make a good man if he is properly trained but he will be nothing but a loafer if he does not get better people than Henry and his wife to raise him." She also insisted that she did not wish to keep William if he wanted to return to the

Elins, but that she had *rescued* William. "I merely took him from the street," she said, "for the sake of humanity."

The local bureau agent saw that the Elins were "very anxious to get [William] back and ought to have him if they take care of him." But if William were forced back, he said, the boy would "run away and stray into vice and misery." "Mrs. Wood," he said, "is represented to me as a respectable lady and has means to take care of the boy." The bureau decided against the Elins, and William Fennison was ordered to remain with Mrs. Wood. It was Henry Elin, however, who best explained the contradictions inherent in this struggle over a freedchild. Despite his effort to accommodate Mary Wood under the new system of wage labor, Henry Elin could not win. "I offered to hire him out to Mrs. Wood," Elin said. "But she don't want to hire him, she wants to raise him."[96] When freedpeople such as the Elins endeavored to work within the system of free labor—being willing to hire William to Wood, but not *give* him to her—they had to confront a revived paternalist ideology, one that played well with the northern agents of the Freedmen's Bureau because it was framed around the best interests of the child.

Since most children are dependent upon adults, the white paternal figure and the dependent black child did not require nearly so much ideological contortion as the slaveholder's relationship to his slaves. It was this relationship to freedchildren that a white southerner described, serving as witness to the state of affairs in Texas and Louisiana before the congressional Joint Committee on Reconstruction in 1866. Responding to the committee's queries about the abuse of freedpeople, he insisted that planters did not use violence to compel freedpeople to fulfill their contracts. But then he offered up the fact that black children *were* whipped by their employers. He justified this abuse as corrective: he "switched" the "little house servants" working in his household just as he "switched" his own children. The context of this abuse of black children, however—that black children were his employees, and his own children were not—was erased in his testimony. The difference between punishing black children for the work they did or did not do as servants, and the disciplining of his own children for their misdeeds, was papered over. The former slaveholder claimed the role of father for both black and white children, even though the only binding relation between himself and his "little house servants" was a contract. The free labor contract, in turn—involving dependent black children and white employers—became a means to obscure the role of black parents as the guardians of their children. As many former slaveholders did, this one also argued his point with a critique of black people as parents. Black parents, he said, "neglect" to discipline their children, and it was up to employers to care for black children: "The negro will not take care of his offspring unless required to do it, as compared with the whites. The little children will die, they do die, and hence the necessity of very vigorous regulations on our plantations which we have adopted in our nursery system."[97] Boasting about the "nursery system" on plantations as evidence of slaveholder benevolence was not new, but its context was. Instead of criticizing black parents as a justification for the system of slavery, this former slaveholder was criticizing them out of a desire to replace them altogether, leaving their children solely in the care of planter families.

This former slaveholder's notions of black parenthood as lethal illustrate the nature of postemancipation paternalism, an ideology that took aim at black parents and relatives. In trying to portray themselves as the best possible caretakers for black children, they sought to discredit freedpeople as parents and guardians. Former slaveholder Elizabeth Callihan had such designs when she tried to preserve the indenture of "William Callihan" against the wishes of William's mother, Maria Reeding. Callihan claimed that the child had been in her charge since 1863, "his Mother having left about that time." Arguing that William should remain with her, she insisted, "this is the first time I have been made aware of the existence of the woman who claims to be the Mother of the said William," since she did not know "whether his Mother was alive or dead." By her own account Callihan told the bureau's headquarters in New Orleans a few months prior "that they must dispose of [William] or bind him," the bureau agreeing to do the latter. Although willing to have William "disposed" of a few months before, when challenged by the boy's mother, she argued that she was "very much attached to him and he appears equally so to me, having never known any other protector." William's mother, by Callihan's report, was an "invalid, unable to care for herself or him," and should William be taken from Callihan's care, "in all probability he will have no one to provide for him." The headquarters, upon reading the case, replied that the indenture was not valid without the mother's consent. But in the interest of pressing labor contracts whenever possible, the local agent was advised by his superiors to "try and induce the mother to give her consent as, if *Mrs. Callihan's* statement is true, the child is contented and doing well and the mother is unable to provide for it."[98] The need of the mother for her child, particularly if she was indeed an invalid, was not considered. And the white woman who had owned the boy—who had once thought him exchangeable for money—was promoted as his best protector.

This pull and tug between parents and relatives and former slave-holders was further complicated by the wants of freedchildren, which were not always easy for bureau agents to discern, even less so for a historian reading children's secondhand testimony in the archives. The possibility that freedchildren were coerced into testifying in favor of the white person who claimed them was quite real. Recall that Mrs. Elin anticipated the child William Fennison's testimony against her but blamed it on the efforts of Mrs. Wood to influence him. As we also saw in the case of William Fennison, however, the boy testified that he did not want to return to the Elins, where, he said, "he never got half enough to eat and was beaten badly." This, too, may have been true. Particularly since the Elins were not kin to William, he may have been reluctant to live with them, a poor working-class couple, instead of Wood, who probably had plenty of food in her house. The choice of leaving a well-stocked pantry for a household where food might at times be scarce was perhaps not so difficult for an orphan to make.[99] The charge of beatings might also have been true. Former slaves have testified that physical punishment was a part of their child rearing, as slaves and as freedchildren. Some historians have tied this to the psychological effects of slavery on parents, others to the idea that parents beat their children to teach them lessons that would preserve them from something worse at the hands of whites. Physical punishment of children was also part of child rearing among many white families.[100]

William's loyalties (if they were, in fact, with Mrs. Wood), and those of other freedchildren toward white guardians, reflect the complicated nature of their childhood in the transition from slavery to freedom—the choice between hunger and plenty of food, between more work or a little less, and between unfamiliar surroundings or the place where they were born. If many adult freedpeople confronted uncertainty in the first days or weeks of freedom—whether to remain in a familiar place where they could earn a living or leave in order to free themselves from former owners—it must have been doubly confusing for freedchildren like William Fennison, without parents, to decide where to go and with whom to align themselves.[101] The story of Pelagea Francis begins to explain the predicament of some freedchildren after the war.

According to bureau agent William Cornelius in New Iberia, Louisiana, he first encountered Pelagea on the plantation of Charles Lastrapes. In a narrative reminiscent of those written by northern reformers and missionaries in the South, Cornelius wrote that the girl caught his attention because of the "filthy appearance of her person scarcely clothing enough to cover her nakedness and that very dirty and ragged and her skin to all appearances had not seen water for many days." Cornelius asked Lastrapes to whom the girl belonged, and Lastrapes said that Pelagea was an orphan with no one to take care of her, that her mother had died and her father "deserted her at the commencement of [the war]" (quite possibly, to enlist) and had since died. Cornelius asked Lastrapes if he would take in the girl as an apprentice, "being acquainted with the family for the past year" and finding them "among the number of most *Loyal Citizens* minded as to the privilege of Freedmen particularly as to the point of *Education*." Lastrapes said he had no use for the child himself but proposed that his widowed mother, "an aged Lady of some 86 years," should take her until the age of fifteen. Cornelius did not authorize the apprenticeship until he had "visited *The Quarters* of the Freed People to be positive that she *Pelagea* had no relations living." There he found "but one aged Freedwoman who claims to be its *God Mother* but made no objections whatever" to binding the child to Mrs. Lastrapes. The girl seemed happy in the arrangement, and on subsequent visits Cornelius "found the child very neat and clean in her appearance perfectly happy, playing with the white children of the family." But Cornelius's rescue effort was nearly foiled by a woman who appeared in his office claiming that Pelagea's uncle had left the child to her: "I immediately visited the Plantation again found the child perfectly happy and questioned her and [away] from the family, if she wished to leave Mrs. Lastrapes and go to New Orleans with this colored woman, She immediately answered *No!*" While Cornelius was at the plantation, the freedpeople there told him that the woman claiming custody of Pelagea "has not the means of providing for her self but wants it only for the benefit she may derive from it[,] child labour."[102]

It is not clear from the record what happened to Pelagea, but most likely she was allowed to remain with the Lastrapes. Her case reflects how freedchildren, particularly orphans, could be caught between the familiar life of the plantation and the unfamiliar world beyond it, and between former slaveholders, a bureau agent, and freedpeople. Although the freedpeople living on the plantation advocated that she remain there, Cornelius's description of Pelagea playing with "the white children of the family" is reminiscent of many stories of slave children who played with whites as children, stories that inevitably ended with the black and white children parting ways when the black child was old enough to work. Told by former slaves, stories of black and white children playing together, then living separate and unequal lives, spoke of the injustice of a racially divided society.[103] But told by former slaveholders, the same stories painted a picture of benevolent paternalism, of "my family white and black." Cornelius's account, then, endorsed the idea that former slaveholders might "raise" both. And, yet, Pelagea had been dirty and untended until her apprenticeship to Lastrape's mother, that is, until she had been bound into a labor contract. The freedwoman who tried to claim her may have wanted Pelagea for her labor, too. But as a freedwoman with little money, she was not a good paternalist. And Pelagea said she did not want to go to New Orleans.

The frequency with which children professed their reluctance to leave white households or their white guardians (or captors), however, makes many cases suspect. When Charles Joseph went to the bureau to complain that his grandson Joe was being held against his grandfather's wishes by a white man named Thomas Kenefie, Joseph encountered resistance similar to what the Elins confronted. Joseph explained to the bureau agent that the boy's parents had left him in his care and that Kenefie was retaining the boy. Kenefie testified to the bureau that Joe had lived with him the previous spring and had come back to Kenefie asking to be hired, explaining "that his grandfather not only used him very harshly but that he actually nearly starved him, he also stated that his parents never gave him up to him, and he does moreover positively state if he is forced to go back to live with him, that he will drown himself." The bureau ordered Kenefie to return the boy to his grandfather, but Kenefie failed to comply. The agent explained to superiors: "The boy always conceals himself when his Father and Grandfather go after him and I firmly believe that Mr. and Mrs. Kenefie encourage the boy to do this." He asked permission "to go and search the house for the boy in order that he may be restored to his grandfather."[104] Given Kenefie's flair for melodrama and intrigue, his case appears fairly suspect. Placing his efforts to keep Joseph alongside other former slaveholders' attempts to hold on to freedchildren suggests that often former slaveholders were not telling the truth in their testimony to bureau agents.

Freedchildren and their labor were the last thing former slaveholders let loose in their struggle to maintain a compulsory system of black labor. Even when children had been apprenticed by freedpeople to former slaveholders, the latter could fail to uphold their end of the agreement and exploit the labor of the children by hiring them out, as if they were still slaves. Such were the circumstances of three children—George Washington, Isabella, and Alonzo—who had been apprenticed to Revilla McDonald after the death of their mother. Isabella Collins petitioned for custody of the children (her niece and nephews) after it was discovered that McDonald "has given up house-keeping and proposes to hire the children out to other parties." Even though McDonald's plan to violate a contract and "hire out" the children made it clear that she was only interested in the profits she could make off of their labor, it was Isabella Collins who was required by the bureau agent to substantiate her claim as aunt and rightful guardian of the children with letters of recommendation from her employers. The agent explained to one of Collins's recommenders, without a hint of irony, that he required the letters from her employers "in order that injustice would not be done to the children."[105]

Like antebellum paternalism, then, this postemancipation strain was rife with contradiction. Perhaps the most specious argument former slaveholders offered for why *they* should have custody of black children was that the children's relatives wanted them only for their labor. As we saw in the case of Porter, bureau agents could also be party to this kind of criticism of freedpeople.[106] But the accusation was even more outlandish when it came from former slaveholders seeking custody of freedchildren. When Lucy Bowles appeared at Sarah Pulliam's house looking for her nieces Alice and Georgiana, for instance, Pulliam insisted that the children rightfully belonged with her. "It is the first time that Lucy Bowles has ever seen them," she wrote, "and she says she wants to have them to wait on her." Pulliam insisted that the girls' mother, on her deathbed, asked Pulliam "to keep and raise her children." "She [Lucy Bowles] did not want them then but now that [they] can do a little such as set the table and wash dishes she wants them and we are not willing for her to have them." For her part, Bowles explained to the agent that not only was she the aunt of the girls, but that they had grandparents living as well. It is not clear from the record that Lucy Bowles succeeded in retrieving her nieces, though given the agent's initial order to Pulliam, Bowles may have been successful. Pulliam, however, continued to protest, and her response to the existence of the children's grandparents was no more charitable than her first letter of complaint. "I do think we ought to be allowed to keep them until they are grown for well I do know that if their relations get them they will suffer for I know they will not get the treatment they now get."[107]

We cannot know whether Pulliam was telling the truth about Alice and Georgiana's mother on her deathbed. But the records of the bureau contain many examples of freedpeople leaving their children with former owners for a time, either informally or by contracting their labor, until the parents or relatives could claim them. There was risk involved in this, however. Often employers and former owners refused to give freedchildren up, even after the contracts their parents signed for their labor had expired. In other cases, employers suddenly moved or left town, leaving parents and relatives unable to discover their children's whereabouts.[108] Enoch Braston, in Mississippi, testified to the bureau that he had been unable to retrieve three of his children from his former master, John Heath. When he left the plantation to get medicine for one of the children, Heath told him that if he came back, "he would put a ball through me." Braston was able to get his wife and four children away from Heath but was still unable to get the other three and was afraid to retrieve them. When he had tried to get them at Christmas, "Heath said buzzards would pick my bones, Fanny Guy his stepdaughter had a doubled barreled gun & said she would shoot me if I came into the yard."[109]

Prince Durant suffered even more abuse when he tried to retrieve his children. Durant testified before a bureau agent that he had left his children in the care of a Mrs. Woodside in 1866 with the understanding that she would keep them for one year. The children, Rose, Willie, and Kate, were fourteen, nine, and seven, respectively, at the time of Durant's testimony. When Durant returned, Mrs. Woodside had died and the children were living with her son, Edward. Durant went to the Woodside residence with three other freedmen (possibly anticipating resistance from the Woodsides). They were met by Woodside's wife and Louisa Lann, his aunt. Lann, inventing an apprenticeship contract on the spot, said that Edward would keep the children until they were twenty-one, despite Durant's insistence that he made no such agreement.

"Uncle you must recollect we are white here," Mrs. Edward Woodside said from an upstairs window, to which Durant replied from the yard, "Madam I am not speaking about white or black, I only want my children." When Mrs. Woodside finally relented and told Louisa Lann to turn over the children, Lann said, "No I'd rather die than let them go," suggesting an attachment that the children clearly did not share. When Durant turned to leave, his children followed him. The whole party was a few miles down the road when Edward Woodside came after them with a shotgun and a constable. Woodside shot at Durant and missed. Then they took Durant into custody, where he was beaten with a hatchet, left tied up for hours, and fined. (The justice of the peace had earlier refused to help Durant, according to the report, saying that he "did not interfere between the negro and his master.") In the meantime, the children returned to the Woodside house. It is unclear when, or if, Durant was able to get his children. The constable and Woodside, in testimony to the local bureau agent, denied any wrongdoing.[110]

Freedwomen, too, encountered violence when they tried to retrieve their children from former owners. The postmaster in New Town, Maryland, wrote to military officials in 1864 that former slaveholders "are threatening Mothers with the severest punishment if they come on their premises." One mother, in particular, was struck on the side of her head when she tried to retrieve her sixteen-year-old son from her former owner. At the time the boy was taken from her, she had already hired him out to someone else for ten dollars a month.[111] But more often, perhaps, single freedwomen seeking custody of their children had to combat representations of themselves as "loose" and unfit for motherhood.[112] In the antebellum South, black women often were characterized by both male and female slaveholders either as faithful, maternal "Mammies" or as "Jezebels," that is, loose women responsible for the sexual transgressions of white men. Both stereotypes served to justify the system of slavery and mask the sexual exploitation of black women by white men.[113] But in the context of freedom, such characterizations took on new meaning. At times bureau agents as well as former slaveholders represented freedwomen as sexually promiscuous and irresponsible in the context of custody battles over black children. What black women faced in such instances was not a slaveholder justifying slavery or sexual exploitation, but both former slaveholders and the state seeking to deny them the right to raise their children, or the children of their relatives.

One bureau agent read the back-and-forth migration of freedwomen from the countryside to New Orleans in search of work after the war as evidence that they were all engaged in prostitution. Citing the "growing uneasiness and dissatisfaction" caused by "loose and imperfect domestic relations," freedwomen, in his view, sought comfort and income elsewhere:

> There is a large and increasing travel on the Railroad to New Orleans, of colored people—a great proportion of them are females—They leave their homes for the city on various pretenses, and are absent a few weeks when in very many cases they return. It does not require great acumen to see what has been the course of their lives, while they have been away. Their new dresses and *general flare* and the *pocket money* are to my mind unmistakable witnesses of the mode by which the means have been obtained.[114]

Freedpeople had plenty of reasons to be "dissatisfied" after the war other than "imperfect domestic relations" (injustice, poverty, and continued abuse to name a few), but what is more, the agent read black women's attempts at finding work and earning money in the city (where domestic labor was in high demand) as signs of lascivious behavior. These sorts of assumptions about black women, in turn, became quite damaging when women sought the custody of their children. In at least once instance, such characterizations appear in a child's apprenticeship contract, supervised by the bureau. Affy Harris was described in the document as a "female of yellow color, aged about 10 years whose father is unknown and whose mother, though living is unfit and unable to raise, take care of, and educate her said child, being of lude and abandoned habits."[115]

What we see in the records of the bureau, in instances in which black women were seeking custody of children from former owners, is an increasingly severe condemnation of black women as unqualified caretakers. As slaves and as freedwomen, black women or "Mammies" were considered maternal when they cared for white children, but not when they cared for their own children. Like poor white women, black mothers and their black children were not included in the cult of domesticity found among white middle-class and planter-class women.[116] A former slave in New Orleans, for instance, recalled being whipped by his owner because he had said to the mistress, "My mother sent me." "We were not allowed to call our mammies 'mother.' It made it come too near the way of the white folks."[117] After emancipation, however, when black women could legally demand the right to care for their children, their rights to motherhood were challenged in ways that those of wealthier white women would not have been.

It seems the only black woman likely to receive praise for her good character by her former owners in such disputes was a dead one, provided she had (by the former owner's account) left her child in the care of her mistress to "raise it as one of her own."[118] The aunt of a child named Celeste was denied custody of the girl in favor of the former owner of the child's deceased mother. "The child in question was *born in the Doctor's family* her mother being the cook," the agent explained, deftly replacing the arrangements of slavery with the arrangements of family. "This girl has been raised with the Doctor's own children, consequently is very much attached to the family." According to the agent, turning Celeste over to her aunt "would be hurling the child into the very depths of perdition as Caroline LeBlanc bears anything but a good name, and especially for chastity and virtue." Celeste's aunt, he wrote, was also "a noted public character and a thief."[119] In another case, after investigating the claims of a mother for her child (though he does not say just how), the same bureau agent denied a woman custody of her son when he "learned the boy's mother is unfit to have care of him. She being known as a drunkard, common thief, and worthless, that when her boy is by his mother taken home he is abused and beat[en] and by her made to steal in order that she may satisfy her appetite with liquor and to live."[120]

There seems to have been less questioning regarding the character or morality of freedmen in struggles over freedchildren. Freedmen who took their complaints before the bureau were characterized by those consulted (freedpeople or whites who knew them) as either "industrious," "hard-working," or simply too poor to support the children. When a father sought custody of his children from their former owner (the mother having died), the agent represented the man as being simply unable to support and school them, but the woman he had since married was believed to be "morally incapable of taking care of them." The agent decided that the former slaveholder ought to have custody, since he and his family had "raised the children." The bureau's rules, however, made the rights of a parent tantamount, and in this case the children were given over to their father.[121]

Not only did former slaveholders and bureau agents sometimes represent black women as prostitutes and unfit mothers, but they also coerced children into their campaigns to destroy black women's credibility. When a mother reported that her son was held against his will by a man named Dodge the agent went to the home of Dodge and found the twelve-year-old boy, "well dressed and clean and neat in appearance." The agent reported that the boy "refused in my presence to go with his mother under any circumstance." Even when agents declared in such cases that they questioned the child away from relatives or parents, it is very likely that former slaveholders bribed or threatened the children to say they wanted to remain with them. Under slavery, slaveholders frequently courted the affections of black children in efforts to undermine slave parents' authority.[122] But in freedom, handling disputes over the upbringing of black children often became the work of the state, and black women also bore the brunt of the prejudices of local agents. The agent sent the boy to the provost marshal, who decided (against the rules of the bureau, which would have given custody to the mother) that the child should remain with Dodge. "Dodge is a good man," the agent declared, adding, "I have since ascertained that the mother is an inmate of a house of ill-fame in New Orleans."[123] The agent sought to discredit the child's mother by giving the role of caregiver to Dodge (the child discovered at Dodge's house, neat and pressed) and declaring the woman a prostitute.

The very public nature of the claims against them made it especially difficult for some black women seeking custody of their children. Black women were the figures most likely to be seen working in the city streets (going to the market for their employers, delivering laundry) and traveling back and forth from city to country on a regular basis, working and then tending to children.[124] Freedwomen's visibility and daily mobility as workers were often used against them when former slaveholders and bureau agents challenged their competency as mothers. This pattern of criticism is clear in the case of Virinda, a woman who had been freed in 1863 by the federal government after providing information about "concealed weapons." She then sought the custody of two of her five children from her former owner, Joseph Soloman, and filed suit against him before the provost marshal in New Orleans. She had left the two children in the charge of her former owner until she could find a new situation and a place to live. One of the children testified that she did "housework" for Soloman. Soloman brought forward witnesses who represented Virinda as "a lewd and abandoned woman" who could not properly care for her children, who were "often in the streets." But by the accounts of a federal officer, she had worked hard to secure a modest house for herself and her children and had been trying for some ten months to regain custody of them. A seamstress who knew her testified that Virinda had been "always at work for nine months" and that she made enough money to support the other two children. Two federal officers also testified on her behalf, agreeing that she was employed for more than a year. One of Virinda's children was then put on the stand and insisted that she wanted to stay with her white employers. "I often told Mr. Soloman that I did not want to go back to my mother," she said. "[I] did not tell anyone I wanted to leave. I did not have enough to eat when I was with my mother," raising, again, hunger as a charge against a freedperson seeking custody against the wishes of a white person.[125] The child was under Soloman's charge at the time, so he could have threatened her with punishment should she testify against him.

The judge in the case decided against Virinda, allowing the children to remain with Soloman while giving visiting rights to their mother. Although there was insufficient evidence against her character, the judge said, he believed Virinda had failed to prove herself capable of caring for all five children. The children were ordered to remain in the custody of Soloman, who, according to the judge, "is admitted to be a fit and proper person, and having ample means to care for the children."[126] Soloman, in turn, refused to permit Virinda, whom he described as a "depraved creature," to visit her children, and he had her arrested for alleged "violent language" against him. She was released from prison only after swearing that she would not visit Soloman's house again. She then placed her case before the commanding general in New Orleans, whose decision does not appear in bureau documents. Virinda's story illustrates the obstacles black women faced in trying to obtain custody of their children. Her status as a working woman was used against her, as were her ardent demands for custody of her children. Those most able to testify to her hard work, however, were other freed working women like herself. In turn, she was displaced in her role as guardian of her own children by her former owner, someone who had more money than she did and who accused her of depravity when she resisted his appropriation of her children.

There are other historical lessons within Virinda's story, however, lessons about freedom and free labor, and the relationship between the two. By demanding that her children leave Soloman's house, Virinda articulated what freedom meant to her: that her children were her own. But with emancipation had come the challenge of supporting her children, so that her notions of freedom from her former owner had to exist side by side with the need to sustain herself and her dependents. Although Virinda had left Soloman's house with three of her children, her other two children remained in his household until she could find work and support them herself. Because of her dependent children, she moved toward freedom in stages, using Soloman's need for her children's labor to her advantage. They would have food and shelter in exchange for their labor until she could take them into her own household. When able, she demanded custody of her children and tried to separate them from the household and conditions in which they had once been enslaved. Through contracting for her children's labor, Virinda worked toward full freedom from her former owner.

Freedwomen, in particular, used the apprenticeship system to their advantage—that is, as both a survival strategy and a means through which, eventually, to separate themselves and their children from the context of their enslavement.[127] In many cases women apprenticed their children to former slaveholders, only to retrieve them once they had the means to care for them again themselves. This arrangement, of course, did not suit most former slaveholders, who intended to keep the children, as the contract typically stated, until they were of age. At least one Freedmen's Bureau agent seemed to have understood what freedwomen were doing. In the cases where mothers were seeking custody of their children, he observed, often "the mother has left the plantation where she and her children lived, and sought and found employment elsewhere, and there made application for her children." There are numerous examples of freedwomen who put their mark on apprenticeship agreements, binding their children to former slaveholders, but many of these contracts were for such long periods (in some cases beginning with infancy) that it is likely the women did not choose to sign or intend to honor the contract.[128] The same bureau agent noted, in fact, that "as a general thing force has been used in making the mother sign the agreement [that bound children until their majority]," and he usually took it upon himself to void such contracts and return the children to their mothers.

But as with most bureau agents, the voiding of a contract, even if it may have been signed under coercion, was no small thing. If he found that the mother had signed the agreement "voluntarily," and was only "induced to take them away through advice from designing persons," then the agent "allowed" the children to remain with the employer.[129] In many cases, however, freedchildren's labor was instrumental in freed-people's efforts to become independent from those who had once owned them. Although they may have continued to work for their former owners for a time, the labor freedchildren performed was an investment their mothers made in the interest of completely dissolving the relations of slavery. Louisa Howard left her son William Turner, binding him to work for Ann Bassett on her plantation for a period of three years. Howard returned to retrieve William before the end of the contract period, and Bassett agreed to cancel the arrangement. In explanation for retrieving the boy before the contract expired, Howard said that she had not understood that he had been bound for any given period, "but only until such a time as she would require his services and as that time had come she claimed the boy."[130] Such a strategy was not unique to freedwomen in the American South. Evidence from emancipations in other slave societies suggests that freedwomen often left their children behind for periods of time, while they went in search of better employment and economic independence elsewhere, usually in cities where their skills as cooks and housekeepers were in demand.[131]

When they could, however, single or widowed freedwomen took their children with them when they left in search of work. Ex-slave Henry Reed, for instance, a child of twelve living on a plantation in Opelousas in 1865, recalled that "there were lots of 'omens left their chellums, when the sojers come. . . . I thank God my maw never left me."[132] Reed's father had died in the war, leaving his mother to care for their three boys. His mother was fortunate and was able to take her children with her when she left the plantation for Morgan City, where she probably found work as a cook or housekeeper. In the testimony of former slaves, the impetus for such a move was many times abuse and no doubt fear. Carlyle Stewart, for instance, stayed with her mother on her former owner's plantation right after the war but remembered the abuse her mother suffered from one of the plantation "bosses" after emancipation. "I was only seven but I remember when Mr. Alfred kicked my maw and make a big lump on her face." After that, her mother, a seamstress, took Carlyle and her siblings to New Orleans in a flatcar.[133] John James, who had had a run-in with Klansmen in Louisiana, narrated his move from the plantation as a story of escape. He and his mother had stayed on the plantation of their old master for a time after the war ended. But after James was chased and threatened with a beating by "white caps" when he was thirteen, mother and son left for the city: "Mammy moved to Baton Rouge soon after dat and works as de housemaid. (My pappy done die befo' I 'member him.) Us stays dere two year and I gits some little jobs and den goes to work for de railroad in Sedalia."[134]

The mothers of Carlyle Stewart and John James, as their grown children told it, left behind abuse and the terrorizing work of groups like the Klan when they left the plantation. But their mothers also broke the claims of former slaveholders when they took their children away to the city. Other freedwomen and freedmen, as we have seen, had to move toward freedom more gradually. It is in the light of such difficult choices, perhaps, that we can better understand the experiences of Dorothula and Tillie Bell. Both stories survive, as most of the past does, in brief scraps, through the words and in categories devised by others. From short pieces of typescript we get only glimpses of the childhoods of the two girls. The testimony of a white woman named Miss Tinsley, interviewed by the Federal Writers' Project, recalled the daily life of a child named Dorothula, who was "Mis' Hester's colored girl." Tinsley said that when Dorothula "was a tiny female piccaninny with her hair tied up in such a way as to remind one of a burnt-over stump field, her mammy had given her to Mis' Hester." From the time she was ten, Dorothula boarded with Hester, tending babies, washing dishes, and sweeping porches.[135] Dorothula's mother is absent in the woman's story, except as the person who relinquishes her child to a white woman. In the terms of the white woman who told it, Dorothula was "given" to the woman who employed her, a term she most likely heard the employer herself use. Though she was not an orphan, by Tinsley's account she became one when she entered the employ of Miss Hester. If we consider the evidence of other freedwomen's efforts to raise their children, then Dorothula's mother perhaps believed Miss Hester's household would be the best place to leave her child, the best way to raise her, at least until something better could be arranged.

Tillie Bell's story is even briefer, preserved in the typescript of a "work song" transcribed by an employee of the Federal Writers' Project. Tillie Bell, a former slave or the child of slaves, shared with her visitors a song that she had learned in childhood from her mother. "My ma used to sing this to us," she said. "They used to sing it on the plantation." The song was both spare and full of meaning:

> You work me all the year long and gine me an old faden
>   handkerchief
> You work me all the year long and gine me an old faden
>   handkerchief
> You work me all the year long and gine me an old faden
>   handkerchief[136]

In the lines, repeated one after another, was a commentary on plantation labor and economic injustice, voicing the sharp grief of laboring for a full year to receive only a token in payment. The distance between Bell's childhood and her mother's life on the plantation was implicit— "the plantation" was a place Bell did not know, or at least not well enough to have sung the song herself. Implied, too, was the contrast between the slaveholder's handkerchief and the demands of black people after emancipation to be justly compensated for their labor, between a paternalist's mere token and a fair wage. Sung to her free child, the song was a mother's pointed response to a brutal system in which trinkets had been exchanged for backbreaking work. It was a lesson, that is, on the difference between slavery and freedom.

5

Schooling
We Ought to Be One People

The lessons that André Grégoire gathered about freedom had not come from plantation work songs. But in early November 1868, at the age of twenty-five, Grégoire arrived in Houma, Louisiana (a town south of New Orleans surrounded by sugar plantations) to receive his teaching assignment at a school for former slaves. He had left New Orleans for Haiti nine years earlier, leaving behind the racial repressions and limitations of the late antebellum South, and the company of his schoolmates at the Catholic Institution. After his departure, his friends addressed several letters to him in Port-au-Prince. Recall, for instance, that John Blandin had asked Grégoire "if you are glad to live there." "As to ourselves," Blandin had explained, "our situation is growing worse every day." He wanted to know whether it was "good" in Haiti or at least better than in Louisiana.[1] That was a question Grégoire had hoped to answer when he sailed for Port-au-Prince. (Before Haiti, there had been Mexico. André's father had gone with an associate on a scouting trip to Veracruz in 1857 before deciding against moving his family there.)[2] Although what Grégoire experienced in Haiti is not certain, his stay there seems to have hinged on the situation in Louisiana. In the fall of 1866, at the age of twenty-three—after slavery's abolition and the Civil War's end—André Grégoire left Port-au-Prince on the *Billy Butts* bound for New Orleans.[3]

Grégoire may have left Louisiana as a student, but he returned an artisan, in the tradition of free men of color in New Orleans. His classmate, John Blandin, had written in his letter addressed to Port-au-Prince that André was working in the English consul's office in Haiti. But on the passenger list of the *Billy Butts*, Grégoire's occupation reads "carpenter," a trade into which he followed his father.[4] By 1868, however, Grégoire was ready to take up the difficult and dangerous occupation of teacher to former slaves in rural Terrebonne Parish.[5] Many teachers in schools for freedpeople, particularly those in rural areas, had already encountered resistance from local white populations. Some had been kidnapped, others shot at and otherwise generally discouraged. According to an agent for the American Home Missionary Society, the white inhabitants of Terrebonne Parish had expressed their opposition to schools for freedpeople in violent ways. In testimony before Congress in 1865, the agent reported that in Terrebonne "one colored school-house had been torn down and another burned after the withdrawal of the troops."[6]

Not only was Grégoire taking a potentially dangerous post, but he also had accepted a poorly paid one, despite the fact that he seems to have arrived in Houma with little money. The agent reported, with some consternation, that Grégoire "had not the means to pay" his stage fare from the train station and that a conveyance also had to be found to take Grégoire to the school on the Bisland Plantation, to which he had been assigned. The bureau agent, M. W. Morris, had requested some months before "a male teacher col'd." "It is the universal desire on the Plantation and as he can only be accommodated by people of that class."[7] (Accommodations had been especially difficult to secure for white teachers in rural areas of the South because white families often refused them room and board.)[8] Given Grégoire's meager finances, however, he must have been especially dismayed to learn that he would not be receiving a government salary. "Mr. Gregoír [*sic*] seems to be very dissatisfied," Morris reported. "He said he was made to understand The Govt would pay him a salary of $50.00 per month and he would not have to depend on the Pupils." "I replied in the negative," Morris explained. "But he has finally concluded to take the school, and I told him if I found him efficient in his duties I would recommend his receiving some assistance from the Bureau."[9]

Grégoire was not alone among schoolteachers needing aid, since by 1868 in Louisiana there was little or nothing to support teacher salaries outside of the small tuition paid by freedpeople themselves. When Grégoire reached Houma, a system of schools for freedpeople had been in operation for four years, since the establishment of a board of education in the Department of the Gulf by General Nathaniel P. Banks in 1864.[10] (It was this system that the sale of Rosa's and Rebecca's photographs, and their tour in the Northeast, helped to support.) By the end of 1865, there were reportedly 150 schools established in the state, with some 14,000 black children enrolled.[11] But when the board schools were turned over to the Freedmen's Bureau in 1865, it soon became clear that supporting them financially would be difficult. Banks had intended that the schools be supported by a general tax, but it had met much opposition and failed to bring in sufficient funds. Freedpeople then asked that they be taxed to support the schools, which led to a 5 percent tax on wages in rural areas and a tuition system ($1.50 or less per student) in towns. The system of schools for freedpeople in southern Louisiana soon declined, because of the inability of most freedpeople to regularly contribute to a teacher's salary.[12] Throughout the rural parishes, teachers lamented that they would no longer be able to keep their schools open because they had no means to support themselves.[13] The bureau's schools for freedchildren in Louisiana were rescued from extinction, however, in large part, by benevolent and missionary societies' stepped-up efforts and by the Republican state legislature, which passed a new state constitution in 1868. By 1869, some 16,000 black pupils were enrolled in bureau schools, although the state's superintendent of education reported that more than one-half of the "colored children" in Louisiana still did not even have minimal schooling.[14]

Grégoire must have performed well at the Bisland Plantation, because in the following month's report the agent made an application for assistance from the bureau on his behalf.[15] At this point, however, André Grégoire slips away again from the record.[16] Yet the knowledge that he returned to New Orleans from Haiti and (at least for a time) dedicated himself to the education of freedpeople, with little monetary compensation, is significant. The search for a good country took him, a free boy of color, out of the antebellum South and toward Haiti—a nation that had been a beacon of freedom for many free people of color before the Civil War.[17] But the search also led him back to Louisiana, after the Civil War and the passage of the Thirteenth Amendment abolishing slavery. That he opted to teach at a Freedmen's Bureau school might be a sign that he intended to convey his transatlantic view of racial struggle to the children of former slaves. But it most certainly points to the political value of freedchildren's education—in ideology and practice—and its importance for the future of people of color, formerly slave and free. Indeed, the politically organized and well-educated Afro-Creoles who had taught Grégoire (himself an Afro-Creole) would make public schooling an essential part of their campaign for racial equality after the Civil War. It is to their struggle on behalf of black children's education, in concert with the efforts of former slaves, that we, like André Grégoire, must return.

We have seen how the black child figured into the politics of antebellum migration for free people of color, and the meanings invested in freedchildren and their futures by reformers, freedpeople, and former slaveholders. But perhaps the most encompassing discussions of the future after slavery came in the form of arguments about freedchildren's education. After the Civil War, black children gained a new role in southern society when their access to schooling became the subject of legislative sessions and editorial columns, and when freedpeople organized to raise school funds for their children throughout the rural South. Freedpeople, formerly free people, and their allies viewed education as fundamental to the political and economic future of all people of color after emancipation. But daily struggles over freedchildren's education also made their schools targets for the Ku Klux Klan, the White League (a Louisiana organization akin to the Klan), and less organized attacks on schoolhouses, teachers, and students. Throughout the South after the Civil War, the creation of schools for the education of freedchildren was met with fierce, often violent opposition. These schools not only challenged the professed superiority of the white race but also threatened the existence of a permanent, unschooled black labor force.[18]

Although such battles occurred throughout the postbellum South, it was in southern Louisiana, and specifically New Orleans, that opposing interests in the struggle over freedpeople's education voiced the most expansive ideas about the racial future of the South and the nation, and about relations between blacks and whites after slavery. This was due, largely, to a politically organized, relatively prosperous, and highly educated population of formerly free people of color. Many of the same Afro-Creoles who had supported and instructed students at the Catholic Institution carried forward their ideals about education and racial equality into the political arena of the postemancipation South. Most of the black political leaders in Louisiana after the Civil War came from the antebellum population of free people of color, and many of these were Afro-Creoles. During Reconstruction, Afro-Creole leaders pressed for equal rights for all blacks in Louisiana, not just those of the formerly free population—rights that included equal access to education.[19] As they had with the Catholic Institution, Afro-Creole activists viewed education in the public schools as critical to the creation of an equal society. (It was this conviction, too, that likely led to André Grégoire's decision to teach in a school for freedpeople in Terrebonne Parish.) Although the activities of Afro-Creole women were not as often recorded, they also organized themselves and worked for the cause of freedpeople's education. An advertisement in the *New Orleans Tribune* in 1865 (a newspaper established in 1864 and edited largely by Afro-Creoles)[20] announced a fair to raise money for the Orphans Industrial and Educational Home for the Children of Freedmen. The fair's organizers—a list that included the wives of many of the prominent Afro-Creole leaders— invited "all benevolent persons and friends of progress" to contribute.[21]

In addition, New Orleans was the only southern city that succeeded in integrating some of its schools between 1871 and 1877, thus making it the only place in the South to experience school segregation and desegregation in both the nineteenth and the twentieth century.[22] The Louisiana Constitutional Convention of 1868, at which at least half of the delegates were formerly free men of color, created a state constitution that ordered the public schools to be open to all children, irrespective of race, color, or previous condition.[23] The political connections and experience of the city's free people of color, and their choice to throw their lot in with former slaves, made such legislation possible. Although the law applied to the whole state, the only possible place to implement it was New Orleans, where the population of black children was dispersed throughout the city and the concentration of both schools and population was relatively high.[24]

Some historians have argued that the racial composition and history of racial interaction in New Orleans made it unique, and therefore not "representative" of the rest of the South. Indeed, in other southern states, the idea of integrated education in the nineteenth century was seldom entertained or attempted.[25] Yet this "unrepresentative" place held the opening scenes in a national story about racial segregation, most notably the landmark U.S. Supreme Court case *Plessy vs. Ferguson* (1896). The *Plessy* case challenged the "Separate Car" laws and ended in the Supreme Court's endorsement of segregation based on the argument that "separate but equal" facilities were not unconstitutional.[26] The members of the Comité de Citoyens, or Citizens' Committee, which organized Homer Plessy's challenge to segregation on railcars, were Afro-Creoles. Although the *Plessy* case was testament to the radicalism and the political organization of the Afro-Creoles in New

Orleans, it was not their first legal challenge to the postbellum segregation of southern society. Public debates and court cases fighting the segregation of public schools at the end of Reconstruction, led by Afro-Creoles, preceded *Plessy* by more than a decade. As historian C. Vann Woodward argued, segregation "in racial and universal form" did not happen immediately with the end of slavery. Rather, "before it appeared in that form there transpired an era of experiment and variety in race relations of the South in which segregation was not the invariable rule."[27] Indeed, as the fight over "mixed schools" in New Orleans well illustrates, there were fervent efforts against segregation, and successful experiments in integration—proof that the system of Jim Crow that eventually claimed the South was far from inevitable.[28]

The battles over the segregation of public schools (like similar battles a hundred years later) were struggles over both space and time. While proponents fought to sustain integrated or (in the words of the Afro-Creole leaders) "common" schools—spaces defined not by race but by function—they also made fervent arguments about the negative, long-lasting consequences of segregation for the future of black and white people in the United States. They saw in 1867—the year the South entered the Radical phase of Reconstruction—the forward edge of an opportunity, the squandering of which would leave black Americans far short of equal in southern, and American, society. But opponents of "mixed schools" (the more negative term those opponents most often used) saw the future there, too, but a future that held dark prospects for the white race—especially the poorest whites. Unable to attend "mixed" public schools, this argument went, poor white children would be left in poverty and ignorance, while black children learned their letters.

In fact, the contest over "mixed" or "common" schools reflected many of the issues that slave emancipation had raised: the prospect of public education in the South, for black as well as white children; the struggles against racial discrimination in public spaces (a fight in which the Afro-Creoles of New Orleans were in the vanguard); the fears of "miscegenation" on the part of white southerners (fears that Rosa's face had once raised for many northerners) and the threat it posed to the future of the "Anglo-Saxon" nation; the concerns of reformers and politicians that integration would bring an end to public education and jeopardize the cause of "civilization" in the South; the fears of some poor whites that their children would fall behind black children because they refused to attend the same schools; and the desires of freedpeople (who were on both sides of the segregation issue, it seems) for their children to learn the skills to make them independent from whites.

At stake in the struggle over where the black child would be educated, according to the contenders in this fight, was the significance of race in the postbellum South and the future of race in the United States. The debates over the education of black children and the threat it allegedly posed to the schooling of poor (or at least nonelite) white children —debates that occurred at the local, state, and national levels—moved quickly from discussions of black children's education to the scope of American citizenship, the long-term effects of segregation, and the defense of the white man's "birthright." If the words "children" and "childhood" disappeared in the ornate language of political debate, it was because they often ceased to be separate, ideologically, from the ideas politicians, government officials, editors, and freedpeople articulated. In political discourse, the education of the black child became an extended metaphor for the future of the South, a metaphor that contained competing claims for civil rights, black equality, and white supremacy.

The debate over the education of black children in Louisiana officially began with a session of the Louisiana legislature called by Major General N. P. Banks in Union-occupied New Orleans in 1864. The assembly's purpose, at President Lincoln's prescription, was to draft a new constitution that would abolish slavery in the state and clear the way for Louisiana's readmission into the Union, in an effort to salvage the battered southern economy and restore order.[29] (The enslaved of Louisiana, by this point, had been emancipated through federal proclamation.) The delegation at the convention was all-white, elected by white male citizens who had taken the "ironclad" oath of loyalty to the Union and had lived in the state for at least a year. Its members did not come exclusively from the planter class, however. A large number came from New Orleans (sixty-three delegates, from a total of ninety-eight) and represented the concerns of the city's white residents: artisans, merchants, and the working classes. In turn, the convention passed legislation that favored small farmers, artisans, and laborers, seeking relief from the overbearing interests of the planter class. The moderate Unionism that guided many of these delegates, however, although it included the abolition of slavery, was largely opposed to any further advancement of black people's interests.[30]

Considerable time on the convention floor was devoted to the question of whether or not the state government should be responsible for the education of freedchildren. Major General Banks, head of the Department of the Gulf, had already issued an order establishing a district system of schools for freedchildren throughout the state.[31] Nevertheless, the argument over taxpayer support of black children's education surfaced throughout the constitutional debates of 1864. Former slaveholder Edmund Abell was the loudest voice in the delegation speaking for the interests of the planter class. Abell resisted the idea that emancipation was on the horizon, or even that the convention's main legislative task was to abolish slavery. (He offered, in the course of his speech making, various plans for gradual emancipation that he argued would be more fair to "masters" than immediate abolition.) Abell opposed any legislation that would allow the "property" of slaveholders to be unjustly "torn" from them and that same "property" then educated at their owner's expense.[32] (Abell refused to cede to the opposition until the final vote on emancipation had passed, and he expressed his annoyance with the education debate that preceded it as "quibbling over the education of slave children.")[33] He also framed the prospect of educating black children in terms of a race war: "The question is upon the education of the black children, and, sir, here is one who will never vote for it. Never will I vote for a measure that will imbrue the hands of the people in blood."[34]

Another representative, Alfred C. Hills (an editor who had come to the South as a writer for the *New York Herald* and an ally of General Banks), responded to Abell's dark premonitions about the education of black children with some of his own:

> I tell you the way to prevent them [from taking revenge on whites] is to educate them. (Applause.) . . . In my opinion it [is] our duty, as a matter of self-preservation, to educate this race. It is a matter of preservation for all of us to do them justice, because a race that has for ages and generations suffered injustice, may at last revolt against it. . . . Do the negro justice and you place between you and insurrection an impenetrable shield. Do them justice and they will never imbrue their hands in your blood, even if they should become stronger, which they never will and never can.[35]

By his own admission, Hills was not concerned about the prospect of racial equality: "I believe that the white race is the dominant race in this country, and always will be."[36] The educated black child, however, would serve as a buffer to protect the white race from the aggression of former slaves. From the beginning, then, black children's education was often viewed by white politicians in terms of how it would affect white people. Schooling for black children would cause a race war, or it would stave off one, but it would not be, in these politicians' view, about the interests of the black child, but rather, the white race.

If his tales of bloody resistance to the education of black children came from his allegiance to the slaveholding class, Abell also spoke for slaveholders in his disregard for public education in general. "In old Kentucky, my native State, for one hundred years, they were without public schools, and the country produced many of the noblest men in the land."[37] In response to Abell's disdain for public education, the other delegates also seized the opportunity to argue in favor of the poor white child. Hills responded to Abell's dismissal of public education by suggesting that the Civil War would never have happened had not "the mass of the people [in the South]—not the blacks, but the whites—the 'poor white trash' as they were called" been "kept down in a state of ignorance by the slaveocracy that rules and oppresses them." Because of "the general diffusion of intelligence" in the North, Hills argued, northerners were loath to enter into a war. The South would have never undertaken such a rebellion, he said, if "the children of the poor as well as the rich" had been educated.[38]

The debate over the education of black children, then, also pivoted on the neglected opportunities of the poor white child. Although some southern states—Louisiana, North Carolina, Alabama, and Kentucky—had public school systems in place before the Civil War, the notion of tax-supported common schools remained unpopular throughout most of the South until after the war.[39] The city of New Orleans had one of the more extensive public school systems in the South, launched in 1842. The Louisiana system, created five years later, grew out of the success of the New Orleans schools. But even the state system had limited reach, given the isolation of outlying parishes, entrenched political corruption, and lack of support from taxpayers.[40] With emancipation, however, the prospect of schooling for black children illuminated the clouds of "ignorance" that had been the climate of working-class, especially rural, white southern childhoods, for generations. Indeed, the story of freedpeople's determination to educate themselves and their children has often been told along with a story about working-class whites' inability to ensure the education of their own children. As W. E. B. Du Bois noted in his landmark book *Black Reconstruction in America* (1935), "The first great mass movement for public education at the expense of the state, in the South, came from Negroes."[41] Historians have argued that poor whites failed to push for the education of their own children because they bowed under the pressure of the planter class, a class on which small farmers depended economically, and a class that did not support the education of laborers, black or white.[42] Such pressure was especially difficult to confront as long as the planter class controlled the appropriation of state funds.[43] In fact, poor whites in the South would not launch an organized campaign for universal education until the Populist movement of the late nineteenth century. And it was not until the turn of the century that child labor reformers successfully lobbied for funding for the education for poor whites, in part by arguing that without it, African Americans would become more educated than whites. It was an argument divorced from reality but it was nonetheless effective.[44]

In the 1864 convention, even though many legislators professed to have no "fear" of "the African," they did have a fear of an educated black population and an uneducated white one, a possibility already raised by the school system established by General Banks, which devoted most of its energies to schools for freedpeople. The federally sponsored education of the poor black child pointed toward the neglected education of the poor white and the alarming idea, in the view of these legislators, that the "supremacy" of the white race was at stake. Some members argued against state support for the education of black children because of a perceived threat to the future of the white child. Representative C. Henry Gruneberg (according to the census, a successful "horse trader" from Lafourche Parish) said his constituents feared "that the orders of the commanding general [Banks] which provide for the education of the colored before the white ones might be followed up by laws from this assembly which would destroy the birth-right of the white man."[45] For Gruneberg and his constituents, immediate emancipation seemed to promise that black children (and eventually the black race) would overtake white ones. (He favored instead, he said, a plan for emancipation in the year 1900.) Another delegate, R. King Cutler, a conservative Unionist, said he supported the abolition of the "odious provisions" of Louisiana law in regard to slavery and was in favor of educating freedpeople, but not in "doing so hastily." Cutler did not want to see the imposition of any educational duties upon the legislature except those that would educate "the superior race of man—the white race."[46] Imposing a tax on "loyal men," Cutler said—thus charging the legislature with the maintenance of free public schools for black children—"[would] be imposing an obligation on the loyal people impossible for them to bear. It is all they can do to get the necessaries of life and educate the white race at present."[47] Another delegate agreed that white people were only responsible for their own, declaring, "I will never tax white men to educate negro children."[48]

The opposition that delegates like Abell and Cutler set up between black children and the white race occurred frequently in the political rhetoric of those opposed to the black child's education. At the very moment when many legislators were desperate to draw lines between black and white children, however, they also created a more pointed relationship between the two, one that would become yet more complicated, as we will see, with debates over school segregation. The amendment finally agreed upon was deliberately vague with regard to where the taxes for free public schools would come from—"the Legislature shall provide for the education of all children . . . by maintenance of free public schools by taxation or otherwise"—but did guarantee the legislature would provide instruction for "all children" of the state.[49]

Freedpeople chose not to wait for the goodwill of legislators before they began setting up their own schools, particularly in places where a bureau school had not yet been established. Their determination to see their children educated astonished even their most ardent advocates. When the school board in Louisiana temporarily suspended collection of the 5 percent school tax, thus promising the closure of schools for freedchildren, Major General E. R. S. Canby received a petition signed by and on behalf of ten thousand freedpeople asking for the tax to be reinstated.[50] In a resolution sent to Canby by freedpeople of East Baton Rouge Parish, they insisted: "The valuable schools now established for our children are in danger of being terminated for lack of means with which to continue them" and pleaded with the general to reinstate the tax. Their "safety," the freedpeople declared, depended upon "a development of the principles fostered in the schoolroom," and they argued that "true manhood and education go hand in hand each to support the other."[51] The strength of freedpeople's activism was witnessed firsthand by the superintendent of schools in Baton Rouge, while he was attending another mass meeting related to the school tax. "I requested that all who were in favor of supporting the school for their children by a system of 'taxation' . . . to stand on their feet. The house was crowded to over flowing, probably 1,000 were present, and *every man and woman* stood erect. I say ERECT and I mean it too, for the motion was received with a shout, and the house fairly trembled."[52]

President Andrew Johnson refused to reinstate the tax, thus cutting off the largest source of funding for freedpeople's schools. In response, freedpeople established their own associations to fund schools, like the Louisiana Relief Association, that aimed to promote the education of black children who could not afford to pay for schooling. Private schools also opened wherever possible, and in New Orleans the number of black students in private schools outnumbered those in bureau schools.[53] Indeed, teachers and bureau agents often noted freedpeople's extraordinary will to educate their children.[54] Throughout the South, freedpeople contributed their labor and what small moneys they could afford to building schoolhouses and hiring teachers. As historian Herbert Gutman suggested, the success of freedpeople's education depended upon "much more than either Yankee benevolence or federal largesse." The "communal values" freedpeople had developed under the system of slavery made the education of their children possible. In some cases, even those people who did not have children of their own to send to school insisted on contributing their labor and their money. Freedpeople in South Carolina who did not have enough money for a schoolhouse decided to set aside a piece of land to cultivate and "devote all its produce to the schools." And, at school meetings, freedpeople urged their fellows to contribute what they could—"each putting in according to his means"—so that the children of widows would have as much opportunity as other children.[55] Such cooperation was not unbroken, however, particularly under the strain of poverty. There were reports of freedpeople resisting the 5 percent tax on their earnings to pay for schools. Sometimes they did not know why their employer withheld part of their wages until an agent of the bureau explained it to them.[56] In other cases, freedpeople without children did not wish to be taxed to support the schools. And disputes arose among parents when bureau teachers admitted some students at full tuition and allowed others, with smaller means, to pay less or nothing.[57] The necessity for a statewide government-funded school system was all too apparent to teachers like André Grégoire (who had hoped to receive a government salary for his efforts) so that teachers need not depend upon students for support.

What the mass meetings and other efforts on the part of freedpeople signified (indeed what white opposition to freedchildren's education signified, too) is that with emancipation, the futures of black children took on new importance. No longer the property of the planter class with a dollar value attached, freedpeople's children had become fully their own. As we have already seen, the economic value of freedchildren, as workers, was a crucial part of freed families' survival. But black children and their education were also a source of political strength, a way out of illiteracy, and a security against the devious nature of planters and managers who would cheat those who could not read and cipher. As one freedman from Louisiana explained, "Leaving learning to your children was better than leaving them a fortune; because if you left them even five hundred dollars, some man having more education than they had would come along and cheat them out of it all."[58]

Concern for the status of white children, however, underwrote much of the political violence in opposition to freedchildren's education. For many working-class whites, especially, freedchildren's schools raised the possibility that black children might achieve a status equal to that of white children—or worse, still, in their view, a generation of black children better educated than white children.[59] Former slave Elizabeth Hite, still a child at emancipation, had personal experience with the hostility of poor whites. When she was a child, missionaries had come to her community to open Sabbath schools in an effort to educate freedpeople and were met by a band of whites determined to shut the school down. As she recalled:

> White people teached de school. Dere was religious people tryin to git de slaves [freedpeople] to go to chirch but some kind of riders came along an tol dem dat dey must not teach niggers. I heahed of de Ku Klux Klans in Texas. Dey didn't com whar I lived [in Louisiana]. Dese riders didn't wear anything over dere faces or heads. Dey was jest lak ev'ryday people. Dey was nothin but de po' white trash. Dese was de people who had nothin.[60]

They had nothing, perhaps, except their identity as white people, and in the South (as elsewhere) that was worth something. If white workers failed to acknowledge their common economic interest with freedpeople, they also chose not to recognize public education as a common cause with the black working class.[61] In turn, the education of the black child, like the freedman's vote, was a force that white people, regardless of class, often united against in order to prevent black equality from becoming a reality.[62]

Black children's education, in this light, was a ground for political struggle and negotiation as surely as electoral battles and labor disputes. When testifying before the Joint Committee on Reconstruction in 1866 (hearings called before Congress to address reports of the continued abuse of freedpeople in the South), Thomas W. Conway, an assistant commissioner with the Freedmen's Bureau in Louisiana, observed that most of the southern white population was "more hostile to the establishment of schools than they were to freedpeople owning land." Local whites had already broken up several schools where he worked, and in other parishes, after the withdrawal of Federal troops, "the freedmen's school-houses . . . were, before night, burnt or pulled down, the schools disbanded, and the teachers frightened away."[63] A black female teacher named Edmonia Highgate, from New York, reported from her post in Vermillionville, Louisiana, in the midst of this kind of violence: "God has wondrously spared me. There has been much opposition to the School. Twice I have been shot at in my room." She lived, she said, under constant threat of having the school and house where she boarded burned down around her.[64] Other teachers were not even so fortunate. Many were kidnapped (these were most often male teachers) and whipped or beaten by Klansmen or White Leaguers.[65] Other times, the perpetrators were simply classed by observers as "ruffians," like those in East Feliciana who arrived in dark of night painted up in blackface, kidnapped the teacher, a "colored" man, and nearly killed him.[66] When a young female teacher working in Donaldsonville, Louisiana, was murdered by a local militia "patrol" (it was deemed an "accident" by local authorities), the Republican *New Orleans Tribune* augured that "the record of the teachers of the first colored schools in Louisiana will be one of honor and blood."[67]

Not every nonwealthy white person who opposed the education of black children joined an organization. There was Mrs. Hyland, for instance, a woman who practiced her own outrages upon a schoolhouse in New Orleans. She was reported to be a "strong secessionist" and frequent abuser of "Unionists," with one son in the rebel army and the other living in the city who supported her. Hyland went into a "colored school" near the house where she boarded, abused the teachers, and threw stones and bricks into the schoolroom.[68] There was William

Savage, too, a man brought into provost court on charges that he had used "incendiary language" with regard to a "colored school." Testifying against Savage were a woman named Esther and a man named Alfred Johnson, both "colored." Johnson said that he had seen some children (their race was not specified) playing with fire in front of the colored schoolhouse. Johnson told the children to put the fire out, that they could "do damage," to which Savage replied that they were children and would not hurt anything. Esther testified to the same, explaining that Savage told the children the fire ought to be put in the schoolyard, and that the schoolhouse ought to be brought down, since "it would make a damned fine light for the city." Esther also testified that she had seen Savage often in front of the engine house, where he was employed to run the fire engine.[69]

Much of the resistance to black children's education took the form of smaller, daily discouragements: a former slaveholding family trying to convince their workers not to pay the school tax; townspeople refusing to offer board to schoolteachers; white boys and grown men throwing stones at freedchildren or letting their dogs loose to terrorize the children on their walk to school.[70] Yet because they had not been whipped up by a swearing mob, their violence and aggression seem more articulate than anything the White League might have orchestrated. Alone, they did not destroy a black school. Instead, their actions were in protest of what those schools represented: an overturning of the antebellum social order and a threat to the dominance of white people.

Many white commentators also saw the education of black children as a threat to their own mastery of the economy. If the black working class became educated, these whites believed, the economic order in the South would be disastrously upended. There was the southern educator we encountered earlier, for instance, who warned that "the sable pickaninny, that has to do his grammar and arithmetic, will leave your boots unblacked and your horse uncurried."[71] Such an upending, some feared, might even endanger the privileged childhoods of planters' children, sending them into a world without servants where the labor once done by black children would have to be done by white children themselves. Nuns who ran a school for wealthy white girls in rural Louisiana, for instance, were inspired to adapt the girls' education to such a course of events at the end of the Civil War. "Foreseeing the future," the nuns reported in their house journal, "we judged it best to initiate these pupils into the new position in life which Divine Providence destined for them, by teaching them to do the work formerly left to the slaves." The nuns divided their charges into teams and instructed them in "all kinds of manual and household work," setting them to chores in the kitchen and to dishwashing and ironing. "And these occupations filled not the class periods," the nuns reported, "but the time formerly given to piano lessons, practice of music and art. The children brought energy and courage to these novel occupations, as their mothers are doing in the midst of the severest reverses of fortune."[72] Most of their students would be spared hard labor because black children, by necessity, took up the cleaning rags and pressing irons that for a short time seemed to threaten the childhoods of wealthy white children. But the nuns, inadvertently perhaps, made the point that the wealth and privilege of many white children, in fact, rested upon the "manual and household" labor of black ones.

That the schooling of black children was as much an economic issue as a political one, there is little doubt. Some freedpeople refused to sign labor contracts unless planters made schooling available for their children. And some planters, in efforts to recruit laborers, set up schools by their own volition. The black child's education, in such cases, became for planters an economic investment that would sustain their labor force.[73] But while some planters recognized that schools on their property would attract workers and encourage them to sign contracts, others sought to discourage schools. There were reports of planters allowing a school for their own workers but not allowing children from surrounding areas to attend, even though the tuition drawn from only one plantation was not large enough to support a teacher.[74] One planter voiced the opinion that "the negroes had better be taught to drag the hoe 'or hold the plow' which would be of more use to them."[75] Some freedpeople were compelled by their employers to withdraw their support for freedchildren's schools if they hoped to keep their jobs.[76] Many white schoolteachers could find no local white family willing to give them board, and others faced considerable harassment from the local population if they did try to open a school in rural areas. A planter named Robert Moore, for instance, directly discouraged the education of freedchildren on his plantation by destroying a government schoolhouse on his property. Moore was reported to have declared: "I don't give a damn for the United States Government! I don't recognize the Freedmen's

Bureau! Look out now! I am going to tear the house down!"[77] For Moore, the schoolhouse was an intrusion of the federal government on his property and marked the end of an unschooled black labor force.

With perseverance, freedpeople, benevolent societies, and the bureau maintained schools for black children and outlasted many white southerners' outright opposition to them. Indeed, violent opposition to the education of black children had dissipated somewhat by the early 1870s.[78] But whereas many white southerners had come to accept schools for black children as an irreversible consequence of emancipation, they could not abide the idea of "mixed schools." The integration question, however, had been somewhat slow to rise. During the war, northern missionaries narrating the progress of their black scholars often commented on the small number of white children who also attended their schools at the request of their parents. Some missionaries admitted the white children on the condition that they attend classes with the black children. A minister in charge of a freedchildren's school during the war agreed to take in white pupils on an integrated basis, noting, "We have often thought that these 'poor whites' stood as great need of school privileges as the negroes, for they are quite as ignorant."[79] But these efforts at integration did not satisfy many poorer whites. To a missionary teacher in South Carolina, a mother explained why she had to withdraw her children from a school for freedchildren, even though there was not a separate school available for white children: "I would not care myself, but the young men laugh at my husband," she said. "They tell him he must be pretty far gone and low down when he sends his children to a 'nigger school.' That makes him mad, and he is vexed with me."[80] With slavery abolished, poor whites in the South may have gained a certain amount of social status by refusing to send their children to schools with freedchildren, cashing in, in a very public way, on their identities as white people.[81] Under such circumstances, some teachers doubled their workload by setting up separate classes for white children and black children at different times of the day.[82] A missionary directing a school for white children in Baton Rouge found poor white parents to be grateful for his efforts. As one parent explained to him, "We have thought it hard that the colored people should have all the free schools."[83] The same missionary, a year later, had to close this school for lack of a teacher and reported that the children's parents were quite anxious about it, since they did not have the money to pay for schooling and were convinced "that the North should care for them as well as for the colored people."[84]

Before the passage of a new state constitution in 1868, the superintendent of schools appointed by the Democratic legislature, Robert Lusher, directed all the resources of his office toward the education of white children, for precisely the reason that the missionary in Baton Rouge described—that is, Lusher believed that the education of white children had been neglected in favor of freed black children. Lusher was a loud proponent of public schools, declaring in his report to the legislature in 1867 that "modern civilization is based on the education of the masses." He appealed to the legislature, explaining: "The war has increased the number of neglected children; the State must, if possible, double her love and tenderness towards them."[85] But Lusher's "neglected children" were white, not black. In a circular sent to all parish assessors in 1866, he wrote: "It is indispensable to the future honor and prosperity of Louisiana, and to the supremacy of the Caucasian race in her councils, that the benefit of a liberal education should be extended to every white child within her limits."[86] (The only mention of freedchildren in his opening remarks in the 1867 report appeared in his discussion of the "now wandering children of freedmen" who would benefit, with the rest of the state's "industrial classes," from the establishment of model farms and mechanical workshops for instruction.)[87] To the sheriffs of the state, in appealing for the collection of taxes, he asked, "Can any such citizen refuse this mite in behalf of the moral, mental, and social improvement *of his own race*?" In response to the "Radical" politicians' criticisms regarding the neglected education of the state's poor whites, perhaps, Lusher predicted that white citizens would "vindicate the *honor and supremacy of the Caucasian race*" and contribute their share of taxes to the school fund.[88] Lusher's concern, like those of the legislators who debated education for freedchildren in 1864, was for the maintenance of white supremacy in the face of perceived challenges to it in the form of education for black children.

Public schools brought black children and nonelite white children into a new relationship to one another, one that hinged on race alone rather than on the legal divide of racial slavery. They raised the possibility that black and white children could be educated together, a possibility that was answered, in most places, by stiff segregation over the course of Reconstruction.[89] The only southern states where integration in public schools could have become a reality were those with black majorities, where blacks held enough votes in the legislatures, namely, Louisiana, Mississippi, and South Carolina. But there was little chance of school integration succeeding in rural areas, where black laborers remained hemmed in economically by the interests of landowners, and black schools vulnerable. The cities of Charleston and New Orleans seem to have been the only possible places to implement school integration. But while South Carolina's Republican legislature required that schools be integrated, this requirement was opposed by powerful state officials and never enforced. In New Orleans, however, a city of two hundred thousand with a diverse population of blacks, immigrant laborers, and whites, the black population was dispersed throughout the city, making "mixed" schools less difficult to sustain. Further, the city's Afro-Creole leaders had the political connections and resources—including a newspaper, the *New Orleans Tribune*, an official organ of the Republican Party founded by Afro-Creoles and published in English and French—to further the cause of integrated schools. As we will see, they also enrolled their own children in the public schools and later challenged school segregation in court.[90]

While only a handful of black leaders in New Orleans during Reconstruction had been enslaved (and many of those had been manumitted as children), the Afro-Creole leadership allied itself with freedpeople in its campaign for racial justice and equality, rather than seek privileges as a caste above former slaves within New Orleans society.[91] When accused of being an elite interest by former abolitionists, the editors of the *Tribune* retorted, in 1864, that it was the "organ of the oppressed, whether black, yellow, or white."[92] At mass meetings the same year calling for the organization of the National Equal Rights League (an idea launched by Frederick Douglass and other black leaders to address the abuses inflicted upon freedpeople in the South that preceded the creation of the Freedmen's Bureau), prominent free black men addressed the issue of unity between freedpeople and the formerly free blacks in Louisiana. They argued that such unity was necessary to protect and defend themselves: "Those very enemies of our political rights are the same who are now denying the freedmen the enjoyment of their natural rights." These leaders viewed themselves as the educated protectors of uneducated former slaves. But they recognized that the relationship would be mutually beneficial:

The emancipated will find, in the old freemen, friends ready to guide them, to spread upon them the light of knowledge and teach them their duties as well as their rights. But, at the same time, the freemen will find in the recently liberated slaves masses to uphold them. And with this mass behind them they will command the respect always bestowed to number and strength.[93]

If their tone was patronizing, it was also politically keen and seems to have been genuine, given that they supported the creation of offices to field complaints from freedpeople regarding abuses and wage disputes. The editors of the *Tribune* also supported the New Orleans Freedmen's Aid Association, formed in 1865, which proposed a plan to buy confiscated land from the government and divide it up into small plots to lease to freedpeople for cultivation.[94]

The sentiment behind this alliance between formerly free people of color and freedpeople was clearly put into practice during debates over "mixed" or "common" schools, with the understanding that the division of schools into "white" and "colored" would harm the chances of all black children. Well before a "mixed-school" controversy erupted in New Orleans, Afro-Creole Republicans and their white allies had begun to speak out against the segregation of schools. In 1865, the state's Democratic legislature passed a school bill declaring that "white and colored children shall not be taught in the same school" and that "they shall be kept separate and distinct *under all circumstances.*"[95] The *Tribune* responded with outrage. (One of the *Tribune*'s editors, Paul Trévigne, who had also been a teacher at the Catholic Institution, would later launch a court case to stop segregation of the schools.)[96] Lashing out at what they perceived was indifference to the question of equality, even by former abolitionists, they wrote: "If we have done [away] with slavery, not so with the aristocracy of color." In the eye of old proslavery Democrats, and even some former abolitionists, "free and freed persons of color are not . . . real and complete men, made in the image of their Creator. They are held as a kind of bastard race, half-way between man and ape, a race that the law has to protect in some form, but that men of Caucasian, and particularly of Anglo-Saxon descent, can only look upon with disdain." According to the *Tribune*, the bill passed by the legislature ordering separate schools was "marked by a kind of repulsion or fear of colored children, in the same manner that the denizens of infested cities feared, during the Middle Ages, the unfortunate leper."[97]

The *Tribune* viewed the segregation of schools not just as an affront to all people of color but also as an intervention by lawmakers that would have long-term consequences for race relations in the South. The editors proclaimed that clearly "it was not enough to perpetuate from childhood the infatuation of the white, and prompt the black to retaliate by inmity [*sic*] or envy; it was not enough to draw a line between two elements of one and the same people, from the cradle itself up to the time of manhood and throughout life." Indeed, the *Tribune* said, the lawmakers had gone further, to declare that the schools for black and white children should be "at least half a mile apart," which suggested that white politicians feared either "moral or physical contagion" would be spread from black child to white. Further still, the law declared that a minimum of fifteen children of any given race would be required for the opening of a school for that group. If there were not enough children of one race in a given area, those children would have to go miles away to the nearest school. The editors argued that "this only show[s] the absurdity of making two peoples with one, two nations without, two bands of enemies with one of brethren."[98]

The long-term consequences of segregated schools, the *Tribune*'s editors argued, were too grave to be ignored. "For colored children," they declared, "we want that they shall be received in the common schools, as it is done in Massachusetts. We want to see our children seated on the same benches with the white girls and boys, so that every prejudice of color may disappear from childhood, and the next generation be aroused to a sentiment of fraternity."[99]

The Afro-Creoles at the *Tribune* got their opportunity to press for integrated schools in 1867, with the passage of the Reconstruction Acts in Congress, against a presidential veto, that would clear the way for a new constitution in every state of the former Confederacy. After the widespread reports of political violence voiced before the Joint Committee on Reconstruction in Congress, and two bloody riots in 1866 in New Orleans and Memphis, Congress had begun to implement a Radical Reconstruction plan to counter the damage done by President Johnson's more lenient policies.[100] The South was divided into five military districts under federal authority and new elections ordered for the creation of legislatures that would pass new state constitutions. Statewide elections in Louisiana brought forty-nine black and Afro-Creole delegates into the state legislature for the first time. The other forty-nine delegates were white, and for the most part Unionist in sympathies. Fourteen of the white delegates were northern "carpetbaggers." Most men of color elected had been free before the war, and many of them were Afro-Creoles from New Orleans. This delegation pressed forward the most radical new state constitution in the South, one that mandated integrated schools, protected the rights of married women, prohibited segregation on public conveyances, mandated state support for the mentally ill and physically impaired, secured pensions for veterans of the War of 1812 (among them, Afro-Creole soldiers), and included a bill of rights modeled on the U.S. Constitution.[101] The Afro-Creole leaders had viewed the Civil War—during which a majority of them had served the Union army, some as officers—in the context of earlier revolutions in the Atlantic World, in Haiti in 1791 and in France in 1848. With the end of the war and the rewriting of the state constitution, they saw an opportunity to fulfill their vision of an equal society, free of slavery and racial inequality.[102]

From the first report of the Education Committee at the convention of 1867, the majority of its members proposed the establishment of integrated schools. Only a handful of delegates (twelve of seventy-three) voted against the final version of Article 135:

> All children of this State between the ages of six (6) and twenty-one (21) shall be admitted to the public school or other institutions of learning sustained or established by the State in common without distinction of race, color, or previous condition. There shall be no separate schools or institutions of learning established exclusively for any race by the State of Louisiana.[103]

Some of those opposed to the article chose to submit their reasons for the record. A physician from Baton Rouge named George Dearing, for instance, insisted that he was in support of tax-supported public schools but believed that "a large number don't want this" and declared himself "unwilling to inaugurate a system of schools in the present immoral state of society which I am forced to believe will have such a demoralizing influence." Others offered the idea that integrated schools would not be "safe" or "practicable" and that making such a system mandatory would "break up our free public school system, or at least virtually exclude the colored children from all participation therein."[104] But

Victor Lange, a black property holder from East Baton Rouge, spoke for the majority of the black delegates when he affirmed his vote in favor of the Constitution and the provision for integrated public schools because in addition to guaranteeing the rights of all citizens, "it follows the free school system, secures to my child and to all children throughout the state their education which their forefathers have been deprived of for two hundred and fifty years, and I shall sign the Constitution without any hesitation."[105]

The editors at the *Tribune* had urged lawmakers during the convention to pass legislation for integrated or "common" schools, pointing to the economic and social consequences of a segregated system. "There is a great object to be carried out by common education of both races. Why should we not inaugurate that move at once—before money is squandered to organized 'star schools.'" The Afro-Creoles (led by Robert Isabelle, one of the first blacks commissioned by the Union army and legislator in the convention of 1867) had successfully defeated attempts to establish "star cars" on the city's streetcar line in 1867, the star intended to designate cars for blacks.[106] There is one mention of these cars, and the dissatisfaction they caused before they were abolished, in one of the student's letters at the Catholic Institution. A student named "Valentine" wrote to "J. R. Slawson, Esq." in 1861, and his letter sheds light on the frustrations of a population experiencing a public system of segregation for the first time:

> Please excuse me of the liberty I take in writing you these words, it is in order to let you know that the colored persons are not satisfied with you for they say that you do not send out enough cracked stars; about three or four times I heard them saying that if there was not more cracked stars at future time they would quit going in, because every time that they want to go in, they must wait half an hour at a corner, so you can see that you will lose if you do not follow that advice.[107]

Valentine's letter clearly explained the frustrating inefficiency of the "star cars" and the effective strategy of a boycott proposed by people of color. And it documents the early experience of segregation for a group that would fight it fiercely in the courts into the 1890s.

But the segregation of schools could not be fought with consumer boycotts or with force. While the article on integrated schools was being debated in the legislature, the editors of the *Tribune* made their own arguments about the importance of the legislation to the reconstruction of the nation as a whole. In this, they saw the creation of "common" schools as critical: "In order to have only one nation and one people, we must educate all children in the same public schools."[108] Where the nation had been divided on the battlefield into Republicans and Democrats, northerners and southerners, school segregation would divide the country by race. For those who insisted that it was "too soon" to teach the black and the white child in the same classroom, the editors of the *Tribune* outlined the dangers of turning a blind eye to the future:

> When will the right time come? Is it, per chance, after we will have separated for ten or twenty years the two races in different schools, and when we shall have realized the separation of this nation into two peoples? The difficulty, then, will be greater than it is to-day. A new order of things, based on separation, will have taken root. It will, then, be TOO LATE.[109]

Taking into account segregation's indelible nature and potential longevity, therefore, the editors framed the question of separate schools in Louisiana—indeed, the segregation of black and white children for generations—in terms of nation rather than region. They used a language of civil rights and nationhood to batter down the idea of segregated education. The figures of children, black and white, held within them the possibility of equal citizenship. "The prosperity and, above all, the strength of this nation, as one of the powers on earth, depends upon our union of classes in patriotism," the editors concluded. "Do not make any longer white and black citizens; let us have but Americans."[110]

The *Tribune*'s editors also decried the opposition to "common" schools offered up by "all the white dailies of the city, the Republican included," which were "opposing the idea of common schools and advocating the principle of race schools." They framed their argument in favor of common schools in the context of other innovations that had been opposed by conservatives but had been proven worthwhile and successful—namely, the arming of black men in the Civil War and universal suffrage for men. The editors accused Republicans who did not endorse the mixed-school idea of playing "into the hands of rebels; experience did not enlighten them. They are still behind time, trying the impossible task of conciliating a class of men who do not want to be conciliated." Further, there was "a national interest in destroying" the "rebel schools" that had educated the sons of the Confederacy. "When the right of suffrage was conferred upon all citizens, the rebels realized the downfall of their political supremacy. Now let them understand by the breaking up of their schools that they will not be allowed to raise a class of rebel children."[111]

Democratic papers like the *New Orleans Daily Picayune*, on the other hand, reviled the idea of "mixed schools" altogether, interpreting them as partisan instruments devised by Radical Republicans for the degradation of white children and white families. They met the *Tribune*'s language of nation and citizenship with the language of a violated domestic circle. In the Democrats' representations, the interests of black children were "political," but the interests of white children were not. The *Picayune*'s editors suggested that the proposed amendment to admit black and white children to the same schools was an attempt "to found and keep up a nursery for the propagation and support of Radicalism, with its train of foul and destructive theories and isms." This would not happen without a fight, the *Picayune*'s editors declared. In their view, the state superintendent of education, Thomas Conway (a veteran of the Freedmen's Bureau), was forcing black equality down the throats of white southerners, something that could not be tolerated. The graveness of this threat, however, was articulated through thinly veiled fears of interracial sex: "Nor will [Conway] and his army of male teachers, or constables, be permitted to seize white children from their parents or guardians, to force them into his miscegenating school houses. If he attempts to do so, it will surely be at the cost of blood; for even tender, timid women will become as brave as stern warriors in the face of such outrage."[112]

The question of integrated schoolrooms led opponents to situate white children within protected domestic space, under the care of "their parents or guardians." Unlike segregation in streetcars or hotels, the segregation of schoolrooms could be framed more easily as a direct challenge to the white domestic sphere. To remove the white child from that space—with an "army of male teachers," no less—was to take the white child out of its "natural" domestic setting. The innocence of the white child, in such representations, was threatened by the political needs of the black one. Hence, the white child was thrust mercilessly into the political ring when forced through the doors of "miscegenating schoolhouses." The sexualizing of integrated schoolrooms further pressed the point that the white domestic sphere was being violated. Indeed, the public debate over separate schools in the nineteenth century was voiced in a political language not so different from that of northern abolitionists pointing to the threat of slavery to seemingly white children like Rosa and Rebecca. The sexual threat to the "purity" of white children ran through both discussions, though after emancipation the roles were reversed: the "perpetrators" were Republicans, and proslavery factions were outraged. Yet in both cases, the interests of the black child slipped from view, while the well-being and "purity" of the white child seemed to be endangered.

It is difficult to know how many freedpeople and free people of color supported the idea of "mixed schools." An investigation launched by the New Orleans school board in 1867 into the opinions of teachers in the schools of the Freedmen's Bureau found educators on both sides of the issue. The results of the investigation were tainted by the fact that both black and white bureau teachers faced losing their jobs when the city school board assumed control of bureau schools, should they voice opposition to segregation. The responses of black teachers were particularly guarded, whereas white teachers seemed quite convinced that having separate schools for white and black children was the only possible arrangement.[113] Integration received most of its support from the downtown section of the city, where the French-speaking Creole population, white and colored, lived. Armand Lanusse, still the head of the Catholic Institution, even refused to speak with the board's investigators, since he opposed the conservative school board and considered it to be illegitimate.[114]

Many of the teachers interviewed in New Orleans, both black and white, reported that the parents of their black pupils were opposed to the idea of segregated schools. A white woman named Cornelia Clarkson teaching at a bureau school reported that when parents found out that the school system was to be integrated, they "requested her to continue her school exclusively for colored children, saying that they did not wish their children to go to school with white children" and assuring her that they would continue to pay tuition if she would keep her school open. Clarkson explained that "none of the colored people except those actively engaged in politics, and those so near white that they are unwilling to associate exclusively with colored persons and thereby acknowledge their race, desire their children to be mixed with whites in the same schools."[115] A pair of white teachers reported that they received a petition from three hundred parents asking them to keep the school open solely for black children. Many of the black teachers, like P. M. Williams, who taught at a bureau school, insisted that black children had the right to attend any public school. But many of these same teachers testified, as Williams did, that "under the circumstances existing in the city at present" it was in the black children's best interest to keep the schools segregated.[116] Some freedpeople with children also feared the violence that might erupt (and did a few years later) and were concerned that mixed schools might also distract their children from getting a good education. One black woman in New Orleans said that she did not want her children to suffer blows at the hands of white children in an integrated school. "I don't want my children to be pounded by dem white boys," she said. "I don't send them to school to fight, I send them to learn."[117]

Even among advocates of freedchildren's education, the question of separate or mixed schools was the subject of debate. In 1867, the Louisiana Educational Association (supported by the American Missionary Association) held a forum on the issue, in response to the impending Constitution of 1868. A "colored" man from Ohio, named Roxborough, "spoke at considerable length in favor of accepting the proposition proposed by the old school board for the education of colored children in New Orleans in separate schools, at the public expense." He believed that the call for integrated schools had "no well founded basis" but, rather, sprang "from a sentimentality rather than a principle." The Reverend Dr. J. B. Smith, on the other hand, a white man, argued that "separate schools would perpetuate distinction of color, and tend to degrade those who attend them." Smith had been a teacher for twenty-six years, and for some part of that, teaching white children. According to the published record of the meeting, he related that the separate school system that had existed in New York resulted in iniquities in terms of school buildings and the quality of teachers provided for black children: "In addressing himself to the colored portion of the audience he said, every right, every privilege, every advantage is due to you, and you never will obtain them for your children in separate schools as you will in schools where there is no distinction of color." Finally, Edmonia Highgate, the black female teacher from New York who had taught in a bureau school in a rural parish, declared that "she would rather starve than to stoop one inch on [the separate school] question," and that she would resign her current post rather than subject it to the rules of the old school board. "If I cannot live in the city I can go into the country as a teacher where I have been before, exposed to rebel bullets which were aimed at my head, but fell harmless at my feet."[118]

In the same spirit as Edmonia Highgate, the Louisiana legislature of 1868 signed into law Article 135, mandating that "all children of this State" should be admitted to the public schools "in common without distinction of race, color or previous condition."[119] The first test of the new law seems to have occurred at the Bayou Road School for girls. After a group of young girls were admitted to the school, the renegade city school board, not yet under Republican control, launched an investigation hoping to discern whether or not the girls were white. When the superintendent inquired about whether or not there were any "colored" children at the school, the principal of the school replied: "When those children were admitted it was never to my knowledge that they were colored; but a few days after their admission, some of our pupils in their neighborhood would report that they were not white." The principal listed twenty-eight girls under suspicion enrolled and closed her letter with: "There may be others unknown to us."[120]

Flying in the face of state law, the board proceeded to search out any nonwhite students from the public schools set aside for white children. In a resolution that revealed the difficulty of finding the kind of children it was looking for, the board pronounced that, based on information from "parents and citizens," it appeared that "*more or less colored* children have been smuggled into the Schools set apart for the education of white children." Principals of white schools were instructed to search out any "children of color" from among their students and transfer them immediately. But, "in the case of grave doubt as to the status of any pupil," then the board would examine the case individually.[121] Several such incidents did arise, and the superintendent sent letters addressed to the children's parents—to be carried home by the children—demanding proof that their children were not of "mixed blood." Apparently this "proof" could take the form of "documentary evidence or testimony of sworn witnesses."[122] Most of these parents refused to provide documentation of their children's racial status, and the girls in question were ordered to leave the school. In the case of Blanche and Julia Dauphine, for instance, the board notified the girls' father that "some well known citizens have denied the right of your children . . . to attend the schools which have been established exclusively for white children." One child, Olivia Edmunds, was reported to have received admittance to the school "upon a certificate of white birth." But the evidence against her "by well known citizens" seems to have "discredited" her proof of all-white lineage.[123]

The difficulties encountered by the board members who took on the role of ethnologist were not novel, especially in Louisiana, as the white-looking Rosa and Rebecca so well illustrated, but the context of their separation of white from black gave the work of reading race new meaning. In trying to separate them, the board deepened and complicated the children's political relationship to one another. In denying black children (who were, by law, equals to their white counterparts) the "privilege" of education with white children, they encouraged what the *Tribune* termed "infatuation of the white" from the perspective of white children and the "inmity [*sic*] or envy" among "colored" children. In fact, the *Tribune* chastised the Republican-controlled legislature for being slow to put forward a school bill that would enforce the 1868 constitution's decree for common schools. "Let our people in the city and parishes understand that without education their rights are never safe," the editors wrote.

> . . . Let not the people be cheated out of their most indispensable blessing. Their eyes are upon you. They watch you[r] proceedings with eager interest. Let them not be disappointed. The children of our State must have the means of a solid education. You, men of the Assembly are legislating about canals and drainage and railroads and such things. We say to you, Give us canals to drain off ignorance, and to convey throughout all the districts the healthful waters of truth. Enforce the educational provisions of the Constitution. We fought hard for that. Let it not be a dead letter.[124]

It was not until 1870 that the system of segregation that had sent Blanche and Julia Dauphine away from the Bayou Road School was dissolved. (By then, members of the state legislature had reordered the entire state school system, and a court order finally led the old school board to disband.)[125] In 1871, the new school board in New Orleans—a board that would, before 1877, contain the prominent Afro-Creoles Victor Eugene McCarthy, Henry Louis Rey, Paul Trévigne, and African American senator P. B. S. Pinchback—began to enforce the state law against separate schools, and several black students were admitted to previously all-white schools.[126] Democratic editors, in turn, interpreted the creation of mixed schools as eminently political acts, ones that were forced upon white parents and children. According to the *Picayune* (under the headline "Infamy Consummated"): "The foul work is completed and our public schools are subjected to that admixture of races which must inevitably destroy them."[127] When this prophecy had not been realized by 1872, the paper's editors tried other arguments. "The schools," the *Picayune* declared, "should not be an instrument in the hands of the educator to break down social barriers and mould the opinion of childhood."[128] Segregation, the editors suggested, might *seem* political in that "the colored race must be considered as a nation by itself so far as it relates to education." But in reality, it was the natural order of things, "a fact most thoroughly fixed in human nature and in our condition, that the children of whites will never be mixed in private or public schools with the children of the colored."[129] Integration (in the interests of black children), in this view, was both against nature and decidedly political, while segregation (in favor of the white child) was "the natural order of things." In what would become a common refrain in the South after Reconstruction, segregation was characterized as the only "natural" means of ordering society and any opposition to it brazenly political.[130] The paradox of segregation—that if segregation was the "natural order of things," it would not need legal force— seemed to have missed the editors altogether. Indeed, this segregation-as-"nature" argument was one southern Democrats would oil and polish over time until, as the *Tribune*'s editors predicted, it was "TOO LATE" and the South had divided into "two peoples."

That an integrated system, which by many accounts seemed to be working, could be interrupted only by violent mobs exposed the absurdity of the "natural" segregation argument. Though many white parents withdrew their children from the public schools in 1870, many of those same children also returned after a time. Historians estimate that nearly a thousand black children attended integrated schools in the city between 1870 and 1877, with the city system divided roughly into thirds, with white, integrated, and black schools.[131] Many educators were of the opinion that the integrated schools were the most successful of all the public schools.[132] Writer George Washington Cable, while touring the city's public schools as a reporter for a Democratic paper, had an epiphany when he witnessed "children and youth of both races standing in the same classes and giving each other peaceable, friendly, effective competition."[133] A similar sentiment was expressed in 1874 by then former superintendent of education for the Freedmen's Bureau

T. W. Conway, who said he had endeavored "to put the system of mixed schools to a thorough, practical test." In the first days of desegregation, all the white pupils left. A few days later, however, "to my surprise [I] found nearly all the former pupils returned to their places; and that the school, like all the schools in the city, reported at the close of the year a larger attendance than any time since the close of the war. The children were simply kind to each other in the school-room as in the streets and elsewhere!" Conway advised: "All that is wanted in this matter of civil rights is to let the foes of the measure simply understand that we mean it. Do this, and as in the case of the enemies of free schools in Louisiana, they will be quiet."[134]

The debate reached the national level after Louisiana and South Carolina both wrote mandates for integrated schools into their state constitutions. Radical Republicans in Washington, led by Senator Charles Sumner of Massachusetts, tried to attach "mixed-school" clauses to legislation multiple times between 1867 and 1874, never with success. "If I should have my way," Sumner said in 1867, "according to the true principle, it would be that the schools, precisely like the ballot-box or the rail cars, should be open to all."[135] In the North, officials had already begun integrating the public schools. Sumner had led the campaign to integrate the schools in his home state of Massachusetts in the 1850s. And after the passage of the Fourteenth Amendment, black children in the North could no longer be denied access to a public education, and some, though not all, large city school systems began to teach black and white children in the same classrooms. (Public schools in Philadelphia were not integrated until the 1930s.)[136]

The heated debates that the prospect of mixed schools in the South produced at the national level, however, were some of the most explicit discussions on record about the political future of race relations after emancipation. Responding to the passage of mixed-school clauses in South Carolina and Louisiana in 1868, Representative James Beck, Democrat from Kentucky, argued that the greatest evil of "compulsory education of girls and boys at the same school as the negroes" was that it would deprive the poor white child of an education. "They are all mixed together. A poor man cannot help himself." The wealthiest in the South could send their children to all-white schools, but after the recent conflict, "few of the most intelligent and respectable people are really able to afford the means of education such as they used to afford" and would be forced to send their children to mixed schools. "I can scarcely conceive of a more despotic, galling and degrading provision in the fundamental law of a State pretending to be free."[137]

When southern Democrats sparred with Radical Republicans over a "mixed-school clause" in state constitutions, however, the southerner often sidestepped this issue of civil rights and instead fixated on "miscegenation." In 1872, during an attempt by Sumner to attach mixed-school legislation as a rider to an amnesty bill directed at the South, Senator Thomas M. Norwood, a Democrat from Georgia, balked. Norwood saw in mixed schools the potential for an (unwelcome) erasure of the color line:

> You propose by the amendment, in the first place, to put the children together in schools. There you make no distinction. There you teach the young and tender mind by this association that you believe there is no distinction between the two races. They grow up under that early impression until they ripen into manhood and womanhood. You then throw open the churches to them. There you allow them to sit in the same pews. The same familiar association continues from childhood up to manhood, and when they have arrived at manhood you then, by your statute, say that if they see fit to join in matrimony there shall be no impediment to it.[138]

Ironically, in his opposition, Norwood echoed the desires of those in favor of mixed schools: "I would ask [Sumner] or any other Senator, if the clause which I have called attention to shall be enacted, what distinction will then exist between the whites and blacks in a social point of view?"[139] Social equality, in white southern parlance, was becoming ever more tightly laced with physical contact and sexual transgression across a color line that was still in its drafting stage.[140] Representative John Thomas Harris, a Virginia Democrat, in the same session, said that mixed schooling "is wrong in principle and contrary to the laws of God." "What relation is so absolutely social as the mingling of children at school?" he asked. "Test this doctrine at your own hearthstones; offer your little children who are not influenced by party or revenge a social entertainment, and tell them they must invite as many black as white children, and see how quick God will speak through their innocent lips, 'Then we will have no party, we will have no party.'"[141]

Republicans took aim at such white southern evasions of their interracial history. For example, William Kelley from Pennsylvania urged his colleague from Virginia not to become overly concerned about the prospect of white children attending school with black ones. Alluding to antebellum sexual relations between white men and black women in the South, he offered the following: "If, as he seems to apprehend, such schools should be forced upon the people of this and other States, it will in the South be but temporary," he quipped. "For all men know that the sun and atmosphere of the southern states soon bleach the blackest African, both in hair and complexion, to the colors characteristic of the purest Saxon lineage."[142] Kelley also spoke of his tour of schools for freedpeople in the southern states, including "the gentlemen's own state of Virginia," and there "found in each and all of them pupils of Saxon hue and Caucasian feature." When he congratulated the teachers for opening their schools to white and black, he was informed that all of the children in attendance were "the children of freedmen": "As the gentleman says there is no intercourse between the children of the different races because white children abhor it, I would like to learn the age at which the abhorrence ceases, or whether it is the effect of the climate of the South that so changed the complexion and features of those Virginians of African descent."[143]

A mixed-schools clause was again attached to legislation before being removed, in 1874, this time from the civil rights bill of 1875. More than one opponent of mixed schools in these congressional debates made the argument that to force (as one politician put it) "this sum of villainies and quintessence of abomination known as the 'coeducation of the races'" would mean the certain end to all public schooling in the South. In an address delivered in Tennessee used in the congressional debate, Senator W. G. Brownlow predicted that "if the civil rights bill should pass without the mixed-school feature being stricken out, the whole school fabric in Tennessee will at once fall to the ground, as it will deserve to do." For Brownlow, "it is not a question as to whether we will have mixed schools, but whether we shall have any system of public education at all."[144] Senator George Edmunds, Republican of Vermont, responded to such arguments with statistics drawn from the southern states to illustrate the great disparity between the moneys spent on black children's education and those of white children. In Georgia, for example, Edmunds stated that where black children made up 43 percent of the school-age population, they could attend only 13 percent of the public schools. In this, he foresaw a danger that through segregated education the state would "feed the white at the expense of the black, in order that the ancient order of things, the aristocracy of the races, may again be restored."[145] For all their pointed arguments, however, Radical Republicans in Congress failed to successfully attach a mixed-school clause to what became the Civil Rights Act of 1875. The clause was defeated by a combination of Democratic opposition and ambivalence among members of the Republican Party, including some moderate black Republicans who insisted that the freedpeople of their states were generally not in favor of mixed schools.[146]

The debate over the Civil Rights Act and its mixed-schools clause in Congress led to a sharp upsurge in activity among Louisiana's White League in 1874, during which vigilante groups aimed to close down New Orleans's integrated schools. That same year, the White League launched a series of attacks on the Republican-controlled state government. When those attacks were put down by Federal troops, the league shifted its focus from government-directed terrorism to an attempt to compel the segregation of the city's schools.[147] Reports of "regulating" bands of high school boys began appearing in the papers. But the *New Orleans Republican,* recognizing their connection to the league, reported them to be "large sized boys" and "white regulators."[148] The league went to a girls' high school on Royal Street, where white girls attended as well as a few black girls and light-skinned mulattoes. Terrorizing the girls, the leader of the group called the class roll and judged them one by one. Once they had (or so they thought) separated the "white" from the "colored," the White Leaguers ordered the "colored" girls expelled from the school. Although the girls left, with the angry mob outside the school, they were reinstated several days later, the law mandating integrated schools being still in effect. A similar "regulating" incident occurred at another girls' school attended by several black students. By this time, white and black people had gathered outside the school, and a fight broke out. In the scuffle several people were injured, and one man was killed.[149]

The regulators, like the school board in the Bayou Road incident in 1868, found it difficult to be certain which girls were white and which were not. This, according to the superintendent's report the next year, was what finally ended their "regulating" spree: "Pupils were forcibly driven from halls of examination and classrooms, under the suspicion of being tainted with colored blood; nor did the acts of violence cease until the 'committee' became unable to decide upon the true lineage of the young ladies, and feared that too much scrutiny would carry them upon dangerous ground."[150] Indeed, they inadvertently insulted white students during their raids. According to an account in *Harper's Weekly,* "The question of color was one that not even the sharpest inquiry could decide. Indignant parents, noted in the gay society of New Orleans, frowned at the insult that had been put upon their children; young maidens of the purest blood were frequently the objects of the mistaken ardor of the young crusaders, and were forced to prove that they were white." The *Harper's* writer argued that the experiment of mixed schools in the city would have continued to run smoothly were it not for the intrusion of the "regulators." "All races and classes were mingled in the mixed schools, or divided, according to the tastes or nationality, as they chose; and it was not until the recent foolish outbreak of the White League, young and old, that any danger threatened the course of education in New Orleans."[151]

The absurdity of their efforts eventually ground the White League raids to a halt. After calm was restored, the schools continued as before, though Democratic newspapers weakly claimed a tentative victory: "All of the pupils in attendance are thought to be white, although concerning a few it is hinted that they may be of negro blood. The color line is, however, so very vaguely defined in their feature that no one cares to assume the task of pronouncing judgment in the matter."[152] The *New Orleans Bulletin* accused the school board superintendent of devising a particular method for integrating the schools: "At first he moved cautiously, and only put in light-colored mulattoes; then he tried children of a darker hue, until finally he succeeded, in a few instances, in placing negro girls as black as ebony side by side with the fairest Caucasian."[153] Several months later, after the riots had dissipated, another Democratic paper expressed horror that a female teacher of one of the public schools had decided that "the daughters of white citizens and the children of their negro employe[e]s" would march through the streets, holding hands. "What pretext is given for this outrage," the editors wrote, "or wherein either child can in the slightest degree be benefitted, we have not the remotest conception."[154] To the disappointment of Democratic editors and politicians, however, integrated schools continued in New Orleans until the end of Reconstruction. By some estimates between five hundred and one thousand students attended mixed schools under the integrated system.[155] The school superintendent who reinstated segregated schools in 1877 estimated that several months after the start of *resegregation,* there were still some three hundred children attending mixed schools.[156]

The compromise in 1877 that put Rutherford B. Hayes, a Republican, in the White House also guaranteed Democrats that the last Federal troops would be pulled out of the South, ultimately leading to the collapse of Republican state governments.[157] With the restoration of Democratic power at the level of state and local government came the appointment of a new school board aimed at the segregation of the public schools.[158] The incoming superintendent, William O. Rogers, had been the head of the renegade school board that had tried to root out colored children from the schools in 1868. Upon his return, he declared rather transparently: "Our Board has already indicated its policy in the matter of color line and has resolved that hereafter there shall be separate schools for whites and blacks. The decision in my judgment is based upon sound Educational ground, irrespective of political or other considerations."[159] The state superintendent, once again Robert Lusher, was pleased to announce the end of mixed schools, but lamented the articles in the 1868 constitution, noting that "no so unwise and unnecessary a mingling of social relations in public schools is to be found in the constitution of any other American state." Attributing the integrated school system to "partisan rancor and blind fanaticism," he declared that such laws had been "dissipated by the sunlight of peace and reconciliation, which, in this purer political era, is happily illumining every interest and all classes of our redeemed commonwealth." The "mental and moral instruction of the two races" would henceforth take place "in separate schools, with equal facilities and advantages for both."[160]

The Afro-Creole leadership in New Orleans did not share Lusher's enthusiasm. The energy and support that many Afro-Creoles had put into the Catholic Institution had been directed to the public schools after emancipation, with most of the formerly free children of color attending the public schools.[161] Perhaps by way of appeasement, the state superintendent offered to set up a three-tiered system of segregation in the schools, suggesting that "the desire to enter white schools in contravention of the natural law, is peculiar to children of mixed white and colored blood, whose parents have always been free. These children undoubtedly merit special considerations; and, as they have a strong aversion to association in the schools with children of a darker hue, it would seem wise to establish a separate, intermediate class of schools for their instruction."[162] But the Afro-Creole leadership never publicly entertained the idea of a three-caste school system. When the school board segregated the schools in 1877, members of the Afro-Creole community were joined by Protestant, English-speaking blacks in protest.[163] The editors at the *Tribune* had voiced their philosophy on this score some years earlier, when discussing a state civil rights bill in 1869. They argued against the notion that the benefits of such a law would apply to only a small number of the colored population. "When one or a few colored men are excluded from certain public rights enjoyed by *all* white men, not the few alone but the entire colored population are wronged. The blow falling directly on a few shoulders also reaches the mass. For it is not . . . so much the practical evils of exclusion which we complain of, as the stigma it puts upon our manhood, the stamp of inferiority which sets upon our color, and this extends to all alike."[164]

Three prominent Afro-Creoles—Paul Trévigne, Arnold Bertonneau, and August Dellande—initiated cases in the courts to stop the resegregation of the public schools. Trévigne, an editor of the *Tribune* and once a member of the city school board and a teacher at the Catholic Institution, started a case that led initially to a temporary injunction to stop resegregation. In his appeal before the state supreme court, Trévigne argued that "this case is one of great magnitude, involving as it does a question of civil liberty and constitutional right, with all the sacred guarantees of citizenship, and is really a test, judicially, of the status of that class termed '*colored*,' whose rights to citizenship ought to be protected."[165] Trévigne and his attorney argued that the separation of schools by race was unconstitutional because "a distinction thus made detracts from their status as citizens and consigns them to the contempt of their fellow men and citizens of this community and elsewhere." In addition, the added burden that separate schools would inflict on taxpayers was also unconstitutional, and further, this economic burden would ultimately deprive "the avenues of education to [Trévigne's] son and the entire colored population because taxes cannot be collected to carry on separate schools, and which would have the effect of closing them up."[166] The judge dismissed the suit with the argument that Trévigne had failed to prove damages and that he had filed his suit too late, after resegregation had already begun.[167]

The other two plaintiffs, Bertonneau and Dellande, both tried to have their children admitted to the Fillmore School, a school designated for white children in 1877. The Fillmore School, plaintiffs charged, was the public school closest to their homes, but its principal had refused to admit the children following the proclamation of the new school board, segregating the public schools. Bertonneau (who had been on the Board of Directors of the Catholic Institution and a member of the legislature during the state convention that produced the constitution of 1868) sued the New Orleans School Board for violating both his civil rights (guaranteed under the Fourteenth Amendment of the Constitution) and the right of his children, under Article 135 of the Louisiana Constitution, to attend any public school "in common" with white children. Bertonneau's case in U.S. District Court was thrown out by the circuit judge, who did not recognize any violation of federal law by the school board; he did not agree, that is, that separate schools violated Bertonneau's civil rights under the Fourteenth Amendment, since the segregation law "applies with equal force to persons of both races."[168]

The Dellande case reached the state supreme court on appeal. Dellande's two sons, Arnold, age fourteen, and Clement, age eleven, were, like Bertonneau's children, denied admittance to the Fillmore School. According to Dellande's testimony, the boys, along with some other children, had been sent home after the school board declared it to be a school for white children only. The Fillmore School stood 150 feet from Dellande's house. "The children had gone off," Dellande testified. "I brought the children back to Mr. Gordon [the principal]. Mr. Gordon stated to me that he could not admit them, as the Fillmore School was assigned for white children, and he would have to get an order from the Superintendent."[169] Dellande lost at the district court level, with the judge's sentiments being quite clear in his written statement. Though unable to overturn it, the judge insisted that Article 135 of the Louisiana Constitution mandating integrated schools "tramples upon the usages of centuries and contains the germs of Social war." The legislation was insufficient, in his view, because of the state power allegedly required to keep it in force.

> It is obvious what a vast instrumentality of agencies coercive and penal were needed to carry into execution a policy against which every instinct of our race revolts, and which does violence to the habits, traditions, the rooted convictions of the people for many generations and yet the bold and reckless men who for so long a time wielded almost unlimited power failed to provide such legislation, so much so [that] men shrink in action from what their madness may proclaim in theory.[170]

Forgotten in the judge's racist, fiercely partisan decision were the periods of mostly peaceful integration in the city. The Republican legislature of 1868 had created a partially integrated system that functioned for most of the 1870s in New Orleans, but this seems to have been deemed irrelevant. The judge instead used "habits" and "traditions" to defend segregation, imagining a southern past in which interaction between black and white children never occurred, a separation drawn, he said, from the "rooted convictions" of southerners for "generations."[171] Though plenty of accounts about the antebellum South record slave children and white children playing together, and despite the daily interaction of slaveholders and slaves in the antebellum household, the judge insisted on a different history of race relations. The lines he drew between black and white children were in the service of naturalizing segregation, making Republican efforts at integrating black and white children into violations of both the natural order and the (imagined) history of southern childhoods.

Dellande appealed to the state supreme court, but the court did not agree to hear the case until 1879, giving the Democratic legislature enough time to invalidate the constitution of 1868 with a new constitution, one that did not mandate integrated schools. Rodolphe Desdunes, in his history and remembrances of the Afro-Creoles, *Nos hommes et notre histoire* (1911), praised the "supreme effort" made by the Afro-Creole leaders to stop school segregation "against the first signs of the reactionary movement whose policy prevails even to this day with the most alarming effects."[172] Placing their struggle—as the editors of the *Tribune* had done—in the context of national rather than local politics, Desdunes and his colleagues saw the segregation of schools as "un premier coup de canif" (a first blow of the knife) to come from the compromise between national Republicans and Democrats in 1877, which put Republican Rutherford B. Hayes in the presidency and brought an end to Reconstruction, with the removal of Federal troops from the South. Desdunes was also very hard on the black delegates "of American birth" who attended the convention of 1879 and adopted the measure that established Southern University expressly for black students: "These men knew that this line of demarcation, once established, largely with their consent, would serve as the basis and the pretext for other measures contrary to the interests and rights of our citizens." They knew, Desdunes wrote, that it was a move backward, sacrificing the progress for which they themselves had labored.[173]

By 1879, without the support of the constitution of 1868, August Dellande was left with the argument that the school board had discriminated against Arnold and Clement "arbitrarily on account to color": "The relator [Dellande], to all intents and purposes, and in so far as social questions are involved, is a white man. This is shown by the evidence. His children are also white. He is a merchant in this city, a man of large family, and all his children are apparently white."[174] Echoing the argument that photographs of white-looking slave children had made during the Civil War, but using it to confront a hardening, postbellum color line, Dellande argued that if a black child can *seem* white, then on what grounds could the black child be excluded from the company of white children? What was race, if not visible? This argument about the arbitrary nature of a color line—an argument in which historians and other scholars trailed far behind nineteenth-century reformers and radicals, who had so much at stake in its formulation—did not rustle the thoughts of the court, however, which decided against Dellande and in favor of the school board and segregated schools.[175] But it was nonetheless an attempt to demonstrate that the system of segregation based on racial categorization had already become, as one scholar describes it, "a radical act of imagination."[176] The case of the Dellande children made clear, as did the images of Rosa and Rebecca, that a division between the black child and the white was arbitrary and constructed rather than real. It was the child who was neither black nor white, who once again demonstrated that the fates of black children and white children were intertwined.

If white southern Democrats were not convinced of Dellande's argument about race, they also failed to acknowledge what plain numbers would have told them. Although the circumstances surrounding integrated schools may have been unique to New Orleans, the consequences of segregated education were not. In his study of school segregation in the South after 1900, historian Louis Harlan found that southern school systems, overburdened by the existence of two schools in every district, lagged far behind those of the northern states into the twentieth century. The average amount spent by the state to send a child to public school in 1900 was 20 cents in Massachusetts, 8.2 cents in Virginia, and 5 cents in South Carolina. With less than one-tenth the nation's population in 1900, the South had more than one-fourth of the country's illiterates, and one-fourth of these were white. Black children, of course, suffered the worst effects of the segregated school system in the South.

They had fewer teachers and fewer schools, and the schools they did have were at greater distances from home than those for white children. Whereas there were 108 black students per teacher in Georgia, there were 61 white students under one instructor. By 1915 in South Carolina, the white child received twelve times as much from the public school fund as the black child.[177] School segregation ostensibly left black and white children on opposite sides of educational opportunity. But because there were two school systems overextending the meager public funds white southerners were willing to spend on public schools, both black children and white children suffered in an underfunded, overburdened, segregated educational system.

As Rodolphe Desdunes's angry account of school segregation reflected, this was not the future that the Afro-Creoles in New Orleans had hoped for for black children. The group's leaders continued their fight against segregation after losing the battle over common schools, pressing their case all the way to the U.S. Supreme Court. Forming the Comité des Citoyens, or Citizens' Committee, in 1891, they staged a challenge to the state's "Separate Car" laws, with the cooperation of a light-skinned man of color named Homer Plessy. The high court did not side with Plessy, and the policy of "separate but equal" would stand until 1954, when the *Brown v. Board of Education* decision declared segregation in public schools unconstitutional.[178] But the lawyer for Homer Plessy, Albion Tourgée, echoed the earlier arguments of the Afro-Creoles against segregation in a brief before the Court: "It is not consistent with reason that the United States, having granted and bestowed *one equal citizenship* of the United States and prescribed *one equal citizenship in each state,* for all, will permit a State to compel a railway conductor to assort them arbitrarily according to his ideas of race, in the enjoyment of chartered privileges."[179]

It may not surprise the reader that several of the men who shared this vision of society—of citizens undivided, of equal rights regardless of race—had long ties to the Catholic Institution. Aristide Mary, onetime candidate for governor who had proposed and fostered the formation of the Comité before his death in 1893, was a longtime supporter of the Catholic Institution. Desdunes, a member of the Comité and the most important chronicler of the Afro-Creoles in New Orleans, was a student at the Catholic Institution when André Grégoire was attending.[180] Paul Trévigne was a teacher at the Catholic Institution, an editor at the *Tribune,* and a collaborator with Rodolphe Desdunes on the *Crusader,* a newspaper edited by the Citizens' Committee.[181] And the president of the Comité, Arthur Estèves, was credited with reviving the Catholic Institution when he was elected to the directorship in 1884.

The school had fallen into disrepair when formerly free people of color, who would have supported the school through tuition, began to send their children to the public schools, so much so that it was already in desperate need of funds by 1868. There are numerous references to the sad state of the Catholic Institution in the minutes of the Board of Directors, none worse, perhaps, than the report that the school was without books, that broken windowpanes in the girls' classroom were letting in the rain ("les pluies continuelles"), and there were holes in the ceiling.[182] The Archdiocese of the Catholic Church nearly confiscated the school and its property in the mid-1880s. (The archbishop of the diocese had been appointed its guardian by Madame Couvent in 1847.) The petition filed with the district court in New Orleans charged that the "*Société pour l'instruction des orphelins dans l'indigence* has failed since the month of September 1874, to carry out the provisions of the will" of Madame Couvent and "has failed to maintain, and carry on any school for the purposes named in the will."[183] But by one account, the church's suit originated because the leaders of the school had planned to "abandon Catholic instruction" in favor of a secular curriculum.[184]

Education, through the Catholic Institution, had been at the center of the Afro-Creoles' efforts to fight the repressions of the 1850s, and its supporters seemed to have considered it a "public" school before the war.[185] With the end of the Civil War and emancipation, they devoted their educational efforts to the cause of public schools, in particular to "common schools," and it was then that the Catholic Institution nearly met its end. A school that had been designated for children of color at a time when the public schools were closed to them, it was revived only after the last efforts to prevent school segregation had been exhausted and the "alarming effects" of segregation had become manifest. Rodolphe Desdunes and the other directors managed to maintain control over the Catholic Institution in the face of legal challenge from the church. According to Desdunes, Estèves was appointed to the directorship with a solemn charge: "pour relever cette institution de ses ruines"

—to lift this institution from ruin.[186] That they succeeded, that the Catholic Institution was revived, even while the South as a whole slid toward its "nadir" in terms of race relations in the 1890s, suggests that the Afro-Creoles' vision for the future remained a positive one, unimpeded by the segregated system they had fought so hard to prevent.

Conclusion
Some Mighty Morning

After Reconstruction, the displacement of the black child as a shared metaphor for the future was near total. Once white supremacy became institutionalized in the South with de jure segregation at the close of the nineteenth century, the notion that the black child might represent a future of racial equality for the nation dissolved. Instead, the debate over the black child after Reconstruction was one carried on mostly among African Americans—whether black children should receive an industrial or a liberal education, or the best ways to promote the propagation of the race in the face of violence and discrimination.[1] Some northern philanthropists and reformers working in the South focused on the creation of an industrial school system for the training of black children, but others turned away from them completely, deserting the welfare of black children in order to rescue white children from dangerous working conditions in the cotton mills that dotted the southern landscape by the turn of the century. In the words of historian Shelley Sallee, "As poor whites became a 'white trash' working class, reformers invented the 'forgotten child' as the country's most promising white, the purest Anglo-Saxon."[2]

Indeed, the black child was a figure transformed from a metaphor for the future to a bellwether for the racial climate of the post-Reconstruction era. Just before and during the sectional strife of the Civil War and its immediate aftermath, the uncertain effects of slavery's abolition upon the racial ordering of American society made the black child a pivotal figure within cultural and political debates. If the potential of that child was feared by white supremacists, it was cultivated and anticipated by those who favored racial equality in the United States. Even the advocates of freedpeople, however, as we have seen with many reformers in the South as well as some agents of the Freedmen's Bureau, proved less than ardent about the notion of equality, in theory or in practice, for former slaves. By the end of Reconstruction, the national discussion had shifted away from the struggle for racial equality.[3] In turn, the role of the black child—freedom's child—became a decidedly smaller one on the national stage.

If the black child lost her hold on the imagination of many in American society in the late nineteenth century, however, she still remained the focus of aspirations for African Americans. Northern black activist and historian W. E. B. Du Bois had his differences with the Afro-Creoles who were his contemporaries—or, rather, they had their differences with him. Rodolphe Desdunes took aim at Du Bois, in print, for his suggestion that all southern blacks were uncultured and uneducated. In a pamphlet published in 1907, Desdunes even criticized Du Bois by drawing a distinction between the "Latin Negro" (or Afro-Creole) and the "Anglo-Saxon Negro": "One hopes, the other doubts. Thus we often perceive that one makes every effort to acquire merits, the other to gain advantage. One aspires to equality, the other to identity."[4] Despite the anger in Desdunes's critique, it reflected, nonetheless, the forward-thinking disposition of Afro-Creole leaders. Yet Desdunes and Du Bois were perhaps not so far apart. Both men shared a certain outlook, founded on hope, that saw promise in the next generation. Du Bois, perhaps the most eloquent African American to describe the darkest hours in the South at the turn of the last century, nonetheless let fall a slant of light near the end of his book, written from "behind the veil" of blackness, *The Souls of Black Folk* (1903). It was a light that Desdunes may have appreciated, in spite of himself: "Surely there shall yet dawn some mighty morning to lift the Veil and set the prisoned free. Not for me—I shall die in my bonds—but for fresh young souls who have not known the night and waken to the morning: a morning when men ask of the workman, not 'Is he white?' but 'Can he work?' When men ask artists, not 'Are they black?' but 'Do they know?' "[5] Du Bois saw the black child, freedom's child, as the best hope for fairness and racial equality in the United States, the bridge between past and present, black and white, disparity and equal opportunity. He left the reader not in despair of present conditions but looking forward. His words are still resonant, still necessary, and a fitting place to close a story that remains unfinished.

Notes

NOTES TO THE INTRODUCTION

1. Eric Foner, *Reconstruction: America's Unfinished Revolution 1863–1877* (New York: Harper and Row, 1988), 1–4; Iver Bernstein, *The New York Draft Riots: Their Significance for American Society and Politics in the Age of the Civil War* (New York: Oxford University Press, 1990).

2. In 1820, Jefferson wrote: "But as it is, we have the wolf by the ear, and we can neither hold him, nor safely let him go. Justice is in one scale, and self-preservation in the other." Paul Leicester Ford, ed., *The Works of Thomas Jefferson*, vol. 12 (New York: Putnam's, 1905), 159. See also Tim Matthewson, "Jefferson and Haiti," *Journal of Southern History* 61 (May 1995): 244; and Peter S. Onuf, "Every Generation Is an 'Independent Nation': Colonization, Miscegenation, and the Fate of Jefferson's Children," *William and Mary Quarterly*, 3rd ser., 57 (January 2000): 159.

3. Lydia Maria Child, *The Right Way, the Safe Way, Proved by Emancipation in the British West Indies, and Elsewhere* (New York, 1860), 93, in "From Slavery to Freedom: The African American Pamphlet Collection, 1824–1909," Rare Book and Special Collections Division, Library of Congress, American Memory, http://memory.loc.gov/ammem/index.html.

4. Testimony of a South Carolina Freedman before the American Freedmen's Inquiry Commission, Beaufort, S.C., June 1863, in Ira Berlin, Thavolia Glymph, Steven F. Miller, Joseph P. Reidy, Leslie S. Rowland, and Julie Saville, eds., *Freedom: A Documentary History of Emancipation 1861–1867*, ser. I, vol. III, *The Wartime Genesis of Free Labor: The Lower South* (Cambridge: Cambridge University Press, 1990), 253.

5. Prof. Bennett Puryear, *The Public School in Its Relation to the Negro* (Richmond, 1877), 11, quoted in Leon F. Litwack, *Been in the Storm So Long: The Aftermath of Slavery* (New York: Knopf, 1979), 486.

6. Thomas C. Holt, *The Problem of Freedom: Race, Labor, and Politics in Jamaica and Britain, 1832–1938* (Baltimore: Johns Hopkins University Press, 1992).

7. Robin D. G. Kelley, *Freedom Dreams: The Black Radical Imagination* (Boston: Beacon Press, 2002), 9.

8. Frederick Douglass, "Speech in Madison Square," 1878, quoted in David Blight, " 'For Something beyond the Battlefield': Frederick Douglass and the Struggle for the Memory of the Civil War," *Journal of American History* 75 (March 1989): 1163. There is a growing literature on memory and the Civil War, particularly on the ways in which the war was commemorated after the end of Reconstruction, in the context of a national "reunion" between the North and the former Confederacy (accompanied by increasing racial repression in the South) that began in the late nineteenth century. See, for example, David Blight, *Beyond the Battlefield: Race, Memory, and the American Civil War* (Amherst: University of Massachusetts Press, 2002); Blight, *Race and Reunion: The Civil War in American Memory* (Cambridge, MA: Belknap Press, 2001); Alice Fahs, *The Memory of the Civil War in American Culture* (Chapel Hill: University of North Carolina Press, 2004); W. Fitzhugh Brundage, *The Southern Past: A Clash of Race and Memory* (Cambridge, MA: Belknap Press, 2005).

9. In her considerations of working-class childhood, historian Carolyn Steedman has proposed a useful analytic distinction between the *idea* of "the child" and the material and emotional world of "children": whereas " 'the child' is a historical construct," the product of adult imagination and projection, "children" are individuals who experience childhood. Carolyn Steedman, *Past Tenses: Writing Autobiography and History* (London: Rivers Oram Press, 1992), 194.

10. Philippe Ariès argued that from the seventeenth through the nineteenth century, "the idea of childhood was bound up with the idea of dependence . . . one could leave childhood only by leaving the state of dependence, or at least the lower degrees of dependence." The notion of adolescence as a separate stage from childhood, he suggested, is largely a twentieth-century notion. Philippe Ariès, *Centuries of Childhood: A Social History of Family Life,* trans. Robert Baldick (New York: Vintage Books, 1962), 26.

11. Roland Barthes, *Camera Lucida: Reflections on Photography,* trans. Richard Howard (New York: Hill and Wang, 1980), 3.

NOTES TO CHAPTER I

1. Wm. H. P. Green to Léon Dupart, Esq., "Mobile, Alabama," June 20, 1857, Catholic Institution Letterbook I (hereafter Letterbook I), Archives of the Archdiocese of New Orleans (hereafter AANO).

2. William entered school in 1852 at the age of eight. His admission was recorded in the minutes of the school's directors. *Journal des Séances de la direction de l'institution Catholique pour l'instruction des Orphelins dans l'indigence,* 3 Septembre 1852, 109 (hereafter Séance Book I), AANO.

3. See Alfred N. Hunt, *Haiti's Influence on Antebellum America: Slumbering Volcano in the Caribbean* (Baton Rouge: Louisiana State University Press,

1988), 170; Donald Everett, "Free People of Color in New Orleans, 1830–1865" (M.A. thesis, Tulane University, 1952), 130. The newspapers in New Orleans reported several voyages of free blacks to Haiti in 1859 and 1860. *New Orleans Daily Picayune,* June 22, 1859; January 15, 1860; November 11, 1860; *New Orleans Daily Delta,* July 21, 1859; *New Orleans Daily Crescent,* June 21, 1859; *New Orleans Commercial Bulletin,* May 4, 1859. I have been unable to find equivalent sources for the migration to Veracruz, though there is documentation from the Mexican government about the free black colony, discussed later.

4. Arthur Denis to J. Leonidas, Esq., "Alexandie, La.," October 21, 1859, Letterbook I, AANO.

5. I determined as many of the boys' ages as possible using census rolls and the existing but incomplete record of admissions to the Catholic Institution found in the minutes of the school's board of directors.

6. L. Dupart to Mr. Green, Esq., "Vicksburg, Miss.," June 26, 1857, Letterbook I, AANO.

7. Bruce Dorsey has argued, however, that African American women played a more active role in emigration than they did in colonization movements. See Bruce Dorsey, *Reforming Men and Women: Gender in the Antebellum City* (Ithaca, NY: Cornell University Press, 2002), 162–163.

8. L. Dupart to Mr. Green, Esq., "Vicksburg, Miss.," June 26, 1857, Letterbook I, AANO.

9. Walter Johnson, *Soul by Soul: Life inside the Antebellum Slave Market* (Cambridge, MA: Harvard University Press, 1998), 6–8.

10. See Rosanne Adderley, " 'A Most Useful and Valuable People?': Cultural, Moral, and Practical Dilemmas in the Use of Liberated African Labour in the Nineteenth-Century Caribbean," in Sylvia R. Frey and Betty Wood, eds., *From Slavery to Emancipation in the Atlantic World* (London: Frank Cass, 1999), 59–80.

11. L. Dupart to A. Frilot, "Attakapas, La.," June 4, 1858, Letterbook I, AANO. Parenthetical words in the children's letters were added by the original transcriber, a fellow student.

12. A. F. Frilot to L. Dupart, "Pointe Marie, La.," June 4, 1858, Letterbook I, AANO.

13. The term "black Atlantic" is borrowed from Paul Gilroy, *The Black Atlantic: Modernity and Double Consciousness* (Cambridge, MA: Harvard University Press, 1993). The idea of an "imagined community" comes from Benedict Anderson, *Imagined Communities: Reflections on the Origin and Spread of Nationalism* (New York: Verso, 1983). On what the act of writing allows children to do, see Carolyn Steedman, *The Tidy House: Little Girls Writing* (London: Virago, 1982). Steedman's work with children's writing influences the readings and interpretations of the students' letters herein.

14. See Michael P. Johnson and James L. Roark, *Black Masters: A Free Family of Color in the Old South* (New York: Norton, 1984).

15. On the debate among African Americans over their racial destiny *after* Reconstruction and into the twentieth century, see Michele Mitchell, *Righteous Propagation: African Americans and the Politics of Racial Destiny after Reconstruction* (Chapel Hill: University of North Carolina Press, 2004).

16. On the biblical interpretation, or "Exodus politics," of the black struggle in the early nineteenth century, see Eddie S. Glaude Jr., *Exodus! Religion, Race, and Nation in Early Nineteenth-Century Black America* (Chicago: University of Chicago Press, 2000), 111–112 and passim.

17. At Couvent's death in 1837, she left land and buildings to be used for a free school for orphans of color in the Faubourg Marigny, in the city's Third District. Rodolphe Lucien Desdunes, *Nos hommes et notre histoire: Notices biographiques accompagnées de réflexions et de souvenirs personnels, hommage à la population créole, en souvenir des grands hommes qu'elle a produits et des bonnes choses qu'elle a accomplies* (Montreal: Arbour and Dupont, 1911), 28–32. *Nos hommes* was published in translation as *Our People and Our History,* trans. Sister Dorothea Olga McCants (Baton Rouge: Louisiana State University Press, 1973), 21–24. Subsequent citations will include page numbers for both editions because they differ somewhat. Roger Baudier, Sr., "The Story of St. Louis School of Holy Redeemer Parish, New Orleans, LA., Formerly St. Louis School for the Colored, l'Institution Catholique pour l'Instruction des Orphelins dans l'Indigence, Widow Couvent's School, 1847–1956," unpublished ms., AANO; "History of the Catholic Indigent Orphan Institute," 1916?, AANO; Marcus B. Christian, "Dream of an African Ex-Slave," *Louisiana Weekly,* February 12, 1938; "New Wine in an Old Bottle," *Colored Harvest* 12 (May–June 1924): 10; Charles Barthelemy Rousseve, *The Negro in Louisiana: Aspects of His History and His Literature* (New Orleans: Xavier University Press, 1937), 43–44; John W. Blassingame, *Black New Orleans 1860–1880* (Chicago: University of Chicago Press, 1973), 108.

18. Donald E. DeVore and Joseph Logsdon, *Crescent City Schools: Public Education in New Orleans, 1841–1991* (Lafayette, LA: Center for Louisiana Studies, 1991), chap. 1; Roger W. Shugg, *Origins of Class Struggle in Louisiana: A Social History of White Farmers and Laborers during Slavery and After, 1840–1875* (Baton Rouge: Louisiana State University Press, 1939), 70–75.

19. According to the census of 1850, 1,008 free colored students attended school in New Orleans. U.S. Bureau of the Census, *Seventh Census of the United States, 1850* (Washington, DC: Government Printing Office, 1850), 853. For enrollment figures, see 15 Avril 1852 and 1 Août 1853, Séance Book I, AANO. On 2 Novembre 1853, there were 96 boys and 98 girls in attendance. Séance Book I, AANO, 77. Apparently the school quickly earned a reputation outside of New Orleans as well. A man from Mobile, Alabama, asked that a

child of that city be admitted as a boarder at the Catholic Institution. The school, however, was unable to accommodate boarders. See 1 Avril 1858, Séance Book I, AANO.

20. "History of the Catholic Indigent Orphan Institute"; Nathan Willey, "Education of the Colored Population of Louisiana," *Harper's New Monthly Magazine* 33 (July 1866): 248; Caryn Cossé Bell, *Revolution, Romanticism, and the Afro-Creole Protest Tradition in Louisiana, 1718–1868* (Baton Rouge: Louisiana State University Press, 1997), 123–127; R. L. Desdunes, "Mme Bernard Couvent," *Negro History Bulletin,* October 1943, 7; Christian, "Dream of an African Ex-Slave"; Desdunes, *Nos hommes et notre histoire,* 139–146; *Our People and Our History,* 101–107; Rousseève, *The Negro in Louisiana,* 43–44; Blassingame, *Black New Orleans,* 108.

21. William H. Green to Armand Nicolas, Esq., "Grand Lake, La.," February 9, 1857, Letterbook I, AANO.

22. Cossé Bell, *Revolution, Romanticism, and the Afro-Creole Protest Tradition in Louisiana,* 115; Ira Berlin, *Slaves without Masters: The Free Negro in the Antebellum South* (New York: New Press, 1974). Berlin, writing about the early nineteenth century, describes the establishment of free black schools and churches as "a means of establishing a new identity as a free people." The situation of free blacks in the South in the late 1850s, however, makes it clear that the significance of education for people of color depends upon its historical context. Rather than seeking a "new identity" in the 1850s, New Orleans's free blacks sought both the survival of their community and the promise of a different future.

23. Donald E. DeVore, "Race Relations and Community Development: The Education of Blacks in New Orleans, 1862–1960" (Ph.D. diss., Louisiana State University, 1989), 2. On the economic status of free blacks in the South, see Loren Schweninger, "Prosperous Blacks in the South, 1790–1880," *American Historical Review* 95 (February 1990): 31–56.

24. 15 Avril 1852, Séance Book I, AANO, 76; Desdunes, *Nos hommes et notre histoire,* 144; *Our People and Our History,* 106. On education for children of color in the antebellum period, see Betty Porter, "The History of Negro Education in Louisiana," *Louisiana Historical Quarterly* 25 (July 1942): 732; Alice Dunbar-Nelson, "People of Color in Louisiana, Part II," *Journal of Negro History* 2 (January 1917): 65; H. E. Sterkx, *The Free Negro in Antebellum Louisiana* (Rutherford, NJ: Fairleigh Dickinson University Press, 1972), 273.

25. ". . . *orphelins reellement indigens passeront toujours avant les autres enfans présentés,*" 28 Septembre 1857, Séance Book I, AANO.

26. Desdunes, *Nos hommes et notre histoire,* 22; *Our People and Our History,* 17. The school's board, however, was not completely free of class prejudice, despite its original mission to educate indigent children. Proof of this comes from an exchange between several of the members of the board concern-

ing the building of a branch of the institution in the Faubourg Trémé (a much poorer neighborhood than the Faubourg Marigny, where the main school was located). When one member, M. Amand, proposed the establishment of a branch in Trémé so that it might be of use "aux familles pauvres, qui habitent cette partie de la ville" (to the poor families living in that part of the city), M. Villard responded that poor children should have to walk if they wanted a free education—"c'est à eux de marcher pour chercher l'education qu'on leur donne gratuitement." Another board member, M. Gonzales, responded to Villard, "vous n'êtes pas humain" (You are not humane). More such words were exchanged until the president called for order, declaring that since the poor also pay taxes on their property, they should get the benefits of the moneys allotted the school by the legislature (which amounted to $2,000 that year). When this was put to a vote, the board decided to look for property in the Faubourg Trémé. There is no evidence, however, that this branch of the institution was ever built. 22 Juillet 1854, Séance Extraordinaire, Séance Book I, AANO.

27. Blassingame, *Black New Orleans,* 108. Recent scholarship suggests that the privileged status of free blacks in New Orleans, as compared with that of free blacks in the rest of the country, has been overstated. Though New Orleans did have the largest percentage of free black professionals and artisans—fully one-quarter of all such persons within the fifteen largest cities in the United States—fresh readings of demographic and economic records suggest that "free persons of color [in New Orleans] were obviously privileged only in comparison to slaves." See Paul Lachance, "The Limits of Privilege: Where Free Persons of Colour Stood in the Hierarchy of Wealth in Antebellum New Orleans," in Jane G. Landers, ed., *Against the Odds: Free Blacks in the Slave Societies of the Americas* (London: Frank Cass, 1996), 66–67. See also Leonard Curry, *The Free Black in Urban America, 1800–1850: The Shadow of a Dream* (Chicago: University of Chicago Press, 1981).

28. 2 Novembre 1854, Séance Book I, AANO; 4 Mai 1853, Séance Extraordinaire, Séance Book I, AANO.

29. On the Afro-Creoles of Louisiana and their intellectual and political activism, see Cossé Bell, *Revolution, Romanticism, and the Afro-Creole Protest Tradition in Louisiana.* On the creation of Afro-Creole culture in the colonial period, see Gwendolyn Midlo Hall, *Africans in Colonial Louisiana: The Development of Afro-Creole Culture in the Eighteenth Century* (Baton Rouge: Louisiana State University Press, 1992). The term "Creole" has a long and intricate history in Louisiana beginning in the early colonial period when it was used to describe slaves born in the French colony rather than in Africa. By the late eighteenth and early nineteenth centuries, black, white, and mixed-race native Louisianans called themselves "Creoles" to distinguish themselves from Anglo-Americans. In the 1820s, members of the growing population of free people of Afro-European descent began to claim a racial and ethnic identity distinct from

both whites and enslaved blacks by referring to themselves as "Creoles of color" or "Afro-Creoles." See Midlo Hall, *Africans in Colonial Louisiana,* 157.

30. DeVore and Logsdon, *Crescent City Schools,* 42; Dunbar-Nelson, "People of Color in Louisiana, Part II," 65.

31. See Robert C. Reinders, "The Free Negro in the New Orleans Economy, 1850–1860," *Louisiana History* 6 (Summer 1965): 273–285; Schweninger, "Prosperous Blacks in the South, 1790–1880," 40.

32. *Prospectus de l'Institution Catholique des Orphelins Indigents encoignure Grands Hommes et Union Troisième Municipalité, Nouvelle-Orleans* (New Orleans: Maitre Desarzant, 1847), Howard Tilton Memorial Library, Louisiana Collection, Tulane University.

33. Desdunes, *Nos hommes et notre histoire,* 141–142; *Our People and Our History,* 104. Desdunes was admitted to the Catholic Institution in 1855, at age six; Séance Book I, 15 Septembre 1855, 1. With private education in antebellum New Orleans, one historian suggests, "color lines were not sharply drawn. The tutor and his students might belong to either race without producing any friction or displeasure thereby." Marcus Christian, "A Black History," chapter 21, "Negro Education," p. 11, Special Collections, Earl K. Long Library, University of New Orleans (hereafter UNO). This meant, of course, that children of color might receive their education from a white instructor.

34. Joanne Pope Melish, *Disowning Slavery: Gradual Emancipation and "Race" in New England, 1780–1860* (Ithaca, NY: Cornell University Press, 1998), 1–2.

35. Cossé Bell, *Revolution, Romanticism, and the Afro-Creole Protest Tradition in Louisiana,* 37, 45.

36. Berlin, *Slaves without Masters,* chap. 1 and 138–157; Thomas D. Morris, *Southern Slavery and the Law, 1619–1860* (Chapel Hill: University of North Carolina Press, 1996), chap. 18.

37. "Local Intelligence, Emigration to Hayti," *New Orleans Daily Delta,* July 21, 1859; Marcus Christian WPA Newspaper Transcriptions, Marcus Christian Collection, UNO. On free people of color in New Orleans and Louisiana, see Sterkx, *The Free Negro in Antebellum Louisiana,* chap. 4; Judith Kelleher Schafer, *Slavery, the Civil Law, and the Supreme Court of Louisiana* (Baton Rouge: Louisiana State University Press, 1994), 20–21; Robert C. Reinders, "The Decline of the New Orleans Free Negro in the Decade before the Civil War," *Journal of Mississippi History* 24 (April 1962): 90. On the cultural and political activities of free black people in colonial Louisiana, see Kimberly S. Hanger, *Bounded Lives, Bounded Places: Free Black Society in Colonial New Orleans, 1769–1803* (Durham, NC: Duke University Press, 1997), esp. the introduction.

38. Dorsey, *Reforming Men and Women,* 160–161; Stanley W. Campbell, *The Slave Catchers: Enforcement of the Fugitive Slave law, 1850–1860* (Chapel

Hill: University of North Carolina Press, 1970), 23–25; Carol Wilson, *Freedom at Risk: The Kidnapping of Free Blacks in America 1780–1865* (Lexington: University Press of Kentucky, 1994), passim.

39. Melish, *Disowning Slavery*, 261–270.

40. Martin R. Delany, *The Condition, Elevation, Emigration, and Destiny of the Colored People of the United States* and *Official Report of the Niger Valley Exploring Party*, introduction by Toyin Falola (Amherst, MA: Humanity Books, 2004 [1852]), 170–171.

41. James M. McPherson, *Battle Cry of Freedom: The Civil War Era* (New York: Oxford University Press, 1988), 78–91.

42. *Dred Scott v. Sanford*, 60 U.S. 393 (1857); Don E. Fehrenbacher, *The Dred Scott Case: Its Significance in American Law and Politics* (New York: Oxford University Press, 1978). See also McPherson, *Battle Cry of Freedom*, 170–178.

43. Philip S. Foner and George E. Walker, eds., *Proceedings of the Black State Conventions, 1840–1865*, vol. 2 (Philadelphia: Temple University Press, 1980), 208–209.

44. Reprinted in Sterling Stuckey, *The Ideological Origins of Black Nationalism* (Boston: Beacon Press, 1972) 199, 204. On similar ideas expressed by James Theodore Holly concerning Liberia, see Floyd John Miller, *The Search for a Black Nationality: Black Emigration and Colonization, 1787–1863* (Urbana: University of Illinois Press, 1975), 235.

45. "Petition of Peter Bestes, Sambo Freeman, Felix Holbrook, and Chester Joie, Boston, April 20th, 1773," in Dorothy Porter, comp., *Early Negro Writing, 1760–1837* (Boston: Beacon Press, 1971), 254–255, cited in Miller, *The Search for a Black Nationality*, 3. On rebellions, see Michael Mullin, *Africa in America: Slave Acculturation and Resistance in the American South and the British Caribbean, 1736–1831* (Urbana: University of Illinois Press, 1992).

46. Miller, *The Search for a Black Nationality*, 4–12.

47. Hunt, *Haiti's Influence on Antebellum America*, 170; Everett, "Free People of Color in New Orleans," 130; Ludwell Lee Montague, *Haiti and the United States, 1714–1938* (New York: Russell and Russell, 1966), 70; Miller, *The Search for a Black Nationality*, viii–ix.

48. Eric Burin, *Slavery and the Peculiar Solution: A History of the American Colonization Society* (Gainesville: University Press of Florida, 2005); Dorsey, *Reforming Men and Women*, 140–142.

49. Foner, *Proceedings of the Black State Conventions*, vol. 2, 219.

50. Delany, *The Condition, Elevation, Emigration, and Destiny of the Colored People*, 58, 186, 200.

51. Miller, *The Search for a Black Nationality*, 268.

52. Quoted in Tom W. Shick, *Behold the Promised Land: A History of Afro-American Settler Society in Nineteenth-Century Liberia* (Baltimore: Johns Hop-

kins University Press, 1977), 3. On the differences between Frederick Douglass and Martin Delany over emigration, particularly their use of language concerning black masculinity to support their positions—that is, whether it was more manly to stay or to go—see Dorsey, *Reforming Men and Women*, 161–162.

53. Delany, *The Condition, Elevation, Emigration, and Destiny of the Colored People*, 200.

54. See, for example, J. A. Claiborne to John Wallace, Esq., "Boston, Mass.," December 5, 1856, and J. A. Claiborne to P. Dufour, Esq., "Marseilles, France," December 18, 1856, Letterbook I, AANO.

55. J. A. Claiborne to P. Dufour, Esq., "Marseilles, France," 18 December 1856, Letterbook I, AANO.

56. A. Grégoire to Joseph Peunel, Esq., "Hartford New Haven," December 12, 1856, Letterbook I, AANO. See also William H. Green to A. Nicolas, Esq., "Galveston, Tex.," December 15, 1856, and J. A. Claiborne to John Franklin, Esq., "Vicksburg, Miss.," December 15, 1856, Letterbook I, AANO.

57. Wm H. Green to Armand Nicolas, Esq., "Grand Lake, La.," February 2, 1857, Letterbook I, AANO.

58. A. Nicolas to Wm. Green, Esq., "Boston, Mass.," December 10, 1856, Letterbook I, AANO.

59. Desdunes, *Nos hommes et notre histoire*, 88–89; *Our People and Our History*, 65; Roussève, *The Negro in Louisiana*, 48; Cossé Bell *Revolution, Romanticism, and the Afro-Creole Protest Tradition in Louisiana*, 85–87. According to Roussève, Mansion contributed funds for migrations to both Mexico and Haiti.

60. *Memoria de la Secretaria de Estado y Del Despacho de Fomento, Colonización, Industria y Comercio de la República Mexicana escrita por el ministro del Ramo C. Manuel Silíceo, para dar cuenta conella al soberano congreso constitutional* (México: Imprenta de Vicente García Torres, 1857), 57. On black Mexicans in Veracruz, see also Patrick J. Carroll, *Blacks in Colonial Veracruz: Race, Ethnicity, and Regional Development* (Austin: University of Texas Press, 1991). Mexico and the United States have markedly different histories of race and racial ideology, however, particularly with regard to *mestizaje*, or racial mixture. New Spain was arguably the New World possession in which Africans, Indians, and Europeans were most fully integrated, both socially and culturally. See Colin M. MacLachlan and Jaime E. Rodriguez O., *The Forging of the Cosmic Race: A Reinterpretation of Colonial Mexico* (Berkeley: University of California Press, 1990 [1980]), introduction; see Patrick J. Carroll, "Los Mexicanos Negros, El Mestizaje, y Los Fundamentos Olvidados De La 'Raza Cósmica': Una Perspectiva Regional," *Historia Mexicana* 44 (January–March 1995): 403–438.

61. William Green to Samuel Green, Esq., "Monterey, Mexico," November 28, 1856, Letterbook I, AANO, 10.

62. The *New Orleans Daily Picayune*'s publisher had a network of pony riders to carry the news from Nicaragua to Veracruz. From there, steamers could reach New Orleans in two weeks' time. George Black, *The Good Neighbor: How the United States Wrote the History of Central America and the Caribbean* (New York: Pantheon Books, 1988), 5.

63. On Walker, his failed adventures, and his popularity among southern slaveholders in favor of slavery's expansion, see McPherson, *Battle Cry of Freedom*, 110–116; Charles H. Brown, *Agents of Manifest Destiny: The Lives and Times of the Filibusters* (Chapel Hill: University of North Carolina Press, 1980), pt. 3; Robert E. May, *The Southern Dream of a Caribbean Empire, 1854–1861* (Baton Rouge: Louisiana State University Press, 1973), chap. 4.

64. J. Alfred Claiborne to C. Claiborne, Esq., "City of Mexico, Mexico," November 27, 1856, Letterbook I, AANO.

65. A. Nicolas to Arthur Nicolas, Esq., "Veracruz, Mexico," November 28, 1856, Letterbook I, ANNO.

66. A. A. Grégoire to Léon Dupart, Esq., "Cincinnati, Ohio," July 5, 1857, Letterbook I, AANO.

67. Armand Nicolas to Léon Dupart, Esq., "Saint Martinville, La.," November 20, 1857, Letterbook I, AANO.

68. W. H. Green to John Green, Esq., "City of Veracruz, Mexico," May 7, 1857, Letterbook I, AANO.

69. Armand Nicolas to M. Lombard, Esq., "Puebla, Mexico," May 8, 1857, Letterbook I, AANO.

70. Armand Nicolas to L. Posthel, Esq., "Cincinnati, Ohio," June 26, 1857, Letterbook I, AANO.

71. The debate over free labor versus slave was at its height in the 1850s. See Eric Foner, *Free Soil, Free Labor, Free Men: The Ideology of the Republican Party before the Civil War* (New York: Oxford University Press, 1970).

72. "A Gregory" and "Louis Duhurt" were on the passenger list of people returning to New Orleans from Veracruz on May 9, 1857, on the ship *Sarah Bartlett*. *Passenger Lists of Vessels Arriving at New Orleans, Louisiana, 1820–1902*, Micropublication M259, RG 036, Rolls 1–93 (Washington, DC: National Archives and Record Administration, 1958), M259_44, accessed through Ancestry.com, *New Orleans Passenger Lists 1820–1945* [online database] (Provo, UT: The Generations Network, 2006).

73. A. Grégoire to George Candiff, Esq., "City of Mexico, Mexico," May 15, 1857, Letterbook I, AANO.

74. L. Dupart to Mr. Green, Esq., "Vicksburg, Miss.," June 26, 1857, Letterbook I, AANO.

75. A. André Grégoire to Ernest Lompré, Esq., "Paris, France," June 26, 1857, Letterbook I, ANNO.

76. Armand Nicolas to L. Homoca, Esq., "Huasacoalca, Mexico," June 19, 1857, Letterbook I, AANO.

77. William H. P. Green to Léon Dupart, Esq., "Mobile, Alabama," June 20, 1857, Letterbook I, AANO.

78. A. André Grégoire to Ernest Lompré, Esq., "Paris, France," June 26, 1857, Letterbook I, AANO.

79. See J. Peunel to A. Grégoire, Esq., "Tampico, Mexico," September 9, 1857; L. Armstrong to L. Dupart, Esq., "Tampico, Mexico," September 11, 1857; W. H. P. Green to Armand Nicolas, Esq., "Tampico, Mexico," September 14, 1857, and M. L. Dupart to E. Brunetter, Esq., "Tlactotalpán, State of Vera Cruz, Mexico," September 18, 1857, Letterbook I, AANO.

80. *New Orleans Daily Delta*, January 16, 1860, cited in Everett, "Free People of Color in New Orleans," 129.

81. *Memoria del Ministerio de Fomento, Colonización, Industria y Comercio Presenta al Congreso de la Union* (México: Imprenta del Gobierno, 1863), 102, 99. These *memorias* were printed annually, but because of the civil war, the government's records are silent for the years between 1857 and 1863, when Eureka and other colonies were in operation in Mexico.

82. The tension between Spain and Mexico appears to have been a diplomatic squabble. This reference, however, serves as further evidence that the students were reading the *Daily Picayune,* since the paper followed the story very closely. See, for instance, the *Daily Picayune,* July 26, July 30, and August 3, 1857.

83. M. L. Dupart to R. Barthelemy, Esq., "Tampico, Mexico," September 11, 1857, Letterbook I, AANO.

84. Antoine Grégoire to Florville Picou, Esq., "Tampico, Mexico," September 18, 1857, Letterbook I, AANO. "Antoine" seems to have been André's first name. See U.S. Bureau of the Census, *Seventh Census of the United States, 1850,* New Orleans Municipality 3, Ward 4, Orleans, LA (Washington, DC: National Archives and Record Administration, 1850), M432, p. 229, accessed through Ancestry.com, *1850 United States Federal Census* [online database] (Provo, UT: The Generations Network, 2005).

85. A. F. Frilot to L. Armstrong, Esq., "Attakapas, La.," May 27, 1858, Letterbook I, AANO.

86. L. Dupart to Wm Green, Esq., "Baton Rouge, La.," May 28, 1858, Letterbook I, AANO.

87. Hunt, *Haiti's Influence on Antebellum America,* 3. Haiti, a former French colony, also had a particular history for the French-speaking population of New Orleans.

88. David Nicholls, *From Dessalines to Duvalier: Race, Colour, and National Independence in Haiti* (Cambridge: Cambridge University Press, 1979), 5.

Evidence of Haiti's importance in the creation of black identity and resistance in other parts of the Americas surfaced throughout the nineteenth century. In Rio de Janiero, for example, slaves wore necklaces with the image of Dessalines etched on them just one year after the Haitian leader declared independence for St. Domingue. João José Reis, *Slave Rebellion in Brazil: The Muslim Uprising of 1835 in Bahia*, trans. Arthur Brakel (Baltimore: Johns Hopkins University Press, 1993), 48.

89. Cossé Bell, *Revolution, Romanticism, and the Afro-Creole Protest Tradition in Louisiana*, 98–99. Cossé Bell points out that although creoles of color in Louisiana did not have the freedom of expression of their French counterparts until the 1860s, the French literary movement "served as a vehicle for the expression of some of their feelings and attitudes" in the decades before the Civil War. See also Dunbar-Nelson, "People of Color in Louisiana, Part II," 52; Hunt, *Haiti's Influence on Antebellum America*, 4, 48; Hanger, *Bounded Lives, Bounded Places*, 163–170.

90. Sterkx, *The Free Negro in Antebellum Louisiana*, 302; Desdunes, *Nos hommes et notre histoire*, 151–152; *Our People and Our History*, 112–113; Cossé Bell, *Revolution, Romanticism, and the Afro-Creole Protest Tradition in Louisiana*, 86.

91. *Daily Picayune* (evening edition), June 22, 1859.

92. Hunt, *Haiti's Influence on Antebellum America*, 177–179.

93. James Redpath, ed., *Guide to Hayti* (Boston: Haytien Bureau of Emigration, 1861), n.p.

94. Cyril E. Griffith, *The African Dream: Martin R. Delany and the Emergence of Pan-African Thought* (University Park: Pennsylvania State University Press, 1975), 61.

95. Redpath, *Pine and Palm*, May 18, 1861, quoted in Hunt, *Haiti's Influence on Antebellum America*, 177–179; Redpath, *Guide to Hayti*, 9, 175.

96. Redpath, *Guide to Hayti*, 168; Cossé Bell, *Revolution, Romanticism, and the Afro-Creole Protest Tradition in Louisiana*, 86.

97. Armand Cloud to A. Lessassier, Esq., "Boston, Mass.," October 28, 1859, Letterbook I, AANO. See also Arthur Denis to W. H. Green, Esq., I. Toussaint to A. Rash (a pun name), I. Bordenave to J. Butler, Esq., L. C. Arthidore to J. Lavigne, Esq., "Boston, Mass," October 28, 1859, Letterbook I, AANO.

98. "Hayti and Immigration Thither," *New Orleans Daily Picayune* (afternoon edition), July 5, 1859.

99. *New Orleans Daily Picayune*, August 14, 1859. Though some did return to New Orleans in the first years of emigration, many of them returned, as the *Picayune* noted, just long enough to gather supplies and equipment. See Everett, "Free People of Color in New Orleans," 128.

100. *New Orleans Daily Picayune*, November 11, 1860.

101. "Local Intelligence, Emigration to Hayti," *New Orleans Daily Delta,* July 21, 1859.

102. L. C. Arthidore to A. Grégoire, Esq., "Port-au-Prince, Hayti," October 7, 1859, and Célicour Bordenave to A. Grégoire, Esq., "Port-au-Prince, Hayti," October 7, 1859, Letterbook I, AANO.

103. Armand Cloud to A. Grégoire, Esq., "Port-au-Prince, Hayti," September 7, 1859, Letterbook I, AANO.

104. John Blandin to A. Grégoire, Esq., "Port-au-Prince, Hayti," October 7, 1859, Letterbook I, AANO.

105. Reprinted in Redpath's *Guide to Haiti* was a list of queries directed to Geffrard, posed on behalf of "certain blacks and persons of color in the United States and Canada who are desirous of emigrating to Hayti." This letter to Geffrard and his response were dated August 1859, which suggests that the children may have seen this document before they wrote their letters to Grégoire. (The *Guide* itself was dated 1861.) The first question read: "Would Emigrants be subject to military duty? If so, how long and what kind of duty?" In the "Reply of the Government," Geffrard states that "the Government, as an evidence of its good intentions in favor of emigration, has resolved to exempt the emigrants from military service. *But this exemption shall not extend to their children when they have attained the proscribed age of drawing lots*" (emphasis added). It is not clear whether children traveling with their parents to Haiti would be considered "emigrants" and therefore exempt from this rule. The boys seem to have wanted very much to know if the rule might pertain to them. Redpath, *Guide to Hayti,* 93–95.

106. Arthur Denis to A. Grégoire, Esq., "Port-au-Prince, Hayti," October 7, 1859, Letterbook I, AANO.

107. I. Toussaint to A. Grégoire, Esq., "Port-au-Prince, Hayti," October 7, 1859, Letterbook I, AANO.

108. John Blandin to A. Grégoire, Esq., "Port-au-Prince, Hayti," October 7, 1859, Letterbook I, AANO.

109. *Journal des Séances de la direction de l'institution Catholique pour l'instruction des Orphelins dans l'indigence commencé le 23 de avril 1859,* 23 décembre 1859, 26 (hereafter Séance Book II), AANO.

110. Arthur Denis to J. Leonidas, Esq., "Alexandrie, La.," October 21, 1859, Letterbook I, AANO.

111. *Douglass's Monthly,* January 1861, 386–387; March, 1861, 420; May 1861, 449–450; quoted in Miller, *The Search for a Black Nationality,* 239–240.

112. On the experiences of American children during the war, see James Marten, *The Children's Civil War* (Chapel Hill: University of North Carolina Press, 1998).

113. John Blandin to H. Vasserot, Esq., "Port-au-Prince Hayti," May 29,

1861, Catholic Institution Letterbook II (hereafter Letterbook II), AANO, 46. Blandin states in another entry that he is seventeen. John Blandin to Francis Richard, Esq., Richmond, VA, July 3, 1861, Letterbook II, AANO, 67–68.

114. On the debate over the reasons free people of color joined the Confederate army, see Cossé Bell, *Revolution, Romanticism, and the Afro-Creole Protest Tradition in Louisiana*, 218, 229–232, and, on free blacks and the War of 1812, 51–60.

115. John Blandin to Henry Vasserot, Esq., "Louisville, Ky.," April 24, 1861, Letterbook II, AANO, 24. See also A.C. to E. Meunier, Esq., "Paris, France," April 24, 1861, Letterbook II, AANO, 23; and H. Relf to A. Pajol, Esq., "Dayton, Ohio," April 24, 1861, Letterbook II, AANO, 26; Joseph P. Logsdon and Caryn Cossé Bell, "The Americanization of Black New Orleans, 1850–1900," in Arnold R. Hirsch and Joseph Logsdon, eds., *Creole New Orleans: Race and Americanization* (Baton Rouge: Louisiana State University Press, 1992), 217–219.

116. John Blandin to H. Vasserot, Esq., "Port-au-Prince Hayti," May 29, 1861, Letterbook II, AANO, 46.

117. John Blandin to Henry Vasserot, Esq., "Louisville, Ky.," April 24, 1861, Letterbook II, AANO, 24.

118. John Blandin to H. Vasserot, Esq., "Port-au-Prince, Hayti," May 29, 1861, Letterbook II, AANO, 46.

119. Armand Cloud to H. Poichare, Esq., "Cincinnati, O.," April 17, 1861, Letterbook II, AANO, 21.

120. Lavigne must have gone to Haiti with his family, since the school directors hired a "Mr. S. Chézan" to replace "Mr. J. Lavigne" (the younger Lavigne's father or brother) "pour cause de départ" in June 1861. Séance Book II, 1 Juin 1861, 53. The students also noted that Lavigne left on the *Laura*, a ship that regularly sailed to Haiti in that period. See *New Orleans Daily Picayune*, January 30, 1861, also cited in Everett, "Free People of Color," 129.

121. J. Bordenave to A. Frilot, Esq., "Metz, France," May 22, 1861, Letterbook II, AANO, emphasis added.

122. T. Richard to J. Lavigne, Esq., "Port-au-Prince, Hayti," October 2, 1861, Letterbook II, AANO.

123. J. Bordenave to R. Pavageau, Esq., "Lavolle, Nand.," December 11, 1861, Letterbook II, ANNO. See also H. Relf to J. Bordenave, Esq., "Bonfouca, La.," December 4, 1861, Letterbook II, AANO.

124. On the Union blockades, see McPherson, *Battle Cry of Freedom*, 379, and chap. 12.

125. H. Relf to E. Fleury, Esq., "Madrid, Spain," December 18, 1861, Letterbook II, AANO.

126. H. Relf to A. Cloud, "Paris, France," October 2, 1861, Letterbook II, AANO.

127. H. Relf to J. Bordenave, Esq., "Bonfouca, La.," December 4, 1861, Letterbook II, AANO.

128. J. Bordenave to L. Lamanière, Esq., "Sienna H'and," January 15, 1862, Letterbook II, AANO.

129. H. Relf to T. Bordenave, Esq., "Madrid, Spain," November 6, 1861, Letterbook II, AANO.

130. H. J. Vasserot to A. Perroux, Esq., "Mobile, Ala.," February 26, 1862, Letterbook II, AANO.

131. Desdunes, *Nos hommes et notre histoire*, 158–159; *Our People and Our History*, 118; Logsdon and Cossé Bell, "Americanization of Black New Orleans," 219.

132. Ira Berlin, Joseph P. Reidy, and Leslie S. Rowland, eds., *Freedom: A Documentary History of Emancipation 1861–1867*, ser. 2, *The Black Military Experience* (Cambridge: Cambridge University Press, 1982), 41–44; Cossé Bell, *Revolution, Romanticism, and the Afro-Creole Protest Tradition in Louisiana*, 231–233.

133. 1 Mai 1862, Séance Book II.

134. Ernest Brunet to L. Mension, Esq., "New York City, N.Y.," September 24, 1862, Letterbook II, AANO.

135. L. Lamanière to B. Couaire, "St. John Baptist, La.," October 15, 1862, Letterbook II, AANO.

136. Cossé Bell, *Revolution, Romanticism, and the Afro-Creole Protest Tradition in Louisiana*, 229–231; Joseph T. Glatthaar, *Forged in Battle: The Civil War Alliance of Black Soldiers and White Officers* (New York: Free Press, 1990), 7–10; Mary Frances Berry, "Negro Troops in Blue and Gray: The Louisiana Native Guards, 1861–1863," *Louisiana History* 8 (Spring 1967): 167–169.

137. E. Pérault to A. Salonich, Esq., October 16, 1862, "Port-au-Prince, Hayti," Letterbook II, AANO.

138. Unknown to R. Duallim, Esq., "Dubuque, Iowa," October 29, 1862, Letterbook II, AANO.

139. E. Brunet to O. Percy, Esq., "Port-au-Prince, Hayti," June 10, 1862, Letterbook II, AANO.

140. L. Lamanière to E. Brunet, Esq., "Dubuque, Iowa," November 26, 1862, Letterbook II, AANO. Deciphering Lucien's use of "Creole" is certainly tricky. But he seems to refer to the Afro-Creoles as "colored men" and distinguishes them from the "Creole" planters, which suggests that the latter were white.

141. Slave emancipation in Cuba was gradual, beginning in 1870. See Rebecca J. Scott, *Slave Emancipation in Cuba: The Transition to Free Labor, 1860–1899* (Princeton, NJ: Princeton University Press, 1985).

142. President Lincoln had proffered the idea before the end of the war that the vote ought to be given to educated free men of color. McPherson, *Battle Cry of Freedom*, 707.

143. E. Pérault to A. Nicolas, Esq., "Port-au-Prince, Hayti," September 24, 1862, Letterbook II, AANO, emphasis added.

144. On the demands of Louisiana's enslaved for their freedom after the start of the war, see Ira Berlin, Barbara J. Fields, Thavolia Glymph, Joseph P. Reidy, and Leslie Rowland, eds., *Freedom: A Documentary History of Emancipation 1861–1867*, ser. I, vol. I, *The Destruction of Slavery* (Cambridge: Cambridge University Press, 1985), chap. 4.

145. L. Lamanière to J. H. Sauvage, Esq., "Tampico, Mexico," November 14, 1862, Letterbook II, AANO.

146. Ibid.

NOTES TO CHAPTER 2

1. Robert Taft, *Photography and the American Scene* (New York: Dover, 1964 [1938]), chap. 8.

2. General Order No. 64, Headquarters, Dept. of the Gulf, New Orleans, August 29, 1863, in *War of the Rebellion: Official Records of the Union and Confederate Armies*, ser. 1, vol. 26 (Washington, DC: Government Printing Office, 1880–1901), 704; Kathleen Collins, "Portraits of Slave Children," *History of Photography* 9 (July–September 1985): 187–188.

3. Banks appointed a Board of Education in March 1864 to direct the establishment of freedpeople's schools. But by then at least seven black schools already had been established and fourteen hundred students enrolled in what was, arguably, the first major effort at public education for freedpeople in the South. See Donald R. DeVore and Joseph Logsdon, *Crescent City Schools: Public Education in New Orleans 1841–1991* (Lafayette: Center for Louisiana Studies, 1991), 57.

4. *Harper's Weekly*, January 30, 1864, 69, 71.

5. Collins, "Portraits of Slave Children," 187–210.

6. Ibid., 203. I have chosen the spelling "Fanny," which was used by the girl's sponsor. However, "Fannie" was often printed on *cartes-de-visite*.

7. Quoted in the *National Anti-Slavery Standard*, December 5, 1863.

8. The suggestion that Isaac and Augusta did not make the trip to Philadelphia comes from photographic historian Kathleen Collins. See Collins, "Portraits of Slave Children," 189.

9. In most instances, I will use the terms "white-looking" and "black-looking" without quotation marks. This is to approximate the perspective of nineteenth-century viewers, rather than to match our current understandings of race as a social construction, dependent on interpretation and context. My choice here is also in the interest of readability.

10. The editors neglected to switch the names, however. Pat Pflieger makes

this observation in "Nineteenth-Century Children & What They Read," http://www.merrycoz.org/yc/WHSLAVES.htm.

11. "White Slaves," *Youth's Companion*, March 9, 1865, 38.

12. *Harper's Weekly*, January 30, 1864, 71. Of all of the children, only Rebecca can be found in the 1860 census or slave schedules with any degree of certainty. J. M. Huger had a mulatto slave girl, aged seven, in his household in the Fifth Ward of New Orleans in 1860. Her grandmother may have been the fifty-year-old mulatto woman in the same house, and her mother either the twenty-eight-year-old or the thirty-five-year-old mulatto woman belonging to Huger. Slave Schedule, Fifth Ward, New Orleans, La., p. 4, U.S. Bureau of the Census, *Eighth Census of the United States, 1860* (Washington, DC: National Archives and Record Administration, 1860), M653, accessed through Ancestry .com, *1860 U.S. Federal Census—Slave Schedules* [online database] (Provo, UT: The Generations Network) (hereafter Ancestry.com). Curators at the Louisiana State Museum traced Rebecca and her relatives to the household of John Huger, a resident of the historic Pontalba Building on Jackson Square in New Orleans's French Quarter.

13. In images, according to W. J. T. Mitchell, "what expression amounts to is the artful planting of certain clues in a picture that allow us to form an act of ventriloquism, an act which endows the picture with eloquence, and particularly with a nonvisual and verbal eloquence." W. J. T. Mitchell, *Iconology: Image, Text, Ideology* (Chicago: University of Chicago Press, 1986), 41. See also Allan Sekula, "On the Invention of Photographic Meaning," in Victor Burgin, ed., *Thinking Photography* (London: MacMillan Education Press, 1982).

14. Thanks to Martha Hodes for this point.

15. The figure of the child can become a metaphor for adult desires and political aims. See Carolyn Steedman, *Past Tenses: Essays on Writing, Autobiography, and History* (London: Rivers Oram Press, 1992), 194. For further explorations of this idea, see Carolyn Kay Steedman, *Landscape for a Good Woman: A Story of Two Lives* (New Brunswick, NJ: Rutgers University Press, 1986); Steedman, *Strange Dislocations: Childhood and the Idea of Human Interiority 1780–1930* (Cambridge, MA: Harvard University Press, 1995).

16. The notion of the United States as a "white nation" was not new. Historian Joanne Pope Melish has noted that in the eighteenth century, many residents of the New England states imagined that gradual emancipation in the North would somehow "restore" the region's homogeneity, that "a free New England would be a white New England." Joanne Pope Melish, *Disowning Slavery: Gradual Emancipation and "Race" in New England, 1780–1860* (Ithaca, NY: Cornell University Press, 1998), 164. On race and emancipation, see Saidiya V. Hartman, *Scenes of Subjection: Terror, Slavery, and Self-Making in Nineteenth-Century America* (New York: Oxford University Press, 1997), 117–118.

Visual images (as well as print media like newspapers, maps, and census rolls) are a vital part of the production of a nation, both as an idea—an "imagined community"—and as a political entity. Benedict Anderson, *Imagined Communities: Reflections on the Origin and Spread of Nationalism* (New York: Verso, 1983), passim; on visual images, race, and nationhood, see Shawn Michelle Smith, "Photographing the 'American Negro': Nation, Race, and Photography at the Paris Exposition of 1900," in Lisa Bloom, ed., *With Other Eyes: Looking at Race and Gender in Visual Culture* (Minneapolis: University of Minnesota Press, 1999.)

17. For a brief discussion of the problem of audience and dissemination in terms of the debate over "white slavery" before the Civil War, see James L. Huston, "Review of Lawrence R. Tenzer, *The Forgotten Cause of the Civil War: A New Look at the Slavery Issue*" *HCivWar*, H-Net Reviews, July 1998, www.h-net.org/reviews/showrev.cgi?path=18608899323509.

18. "Slave Girl Sold by Beecher Found," *New York Times*, May 11, 1927, 28; "Freed Slave Tells of 'Sale' by Beecher," *New York Times*, May 16, 1927, 21; "Mrs. Rose Hunt" (Pinky) photo, *Brooklyn Daily Eagle*, May 16, 1927.

19. Iver Bernstein, *The New York City Draft Riots: Their Significance for American Society and Politics in the Age of the Civil War* (New York: Oxford University Press, 1990). Most abolitionists came from the middle class, though there were significant numbers of "skilled" workers and artisans and a very small percentage of "unskilled" workers involved in the movement as well. See Paul Goodman, *Of One Blood: Abolitionism and the Origins of Racial Equality* (Berkeley: University of California Press, 1998), chap. 11, esp. 145–147; Edward Magdol, *The Antislavery Rank and File: A Social Profile of the Abolitionist Constituency* (Westport, CT: Greenwood Press, 1986), chap. 6.

20. The "displacement" of class issues with the language of race and gender was characteristic of antebellum sentimental fiction. See Amy Schrager Lang, "Class and the Strategies of Sympathy," in Shirley Samuels, ed., *The Culture of Sentiment: Race, Gender, and Sentimentality in Nineteenth-Century America* (New York: Oxford University Press, 1992), 128–142. Ex-slave and abolitionist Frederick Douglass believed that the defeat of slavery could only come with the support of the working class. "It is not to the rich that we are to look," he said in 1852, "but to the poor, to the hardhanded working men of the country; these are to come to the rescue of the slave." Quoted in Herbert Aptheker, *Abolitionism: A Revolutionary Movement* (Boston: Twayne, 1989), 36.

21. William Lloyd Garrison, "Address to the American Colonization Society," July 4, 1829, in William E. Cain, ed., *William Lloyd Garrison and the Fight against Slavery: Selections from the Liberator* (Boston: Bedford Books, 1995), 66–67.

22. On Garrison's editorials, see Carol Wilson and Calvin D. Wilson, "White Slavery: An American Paradox," *Slavery and Abolition* 19 (April 1998):

13–14; Lydia Maria Child, "Mary French and Susan Easton," *Juvenile Miscellany*, 3rd ser., 6 (May–June 1834): 186–202.

23. Wilson and Wilson, "White Slavery," 4–6; on Miller's case, see Carol Wilson, *The Two Lives of Sally Miller: A Case of Mistaken Racial Identity in Antebellum New Orleans* (New Brunswick, NJ: Rutgers University Press, 2007); and John Bailey, *The Lost German Slave Girl: The Extraordinary True Story of Sally Miller and Her Fight for Freedom in Old New Orleans* (New York: Atlantic Monthly Press, 2003).

24. On the Fugitive Slave Act, see chapter 1. See also Lawrence R. Tenzer, *The Forgotten Cause of the Civil War: A New Look at the Slavery Issue* (Manahawkin, NJ: Scholars' Publishing House, 1997).

25. George H. Fitzhugh, "Southern Thought," *DeBow's Review* 23 (October 1857): 339.

26. Wilson and Wilson, "White Slavery," 1–23.

27. Melish, *Disowning Slavery*, 269–277. The term "white slavery" had been used in the 1830s and 1840s as a critique of the wage labor system in the North. But by the outbreak of the Civil War, labor advocates had dropped the term in favor of "free labor." See David R. Roediger, *The Wages of Whiteness: Race and the Making of the American Working Class*, rev. ed. (New York: Verso, 1999), 85. In the late nineteenth century, it was used to describe prostitution.

28. "A White Woman Sold into Slavery," Correspondence of the *Tribune* reprinted in *National Anti-Slavery Standard*, January 3, 1863.

29. Mary Langdon [Mary Hayden Green Pike], *Ida May: A Story of Things Actual and Possible* (New York: Ward, Lock, and Co., 1854), 111.

30. "A White Slave," Correspondence of the *Tribune* reprinted in *National Anti-Slavery Standard*, April 4, 1863.

31. Another fictional account of white slavery was William Wells Brown's *Clotel; or The President's Daughter* (1853). See Joanne Pope Melish's discussion of *Clotel* in Melish, *Disowning Slavery*, 272–277.

32. "Sold at Savannah, in Two Chapters," reprinted from *Chamber's Journal* in the *National Anti-Slavery Standard*, September 12 and 19, 1863.

33. "The White Slaves of the South," Correspondence of the *Grand Rapids Eagle* reprinted in the *National Anti-Slavery Standard*, September 5, 1863. Another story involved a white soldier in the Seventy-eighth Ohio Regiment who had been sold into slavery "out of some charitable institute [in Kentucky] to which he had been committed as a vagrant." "Peculiarities of the Peculiar Institution," Correspondence of the *Cincinnati Commercial* reprinted in the *National Anti-Slavery Standard*, April 11, 1863.

34. Historian Martha Hodes, writing about sexual relations between white women and black men in the nineteenth-century South, notes: "It was the problem of the child that brought the illicit liaison into the public realm, beyond the

confines of gossip and scandal." Hodes, *White Women, Black Men: Illicit Sex in the 19th-Century South* (New Haven, CT: Yale University Press, 1997), 48.

35. C. Vann Woodward, ed., *Mary Chesnut's Civil War,* (repr., New Haven, CT: Yale University Press, 1993), 19.

36. The life of Alexina Morrison well illustrates the furor that racially ambiguous people could create in the antebellum South. See Walter Johnson, "The Slave Trader, the White Slave, and the Politics of Racial Determination in the 1850s," *Journal of American History* 87 (June 2000): 13–38.

37. Jennifer Green-Lewis, *Framing the Victorians: Photography and the Culture of Realism* (Ithaca, NY: Cornell University Press, 1996), 100, 3–4.

38. Kenneth E. Nelson, "A Thumbnail History of the Daguerreotype," the Daguerreian Society, http://www.daguerre.org.

39. Elizabeth B. Clark, "Sacred Rights of the Weak: Pain and Sympathy in Antebellum America," *Journal of American History* 82 (September 1995): 467–468.

40. S. K. Towle, Surgeon, 30th Regiment, Massachusetts Volunteers, to W. J. Dale, Surgeon-General of the State of Massachusetts, April 16, 1863, cited in Kathleen Collins, "The Scourged Back," *History of Photography* 9 (January–March 1985): 44. Towle's comments were printed on the verso of the *carte-de-visite* made of Gordon, printed in Philadelphia. The photographic printers titled the image "Scourged Back."

41. Quoted in the *National Anti-Slavery Standard,* June 20, 1863, beneath the heading "The 'Peculiar Institution' Illustrated." Like the group portrait of "Emancipated Slaves White and Colored," this photograph was made into an illustration and printed in *Harper's Weekly,* appearing on July 4, 1863. See Collins, "The Scourged Back," 43–45.

42. Abigail Solomon-Godeau, "The Legs of the Countess," *October* 39 (Winter 1996): 98.

43. Karen Sánchez-Eppler, *Touching Liberty: Abolition, Feminism, and the Politics of the Body* (Berkeley: University of California Press, 1993), 18, 23. On southerners' readings of a "white" woman enslaved, see Johnson, "The Slave Trader, the White Slave, and the Politics of Racial Determination in the 1850s"; and of slaves in the market, see Walter Johnson, *Soul by Soul: Life inside the Antebellum Slave Market* (Cambridge, MA: Harvard University Press, 2000).

44. John Tagg, *The Burden of Representation: Essays on Photographies and Histories* (Amherst: University of Massachusetts Press, 1988), 78. The phrase "mute testimony" comes from Allan Sekula, "The Body and the Archive," *October* 39 (Winter 1986): 6. The invention and proliferation of photography in the nineteenth century were part of the developing system of surveillance and subjection of particular groups of society, especially children, workers, the insane, and criminals. Michel Foucault, *Discipline and Punish: The Birth of the Prison,* trans. Alan Sheridan (New York: Vintage Books, 1977), 170–194.

45. H. W. Diamond, *Lancet,* January 22, 1859, 89, quoted in Tagg, *The Burden of Representation,* 79.

46. For a history of the "American school," see William Stanton, *The Leopard's Spots: Scientific Attitudes toward Race in America, 1815–1859* (Chicago: University of Chicago Press, 1960). Agassiz quoted in Stephen Jay Gould, *The Mismeasure of Man* (New York: Norton, 1996 [1981]), 77. See also Gould's analysis of Agassiz, Morton, and their "evidence"; *The Mismeasure of Man,* chap. 2.

47. Photography, by the late nineteenth century, became part of a systematic effort to classify criminal and racial "types" on the premise that the medium allowed viewers to read the "true essence" of the sitter. See Shawn Michelle Smith, *American Archives: Gender, Race, and Class in Visual Culture* (Princeton, NJ: Princeton University Press, 1999), 68–93; and Brian Street, "British Popular Anthropology: Exhibiting and Photographing the Other," in Elizabeth Edwards, ed., *Anthropology and Photography 1860–1920* (New Haven, CT: Yale University Press, 1992), 130.

48. These images, found in a cabinet in 1976, were never published by Agassiz. Brian Wallis, "Black Bodies, White Science: Louis Agassiz's Slave Daguerreotypes," *American Art* 9 (Summer 1995); 38–61. See also Alan Tractenberg, *Reading American Photographs: Images as History, Matthew Brady to Walker Evans* (New York: Hill and Wang, 1989), 53–56; Nell Irvin Painter, *Sojourner Truth: A Life, a Symbol* (New York: Norton, 1996), 196–197.

49. Green-Lewis, *Framing the Victorians,* 3–4; Jonathan Crary, *Techniques of the Observer: On Vision and Modernity in the Nineteenth Century* (Cambridge, MA: MIT Press, 1990), 23–24.

50. Viviana A. Zelizer, *Pricing the Priceless Child: The Changing Social Value of Children* (Princeton, NJ: Princeton University Press, 1985), passim.

51. Leslie Williams, "The Look of Little Girls: John Everett Millais and the Victorian Art Market," and Carol Mavor, "Dream Rushes: Lewis Carroll's Photographs of the Little Girl," both in Claudia Nelson and Lynne Vallone, eds., *The Girl's Own: Cultural Histories of the Anglo-American Girl, 1830–1915* (Athens: University of Georgia Press, 1994); Anne Higonnet, *Pictures of Innocence: The History and Crisis of Ideal Childhood* (New York: Thames and Hudson, 1998), chap. 3; Karin Calvert, *Children in the House: The Material Culture of Early Childhood, 1600–1900* (Boston: Northeastern University Press, 1992).

52. Taft, *Photography and the American Scene,* 140; Maurice Rickards, *The Encyclopedia of Ephemera: A Guide to the Fragmentary Documents of Everyday Life for the Collector, Curator, and Historian* (New York: Routledge, 2000), 75–77. See also Michel Frizot, ed., *A New History of Photography* (Cologne: Köneman, 1998), esp. 109–114; Beaumont Newhall, *The History of Photography* (New York: Museum of Modern Art, 1982); Naomi Rosenblum,

A World History of Photography (New York: Abbeville Press, 1989), 62–73, 352–356, 443; Heinz K. Henisch and Bridget A. Henisch, *The Photographic Experience 1839–1914: Images and Attitudes* (University Park: Pennsylvania State University Press, 1994), chap. 2; Gregory Fried, "True Pictures," *Common-Place* 2 (January 2002),pt. 1, http://www.common-place.org. For a technical index of *cartes-de-visite* and their uses, see William C. Darrah, *Cartes de Visite in 19th-Century Photography* (Gettysburg, PA: William C. Darrah, 1981).

53. Shawn Michelle Smith has discussed the nineteenth-century family photograph album (a rather new invention at the time) as something that "offered individuals a colloquial space in which to display practices of national belonging." See Smith, *American Archives*, 6. Nell Irvin Painter has noted the importance of dress and "props" in *carte-de-visite* portraits "self-fashioned" by antislavery activist and former slave Sojourner Truth. Truth used knitting yarn, reading glasses, and books to convey motherliness and wisdom. Sojourner Truth was also one of the first antislavery activists to employ the camera's potential for representation (through portraiture) and the *carte-de-visite* as a means of fund-raising. Painter, *Sojourner Truth,* 196; Painter, "Representing Truth: Sojourner Truth's Knowing and Becoming Known," *Journal of American History* 81 (September 1994): 461–492. Fund-raising through the sale of photographs, especially propaganda, became popular during the Civil War. Kathleen Collins, "Photographic Fundraising: Civil War Philanthropy," *History of Photography* 11 (July–September 1987): 173–187; and Collins, "Living Skeletons: *Carte-de-visite* Propaganda in the American Civil War," *History of Photography* 12 (April–June 1988): 103–120. On the invention of the photograph album to display *cartes-de-visite,* see Taft, *Photography and the American Scene,* 140 and chap. 8; Frilot, *A New History of Photography,* 109–114.

54. Gillian Brown, "Getting in the Kitchen with Dinah: Domestic Politics in *Uncle Tom's Cabin,*" *American Quarterly* 36 (Fall 1984): 505; Harriet A. Jacobs, *Incidents in the Life of a Slave Girl, Written by Herself,* ed. L. Maria Child (Boston, 1861), reprinted, edited by Jean Fagan Yellin (Cambridge, MA: Harvard University Press, 1987). What made Jacobs's narrative so effective was her description of the domestic realm in the slaveholding South as "the ground of the institution's most terrifying intimacies." See Hortense J. Spillers, "Changing the Letter: The Yokes, the Jokes of Discourse or, Mrs. Stowe, Mr. Reed," in Deborah E. McDowell and Arnold Rampersad, eds., *Slavery and the Literary Imagination,* Selected Papers from the English Institute (Baltimore: Johns Hopkins University Press, 1987), 28. See also Philip Fisher, *Hard Facts: Setting and Form in the American Novel* (New York: Oxford University Press, 1987), chap. 2.

55. Laura Wexler, "Seeing Sentiment: Photography, Race, and the Innocent Eye," in Marianne Hirsch, ed. *The Familial Gaze* (Hanover, NH: University Press of New England, 1999), 256. On the "geographic distance" (more felt

than real) between the North and South in this period, see Ronald G. Walters, *The Antislavery Appeal: American Abolitionism after 1830* (Baltimore: Johns Hopkins University Press, 1976), 59.

56. Clark, "Sacred Rights of the Weak," 476. Similar expressions of empathy arose in the writings of antislavery feminists, who paralleled their plight as women with that of the enslaved population in the South. See Jean Fagan Yellin, *Women and Sisters: The Antislavery Feminists in American Culture* (New Haven, CT: Yale University Press, 1989), 50; and Marianne Hirsch, "Introduction: Familial Looking" in Hirsch, ed., *The Familial Gaze.*

57. Bernard Wishy, *The Child and the Republic* (Philadelphia: University of Pennsylvania Press, 1968); Mary Ryan, *Cradle of the Middle Class: The Family in Oneida County, New York, 1790–1865* (Cambridge, MA: Harvard University Press, 1981); Mary Ryan, *The Empire of the Mother: American Writing about Domesticity 1830–1860* (New York: Institute for Research in History and the Haworth Press, 1982); Richard Broadhead, "Sparing the Rod: Discipline and Fiction in Antebellum America," *Representations* 21 (Winter 1988): 67–96.

58. Karen Sánchez-Eppler, "Temperance in the Bed of a Child: Incest and Social Order in Nineteenth-Century America," *American Quarterly* 47 (March 1995): 4. The figure of the "daughter-as-redeemer" displayed both moral purity and strength of character. See Deborah Gorham, *The Victorian Girl and the Feminine Ideal* (Bloomington: Indiana University Press, 1982), 42.

59. Though her concern is not race, Deborah Gorham notes that the image of the good girl in Victorian culture was often contrasted with her opposite. Gorham, *The Victorian Girl,* 49.

60. Elsa Barkley Brown has written about "the relational nature of difference" between white women and black women in U.S. history. See Barkley Brown, "Polyrhythms and Improvisation: Lessons for Women's History," *History Workshop* 31 (Spring 1991): 86, 88.

61. Harriet Beecher Stowe, *Uncle Tom's Cabin or, Life among the Lowly* (New York: Harper and Row, 1965 [1852]), 247. See also the introduction to Ann Douglas, *The Feminization of American Culture* (New York: Knopf, 1977), on "The Meaning of Little Eva."

62. Stowe, *Uncle Tom's Cabin,* 249. See also examples of the popular imagery created for Stowe's novel, which often featured Topsy and Eva together, reprinted in Harriet Beecher Stowe, *The Annotated Uncle Tom's Cabin,* ed. Henry Louis Gates Jr. and Hollis Robins (New York: Norton, 2007), chap. 20.

63. *Freedmen's Journal,* quoted in the *American Missionary,* November 1864, 276.

64. *American Missionary,* June 1865, 126.

65. *American Missionary,* March 1859, 68.

66. *American Missionary,* October 1860, 234.

67. Hartman, *Scenes of Subjection,* 5. In the early nineteenth century, Sarah Roth has argued that "black characters of all ages" were given "childlike qualities" both to make it easier for white children to relate to them and to promote a sense of "superiority" among white children over black people. The work of children's antislavery literature in the later antebellum period, arguably, was more interested in the white child identifying with the slave child. Yet by that same token, such propaganda created a greater social distance between them. Sarah N. Roth, "The Mind of the Child: Images of African Americans in Early Juvenile Fiction," *Journal of the Early Republic* 25 (Spring 2005): 93

68. *American Missionary,* March 1859, 67.

69. Stowe, *Uncle Tom's Cabin,* 43, 496.

70. Ibid., 242.

71. "White and Colored Slaves," *Harper's Weekly,* January 30, 1864, 71. Charles Taylor could have been the five-year-old male slave in the household of John Thornhill, although the child was listed as "black." Thornhill did own a "mulatto" woman of thirty-six who could have been Charles's mother. Slave Schedule, 1st Ward, New Orleans, La., p. 5, U.S. Bureau of the Census, *Eighth Census of the United States, 1860* (Washington, DC: National Archives and Record Administration, 1860), M653, accessed through Ancestry.com.

72. Ex-slave narrators throughout the nineteenth century had to concern themselves with the authentication of their narratives. This involved using specific names and places in their accounts and providing a written introduction by a white sponsor, in order to prove their autobiographies were true and not simply the creation of abolitionists. William L. Andrews, *To Tell a Free Story: The First Century of Afro-American Autobiography, 1760–1865* (Urbana: University of Illinois Press, 1986), 26; see also Charles T. Davis and Henry Louis Gates Jr., *The Slave's Narrative* (New York: Oxford University Press, 1985); John Sekora, "Black Message/White Envelope: Genre, Authenticity, and Authority in the Antebellum Slave Narrative," *Callaloo* 32 (Summer 1987): 482–515; Marion Wilson Starling, *The Slave Narrative: Its Place in American History,* 2nd ed. (Washington, DC: Howard University Press, 1988), chap. 4.

73. Hartman, *Scenes of Subjection,* esp. 19–21. On the imaginings of abolitionists, see Clark "Sacred Rights of the Weak," 479.

74. "A White Slave from Virginia," *New York Daily Times,* March 9, 1855, 4.

75. "Letter from Hon. Charles Sumner—Another Ida May, from the Boston Telegraph, Feb. 27," *New York Daily Times,* March 1, 1855, 1. I am looking further into Charles Sumner's interest in Mary Botts. Mary Niall Mitchell, "The Real Ida May: Truth, Fiction, and Daguerreotypes in a Story of Antislavery" (paper presented at the annual meeting of the Organization of American Historians, New York City, March 2008).

76. Pike had written *Ida May* under the pseudonym Mary Langdon. It was published in 1854 (two years after *Uncle Tom's Cabin*), selling some sixty thousand copies. Donald E. Liedel, "The Puffing of *Ida May*: Publishers Exploit the Antislavery Novel," *Journal of Popular Culture* 3 (Fall 1969), 288; Roth, "The Mind of the Child," 105.

77. "Diary of Hannah Marsh Inman," Manuscript Collection, Worcester Historical Museum, Worcester Women's History Project, www.wwhp.org/Resources/hmdiary.html. According to her diary, Inman had read Langdon's *Ida May* a few months earlier.

78. "Letter from Hon. Charles Sumner," 1.

79. Ibid.

80. "A White Slave from Virginia," 4.

81. "Letter from Hon. Charles Sumner," 1.

82. Fagan Yellin, *Women and Sisters*, 100.

83. Joy S. Kasson, *Marble Queens and Captives: Women in Nineteenth-Century American Sculpture* (New Haven, CT: Yale University Press, 1990), chap. 3; Fagan Yellin, *Women and Sisters*, chap. 5.

84. Kasson, *Marble Queens and Captives*, 75, 82. The quotation from *Harper's Weekly* is also from Kasson, *Marble Queens and Captives*, 82.

85. Ibid., 55.

86. The quotations from Palmer and a nineteenth-century viewer (responding to *The White Captive*) are taken from ibid., 75–76.

87. Sánchez-Eppler, "Temperance in the Bed of a Child," 15; James Kincaid, *Child Loving: The Erotic Child and Victorian Culture* (New York: Routledge, 1992), 13; Higonnet, *Pictures of Innocence*, 36–39, 122–132. These views of girl children as sexually alluring dispute Deborah Gorham's idea that little girls somehow resolved the "tensions inherent in the Victorian view of female sexuality" and that idealized womanhood (in which women were seen as "pure" or "innocent") could "more appropriately be applied to daughters than to wives." I think there is truth in both interpretations of white little girls in the nineteenth century. Gorham, *The Victorian Girl*, 6–7.

88. Williams, "The Look of Little Girls," 124.

89. Millais's *Cherry Ripe* sold six hundred thousand copies in England when it was reproduced as a color centerfold in a Christmas annual. Higonnet, *Pictures of Innocence*, 51. See also Pamela Tamarkin Reis and Laurel Bradley, "Victorian Centerfold: Another Look at Millais's *Cherry Ripe*," *Victorian Studies* 35 (Winter 1992): 201–206; Robert M. Polhemus, "John Millais's Children: Faith, Erotics, and *The Woodsman's Daughter*," *Victorian Studies* 7 (Spring 1994): 433–450.

90. Nina Auerbach, *Romantic Imprisonment: Women and Other Glorified Outcasts* (New York: Columbia University Press, 1985), chap. 9. See also David

M. Lubin's discussion of Guy and Carroll in Lubin, *Picturing a Nation: Art and Social Change in Nineteenth-Century America* (New Haven, CT: Yale University Press, 1994), chap. 5.

91. Ronald J. Walters, "The Erotic South: Civilization and Sexuality in American Abolitionism," in John R. McKivigan, ed., *History of the American Abolitionist Movement*, vol. 1, *Abolitionism and American Reform* (New York: Garland , 1999).

92. On the literature of the "tragic mulatto," see Fagan Yellin, *Women and Sisters*, 71–76; Sánchez-Eppler, *Touching Liberty*, chap. 1; and Susan Gillman, "The Mulatto, Tragic or Triumphant? The Nineteenth-Century American Race Melodrama," in Samuels, ed., *Culture of Sentiment*, 221–244.

93. "An Affecting Incident at Mr. Beecher's Church—a Slave Girl upon the Platform—$883 Contributed on the Spot for Her Redemption," *New York Daily Times*, June 3, 1856, 3.

94. "Mr. Beecher Selling a Beautiful Slave Girl in His Pulpit," ca. 1856, Brooklyn Historical Society, www.brooklynpubliclibrary.org/civilwar/cwdoc007 .html.

95. "An Affecting Incident at Mr. Beecher's Church," 3.

96. "Purchase of a Slave in Plymouth Church," *Brooklyn Daily Eagle*, February 6, 1860.

97. "The White Slave at Mr. Beecher's Church, A True History of the Case," *New York Times*, February 9, 1860, 2.

98. "Brooklyn Intelligence: An Interesting Scene in Plymouth Church," *New York Times*, February 6, 1860, 8.

99. *American Missionary*, March 1860, 68–69.

100. Ibid., 69.

101. "The White Slave at Mr. Beecher's Church," 2. Beecher also commissioned a portrait of her, entitled *Freedom Ring* (with Pink seated on the floor gazing at her ring) by the well-known painter Eastman Johnson. The painting now seems to be lost. See Nona Martin, "Civil War Symbolism," *Carnegie Magazine Online* 63 (January/February 1997), http://www.carnegiemuseums.org/ cmag/bk_issue/1997/janfeb/feat3.htm.

102. "Freed Slave Tells of 'Sale' by Beecher," *New York Times*, May 16, 1927, 21.

103. *American Missionary*, June 1863, 131.

104. Catherine S. Lawrence, *Autobiography or Sketch of Life and Labors of Miss Catherine S. Lawrence Who in Early Life Distinguished Herself as a Bitter Opponent of Slavery and Intemperance, and Later in Life as a Nurse in the Late War; and for Other Patriotic and Philanthropic Services*, rev. ed. (Albany, NY: James B. Lyon Printer, 1896), 140. Thanks to Mary L. White, a participant at the 1999 Berkshire Conference for the History of Women and Gender, for bringing Lawrence's memoir to my attention.

105. "Is It a Sell?" *Brooklyn Daily Eagle*, February 7, 1860, 3. Agnes Moorehead was a Scottish actress who starred in *The Octoroon* in 1859. On the play and its engagement with mid-nineteenth-century questions of race and blood, see Jennifer DeVere Brody, *Impossible Purities: Blackness, Femininity, and Victorian Culture* (Durham, NC: Duke University Press, 1998), 46–58.

106. CHUR 0104 and 0105, Brooklyn Public Library, Brooklyn Collection.

107. *American Missionary*, June 1863, 132.

108. Sentimental fiction was intended to have similar effects on readers. Samuels, ed., *Culture of Sentiment*, passim; and Fisher, *Hard Facts*, chap. 2.

109. *American Missionary*, June 1863, 132.

110. Johnson, *Soul by Soul*, passim.

111. Ibid., chap. 5.

112. *National Antislavery Standard*, February 21, 1863. New Orleans was particularly well known for its light-skinned slave women and free women of color, glamorized by stories of "quadroon balls" where white men chose mistresses from among fair-skinned young women of color. Monique Guillory, "Some Enchanted Evening on the Auction Block: The Cultural Legacy of the New Orleans Quadroon Balls" (Ph.D. diss., New York University, 1999); Caryn Cossé Bell, *Revolution, Romanticism, and the Afro-Creole Protest Tradition in Louisiana, 1718–1868* (Baton Rouge: Louisiana State University Press, 1997), 112–114.

113. Quoted in *Harper's Weekly*, February 28, 1863, 143.

114. "White and Colored Slaves," *Harper's Weekly*, January 30, 1864, 71.

115. Thanks to an anonymous reviewer for this point.

116. *Harper's Weekly*, January 30, 1864, 71.

117. My reading of this image differs somewhat from that of literary scholar Caroline Levander. See Levander, " 'Let Her White Progeny Offset Her Dark One': The Child and the Racial Politics of Nation Making," *American Literature* 76 (June 2004): 221–223; and Mary Niall Mitchell, "Rosebloom and Pure White, or So It Seemed," *American Quarterly* 54 (September 2002): 398–399. On white nationalism and "free soil" ideology in the antebellum and Civil War years, see George M. Frederickson, *The Black Image in the White Mind: The Debate on Afro-American Character and Destiny 1817–1914* (Hanover, NH: Wesleyan University Press, 1987 [1971]), chap. 5.

NOTES TO CHAPTER 3

1. As one writer observed about this particular photograph, Murray's arm around the smallest child, Elsie, "compels her attention as much as it embraces." Karen Sánchez-Eppler, *Touching Liberty: Abolition, Feminism, and the Politics of the Body* (Berkeley: University of California Press, 1993), 7. One can find similar images of white women and black slaves in antislavery literature.

See, for example, the frontispiece to an almanac printed in London in 1853 in honor of Harriet Beecher Stowe's *Uncle Tom's Cabin,* of Liberty reading from the Bible to a group of black children with chains around their feet. Reprinted in Clare Midley, *Women against Slavery: The British Campaigns, 1780–1870* (London: Routledge, 1992), 147.

2. The federal Freedmen's Bureau, established in 1865, tried to counter these and other rumors (e.g., "[the freedpeople] are dying off," "they are killing their children") with published reports from military officials in the field. *Letters from the South, relating to the condition of freedmen, addressed to Major General O. O. Howard, commissioner Bureau R., F., and A.L. by J. W. Alford, gen. sup't education, Bureau R., F., & A.L.* (Washington, DC: Howard University Press, 1870), in "From Slavery to Freedom: The African American Pamphlet Collection, 1824–1909," Rare Book and Special Collections Division, Library of Congress, American Memory, http://memory.loc.gov/ammem/aapchtml/ aapchome.html. See also Heather Cox Richardson, *The Death of Reconstruction: Race, Labor, and Politics in the Post–Civil War North, 1865–1901* (Cambridge, MA: Harvard University Press, 2001), 12.

3. S. G. Howe, *Report to the Freedmen's Inquiry Commission, 1864: The Refugees from Slavery in Canada West* (Boston: Wright and Potter, 1864), iii. The *New York Times,* for instance, often ran columns addressing this theme, such as "The Freedmen of the South—What Shall Be Done with Them?" *New York Times,* March 6, 1862, 3, and "The Future of the Southern Negro" *New York Times,* March 23, 1862, 4.

4. Murray had been in South Carolina since at least 1864. Rupert Sargent Holland, ed., *Letters and Diary of Laura Towne Written from the Sea Islands of South Carolina 1862–1884* (New York: Negro Universities Press, 1969 [1912]), 136. The first boatload of plantation superintendents and teachers to reach Port Royal numbered just forty-one men and twelve women, many of whom lasted but briefly in the heat and mosquitoes before returning home. The freed population in the region, on the other hand, numbered some eight thousand. Robert C. Morris, *Reading, 'Riting, and Reconstruction: The Education of Freedmen in the South, 1861–1870* (Chicago: University of Chicago Press, 1976), 4–5; Ira Berlin, Thavolia Glymph, Steven F. Miller, Joseph P. Reidy, Leslie S. Rowland, and Julie Saville, eds., *Freedom: A Documentary History of Emancipation 1861–1867,* ser. I, vol. III, *The Wartime Genesis of Free Labor: The Lower South* (Cambridge: Cambridge University Press, 1990), 89.

5. *Circular of the Port Royal Relief Committee, Signed March 17, 1862* (Philadelphia: Port Royal Relief Committee, 1862), quoted in Morris, *Reading, 'Riting, and Reconstruction,* 4.

6. Charles Nordhoff, *The Freedmen of South-Carolina: Some Account of Their Appearance, Character, Condition, and Peculiar Customs* (New York:

Charles T. Evans, 1863), 4; Morris, *Reading, 'Riting, and Reconstruction,* 7; James M. MacPherson, *The Struggle for Equality: Abolitionists and the Negro in the Civil War and Reconstruction* (Princeton, NJ: Princeton University Press, 1964), 164. On the transition from slavery to freedom in the South Carolina Low Country, see Julie Saville, *The Work of Reconstruction: From Slave to Wage Laborer in South Carolina, 1860–1870* (Cambridge: Cambridge University Press, 1996).

7. Adam Gurowski, *Diary,* vol. 1, *March 4, 1861 to November 12, 1862* (Boston: Lee and Shepard, 1862), 47, quoted in Willie Lee Rose, *Rehearsal for Reconstruction: The Port Royal Experiment* (New York: Bobbs-Merrill, 1964), 31.

8. Anne McClintock, *Imperial Leather: Race, Gender, and Sexuality in the Colonial Conquest* (New York: Routledge, 1995), 24, 44–45; Sánchez-Eppler, *Touching Liberty,* intro and chap. 1.

9. Wilma King, *Stolen Childhood: Slave Youth in Nineteenth-Century America* (Bloomington: Indiana University Press, 1995), chap. 2; Marie Jenkins Schwartz, *Born in Bondage: Growing Up Enslaved in the Antebellum South* (Cambridge, MA: Harvard University Press, 2000), chap. 5; Gwyn Campbell, "Children and Slavery in the New World: A Review," *Slavery and Abolition* 27 (August 2006): 264–266.

10. As one of the most thoughtful students of abolitionism, Ronald Walters, once suggested, "For reform to have a constituency, it must be intelligible, and it can only be if it draws upon conventional symbols and articulates acceptable themes. Anything else would be gibberish." In turn, Walters argued the usefulness of abolitionist propaganda for the cultural historian: "The power of antislavery propaganda was in its ability to *explain* (sometimes rightly, sometimes wrongly) and explanation is impossible unless reformer and audience operate with a shared structure of assumptions." Ronald G. Walters, "The Boundaries of Abolitionism," in Lewis Perry and Michael Fellman, eds., *Antislavery Reconsidered: New Perspectives on the Abolitionists* (Baton Rouge: Louisiana State University Press, 1979), 21–22.

11. Sumner quoted in George Frederickson, *The Black Image in the White Mind: The Debate on Afro-American Character and Destiny, 1817–1914* (Hanover, NH: Wesleyan University Press, 1987), 109. For more examples of this "romantic racialism," see Frederickson *The Black Image,* chap. 4.

12. Lydia Maria Child, *The Right Way, the Safe Way, Proved by Emancipation in the British West Indies, and Elsewhere* (New York, 1860), chap. 5, in "From Slavery to Freedom: The African American Pamphlet Collection, 1824–1909," Rare Book and Special Collections Division, Library of Congress, American Memory, http://memory.loc.gov/ammem/aapchtml/aapchome.html. Specifically, Child dismissed the idea of gradual emancipation accomplished through

a system of apprenticeship. Apprenticeship, in its Caribbean incarnation, was a system intended to smooth the transition to free labor, in effect "training" former slaves for freedom. It required them to pay for their freedom with continued labor on the plantation. This system was viewed by many abolitionists as a failure because it kept former slaves in an ameliorated state of bondage, still subject to abuse by overseers and planters and unable to "advance" as rapidly as former slaves under immediate emancipation. Child's promotion of immediate emancipation highlighted the activities of fully freed populations in the Caribbean. On Caribbean apprenticeship, see Thomas C. Holt, *The Problem of Freedom: Race, Labor, and Politics in Jamaica and Britain, 1832–1938* (Baltimore: Johns Hopkins University Press, 1992), chap. 2.

13. Child, *The Right Way, the Safe Way*, 13–14.

14. Child, *The Right Way, the Safe Way*, 19. Throughout the Caribbean, freedpeople often resisted the plantation mode of production after emancipation and sought to establish their own "peasant communities," rather than to work for their former owners. Sidney W. Mintz, *Caribbean Transformations* (New York: Columbia University Press, 1974), chaps. 5–9; Holt, *The Problem of Freedom*, chap. 5.

15. Child, *The Right Way, the Safe Way*, 36.

16. Ibid., 80.

17. Nordhoff, *The Freedmen of South-Carolina*, 18.

18. Edward Philbrick, letter to the Boston *Daily Advertiser*, July 20, 1863, in Elizabeth Ware Pearson, ed., *Letters from Port Royal 1862–1868* (New York: Arno Press, 1969), 220, originally published as *Letters from Port Royal Written at the Time of the Civil War* (Boston: W. B. Clarke Company, 1906). The language of liberalism, encouraging "industry" and "thrift," Thomas Holt has noted, was common to both British and U.S. emancipation. Thomas C. Holt, " 'An Empire over the Mind': Emancipation, Race, and Ideology in the British West Indies and the American South," in J. Morgan Kousser and James M. McPherson, eds., *Region, Race, and Reconstruction: Essays in Honor of C. Vann Woodward* (New York: Oxford University Press, 1982), 283–313.

19. As we will see, similar arguments would surface again concerning Native Americans in the 1880s. See David Wallace Adams, *Education for Extinction: American Indians and the Boarding School Experience 1875–1928* (Lawrence: University Press of Kansas, 1995), 23.

20. Edward L. Pierce, "The Freedmen at Port Royal," *Atlantic Monthly* 12 (September 1863): 306–307.

21. Ibid., 307. On postbellum labor struggles in South Carolina, see Saville, *The Work of Reconstruction*.

22. "Children's Department," *American Missionary*, November 1858, 285.

23. See, for instance, "Children's Department," letter from Mount Tappan, April 23, 1862, *American Missionary*, August 1862, 188–189; "Letter from

Mr. Fee" and "Children's Department," *American Missionary,* November 1859, 260–263.

24. "Capacity of the Negro for Improvement," *American Missionary,* June 1861, 129.

25. Letter published in the *Boston Transcript,* January 27, 1862, quoted in McPherson, *The Struggle for Equality,* 160.

26. George W. Stocking Jr., *Victorian Anthropology* (New York: Free Press, 1989), 10–11. See also Adams, *Education for Extinction,* 12–13. From here, I will use the terms "civilization," "uncivilized," and "civilizing" without quotation marks, as nineteenth-century reformers would have understood them, in the interest of readability.

27. *National Freedmen's Relief Association Organized in the City of New York on 22nd February 1862* (New York: National Freedmen's Relief Association, 1862), quoted in Morris, *Reading, 'Riting, and Reconstruction,* 4.

28. Susan Thorne, *Congregational Missions and the Making of an Imperial Culture in 19th-Century England* (Stanford, CA: Stanford University Press, 1999), 95–97; Peggy Pascoe, *Relations of Rescue: The Search for Female Moral Authority in the American West, 1874–1939* (Oxford: Oxford University Press, 1990), passim.

29. McClintock, *Imperial Leather,* 24.

30. Christine Stansell, *City of Women: Sex and Class in New York, 1789–1860* (Urbana: University of Illinois Press, 1982), 197 and chaps. 9–10; Jean Fagan Yellin and John C. Van Horne, eds., *The Abolitionist Sisterhood: Women's Political Culture in Antebellum America* (Ithaca, NY: Cornell University Press, 1994), passim; Mary Ryan, *The Cradle of the Middle Class: The Family in Oneida County, New York, 1790–1865* (Cambridge: Cambridge University Press, 1981), chaps. 3 and 5; Catherine Hall, *Civilising Subjects: Metropole and Colony in the English Imagination 1830–1867* (Chicago: University of Chicago Press, 2002), 91–96; Julie Roy Jeffrey, *Frontier Women: "Civilizing" the West? 1840–1880,* rev. ed. (New York: Hill and Wang, 1998), passim; Pascoe, *Relations of Rescue,* passim.

31. Mrs. A. M. French, *Slavery in South Carolina and the Ex-Slaves; Or, The Port Royal Mission* (New York: Winchell M. French, 1862; repr., Negro Universities Press, 1969), 48.

32. Morris, *Reading, 'Riting, and Reconstruction,* chap. 1.

33. Jacqueline Jones, *Soldiers of Light and Love: Northern Teachers and Georgia Blacks, 1865–1873* (Chapel Hill: University of North Carolina Press, 1980), 20. Also on the AMA, see Joe M. Richardson, *Christian Reconstruction: The American Missionary Association and Southern Blacks, 1861–1890* (Athens: University of Georgia Press, 1986); Clifton Herman Johnson, "The American Missionary Association, 1841–1861: A Study of Christian Abolitionism" (Ph.D. diss., University of North Carolina, 1958).

34. Morris, *Reading, 'Riting, and Reconstruction*, 2–5, 12–14; *The Thirtieth Annual Report of the Association for the Care of Colored Orphans* (Philadelphia: William K. Bellows, 1866), 5–7.

35. Eric Foner, *Reconstruction: America's Unfinished Revolution, 1863–1877* (New York: Harper and Row, 1988), 68–70.

36. Morris, *Reading, 'Riting, and Reconstruction*, xi, 43. On the Freedmen's Bureau, see Foner, *Reconstruction*, 142–170; and Paul A. Cimbala and Randall M. Miller, eds., *The Freedmen's Bureau and Reconstruction: Reconsiderations* (New York: Fordham University Press, 1999).

37. Morris, *Reading, 'Riting, and Reconstruction*, 57. Morris asserts that "northern whites constituted the predominant element of the teaching force," but government statistics for 1868 count 3,791 whites and 4,213 black teachers. John W. Alvord, *Fifth Semi-annual Report on Schools for Freedmen* (Washington, DC: Government Printing Office, 1868), 7, reprinted in Robert C. Morris, ed., *Freedmen's Schools and Textbooks*, vol. 1, *Semi-annual Report on Schools for Freedmen* by John W. Alvord, Nos. 1–10, January 1866–July 1870 (New York: AMS Press, 1980). On the incomplete nature of bureau figures on education, see Heather Andrea Williams, *Self-Taught: African American Education in Slavery and Freedom* (Chapel Hill: University of North Carolina Press, 2005), 98–100. The superintendent of education for freedmen himself noted that many schools and teachers, particularly just after the war, went unreported. For varying historical treatments of northern missionaries in the South, see Henry Lee Swint, *The Northern Teacher in the South, 1862–1870* (Nashville: Vanderbilt University Press, 1941); Rose, *Rehearsal for Reconstruction*; Jones, *Soldiers of Light and Love*; Richardson, *Christian Reconstruction*; Margaret Washington Creel, *"A Peculiar People": Slave Religion and Community-Culture among the Gullahs* (New York: New York University Press, 1988).

38. Williams, *Self-Taught*, 99 and chap. 6. See also Judith Weisenfeld, "'Who Is Sufficient for These Things?': Sara G. Stanley and the American Missionary Association, 1864–1868," *Church History* 60 (December 1991): 493–507; Clara DeBoer, "The Role of Afro-Americans in the Work of the American Missionary Association" (Ph.D. diss., Rutgers University, 1973).

39. Ronald Butchart puts the number of southern whites who taught in black schools in this period at upwards of three thousand. Butchart is compiling information on some eleven thousand teachers who taught in schools for freedpeople between 1861 and 1875. See http://www.coe.uga.edu/ftp. Ronald E. Butchart, "Remapping Racial Boundaries: Teachers as Border Police and Boundary Transgressors in Post-emancipation Black Education, USA, 1861–1876," *Paedagogica Historica* 43 (February 2007): 61–78.

40. W. E. B. Du Bois, *The Souls of Black Folk*, introduction by Henry Louis Gates Jr. (New York: Bantam Books, 1989 [1903]), 19.

41. See Carol Faulkner's reexamination of women's work in this regard.

Carol Faulkner, *Women's Radical Reconstruction: The Freedmen's Aid Movement* (Philadelphia: University of Pennsylvania Press, 2004), 2 and passim. On northern women's engagement in the antislavery movement, in numerous ways, see Bruce Dorsey, *Reforming Men and Women: Gender in the Antebellum City* (Ithaca, NY: Cornell University Press, 2002), 164–186; and Beth A. Salerno, *Sister Societies: Women's Antislavery Organizations in Antebellum America* (De Kalb: Northern Illinois University Press, 2005).

42. Foner, *Reconstruction,* 97. See also Carter G. Woodson, *The Education of the Negro Prior to 1861* (New York: Arno Press, 1968 [1919]; Williams, *Self-Taught,* chap. 1; Janet Duitsman Cornelius, *When I Can Read My Title Clear: Literacy, Slavery, and Religion in the Antebellum South* (Columbus: University of South Carolina Press, 1991).

43. Testimony of Miss Lucy Chase to the American Freedmen's Inquiry Commission, Portsmouth, Virginia, May 10, 1863, in Ira Berlin, Steven F. Miller, Joseph P. Reidy, and Leslie S. Rowland, eds., *Freedom: A Documentary History of Emancipation 1861–1867,* ser. I, vol. II, *The Wartime Genesis of Free Labor: The Upper South* (Cambridge: Cambridge University Press, 1993), 152; William Shields to William N. Mercer, September 21, November 28, and December 1, 12, 1866, William N. Mercer Papers, Special Collections, Hill Memorial Library, Louisiana State University, cited in Foner, *Reconstruction,* 140. See also James Anderson, *The Education of Blacks in the South, 1860–1935* (Chapel Hill: University of North Carolina Press, 1988); and Morris, *Reading, 'Riting, and Reconstruction.*

44. Testimony of Harry McMillan (colored) to the American Freedman's Inquiry Commission, June 1863, Beaufort, S.C., in Berlin et al., eds., *Freedom,* ser. I, vol. III, *The Wartime Genesis of Free Labor: The Lower South,* 250–252.

45. According to the census of 1860, there were 2,213,209 enslaved people under the age of twenty in the United States. *Historical Statistics of the United States, Colonial Times to 1970,* Bicentennial ed., pt. 1 (Washington, DC: U.S. Department of Commerce, Bureau of the Census, 1975), 18, http://www2 .census.gov/prod2/statcomp/documents/CT1970p2-01.pdf.

46. "A New Sanitary Commission," *Harper's Weekly,* October 10, 1866, 659; Jones, *Soldiers of Light and Love,* 3, 229.

47. J. W. Alvord, *Tenth Semi-annual Report on Schools for Freedmen, July 1, 1870* (Washington, DC: Government Printing Office, 1870), 3, reprinted in Morris, ed., *Freedmen's Schools and Textbooks*; Morris, *Reading, 'Riting, and Reconstruction,* chap. 7.

48. See Williams, *Self-Taught,* chaps. 4–5.

49. *American Missionary,* August 1865, 180.

50. Morris, *Reading, 'Riting, and Reconstruction,* 187 and chap. 6; Lydia Maria Child, *The Freedmen's Book* (New York: Arno Press, 1968 [1865]).

51. Jacob R. Shipherd to Lyman Abbott, February 24, 1866, Jacob R.

Shipherd Letterbook, February 13, 1866–June 14, 1866, Cornell University Library, quoted in Morris, *Reading, 'Riting, and Reconstruction,* 53.

52. Hugh Cunningham, *Children of the Poor: Representations of Childhood since the Seventeenth Century* (London: Blackwell, 1991), 134–142.

53. Steven Mintz, *Huck's Raft: A History of American Childhood* (Cambridge, MA: Belknap Press, 2004), 157–158.

54. Charles Loring Brace, *The Dangerous Classes of New York and Twenty Years Work among Them,* 3rd ed. (New York: Wynkoop and Hallenbeck, 1880), 91–92. See also Stansell, *City of Women,* 194–197, 204–205.

55. Rev. Thomas Guthrie, *A Plea for Ragged Schools, or Prevention Better Than Cure,* 14th ed. (Edinburgh: John Elder, 1849), 24.

56. "Children's Department," letter from Mount Tappan, April 23, 1862, *American Missionary,* August 1862, 188–189.

57. Ibid.

58. Children's Aid Society, *Third Annual Report* (1856), 8, quoted in Stansell, *City of Women,* 211.

59. Mintz, *Huck's Raft,* 164–167; Clay Gish, "Rescuing the 'Waifs and Strays' of the City: The Western Emigration Program of the Children's Aid Society," *Journal of Social History* 33 (1999): 121–141; Linda Gordon, *The Great Arizona Orphan Abduction* (Cambridge, MA: Harvard University Press, 2001).

60. Annual Report of the Commissioner of Indian Affairs, 1878, 649, quoted in Adams, *Education for Extinction,* 29.

61. Anderson, *The Education of Blacks in the South,* chap. 2; Adams, *Education for Extinction,* passim.

62. Due to the efforts of benevolent societies responding to the large numbers of orphaned children, white and black, during the Civil War, the 1860s saw the establishment of the same number of orphanages as in the previous two decades combined. James Marten, *The Children's Civil War* (New York: New York University Press, 1998), 211.

63. See Wilma King, *Stolen Childhood: Slave Youth in Nineteenth-Century America* (Bloomington: Indiana University Press, 1995), 148.

64. Elvira C. Williams to Mr. G. Whiting, Parish of Orleans, R.B., five miles below Algiers, July 24, 1867, AMA microfilm, Louisiana, Reel 1 [45716].

65. Morris, *Reading, 'Riting, and Reconstruction,* 159–164; see also Anderson, *The Education of Blacks in the South,* chap. 2; and James L. Leloudis, *Schooling the New South: Pedagogy, Self, and Society in North Carolina 1880–1920* (Chapel Hill: University of North Carolina Press, 1996), chap. 6.

66. Elizabeth Hyde Botume, *First Days amongst the Contrabands* (New York: Arno Press, 1968 [1893]), 283.

67. Elizabeth B. Clark, " 'Sacred Rights of the Weak': Pain, Sympathy, and

the Culture of Individual Rights in Antebellum America," *Journal of American History* 82 (September 1995): 463–493.

68. See the end of this chapter and chapter 4.

69. Matthew Frye Jacobsen, *Barbarian Virtues: The United States Encounters Foreign Peoples at Home and Abroad 1876–1917* (New York: Hill and Wang, 2000), chap. 3; Stansell, *City of Women*, 196, 201.

70. Mary Louise Pratt, *Imperial Eyes: Travel Writing and Transculturation* (London: Routledge, 1992), 7.

71. Lydia Maria Child, "Letter XIV," February 17, 1842, in *Letters from New York* (New York: Charles S. Francis and Co., 1843), 83; New York Assembly, *Report . . . into the Condition of Tenement Houses*, 14, quoted in Stansell, *City of Women*, 201. See also Karen Sánchez-Eppler, "Playing at Class," *ELH* 67 (2000): 822. On Henry Mayhew's oft-cited encounter with a young watercress seller, see Carolyn Steedman, *Past Tenses: Essays on Writing, Autobiography, and History* (London: Rivers Oram Press, 1992), chap. 13.

72. Charles Dickens, *Bleak House* (New York: Modern Library, 2002 [1853]), 147, 217.

73. Ibid., 217.

74. Pratt, *Imperial Eyes*, 7.

75. French, *Slavery in South Carolina*, 46.

76. Ibid., 46–47.

77. Ibid., 48.

78. Ibid. Peggy Pascoe has studied similar episodes in terms of women's moral authority and intercultural interaction between Protestant mission women and the women they aimed to help. See Pascoe, *Relations of Rescue*.

79. Guthrie, *A Plea for Ragged Schools*, 19, 12; Thomas Beggs, *An Inquiry into the Extent and Causes of Juvenile Depravity* (London: C. Gilpin, 1849), 49, quoted in Cunningham, *Children of the Poor*, 108; Brace, *The Dangerous Classes of New York*, 97. On Brace's adoption of the term "street Arab," see also Sánchez-Eppler, "Playing at Class," 10–13.

80. Roger Daniels, *Coming to America: A History of Immigration and Ethnicity in American Life* (New York: Perennial, 1990), 140–141.

81. Stocking, *Victorian Anthropology*, 79; Cunningham, *Children of the Poor*, 100, 123–132. Stephen Jay Gould, *Ontogeny and Phylogeny* (Cambridge, MA: Belknap Press, 1985); Gail Bederman, *Manliness and Civilization: A Cultural History of Gender and Race in the United States, 1880–1917* (Chicago: University of Chicago Press, 1996), chap. 3. On other theories of racial development, see Jacobsen, *Barbarian Virtues*, chap. 4.

82. Richardson, *Christian Reconstruction*, viii.

83. Jacobsen, *Barbarian Virtues*, 116–117.

84. "Letter from an Applicant," *American Missionary*, June 1864, 149.

85. "Picturesque Scene," from the *Springfield Republican,* reprinted in the *National Anti-Slavery Standard,* June 27, 1863.

86. Letter from Miss Caroline E. Jocelyn, Stoney Plantation, Hilton Head, S.C., July 20, 1864, *American Missionary,* October 1864, 238.

87. Pratt, *Imperial Eyes,* 201.

88. This professed inexperience with slaves and former slaves, one historian has argued, may have had its roots in the North's own experience with slavery and emancipation. From the collective denial of the history of slavery in the North and a blindness to the population of free people of color in the northern states arose the fantastic notion of a "whites-only New England." This way of thinking of the North as a land of white people "untainted" by the evils of slavery was shared by both intellectuals and the northern white populace at large and served to paint New England and the rest of the North as a region distinct —both morally and racially—from the slave-owning South. Joanne Pope Melish, *Disowning Slavery: Gradual Emancipation and "Race" in New England, 1780–1860* (Ithaca, NY: Cornell University Press, 1998), chap. 6 and p. 218.

89. Botume, *First Days amongst the Contrabands,* 4, italics in original.

90. Botume was not the only northerner to make this observation about the enslaved population of coastal South Carolina. The notion that they were the most "degraded" of all enslaved populations had much to do with the fact that they were also among the most African. The black population there, isolated from other enslaved populations, spoke Gullah, a pigeon language combining African and English forms. See Washington Creel, *"A Peculiar People."*

91. Botume, *First Days amongst the Contrabands,* 35.

92. On similar travel narratives of British missionaries and abolitionists in pre- and postemancipation Jamaica, see Hall, *Civilising Subjects,* esp. chap. 3. British journalists and urban reformers used such tactics in the 1880s, comparing London's slums to the darkest reaches of Africa. See McClintock, *Imperial Leather,* 120–121.

93. French, *Slavery in South Carolina,* 41–42.

94. Edward Philbrick to Mrs. Philbrick, March 9, 1862, in Pearson, ed., *Letters from Port Royal 1862–1868,* 7.

95. *Harper's Weekly,* June 14, 1862, 372–373.

96. Ex-slave Calvin Kennard recalled being fed this way as a child: "We negro kids, which they call us, dey would have the negro wench, as dey called deir cook, to put us chillun's food in a large pan, gib us all a spoon to eat wid an' all us negro kids would git 'round dat pan like a lot of pigs an' dat slop it good to me." George Rawick, ed., *The American Slave: A Composite Autobiography,* suppl. ser. 2, vol. 6 (Texas), pt. 5 (Westport, CT: Greenwood Press, 1979), 2178–2179. See also Laura Smalley's account; she recalled eating with other children, using a wooden spoon, out of a large tray "made just like a hog trough." Ira Berlin, Marc Favreau, Steven Miller, and Robin D. G. Kelly, eds.,

Remembering Slavery: African Americans Talk about Their Personal Experiences of Slavery and Freedom (New York: New Press, 1998), 135. See also the account of Mae D. Moore, quoted in John B. Cade, "Out of the Mouths of Ex-Slaves," *Journal of Negro History* 20 (1935): 300.

97. On the difficulties of missionaries' "early publicity" in the South, see Willie Lee Rose, " 'Iconoclasm Has Had Its Day': Abolitionists and Freedmen in South Carolina," in Martin Duberman, ed. *The Antislavery Vanguard: New Essays on the Abolitionists* (Princeton, NJ: Princeton University Press, 1965), 201.

98. My reading of this image draws on the work of anthropologists. See Catherine A. Lutz and Jane L. Collins, *Reading National Geographic* (Chicago: University of Chicago Press, 1993), chap. 5.

99. Thanks to Tony Seideman for sharing this image from his private collection with me.

100. Gillian Beer, *Darwin's Plots: Evolutionary Narrative in Darwin, George Eliot, and Nineteenth-Century Fiction,* 2nd ed. (Cambridge: Cambridge University Press, 2000), chap. 4.

101. Horatio Alger Jr., *Ragged Dick, or, Street life in New York with the Boot-blacks,* introduction by David K. Shipler (New York: Modern Library, 2005), 4.

On Alger's story and its ambivalent relation to capitalism, see Aaron Shaheen, "Endless Frontiers and Emancipation from History: Horatio Alger's Reconstruction of Place and Time in *Ragged Dick,*" *Children's Literature* 33 (2005): 20–40. See also Sánchez-Eppler, "Playing at Class," 825–826.

102. Harriet Beecher Stowe, *Uncle Tom's Cabin, or, Life among the Lowly,* ed. Ann Douglas (New York: Penguin, 1981 [1852]), 351–352.

103. Ibid., 353–358.

104. Ibid., 414–415. See Harry Birdoff, *The World's Greatest Hit: Uncle Tom's Cabin* (New York: S. F. Vanni, 1947), 219–224; Jim O'Loughlin, "Grow'd Again: Articulation and the History of Topsy," http://www.iath.virginia.edu/utc/interpret/exhibits/oloughlin.

105. Stowe's novel was a touchstone for many Americans in the nineteenth century. As one literary scholar has noted, "Americans could live in *Uncle Tom's Cabin* because it became a way of structuring experience." Jim O'Loughlin, "Articulating Uncle Tom's Cabin," *New Literary History* 31 (Summer 2000): 573. By the 1860s, Topsy had taken on a life of her own on the "legitimate" stage and on the minstrel circuit. *Uncle Tom's Cabin* was not only a national but also an international sensation. The white actresses who played the part of Topsy competed with one another for the most accurate portrayal. One critic, who had once played Eva, compared the performances of two actresses in the role of Topsy: "True, both are great. Mrs. Howard is more like a minstrel wench, thoroughly Northern. Mrs. Chapman is the *bona fide* little nigger, and I fancy, has seen a great deal of plantation life." When "Mrs. Howard" took her

performance of Topsy's abroad, however, a London critic declared that Howard had achieved "not merely the droll, half idiot, wholly ignorant Topsy of the English stage, but the shrewd, cunning, naturally wicked, almost impish Topsy of reality—the child for whom nobody cared, that in a figurative sense may be said with perfect truth 'never to have been born,' that 'never no fader, nor moder, nor broder, nor sister, nor aunt—no, none one em—that never had nothin' nor nobody.'" Quoted in Birdoff, *The World's Greatest Hit,* 197, 162–163. Jim O'Laughlin argues that Stowe drew upon minstrel stereotypes in her creation of Topsy, which in turn made Topsy a natural for the minstrel stage. O'Laughlin, "Articulating *Uncle Tom's Cabin,*" 581.

106. From the *Evening Post,* quoted in the *National Antislavery Standard,* November 28, 1863.

107. Letter "From a Teacher [in Georgia] to Her Sister at the North," *American Missionary,* June 1865, 123, emphasis in the original.

108. Towne, *The Letters and Diary of Laura M. Towne,* 219.

109. "Incidents of Hospital Life," from the *Evening Post,* reprinted in *National Antislavery Standard,* November 28, 1863.

110. Botume, *First Days amongst the Contraband,* 41.

111. Letter from Pope's Plantation, St. Helena, S.C., April 21, 1862, in Towne, *Letters and Diary of Laura M. Towne,* 11.

112. "The Negro in South Carolina, Social, Religious, and Military Aspects of the Negro Question at Port Royal," *New York Times,* July 19, 1862, 2.

113. Janet S. Byrne, "American Ephemera," *Metropolitan Museum of Art Bulletin,* n.s., 34 (Spring 1976): 49–50; Maurice Rickards, *The Encyclopedia of Ephemera: A Guide to the Fragmentary Documents of Everyday Life for the Collector, Curator, and Historian* (New York: Routledge, 2000), 8–9. In the eighteenth century, children's literature adopted mechanical or metamorphic designs in the form of pop-up books. See Gillian Brown, "The Metamorphic Book: Children's Print Culture in the Eighteenth Century," *Eighteenth-Century Studies* 39 (2006): 351–362.

114. See Robert Jay, *The Trade Card in Nineteenth-Century America* (Columbia: University of Missouri Press, 1987); and Ben Crane, *The Before and After Trade Card* (Dexter, MI: Ephemera Society of America, 1995).

115. McClintock, *Imperial Leather,* 214 and chap. 5.

116. J. H. T. Connor and Michael G. Rhode, "Shooting Soldiers: Civil War Medical Images, Memory, and Identity in America," *Invisible Culture* 5 (2003), http://www.rochester.edu/in_visible_culture/Issue_5/ConnorRhode/ConnorRhode.html; Blair Rogers, "Reed B. Bontecou, M.D.: His Role in Civil War Surgery and Medical Photography," *Aesthetic Plastic Surgery* 24 (March/April 2000): 114–129; Blair O. Rogers, "The First Pre-and Post-operative Photographs of Plastic and Reconstructive Surgery: Contributions of Gurdon Buck, 1870–1877," *Aesthetic Plastic Surgery* 15 (1991): 19–33.

117. Gillian Wagner, *Barnardo* (London: Weidenfeld and Nicolson, 1979), 42–44.

118. Here I am drawing on John Tagg's discussion of realism. John Tagg, *The Burden of Representation: Essays on Photographies and Histories* (Amherst: University of Massachusetts Press, 1988), 99.

119. Seth Koven, "Dr. Barnardo's 'Artistic Fictions': Photography, Sexuality, and the Ragged Child in Victorian London," *Radical History Review* 69 (Fall 1997): 25, 31; Wagner, *Barnardo,* 140–152.

120. Koven, "Dr. Barnardo's 'Artistic Fictions,'" 13, 29.

121. Jackson Lears, *Fables of Abundance: A Cultural History of Advertising in America* (New York: Basic Books, 1994), 56–63; Pamela Walker Laird, *Advertising Progress: American Business and the Rise of Consumer Marketing* (Baltimore: Johns Hopkins University Press, 1998), chap. 1.

122. The Quakers had been active in the education of blacks and Native Americans in the United States since the seventeenth century. The "Orphans Shelter" was established in Philadelphia by an association of women "Friends" in 1822 "for the purpose of relieving the necessities of the poorest of the poor; for where do we find, even in populous cities, a class of the human family more abject, or more deserving of the fostering hand of benevolence, than the parentless children of the African race of this country." *Annual Report of the Association for the Care of Coloured Orphans for 1836* (Philadelphia, 1836), iii–iv. "Going to School," *Harper's Weekly,* June 10, 1876, 484. During the Civil War, the Society of Friends established and funded orphanages and schools for freedchildren in Mississippi, South Carolina, North Carolina, Virginia, Tennessee, and Washington, D.C., U.S. Office of Education, *History of Schools for the Colored Population* (New York: Arno Press, 1969 [1871]), 378.

123. *The Thirtieth Annual Report of the Association for the Care of Colored Orphans* (Philadelphia: William K. Bellows, 1866), 5–7.

124. Beer, *Darwin's Plots,* 105; McClintock, *Imperial Leather,* 122.

125. Williams, *Self-Taught,* 141–147.

126. Jim Downs, "The Other Side of Freedom: Destitution, Disease, and Dependency among Freedwomen and Their Children during and after the Civil War," in Catherine Clinton and Nina Silber, eds., *Battle Scars: Gender and Sexuality in the American Civil War* (New York: Oxford University Press, 2006), 78–103; Testimony of Miss Lucy Chase before the American Freedmen's Inquiry Commission, Portsmouth, Va., May 10, 1863, in Berlin et al., *Freedom,* ser. I, vol. II, *The Wartime Genesis of Free Labor: The Upper South,* 152; Foner, *Reconstruction,* 82; Robert Harrison, "Welfare and Employment Policies of the Freedmen's Bureau in the District of Columbia," *Journal of Southern History* 72 (February 2006): 75–110.

127. "Orphans among the Freedmen," *American Missionary,* April 1866, 73, emphasis in original.

128. "The Escaped Slave" and "The Escaped Slave in the Union Army," *Harper's Weekly*, July 2, 1864, 428; "A Typical Negro," *Harper's Weekly*, July 3, 1863, 429.

129. Joseph T. Glatthaar, *Forged in Battle: The Civil War Alliance of Black Soldiers and White Officers* (New York: Free Press, 1990). Heather Williams describes the photos of Jackson as illustrations of the destitute nature of freed-children in *Self-Taught*, 143.

130. Samuel Canby Rumford, "Life along the Brandywine between 1880 and 1895," in Claudia L. Bushman, ed., *Delaware History* 23 (Fall–Winter 1988): 105.

131. Previous historians have taken the image of "Slaves" at face value, assuming that the boys were, in fact, slave children. See, for instance, Rose, *Rehearsal for Reconstruction*, 142–143. It is not clear who wrote the word "slaves" on the portrait, nor is it clear when they wrote it.

132. Jones, *Soldiers of Light and Love*, 109.

133. Office of the Commission of Enrollment, Dept. of the Gulf to Major General Banks, Commander, Dept. of the Gulf, New Orleans, February 24, 1864, AMA microfilm, Louisiana, Reel 1 [45386], emphasis added. The bracketed number in this and later AMA citations denotes the frame number on the microfilm reel.

134. "Education of the Freedmen in Louisiana," *American Missionary*, (November 1864, 258; Morris, *Reading, 'Riting, and Reconstruction*, chap. 5; Saidiya V. Hartman, *Scenes of Subjection: Terror, Slavery, and Self-Making in Nineteenth-Century America* (New York: Oxford University Press, 1997), chap. 4.

135. Williams, *Self-Taught*, 153.

136. "Testimony of a Teacher," Baton Rouge, February 13, 1865, AMA microfilm, Louisiana, Reel 1 [45614].

137. Josiah Beardsley to Rev. George Whipple, Baton Rouge, 7 June 1864, AMA microfilm, Louisiana, Reel 1 [45470G]; Patricia Brady, "Trials and Tribulations: American Missionary Association Teachers and Black Education in Occupied New Orleans, 1863–1864," *Louisiana History* 31 (Winter 1990): 8.

138. E. M. Birge to Rev. George Whipple, New Orleans, June 2, 1864, AMA microfilm, Louisiana, Reel 1 [45467]; E. M. Birge to Rev. George Whipple, New Orleans, June 27, 1864, AMA microfilm, Louisiana, Reel 1 [45489A].

139. Susan M. Ryan, "Misgivings: Melville, Race, and the Ambiguities of Benevolence," *American Literary History* 12 (Winter 2000): 686. According to historian Anna Davin, in London schools in the nineteenth century, "the question of appearance was closely connected [to training in orderly habits]: it became the visible proof of educational success or failure." Anna Davin, *Growing Up Poor: Home, School, and Street in London 1870–1914* (London: Rivers Oram Press, 1996), 134.

140. "Sunday School Meeting in Beaufort, Abridged from the 'Free South' of April 25th," *American Missionary* 7 (June 1863): 126.

141. "Pictures of the South," *Harper's Weekly,* June 23, 1866, 398.

142. See Tera Hunter's discussion of freedwomen's dress in *To 'Joy My Freedom: Southern Black Women's Lives and Labors after the Civil War* (Cambridge, MA: Harvard University Press, 1998), 1–3.

143. E. B. Eveleth to Rev. George Whipple, April 29, 1865, quoted in Joe M. Richardson, " 'We Are Truly Doing Missionary Work': Letters from American Missionary Association Teachers in Florida, 1864–1874," *Florida Historical Quarterly* 54 (October 1975): 185–186, http://palmm.fcla.edu/FHQ/index .shtml. Portions of this letter were also printed in the *American Missionary.* Letter from Miss Eveleth, Jacksonville, FL, February 4, 1865, *American Missionary,* March 1865, 79.

144. McClintock, *Imperial Leather,* 35, 209; Jacobsen, *Barbarian Virtues,* pt. 2.

145. *American Missionary,* June 1865, 124.

146. Jones, *Soldiers of Light and Love,* chap. 5.

147. Rev. E. H. Alden to Rev. George Whipple, New Orleans, June 11, 1864, AMA microfilm, Louisiana, Reel 1 [45472].

148. The AMA's editors, fond of such accounts of swift success, encouraged reports like Alden's. After studying contributions to the *American Missionary* from teachers in Georgia, historian Jacquelyn Dowd Hall concluded that "the descriptions of the children's performances are so glowing, so predictable in both style and content, that they are rendered highly suspect as true reflections of the educational process." Jones, *Soldiers of Light and Love,* 116.

149. "Education of the Freedmen in Louisiana," *American Missionary,* (November 1864, 257.

150. Edward Philbrick, November 16, 1862, in Ware, ed., *Letters from Port Royal,* 110.

151. Letter from Miss Eveleth, Jacksonville, FL, *American Missionary,* February 1865, 79.

152. Towne, Letter from St. Helena, March 9, 1866, *Letters and Diary of Laura M. Towne,* 172.

153. Washington Creel, *"A Peculiar People,"* 287–288.

154. Letter from St. Helena, March 9, 1866, in Towne, *Letters and Diary of Laura M. Towne,* 172.

155. See chapter 4.

156. Letter, April 27, 1867, in Towne, *Letters and Diary of Laura M. Towne,* 182.

157. Letter, April 12, 1868, in Towne, *Letters and Diary of Laura M. Towne,* 192–194.

158. Letter, February 13, 1874, in Towne, *Letters and Diary of Laura M. Towne,* 234.

159. Rebecca M. Craighead to Rev. E. Smith, May 5, 1867, Georgia, Archives of the AMA, Amistad Research Center, quoted in Hunter, *To 'Joy My Freedom,* 36.

160. Jones, *Soldiers of Light and Love,* 152.

161. John F. Maxfield to T. W. Conway, New York, 29 June 1865, Letters Received, Asst. Comr., Bureau of Refugees, Freedmen, and Abandoned Lands, National Archives (hereafter BRFAL), microfilm, M-1027, Reel 11. On slaveholders' painfully similar behavior in the slave market, see Walter Johnson, *Soul by Soul: Life inside the Antebellum Slave Market* (Cambridge, MA: Harvard University Press, 1998).

162. Clarke J. Hepburn to T. W. Conway, Brooklyn, NY, 29 June 1865, Letters Received, Asst. Comr., RG 105, BRFAL, microfilm, M-1027, Reel 8.

163. Harrison, "Welfare and Employment Policies of the Freedmen's Bureau," 75–76.

164. "Southern Emigrants," *Harper's Weekly,* August 3, 1867, 492–493.

165. Laura Smith Haviland, *A Woman's Life-Work* (New York: Arno Press, 1969 [1881]), 377.

166. Ibid., 377–378.

167. Catherine S. Lawrence, *Autobiography, or, Sketch of Life and Labors of Miss Catherine S. Lawrence Who in Early Life Distinguished Herself as a Bitter Opponent of Slavery and Intemperance, and Later in Life as a Nurse in the Late War; and for Other Patriotic and Philanthropic Services,* rev. ed. (Albany, NY: James B. Lyon, Printer, 1896), 184–190.

168. Phillip C. Garrett to George Dixon, October 19, 1867, Friends Freedmen's Association, letters sent, 1867–1868, Friends Freedmen's Association Records, quoted in Morris, *Reading, 'Riting, and Reconstruction,* 243.

169. Alvord, *Tenth Semi-annual Report,* 3–4, reprinted in Morris, ed., *Freedmen's Schools and Textbooks.*

170. Mott to Josephine Griffing, December 25, 1869 and May 17, 1870, in Josephine Sophia Griffing Papers, Rare Book and Manuscript Library, Columbia University, quoted in Lori D. Ginzburg, *Women and the Work of Benevolence: Morality, Politics, and Class in the 19th-Century United States* (New Haven, CT: Yale University Press, 1990), 179.

171. Adams, *Education for Extinction,* 63. See also Frederick E. Hoxie, *The Final Promise: The Campaign to Assimilate the Indians 1888–1920* (Lincoln: University of Nebraska Press, 1984); K. Tsianina Lomawaima, *They Called It Prairie Light: The Story of the Chilocco Indian School* (Lincoln: University of Nebraska Press, 1994).

172. Adams, *Education for Extinction,* 36–51. Pratt also worked closely with General Samuel Chapman Armstrong of the Hampton Institute, in Vir-

ginia, an industrial school established for the children of former slaves that also began accepting Native Americans in the 1870s. Lonna M. Malmsheimer, " 'Imitation White Man': Images of Transformation at the Carlisle Indian School," *Studies in Visual Communication* 11, no. 4 (Fall 1985): 54–75. See also Laura Turner, "John Nicholas Choate and the Production of Photography at the Carlisle Indian School," and Molly Faust, "Visual Propaganda at the Carlisle Indian School," both printed in the exhibition catalog *Visualizing a Mission: Artifacts and Imagery of the Carlisle Indian School 1879–1918* (Carlisle, PA: Dickinson College, 2004), 14–23. Such photographs were also reproduced as illustrations. See "Indian Education at Hampton and Carlisle," *Harper's New Monthly Magazine* 62 (April 1881): 659–675, accessed through "The Making of America," http://cdl.library.cornell.edu.

173. Despite Pratt's claims, many Native American children struggled to preserve their own identity in the face of his civilizing mission. See Adams, *Education for Extinction,* chap. 7.

174. Quoted in Adams, *Education for Extinction,* 23; on Pratt's philosophy, 52.

NOTES TO CHAPTER 4

1. Cyntha Nickols to the Chief Agent of the FB at N Orleans, 10 Jan. 1867, N-1 1867, Letters Received, ser. 1303, East Feliciana, LA, Asst. Comr., RG 105, BRFAL, Freedmen and Southern Society Project Archives (hereafter FSSP) [A8620].

2. See discussion of the bureau's role in indentures, below.

3. Cyntha Nickols to the Chief Agent of the FB at N Orleans, 10 Jan. 1867, N-1 1867, Letters Received, ser. 1303, East Feliciana, LA, Asst. Comr. Endorsement Lt. James DeGrey, FB agent, to Capt. Wm H. Sterling Act. Asst. Adjt. Genl., Parish of East Feliciana, LA, Clinton, LA, 29 Jan. 1867, RG 105, BRFAL, FSSP [A8620].

4. Thomas C. Holt, *The Problem of Freedom: Race, Labor, and Politics in Jamaica and Britain, 1832–1938* (Baltimore: Johns Hopkins University Press, 1992), 66; Bridget Brereton, "Family Strategies, Gender, and the Shift to Wage Labor in the British Caribbean," in Pamela Scully and Diana Paton, eds. *Gender and Slave Emancipation in the Atlantic World* (Durham, NC: Duke University Press, 2005), 144, 152–154.

5. In Cuba, the Moret Law, passed in 1870, freed all children born to slaves after 1868. In 1871, Brazilian legislators passed "The Law of the Free Womb," which freed all children born to slave mothers. Rebecca Scott, *Slave Emancipation in Cuba: The Transition to Free Labor, 1860–1899* (Princeton, NJ: Princeton University Press, 1985), chap. 3; Martha Abreu, "Slave Mothers and Freed Children: Emancipation and Female Space in Debates on the 'Free Womb' Law,

Rio de Janiero, 1871," *Journal of Latin American Studies* 28 (October 1996): 567–580.

6. Interview with Caroline Hunter, in Charles L. Perdue Jr., Thomas E. Barden, and Robert K. Phillips, eds., *Weevils in the Wheat: Interviews with Virginia Ex-Slaves* (Charlottesville: University of Virginia Press, 1979), 150. See also Brenda Stevenson, "Distress and Discord in Virginia Slave Families, 1830–1860," in Carol Bleser, ed. *In Joy and Sorrow: Women, Family, and Marriage in the Victorian South, 1830–1860* (New York: Oxford University Press, 1991), 111; Nell Irvin Painter, "Soul Murder and Slavery: Toward a Fully Loaded Cost Accounting," in Nell Irvin Painter, *Southern History across the Color Line* (Chapel Hill: University of North Carolina Press, 2002), 23; Marie Jenkins Schwartz, *Born in Bondage: Growing Up Enslaved in the Antebellum South* (Cambridge, MA: Harvard University Press, 2000), 1.

7. This was particularly true when freedpeople sought to earn money on their own, apart from an employer. On freedpeople's self-employment, see Sharon Ann Holt, "Making Freedom Pay: Freedpeople Working for Themselves in North Carolina, 1865–1900," *Journal of Southern History* 60 (May 1994): 229–262.

8. Joseph Hall to General Howard or those having charge of freedmen at Washington, D.C., 14 Sept. 1865, #16 1865, Letters Received, ser. 456, DC Asst. Comr., RG 105, BRFAL, FSSP [A-9720], in Ira Berlin, Steven F. Miller, Joseph P. Reidy, and Leslie Rowland, eds., *Freedom: A Documentary History of Emancipation, 1861–1867*, ser. I, vol. II, *The Wartime Genesis of Free Labor: The Upper South* (Cambridge: Cambridge University Press, 1993), 545.

9. Peter W. Bardaglio, *Reconstructing the Household: Families, Sex, and the Law in the Nineteenth-Century South* (Chapel Hill: University of North Carolina Press, 1995), 116–119.

10. On violence against blacks interpreted as violence against a freed black *household* (told through a particularly graphic story), see Marek Steedman, "Gender and the Politics of the Household in Reconstruction Louisiana, 1865–1878," in Scully and Paton, eds., *Gender and Slave Emancipation in the Atlantic World*, 310–327.

11. Bardaglio, *Reconstructing the Household*, 119; Elizabeth Fox-Genovese, *Within the Plantation Household: Black and White Women of the Old South* (Chapel Hill: University of North Carolina Press, 1988), 29–32 and chap. 2; Lee Ann Whites, "The Civil War as a Crisis in Gender," in Catherine Clinton and Nina Silber, eds., *Divided Houses: Gender and the Civil War* (New York: Oxford University Press, 1992), 6; Stephanie McCurry, *Masters of Small Worlds: Yeoman Households, Gender Relations, and the Political Culture of the Antebellum South Carolina Low Country* (New York: Oxford University Press, 1995), 7. On the divided experiences of black and white families, see Brenda E.

Stevenson, *Life in Black and White: Family and Community in the Slave South* (New York: Oxford University Press, 1996).

12. Dylan C. Penningroth, *The Claims of Kinfolk: African American Property and Community in the Nineteenth-Century South* (Chapel Hill: University of North Carolina Press, 2003), 166; Wilma King, *Stolen Childhood: Slave Youth in Nineteenth-Century America* (Bloomington: Indiana University Press, 1995), 154–158.

13. As E. P. Thompson suggested, "Feeling might be more, rather than less, tender or intense because relations are 'economic' and critical to mutual survival." E. P. Thompson, "Happy Families" (review of Lawrence Stone, *The Family, Sex, and Marriage in England, 1500–1800*), *New Society* 8 (September 1977): 501.

14. Steven Mintz, *Huck's Raft: A History of American Childhood* (Cambridge, MA: Harvard/Belknap Press, 2004), 158.

15. Laura Smith Haviland, *A Woman's Life-Work* (New York: Arno Press, 1969 [1881]), 377.

16. As historian Julie Saville has observed regarding the period of Reconstruction, "struggles over the immediate terms of human labor proved to be inseparable from conflict over envisioned human possibilities." Julie Saville, *The Work of Reconstruction: From Slave to Wage Laborer in South Carolina, 1860–1870* (Cambridge: Cambridge University Press, 1994), 4. Michele Mitchell has studied the importance of black children to African American ideas about racial destiny in a later period. Michele Mitchell, *Righteous Propagation: African Americans and the Politics of Racial Destiny after Reconstruction* (Chapel Hill: University of North Carolina Press, 2004).

17. W. J. Rorabaugh, *The Craft Apprentice: From Franklin to the Machine Age in America* (New York: Oxford University Press, 1986), vii, passim; James D. Schmidt, " 'Restless Movements Characteristic of Childhood': The Legal Construction of Child Labor in Nineteenth-Century Massachusetts," *Law and History Review* 23 (Summer 2005): 315–150; Gillian Hamilton, "The Decline of Apprenticeship in North America: Evidence from Montreal," *Journal of Economic History* 60 (September 2000): 627–664; Mintz, *Huck's Raft*, 137–140.

18. Bardaglio, *Reconstructing the Household*, 100, 104; Victoria E. Bynum, *Unruly Women: The Politics of Social and Sexual Control in the Old South* (Chapel Hill: University of North Carolina Press, 1992), 99–103; Laura F. Edwards, *Gendered Strife and Confusion: The Political Culture of Reconstruction* (Urbana: University of Illinois Press, 1997), 40–42; Stevenson, *Life in Black and White*, 132–133, 98–99, 258–259; Karin L. Zipf, *Labor of Innocents: Force Apprenticeship in North Carolina, 1715–1919* (Baton Rouge: Louisiana State University Press, 2005), 24–29.

19. *Midgett v. McBride*, 48 N.C. 36 (1855), quoted in Bynum, *Unruly Women*, 101.

20. See Barbara Jeanne Fields, *Slavery and Freedom on the Middle Ground: Maryland during the Nineteenth Century* (New Haven, CT: Yale University Press, 1985), 139–142, 153–156.

21. Otho Scott and Hiram M'Cullough, comps., *The Maryland Code: Public General Laws and Public Local Laws* (Baltimore: John Murphy and Co., 1860), 38, Archives of Maryland Online, http://aomol.net/megafile/msa/speccol/sc2900/sc2908/000001/000145/html/am145-38.html, accessed December 16, 2006. On antebellum apprenticeship in other southern states, see Karin L. Zipf, "Reconstructing 'Free Woman': African American Women, Apprenticeship, and Custody Rights during Reconstruction," *Journal of Women's History* 12 (Spring 2000): 20; and Zipf, *Labor of Innocents*. On poor white children and apprenticeship in South Carolina, see John E. Murray, "Fates of Orphans: Poor Children in Antebellum Charleston," *Journal of Interdisciplinary History* 33 (Spring 2003): 528–530.

22. Berlin et al., eds. *Freedom*, ser. I, vol. II, *The Wartime Genesis of Free Labor: The Upper South*, 494, 510, 74.

23. Interview with Millie Randall, n.d., in George Rawick, ed., *The American Slave: A Composite Autobiography*, suppl. ser. 2, vol. 8 (Texas), pt. 7 (Westport, CT: Greenwood Press, 1979).

24. Statement of Jane Kamper, 14 Nov. 1864, filed with M-1932 1864, Letters Received, ser. 12, RG 94 [K-4], given at the headquarters of the Middle Department and 8th Army Corps, in Berlin et al., eds., *Freedom*, ser. I, vol. II, *The Wartime Genesis of Free Labor: The Upper South*, 519.

25. William Cohen, *At Freedom's Edge: Black Mobility and the Southern White Quest for Racial Control, 1861–1915* (Baton Rouge: Louisiana State University Press, 1991), 29–37; Eric Foner, *Reconstruction: America's Unfinished Revolution, 1863–1877* (New York: Harper and Row, 1988), 200–201.

26. Berlin et al., eds., *Freedom*, ser. I, vol. II, *The Wartime Genesis of Free Labor: The Upper South*, 495; Fields, *Slavery and Freedom on the Middle Ground*, 142; Rebecca J. Scott, "The Battle over the Child: Child Apprenticeship and the Freedmen's Bureau in North Carolina," *Prologue* 10 (Summer 1978): 100–113.

27. *Laws of the State of Mississippi: Passed at a Regular Session of the Mississippi Legislature: Held in the City of Jackson, October, November and December, 1865* (Jackson: J. J. Shannon, State Printers, 1866), 82–93.

28. On the Black Codes, see Foner, *Reconstruction*, 372. It was not until 1909, for instance, that North Carolina eliminated apprenticeship laws in favor of the Child Welfare Act with broadened state powers and responsibilities regarding children. Zipf, *Labor of Innocents*, chap. 6.

29. Capt. N. G. Gill to Capt. & Pro. Mar., 19 Feb. 1865, Prov. Mar. Letters Received, ser. 1488, Lafourche Parish, LA, RG 393, pt. 4, BRFAL.

30. Lucy Lee to Lt. Col. W. E. W. Ross, 10 Jan. 1865, in "Communication from Major Gen'l Lew. Wallace, in Relation to the Freedmen's Bureau, to the General Assembly of Maryland," *Maryland House Journal and Documents* (Annapolis, 1865), document J, pp. 68–69, in Berlin et al., eds., *Freedom*, ser. I, vol. II, *The Wartime Genesis of Free Labor: The Upper South*, 498; Charles M. Hooper to Wager Swayne, April 20, 1867, Wager Swayne Papers, Alabama State Department of Archives and History, quoted in Foner, *Reconstruction*, 201. On freedpeople's view of apprenticeship as slavery, see also Edwards, *Gendered Strife and Confusion*, 48.

31. The first circular concerning apprenticeships stated the ages of majority for girls and boys to be eighteen and twenty-one, respectively. See Circular No. 25, War Dept., Washington, DC, 4 Oct. 1865, BRFAL. But a random survey of indentures signed in Louisiana state the ages of majority to be eighteen and fifteen.

32. Indentures, Parishes of Sabine and Natchitoches, ser. 1776, box 23, Natchitoches, LA, Agent & Asst. Subasst. Comr., RG 105, BRFAL.

33. Amy Dru Stanley, *From Bondage to Contract: Wage Labor, Marriage, and the Market in the Age of Slave Emancipation* (Cambridge: Cambridge University Press, 1998), x and passim. See also Rebecca J. Scott, "Defining the Boundaries of Freedom in the World of Cane: Cuba, Brazil, and Louisiana after Emancipation," *American Historical Review* 99 (February 1994): 70–102. Scott writes: "Struggles over labor arrangements in the postemancipation world were also struggles over values. Moreover, the different parties to those struggles had 'incongruous notions' of how and where to define the boundaries of freedom." Scott, "Defining the Boundaries of Freedom," 70.

34. Bardaglio, *Reconstructing the Household*, chap. 3.

35. Stanley, *From Bondage to Contract*, xi–xiii, and chap. 4.

36. On slave men and women's manipulation of the market, see Walter Johnson, *Soul by Soul: Life inside the Antebellum Slave Market* (Cambridge, MA: Harvard University Press, 1998).

37. Thomas Calahan, Asst. Supt. to Thomas W. Conway, Asst. Comr., 6 Sept. 1865, Unregistered Letters Received, ser. 1304, Shreveport, LA, Asst. Comr., RG 105, BRFAL, FSSP [A-8549].

38. Capt. J. W. Keller to Lt. Hayden, 2 July 1866, Unregistered Letters Received, ser. 1602, Franklin, LA, Asst. Subasst. Comr., RG 105, BRFAL, FSSP [A-8523].

39. Scott, "Battle over the Child," 102; Noralee Frankel, *Freedom's Women: Black Women and Families in Civil War Era Mississippi* (Bloomington: Indiana University Press, 1999), 138–143; Barry A. Crouch, "'To Enslave the Rising Generation': The Freedmen's Bureau and the Texas Black Code," in Paul A. Cimbala and Randall M. Miller, eds., *The Freedmen's Bureau and Reconstruction: Reconsiderations* (New York: Fordham University Press, 1999), 269.

40. Chaplain L. S. Livermore to Lt. Col. R. S. Donaldson, 10 Jan. 1866, "L" 1866, Registered Letters Received, ser. 2188, Jackson MS Act. Asst. Comr. of the Northern District of Mississippi, BRFAL, FSSP [A-9328], in Ira Berlin and Leslie S. Rowland, eds., *Families and Freedom: A Documentary History of African-American Kinship in the Civil War Era* (New York: New Press, 1997), 221.

41. W. H. R. Hangen, Asst. Subasst. Comr. to 1st Lt. J. M. Lee, 3 Oct. 1867, Madisonville, LA, Letters Received, Asst. Comr., RG 105, BRFAL, microfilm, M-1027, Reel 16 [999].

42. E. W. Dewees Asst. Subasst. Comr. to 1st Lt. J. M. Lee, Trimonthly Report, 10 Oct. 1867, Sparta, LA, Letters Received, Asst. Comr., RG 105, BRFAL, microfilm, M-1027, Reel 14 [1419].

43. Robert Harrison, "Welfare and Employment Policies of the Freedmen's Bureau in the District of Columbia," *Journal of Southern History* 72 (February 2006): 75–110.

44. See, for instance, the cases of Adeline Williams, Mary and Georgiana Smith, and Sarah Minor. William W. Rogers to Capt. J. P. Lee Sub. Asst. Comr. 10th Dist VA, 28 June 1867, Washington, D.C., Letters Received, Asst. Comr., RG 105, BRFAL, microfilm, M-1055, Reel 1 [304]; William W. Rogers to Miss Eliza Heacock, 21 June 1867 and 27 June 1867, Washington, D.C., Letters Sent, Asst. Comr., RG 105, BRFAL, microfilm, M-1055, Reel 1 [294, 300]. Thanks to Robert Harrison for publishing these citations. See Harrison, "Welfare and Employment Policies of the Freedmen's Bureau in the District of Columbia."

45. Wm W. Rogers, AAAG to Maj. J. V. W. Vandenburgh, Local Supt. D.C., Washington, D.C., 12 July 1867, Letters Sent, Asst. Comr., RG 105, BRFAL, microfilm, M-1055, Reel 1 [332].

46. Carol Faulkner, *Women's Radical Reconstruction: The Freedmen's Aid Movement* (Philadelphia: University of Pennsylvania Press, 2004), chap. 7; Nell Irvin Painter, *Sojourner Truth: A Life, a Symbol* (New York: Norton, 1996), chap. 22.

47. Faulkner, *Women's Radical Reconstruction,* 128.

48. Bvt. Maj. Clark to Headquarters BRFAL, 13 Feb. 1868, Letters Received, DC Asst. Comr., RG 105, BRFAL, microfilm, M-1055, Reel 10 [430]; Ann B. Earle to Genl. O. O. Howard, 24 Jan. 1868, Letters Received, DC Asst. Comr., RG 105, BRFAL, microfilm, M-1055, Reel 10 [430]. Carol Faulkner also discusses this particular episode. See Faulkner, *Women's Radical Reconstruction,* 126–127. According to Faulkner, although Griffing was "a strong defender of migration, she was unwilling to force freedpeople to leave Washington, especially if emigration would divide families," but inadvertent or not, Griffing also seemed to be at the center of a fair number of complaints about children separated from their families.

49. As historian Robert Harrison has pointed out, the bureau's approach to

"free labor" was a strange conjoining of home, employment, and long-term contracts, one that could function in the South but did not work as easily for bureau agents in Washington, D.C., and for the settling of freedpeople to points north. See Harrison, "Welfare and Employment Policies of the Freedmen's Bureau," 107–108.

50. See Mintz, *Huck's Raft,* 164.

51. Journal of Business, 22 June 1867, vol. 494, ser. 1924, p. 21, Vermillionville, LA, Agent & Asst. Subasst. Comr., RG 105, BRFAL; Foner, *Reconstruction,* 201.

52. Capt. Edward Bigelow to Thomas W. Conway Genl. Supt. of Fmen, 10 June 1865, Letters Sent, ser. 1486, Thibodeaux, LA, Pro. Mar. (376/931 DG), RG 393 Pt. 4, pp. 57–58, BRFAL.

53. On fictive kinship and family structure among North American slave communities, see Herbert G. Gutman, *The Black Family in Slavery and Freedom 1750–1925* (New York: Vintage Books, 1976), pt. 1; Herbert G. Gutman, "The Black Family in Slavery and Freedom, A Revised Perspective," in Ira Berlin, ed., *Power and Culture: Essay on the American Working Class* (New York: Pantheon Books, 1987), 365–367; Penningroth, *The Claims of Kinfolk,* 170–171; A. J. Russell-Wood, "The Black Family in the Americas," *Societas* 8 (1978): 1–38. On the "female slave network," through which slave women shared the responsibilities of motherhood, see Deborah Gray White, *Ar'n't I a Woman? Female Slaves in the Plantation South* (New York: Norton, 1985), chap. 4. Gutman later stressed the need for further research into the use of these "passageways" by emancipated slaves. See Gutman, "Afro-American Kinship before and after Emancipation in North America," in Hans Medick and David Warren Sabean, eds., *Interest and Emotion: Essays on the Study of Family and Kinship* (Cambridge: Cambridge University Press, 1984), 241–265.

54. Affidavit of Adam Woods, 11 Nov. 1867, No. 569 1867, Letters Received, ser. 1208, Louisville, KY, Subasst. Comr., BRFAL, FSSP [A-4513], in Berlin and Rowland, eds., *Families and Freedom,* 228–230.

55. Martin Lee to Mr. Tillson, 7 Dec. 1866, Unregistered Letters Received, ser. 632, GA Asst. Comr., BRFAL, FSSP [A-5416], in Berlin and Rowland, eds., *Families and Freedom,* 233.

56. Bvt. Maj. & Agent Thomas H. Hopwood to Whom It May Concern, 29 May 1866, Letters Sent, ser. 1826, vol. 390, p. 29, New Roads, LA, Asst. Subasst. Comr., RG 105, BRFAL.

57. H. C. Seymour 1st Lt. & Pro. Mar. to Whom It May Concern, 17 April 1866, New Orleans, LA, Letters Received, Asst. Comr., RG 105, BRFAL, microfilm, M-1027, Reel 14 [84]. For a similar case, see Register of Court Trials, ser. 1466, vol. 197, p. 75, Algiers, LA, Provost Marshal, RG 393, pt. 4, BRFAL.

58. Journal of Business, 10 Dec. 1867, ser. 1924, vol. 494, pp. 67–68, Vermillionville, LA, Agent & Asst. Subasst. Comr., RG 105, BRFAL.

59. Journal of Business, 17 Aug. 1867, ser. 1924, vol. 494, p. 42, Vermillionville, LA, Agent & Asst. Subasst. Comr., RG 105, BRFAL; Capt. Edward Lindemann to Capt. Wm Sterling, 20 Aug. 1867, Letters Received, Vermillionville, LA, Asst. Comr., RG 105, BRFAL, microfilm, M-1027, Reel 17 [0920].

60. William F. Mugleston, "The Freedmen's Bureau and Reconstruction in Virginia: The Diary of Marcus Sterling Hopkins, a Union Officer," *Virginia Magazine of History and Biography* 86 (1978): 55, quoted in Penningroth, *The Claims of Kinfolk*, 168.

61. King, *Stolen Childhood*, 102.

62. Register of Complaints, 13 May 1867, ser. 1807, vol. 404, p. 2, New Orleans, L.B. [Left Bank] Asst. Subasst. Comr.; Register of Complaints, 14 May 1867, ser. 1807, vol. 404, p. 8, New Orleans, L.B., Asst. Subasst. Comr., RG 105, BRFAL.

63. Josephine Griffing to Sojourner Truth and Amy Post, March 26, 1867, quoted in Faulkner, *Women's Radical Reconstruction*, 122.

64. King, *Stolen Childhood*, 160; Jacqueline Jones, *Labor of Love, Labor of Sorrow: Black Women, Work, and the Family from Slavery to the Present* (New York: Basic Books, 1985), 61–62, 87–88, 91, 94; Priscilla Ferguson Clement, *Growing Pains: Children in the Industrial Age, 1850–1890* (New York: Twayne, 1997), 129–131; Albert Camarillo, *Chicanos in a Changing Society: From Mexican Pueblos to American Barrios in Santa Barbara and Southern California, 1848–1930* (Cambridge, MA: Harvard University Press, 1979), 6–14.

65. See, for instance, L. Jolissant to Assistant Commissioner, 31 Oct. 1867, Letters Received, New Orleans, LA, Asst. Comr., RG 105, BRFAL, microfilm, M-1027, Reel 17 [0155].

66. "Labor Regulations," May 25, 1865, Undated *Daily Picayune* (?) Letters Received, Asst. Comr., RG 105, BRFAL, microfilm, M-1027, Reel 11 [0042].

67. Lt. James DeGrey to Capt. William H. Sterling, 30 April 1867, Letters Received, Clinton, LA, Asst. Comr., RG 105, BRFAL, microfilm, M-1027, Reel 14 [861].

68. Bvt. Capt. Richard Folles to Assistant Commissioner, 20 July 1867, Trimonthly Report, Letters Received, Algiers, LA, Asst. Comr., RG 105, BRFAL, microfilm, M-1027, Reel 15 [0342].

69. Historians have spilled much ink assessing the flaws and the strengths of these interviews as a source. I make use of them here with the understanding that memory can be foggy and the circumstances under which the interviews were conducted—mostly by white interviewers in the segregated South in the 1930s and 1940s—shaped the responses of former slaves telling their stories. One of the larger criticisms of these interviews, as sources on slavery, however, is that two-thirds of the respondents were children at the time of emancipation. That, of course, makes them particularly useful here. For further discussion, see

the introduction to Ira Berlin, Marc Favreau, Stephen F. Miller, and Robin D. G. Kelley, eds., *Remembering Slavery: African Americans Talk about Their Personal Experiences of Slavery and Emancipation* (New York: New Press, 1988), xiii–xliii. For a detailed analysis of these sources, see Paul D. Escott, *Slavery Remembered: A Record of Twentieth-Century Slave Narratives* (Chapel Hill: University of North Carolina Press, 1979). Antebellum slave narratives have parallel, if different, flaws as sources. See John Sekora, "Black Message/White Envelope: Genre, Authenticity, and Authority in the Antebellum Slave Narrative," *Callaloo* 32 (Summer 1987): 482–515.

70. Interview with Albert Patterson, 22 May 1940, Watson Memorial Library, Cammie G. Henry Research Center, Northwestern State University of Louisiana (hereafter NSUL), Papers of the Federal Writers' Project for Louisiana (hereafter FWPLA), folder 19. For similar statements on education, see interview with Hannah Kelly, 27 May 1940, NSUL, FWPLA, folder 19; interview with Silas Spotfore, 15 May 1940, NSUL, FWPLA, folder 19; interview with Pauline Johnson and Felice Boudreaux, 12 Sept. 1937, *American Slave*, suppl. ser. 2 vol. 6 (Texas), pt. 5, p. 2038.

71. Interview with Millie Randall, n.d., in Rawick, ed., *American Slave*, suppl. ser. 2, vol. 8 (Texas), pt. 7.

72. Interview with John Moore, May 8, 1937, in George Rawick, ed., *American Slave*, suppl. ser. 2, vol. 7 (Texas), pt. 6, p. 2737; interview with Ella Washington, April 13, 1937, in Rawick, ed., *American Slave*, suppl. ser. 2, vol. 10 (Texas), pt. 9, p. 3974; interview with Ellen Broomfield, 20 Feb. 1941, NSUL, FWPLA, folder 19; interview with Calvin Kennard, 11 Aug. 1937, *American Slave*, suppl. ser. 2, vol. 6 (Texas), pt. 5, p. 2180; interview with La San Mire, n.d., *American Slave*, vol. 5 (Texas), pts. 3 and 4, p. 107. See also Pauline Johnson and Felice Boudreaux, 12 Sept. 1937, *American Slave*, suppl. ser. 2 vol. 6 (Texas), pt. 5, p. 2038; John Zeno, 13 Sept. 1937, *American Slave*, suppl. ser. 2 vol. 6 (Texas), pt. 5, p. 1951; and interviews with Henry Reed, Odel Jackson, Verial Brown, Rev. Tennessee Johnson, Ceceil George, Jordon Waters, Ed De Buiew, and Mary Ann John, NSUL, FWPLA, folder 19.

73. Diana Paton and Pamela Scully, "Introduction: Gender and Slave Emancipation in Comparative Perspective," in Scully and Paton, eds., *Gender and Slave Emancipation in the Atlantic World*, 7.

74. Interview with Carlyle Stewart, 3 May 1940, NSUL, FWPLA, folder 19.

75. Interview with Janie Sienette, 25 Nov. 1940, NSUL, FWPLA, folder 19.

76. Journal of Business, 5 Sept. 1868, ser. 1924, vol. 493, p. 6, Vermillionville, LA, Agent & Asst. Subasst. Comr., RG 105, BRFAL.

77. Journal of Business, 5 Feb. 1868, ser. 1799, vol. 449, p. 104, New Iberia LA, Asst. Subasst. Comr., RG 105, BRFAL.

78. No. 77 U.S. Leath v. Jackson, Register of Court Trials, 19 June 1867, ser. 1466, vol. 197, p. 193, Algiers, LA, Office of Asst. Subasst. Comr., RG 105,

BRFAL; see also William H. Cornelius to Capt. A. F. Hayden, 10 March 1866, Letters Sent, ser. 1784, vol. 447, pp. 9–10, New Iberia, LA Asst. Subasst. Comr., RG 105, BRFAL, FSSP [A-8737a]; Robert and Amy Johnson v. Jerry Taylor, Register of Complaints, 3 Aug.–23 Oct. 1866, ser. 1479, vol. 204, p. 165, Amite City, LA, Asst. Subasst. Comr., RG 105, BRFAL; No. 57 U.S. v. Basil Murphy, Register of Court Trials, 27 Oct. 1866, ser. 1466, vol. 197, p. 103, Algiers, LA, Asst. Subasst. Comr., RG 105, BRFAL.

79. Journal of Business, Court Cases, 22 July 1867, ser. 1586, vol. 267, p. 8, Donaldsonville, LA Asst. Subasst. Comr., RG 105, BRFAL; Capt. John H. Brough to Lt. L. O. Parker, 1 Aug. 1867, Donaldsonville, LA, Letters Sent, Asst. Comr., RG 105, BRFAL, microfilm, M-1027, Reel 14 [692].

80. Ira D. McClary to Capt. William Sterling, 21 Feb. 1867, Letters Received, St. Bernard & Plaquemines (L.B.) LA, Asst. Comr., RG 105, BRFAL, microfilm, M-1027, Reel 18 [70].

81. Edward Lindemann to Capt. William Sterling, 20 May 1867, Vermillionville, LA, Letters Received, Asst. Comr., RG 105, BRFAL, microfilm, M-1027, Reel 17 [733].

82. Agreement between Mary and Kitty before Capt. E. Bigelow Pro. Mar., 26 Dec. 1864, Letters Received, ser. 1488, Lafourche, LA, Pro. Mar., RG 393, Pt. 4, BRFAL. See also Agreement between Bill and Minerva before Capt. E. Bigelow Pro Mar, 28 Dec. 1864, Letters Received, ser. 1488, Lafourche, LA, Pro. Mar., RG 393, Pt. 4, BRFAL.

83. See Bardaglio, *Reconstructing the Household,* 102.

84. Sallie Harris to Mr. Barnz, 11 June 1866, Letters & Orders Received, ser. 3881, Amelia Courthouse VA Asst. Supt., BRFAL [A-8116], in Berlin and Rowland, eds., *Families and Freedom,* 237.

85. Wister Miller to Capt. Barns, 12 June 1866, Letters & Orders Received, ser. 3881, Amelia Courthouse VA Asst. Supt., BRFAL, FSSP [A-8116], in Berlin and Rowland, eds., *Families and Freedom,* 237.

86. Capt. W. F. White to Capt. Stuart Barnes, 12 June 1866, vol. 102, pp. 150–51, Letters Sent, ser. 3879, Amelia Courthouse VA Asst. Supt., BRFAL, FSSP [A-8116], in Berlin and Rowland, eds., *Families and Freedom,* 237–239.

87. On paternalism in the antebellum South, see Johnson, *Soul by Soul,* esp. 28–29, 35–36, 107–112; Eugene D. Genovese, *Roll, Jordon, Roll: The World the Slaves Made* (New York: Vintage Books, 1972), 3–6, and *The World Slaveholders Made: Two Essays in Interpretation* (Middletown, CT: Wesleyan University Press, 1988), 30–31, 100–101; Fox-Genovese, *Within the Plantation Household,* 32, 100–101.

88. Tera W. Hunter, *To 'Joy My Freedom: Southern Women's Lives and Labors after the Civil War* (Cambridge, MA: Harvard University Press, 1997), chap. 1; Leon F. Litwack, *Been in the Storm So Long: The Aftermath of Slavery* (New York: Vintage Books, 1979), chap. 4.

89. Mrs. Mary Golbert to Maj. Genl. Banks, 26 Jan. 1863, Letters Received, ser. 1920, Civil Affairs, Dept. of the Gulf, box 2, RG 393, pt. 1, BRFAL.

90. Thanks to Rebecca Scott for this point.

91. Mr. Edward Lindemann ASAC to Capt. Wm Sterling, AAAG, 31 May 1867, Vermillionville, LA, Letters Received, Asst. Comr., RG 105, BRFAL, microfilm, M-1027, Reel 18 [1440]; Journal of Business, 24 Feb. 1868, ser. 1924, vol. 494, pp. 85–86, Vermillionville, LA, Asst. Subasst. Comr., RG 105, BRFAL. For a similar case, see Journal of Business, 7 June 1867, ser. 1924, Vermillionville, LA Asst. Subasst. Comr., RG 105, BRFAL, and Edward Lindemann ASAC to Capt. Wm Sterling, 30 June 1867, Letters Received., Asst. Comr., RG 105, BRFAL, microfilm, M-1027, Reel 17 [0845].

92. For use of similar paternalist arguments in favor of former slaveholders as custodians, see Frankel, *Freedom's Women*, 142.

93. Capt. Geo. W. Curry to Col. Adrian R. Root, 23 Nov. 1864, enclosing Philip Pettebone et al. to Geo W. Curry, Esq., 22 Nov. 1864, C-643 1864, Letters Received, ser. 2343, Middle Dept. & 8th Army Corps, RG 393 Pt. I, BRFAL, FSSP [C-4133], in Berlin et al., eds., *Freedom*, ser. I, vol. II, *The Wartime Genesis of Free Labor: The Upper South*, 520–521.

94. On the role of bureau agents as brokers between freedpeople and former slaveholders, see Scott, "The Battle over the Child," passim.

95. Bvt. Capt. R. Folles to the Assistant Commissioner, Trimonthly Report, 10 May 1867, Letters Received, Algiers, LA, Asst. Comr., RG 105, BRFAL, microfilm, M-1027, Reel 15 [437].

96. Bvt. Capt. R. Folles to Lt. L. O. Parker, 24 Sept. 1867, Registered Letters Received, F-194 ser. 1451 [box 2 of 1452] Algiers, LA, Agent Orleans & Jefferson Parish, RG 105, BRFAL. Enclosure: Case No. 188 U.S. Elin vs. Wood.

97. Testimony of Caleb G. Forshey, resident of Texas, in Confederate service in trans-Mississippi, especially Louisiana and Texas as an officer of engineers, in *Report of the Joint Committee on Reconstruction at the First Session 39th Congress* (Washington, DC: Government Printing Office 1866), 129. On criticisms of freedpeople as parents, and of black mothers in particular, see Leslie A. Schwalm, *A Hard Fight for We: Women's Transition from Slavery to Freedom in South Carolina* (Urbana: University of Illinois Press, 1997), 211–214.

98. Elizabeth Callihan to Maj. H. W. Wallace, 15 Aug. 1867, Registered Letters Received, ser. 1829, vol. 387, New Roads, LA, Asst. Subasst. Comr., RG 105, BRFAL; Enclosures: R. A. Simms Atty at Law to Elizabeth Callihan, 21 July 1867, Donaldsonville, LA; Indenture of William Callihan to Mrs. E. Callihan, 15 Aug. 1867, granted by Gen. A. Baird; Endorsements: Maj. H. F. Wallace to J. A. Mower, 22 Aug. 1867, New Roads, LA; 2nd Lt. L. O. Parker, 29 Aug. 1867, New Orleans.

99. Stephanie Shaw addresses the issue of child rearing and the family economy in poor black households in the Jim Crow era. See Stephanie J. Shaw,

What a Woman Ought to Be and to Do: Black Professional Women Workers during the Jim Crow Era (Chicago: University of Chicago Press, 1996), 16–20.

100. On the effects of slavery and violence on the rearing of slave children and freedchildren, see Painter, "Soul Murder and Slavery," 23–25; Penningroth, *Claims of Kinship,* 175–176. On physical punishment of children in general in the nineteenth century and eventual reforms aimed to curtail it, see Mintz, *Huck's Raft,* 168–169.

101. Some ex-slaves testified to the feelings of uncertainty they experienced after emancipation. See Litwack, *Been in the Storm So Long,* 212–216.

102. Lt. Wm H. Cornelius to Capt. William H. Sterling, 26 March 1867, New Iberia LA, Letters Sent, ser. 1784, vol. 447, pp. 119–121, Asst. Subasst. Comr., RG 105, BRFAL.

103. David K. Wiggins, "The Play of Slave Children in the Plantation Communities of the Old South, 1820–60," in N. Ray Hiner and Joseph M. Hawes, eds., *Growing Up in America: Children in Historical Perspective* (Urbana: University of Illinois Press, 1985), 183–188.

104. Register of Court Trials, 24 June 1867, ser. 1466, vol. 197, pp. 208–209, Algiers, LA, Asst. Subasst. Comr., RG 105, BRFAL; Capt. R. Folles to Capt. W. W. Tyler, 28 June 1867(?), Letters Sent, ser. 1447 vol. 187 p. 166, Algiers, LA, Asst. Subasst. Comr., RG 105, BRFAL; Thomas Kenefie to L. O. Parker, 29 June 1867, Letters Received, Algiers, LA, R.B. [Right Bank] Asst. Comr., RG 105, BRFAL, microfilm, M-1027, Reel 17 [357]; endorsement of Capt. R. Folles to L. O. Parker, 1 July 1867, F-161, Letters Received, Algiers, LA, RG 105, BRFAL, microfilm, M-1027, Reel 15 [850]; enclosure L. O. Parker to R. Folles, 28 June 1867, Letters Received, New Orleans, LA, Asst. Comr., RG 105, BRFAL, microfilm, M-1027, Reel 15, [850].

105. Daily Journal, 14 September 1867, ser. 1556, vol. 251, p. 112, Clinton, LA, Asst. Subasst. Comr., RG 105, BRFAL; 1st Lt. James DeGrey to Lucius Green, 29 Sept. 1867, Letters Sent, ser. 1546, vol. 246, p. 131, Clinton, LA, Asst. Subasst. Comr., RG 105, BRFAL; L. Green to Lt. James DeGrey, 28 Sept. 1867, Registered Letters Received, ser. 1548, vol. 243, Clinton, LA, Asst. Subasst. Comr., RG 105, BRFAL; Dr. Jno M. Moore to Lt. James DeGrey, 26 Sept. 1867, Registered Letters Received, ser. 1548, vol. 243, Clinton, LA, Asst. Subasst. Comr., RG 105, BRFAL.

106. Cyntha Nickols to the Chief Agent of the FB at N Orleans, 10 Jan 1867, N-1 1867, Letters Received, ser. 1303, East Feliciana, LA, Asst. Comr., RG 105, BRFAL, FSSP [A8620].

107. Complaints, 28–30 Nov. 1866, ser. 1837, vol. 396, pp. 21–22, New Roads, LA, Asst. Subasst. Comr., RG 105, BRFAL.

108. Jacob Taylor vs. Doc Tilly for the custody of his three children, E. W. Dewees to Capt. Wm. H. Sterling, Trimonthly Report, 30 Sept. 1867, Asst. Comr., Letters Received, Sparta, LA, M-1027, Reel 14 [1402], RG 105, BRFAL;

Mary Ann Johnston vs. Emily Wiley for word of Lavinia Johnson, 1st Lt. William H. Webster to Col. Martin Flood (7th Subdistrict) 7 Aug. 1867, Subasst. Comr. Letters Sent, ser. 1486, vol. 216, Baton Rouge, LA, RG 105, BRFAL; Felix Dixie vs. John Long for custody of his daughter, E. W. Dewees to Capt. William H. Sterling, Trimonthly Report, 20 Sept. 1867, Letters Received, Sparta, LA, Asst. Comr., RG 105, BRFAL, microfilm, M-1027, Reel 14 [1397]; Nelson Cole vs. Dodge, Register of Court Trials, 24 June 1867, ser. 1466, vol. 197, pp. 209–210, Algiers, LA, Asst. Subasst. Comr., RG 105, BRFAL.

109. Affidavit of Enoch Braston, 10 Jan. 1866, enclosed in Chaplain L. S. Livermore to Lt. Col. R. S. Donaldson, 10 Jan. 1866, "L" 1866, Registered Letters Received, ser. 2188, Jackson, MS, Act. Asst. Comr. of the Northern District of Mississippi, BRFAL, FSSP [A-9328], in Berlin and Rowland, eds., *Families and Freedom*, 222–223. For similar complaints, see Capt. and Pro. Mar. Alex D. Bailie to T. W. Conway, 30 July 1865, Letters Received, Port Hudson, LA, Asst. Comr., RG 105, BRFAL, microfilm, M-1027, Reel 7; W. H. R. Hangen to Capt. Wm. Sterling, 31 Dec. 1867, Madisonville LA, Letters Sent, ser. 1679, vol. 331, p. 74, Asst. Subasst. Comr., RG 105, BRFAL; Lt. James DeGrey to George F. Schayer, 20 May 1867, Letters Received, Clinton, LA, Asst. Comr., RG 105, BRFAL, microfilm, M-1027, Reel 14 [959]; Register of Complaints, 20 Oct. 1867, ser. 1906, vol. 476, p. 6, Thibodeaux, LA, Asst. Subasst. Comr., RG 105, BRFAL.

110. Evidence of Prince Durant (col) against D. Toadvine, E. L. Woodside, and G. W. Catlett, enclosed in William H. Webster to Wm. H. Sterling, 10 May 1867, Letters Received, ser. 1303, box 14, S-37, Baton Rouge, LA, Asst. Comr., BRFAL, FSSP [A-8626].

111. James Murray to Major General Lew. Wallace, 5 Dec. 1864, M-838 1864, Letters Received, ser. 2343, Middle Dept. & 8th Army Corps, RG 393, pt. 1, BRFAL, FSSP [C-4141]; in Berlin et al., eds., *Freedom*, ser. I, vol. II, *The Wartime Genesis of Free Labor: The Upper South*, 524–525.

112. Hunter, *To 'Joy My Freedom*, 161–166.

113. White, *Ar'n't I a Woman?* chap. 1.

114. William Fiske to T. W. Conway, 29 July 1865, Letters Received, Lafourche Crossing, LA, Asst. Comr., RG 105, BRFAL, microfilm, M-1027, Reel 8 [1001], emphasis in original.

115. Indentures, Parishes of Sabine & Natchitoches, ser. 1776, box 23, Natchitoches, LA, Asst. Subasst. Comr., RG 105, BRFAL.

116. White, *Ar'n't I a Woman?* 58–61; Bynum, *Unruly Women*, chap. 2. Tera Hunter, however, documents the lengths to which freedwomen went, usually through cooperation with other freedwomen, to provide for their families. See Hunter, *To 'Joy My Freedom*, chap. 6.

117. David Macrae, *The Americans at Home* (Edinburgh, 1870; repr., New York, 1952), 318, quoted in Litwack, *Been in the Storm So Long*, 238.

118. Capt. Edward Bigelow to Thomas W. Conway, Genl. Supt. of Fmen, 10 June 1865, Letters Sent, Thibodeaux, LA, Pro. Mar., ser. 1486 (376/931 DG), RG 393 pt. 4, pp. 57–58, BRFAL. See also Ann J. Frisby to Capt. Agt. of FB at St. Joseph, LA, 22 Jan. 1867, Unregistered Letters Received, St. Joseph, LA, Asst. Subasst. Comr., RG 105, BRFAL; John T. White ASAC to Lt. J. M. Lee AAAG, 14 Jan. 1868, Unregistered Letters Received, ser. 1788, New Iberia, LA, Asst. Subasst. Comr., RG 105, BRFAL.

119. Bvt. Capt. John H. Brough ASAC to Capt. W. W. Tyler SAC, 5 July 1867, Letters Sent, ser. 1577, vol. 263, p. 45, Donaldsonville, LA, Asst. Subasst. Comr., RG 105, BRFAL, emphasis added.

120. Bvt. Capt. John H. Brough to Lt. G. A. H. Clement, 11 Dec. 1867, Letters Sent, ser. 1577, vol. 263, p. 153, Donaldsonville, LA, Asst. Subasst. Comr., RG 105, BRFAL. It is possible that the agent's decision was later reversed by his superiors, since a parent's consent was required with such arrangements, but at the time the agent took it upon himself to forbid the woman to retrieve her son.

121. W. H. R. Hanger to Capt. Wm. Sterling SAC, 27 March 1867, Letters Sent, ser. 1678, vol. 331, p. 8, Madisonville, LA, Asst. Subasst. Comr., RG 105, BRFAL. For other examples of planters claims to "raising" freedchildren, see Ann J. Frisby to Capt. Agt of FB at St. Joseph, LA, 22 Jan. 1867, Unregistered Letters Received, St. Joseph, LA, Asst. Subasst. Comr., RG 105 [1863], BRFAL; John T. White ASAC to Lt. J. M. Lee AAAG, 14 Jan. 1868, Unregistered Letters Received, ser. 1788, New Iberia, LA, Asst. Subasst. Comr., RG 105, BRFAL; Lt. William E. Dougherty to Assistant Commissioner, 20 Jan. 1866, Trimonthly Report, ser. 1455, Algiers, LA, Asst. Comr., RG 105, BRFAL, FSSP [A-8690].

122. Schwartz, *Born in Bondage,* 8.

123. Lt. William E. Dougherty to Assistant Commissioner, 20 Jan. 1866, Trimonthly Report, ser. 1455, Algiers, LA, Asst. Comr., RG 105, BRFAL, FSSP [A-8690].

124. This is a theme in many histories of black women in the nineteenth century, throughout the Americas. See, for instance, Maria Odila Silva Dias, *Power and Everyday Life: The Lives of Working Women in Nineteenth-Century Brazil* (New Brunswick, NJ: Rutgers University Press, 1995); Sandra Lauderdale Graham, *House and Street: The Domestic World of Servants and Masters in Nineteenth-Century Rio de Janiero* (Austin: University of Texas Press, 1988); Hunter, *To 'Joy My Freedom*; Bynum, *Unruly Women,* 79–80.

125. Testimony in claim of Virinda [3 Oct. 1863], vol. 24 no. 341, ser. 1683, Provost Court, New Orleans, LA, Pro. Mar., RG 393 pt. 4, BRFAL, FSSP [C-1018].

126. Clipping from an unidentified newspaper [Oct? 1863] enclosed in Col. Geo. Hanks to Maj. G. Norman Lieber, 20 Jan. 1864, Letters Received, ser. 920, Civil Affairs, Dept. of the Gulf, RG 393 pt. 1, BRFAL, FSSP [C-735].

127. Schwalm, *Hard Fight for We*, 250–254, 258–259.

128. William M. Todd to Capt. Wm. H. Sterling, 20 Feb. 1867, Narrative Trimonthly Reports of Operations from Subordinate Officers, Letters Received, ser. 1310, Franklin, LA, Asst. Comr., RG 105, BRFAL, FSSP [A-8538]. See, for instance, Indentures, ser. 1481, box 4, Amite City, LA; ser. 1698, box 29, Sparta, LA; and ser. 1698, Marksville, LA, Asst. Subasst. Comr., RG 105, BRFAL.

129. William M. Todd to Capt. Wm. H. Sterling, 20 Feb. 1867, Narrative Trimonthly Reports of Operations from Subordinate Officers, Letters Received, ser. 1310, Franklin, LA, Asst. Comr., RG 105, BRFAL, FSSP [A-8538].

130. Lt. Ira D. McClary to Capt. W. W. Tyler, 29 June 1867, Letters Received, New Orleans, LA, Asst. Comr., RG 105, BRFAL, microfilm, M-1027, Reel 18 [0544].

131. In Latin American and Caribbean countries, such as Peru, Cuba, or Brazil, where slaves could buy themselves out of slavery, freedom had been the work of women even before emancipation. Once they had bought their own freedom, they went to the city to earn money as laundresses, housekeepers, or cooks. From their earnings, they could then buy the freedom of their husbands and children. A common figure in Peru in the 1850s, for instance, was a freed mother working in Lima whose slave children lived and worked on the hacienda. Christine Hünefeldt, *Paying the Price of Freedom: Family and Labor among Lima's Slaves 1800–1854* (Berkeley: University of California Press, 1994), 16–17, 80; see also Scott, *Slave Emancipation in Cuba*, chap. 10; Graham, *House and Street*.

132. Interview with Henry Reed, June 1940, NSUL, FWPLA, folder 19.

133. Interview with Carlyle Stewart, n.d., NSUL, FWPLA, folder 19.

134. Interview with John James, n.d., *American Slave*, vol. 4 [Texas], pts. 3 and 4. In addition to the Klan, the Knights of the White Camelia and the White League terrorized freedpeople in rural Louisiana parishes. Allen W. Trelease, *White Terror: The Ku Klux Klan Conspiracy and Southern Reconstruction* (Baton Rouge: Louisiana State University Press, 1971), chap. 8; George C. Rable, *But There Was No Peace: The Role of Violence in the Politics of Reconstruction* (Athens: University of Georgia Press, 1984).

135. Unattributed excerpt from the Tinsley Collection, NSUL, FWPLA, folder 7.

136. "Work Song," from an interview with Tillie Bell [former slave and/or the child of slaves], NSUL, FWPLA, folder 8. On work songs as sources, see Lawrence W. Levine, *Black Culture and Black Consciousness: Afro-American Folk Thought from Slavery to Freedom* (New York: Oxford University Press, 1977), 202–216.

NOTES TO CHAPTER 5

1. John Blandin to A. Grégoire, Esq., Port-au-Prince, Hayti, October 7, 1859, Catholic Institution Letterbook I, Archives of the Archdiocese of New Orleans (hereafter AANO).

2. The students' letters made mention of the Mexican travels of André Grégoire (senior) and Louis Duhart, his associate. See discussion of migration to Veracruz in chapter 1.

3. *Passenger Lists of Vessels Arriving at New Orleans, Louisiana, 1820–1902*, Micropublication M259, RG 036, Rolls 1–93 (Washington, DC: National Archives and Record Administration, 1958), accessed through Ancestry .com, *New Orleans Passenger Lists, 1820–1945* [online database] Provo, UT: The Generations Network, 2006).

4. André's father was listed as "housebuilder" in New Orleans in 1850. He also had property valued at $2,000. U.S. Bureau of the Census, *Seventh Census of the United States, 1850,* New Orleans Municipality 3, Ward 4, Orleans, LA (Washington, DC: National Archives and Record Administration, 1850), Roll M432, p. 229, accessed through Ancestry.com, *1850 United States Federal Census* [online database] (Provo, UT: The Generations Network, 2005).

5. On southern Louisiana after emancipation, see Rebecca J. Scott, *Degrees of Freedom: Louisiana and Cuba after Slavery* (Cambridge, MA: Harvard/Belknap Press, 2005), chaps. 1–2.

6. Testimony of Rev. Joseph E. Roy, *Report of the Joint Committee on Reconstruction at the First Session 39th Congress* (Washington, DC: Government Printing Office, 1866), 63; Ronald E. Butchart, "Remapping Racial Boundaries: Teachers as Border Police and Boundary Transgressors in Post-emancipation Black Education, USA, 1861–1876," *Paedagogica Historica* 43 (February 2007): 67.

7. M. W. Morris to Lt. H. H. Pierce, Genl. Supt. of Education, 5 Sept. 1868, Letters Sent, ser. 1634, vol. 295, p. 10, Houma, LA, Asst. Subasst. Comr., BRFAL.

8. Howard A. White, *The Freedmen's Bureau in Louisiana* (Baton Rouge: Louisiana State University Press, 1970), 184. On the challenges for black teachers, from the North and South, see Butchardt, "Remapping Racial Boundaries," 68–75.

9. M. W. Morris to Bvt. Capt. H. H. Pierce, Genl. Supt. of Education, 9 Nov. 1868, Letters Sent, ser. 1634, vol. 295, pp. 83–84, Houma, LA, Asst. Subasst. Comr., RG 105, BRFAL.

10. General Order No. 38, New Orleans, March 22, 1864, in *The War of the Rebellion: A Compilation of the Official Records of the Union and Confederate Armies,* ser. 3, vol. 4 (Washington, DC: Government Printing Office, 1880–1901), 193–194.

11. John. W. Alvord, *First Semi-annual Report on Schools and Finances of Freedmen* (Washington, DC: Government Printing Office, 1866), 6, in Robert C. Morris, ed., *Freedmen's Schools and Textbooks,* vol. 1, *Semi-annual Report on Schools for Freedmen* by John W. Alvord, Nos. 1–10, January 1866–July 1870 (New York: AMS Press, 1980); C. Peter Ripley, *Slaves and Freedmen in Civil War Louisiana* (Baton Rouge: Louisiana State University Press, 1976), 145; James D. Anderson, *The Education of Blacks in the South, 1860–1935* (Chapel Hill: University of North Carolina Press, 1988), 9.

12. White, *The Freedmen's Bureau in Louisiana,* 167–177.

13. Lt. James DeGrey to Lt. J. M. Lee, 30 Nov. 1867, Trimonthly Report, Clinton, LA, Letters Received, Asst. Comr., RG 105, BRFAL, microfilm, M-1027, Reel 14 [1565]; Lt. James DeGrey to Lt. J. M. Lee, 20 Dec. 1867, Trimonthly Report, Clinton, LA, Letters Received, Asst. Comr., RG 105, BRFAL, microfilm, M-1027, Reel 14 [1589]; Lt. James DeGrey to Lt. J. M. Lee, 31 Dec. 1867, Trimonthly Report, Clinton, LA, Letters Received, Asst. Comr., RG 105, BRFAL, microfilm, M-1027, Reel 14 [1608]; P. M. Moore to Capt. A. Finch, 4 March 1868, Bayou Sara, LA, Unregistered Letters Received, ser. 1516, box 7, Asst. Subasst. Comr., RG 105, BRFAL; Bvt. Capt. Frank Osburne to Lt. J. M. Lee, 20 Dec. 1867, Letters Received, Iberville, West Baton Rouge, and Plaquemine, LA, Asst. Comr., RG 105, BRFAL, microfilm, M-1027, Reel 18 [1220]; Edward Henderson to J. M. Lee, 20 Nov. 1867, Letters Received, St. Joseph, LA, Asst. Comr., RG 105, BRFAL, microfilm, M-1027, Reel 16 [1160]; William Woods to Lt. H. H. Pierce Genl. Supt. of Education, 18 Aug. 1868, Letters Sent, ser. 1634, vol. 294, p. 118, Houma, LA, Asst. Subasst. Comr., RG 105, BRFAL; Capt. R. Folles to B. Labraunche, 10 April 1868, Letters Sent, ser. 1447, vol. 189, p. 27, Algiers, LA, Asst. Subasst. Comr., RG 105, BRFAL.

14. *Constitution Adopted by the State Constitutional Convention of the State of Louisiana March 7, 1868* (New Orleans: New Orleans Republican, 1868), art. 135; John. W. Alvord, *Ninth Semi-annual Report on Schools for Freedmen* (Washington, DC: Government Printing Office, 1870), 39–40, reprinted in Morris, ed., *Freedmen's Schools and Textbooks.*

15. M. W. Morris to Bvt. Capt. H. H. Pierce, Genl. Supt. of Education, 15 Dec. 1868, Letters Sent, ser. 1634, vol. 295, pp. 83–84, Houma, LA, Asst. Subasst. Comr., RG 105, BRFAL.

16. More research, under way, hopefully will retrieve the rest of Grégoire's story.

17. William Seraille, "Afro-American Emigration to Haiti during the American Civil War," *The Americas* 35 (October 1978): 185–200. See discussion of Haitian emigration in chapter 1.

18. Anderson, *The Education of Blacks in the South,* 20–21. On opposition during the war, see C. Peter Ripley, *Slaves and Freedmen,* 139–141; Butchardt, "Remapping Racial Boundaries," passim.

19. On black political leaders in New Orleans after the Civil War, see David Rankin, "The Origins of Black Leadership in New Orleans during Reconstruction," *Journal of Southern History* 40 (August 1974): 417–440. On their alliance with the cause of former slaves, see Donald Everett, "Demands of the New Orleans Free Colored Population for Political Equality, 1862–1865," *Louisiana Historical Quarterly* 38 (April 1955): 55–64. On the Afro-Creoles' view of Reconstruction, see Caryn Cossé Bell, "'*Une Chimère*': The Freedmen's Bureau in Creole New Orleans," in Paul A. Cimbala and Randall M. Miller, eds., *The Freedmen's Bureau and Reconstruction: Reconsiderations* (New York: Fordham University Press, 1999), 140–160.

20. Jean-Charles Houzeau, *My Passage at the New Orleans* Tribune: *A Memoir of the Civil War Era,* trans. Gerard F. Denault, ed. David C. Rankin (Baton Rouge: Louisiana State University Press, 1984), 22–23. Houzeau was the exception on the editorial staff. Although he often passed as an Afro-Creole, and many historians have recorded him as such, he was, in fact, a white socialist from Belgium.

21. "A Fair for the Benefit of the Orphans of Freedmen," *New Orleans Tribune,* April 19, 1865, 1.

22. Louis R. Harlan, "Desegregation in New Orleans Public Schools during Reconstruction," *American Historical Review* 67 (April 1962): 663–675.

23. Charles M. Vincent, "Black Constitution Makers: The Constitution of 1868," in Warren Billings and Edward F. Haas, eds., *In Search of Fundamental Law: Louisiana's Constitutions, 1812–1974* (Lafayette, LA: Center for Louisiana Studies, 1993), 73; *Constitution Adopted by the State Constitutional Convention of the State of Louisiana March 7, 1868* (New Orleans: New Orleans Republican, 1868), Art. 135; Harlan, "Desegregation in New Orleans," 664; Roger W. Shugg, *Origins of Class Struggle in Louisiana: A Social History of White Farmers and Laborers during Slavery and After, 1840–1875* (Baton Rouge: Louisiana State University Press, 1939), 206–207.

24. Harlan, "Desegregation in New Orleans," 673.

25. Howard N. Rabinowitz, *Race Relations in the Urban South 1865–1890* (Athens: University of Georgia Press, 1978), xxiii; Harlan, "Desegregation in New Orleans," 673.

26. On the *Plessy* case: Otto H. Olsen, *The Thin Disguise: Plessy v. Ferguson, a Documentary Presentation* (New York: Humanities Press, 1967); C. Vann Woodward, *American Counterpoint: Slavery and Racism in the North-South Dialogue* (Boston: Little, Brown, 1971), 212–233; Charles Lofgren, *The Plessy Case: A Legal-Historical Interpretation* (New York: Oxford University Press, 1987); Eric J. Sundquist, *To Wake the Nations: Race in the Making of American Literature* (Cambridge, MA: Harvard University Press, 1993), 233–270; Keith Weldon Medley, *We as Freemen: Plessy v. Ferguson* (Gretna, LA: Pel-

ican Publishing, 2003); Rebecca J. Scott, "Se batter pour ses droits: Écritures, litiges et discrimination raciale en Louisiane (1888–1899)," *Cahiers du Brésil Contemporain* (Paris) 53/54 (2003): 175–206.

27. Woodward, *American Counterpoint*, 237. This is a restatement of Woodward's thesis, first written in C. Vann Woodward, *The Strange Career of Jim Crow: A Commemorative Edition* (New York: Oxford University Press, 2002 [1955]).

28. In New Orleans, at least, C. Vann Woodward's segregation thesis, mentioned earlier, is the most applicable. Howard Rabinowitz, who voiced perhaps the loudest opposition to the idea that there were significant alternatives to segregation and that it was a fluid, shifting phenomenon in the postemancipation period (suggesting that blacks and many of their northern allies favored segregation to all-out exclusion), did not include New Orleans in his study of the urban south. On the debate between Woodward and Rabinowitz, as well as the arguments of other historians on this issue, see Howard N. Rabinowitz, "More Than the Woodward Thesis: Assessing the Strange Career of Jim Crow," *Journal of American History* 75 (December 1988): 842–856; and C. Vann Woodward, "Strange Career Critics: Long May They Persevere," *Journal of American History* 75 (December 1988): 857–868. Numerous scholars since Woodward and Rabinowitz have integrated the history of segregation more fully into the social and cultural history of the South, including more theoretical perspectives on race, gender, and class. See, for instance, Barbara Jeanne Fields, "Ideology and Race in American History," in J. Morgan Kousser and James M. McPherson, eds., *Region, Race, and Reconstruction: Essays in Honor of C. Vann Woodward* (New York: Oxford University Press, 1982), 143–177; Glenda Elizabeth Gilmore, *Gender and Jim Crow: Women and the Politics of White Supremacy in North Carolina, 1896–1920* (Chapel Hill: University of North Carolina Press, 1996); Grace Elizabeth Hale, *Making Whiteness: The Culture of Segregation in the South, 1890–1940* (New York: Vintage Books, 1999); Robin D. G. Kelley, *Race Rebels: Culture, Politics, and the Black Working Class* (repr., New York: Free Press, 1996), esp. pt. 1; Martha Hodes: *White Women, Black Men: Illicit Sex in the Nineteenth-Century South* (repr., New Haven, CT: Yale University Press, 1999); and Kenneth W. Mack, "Law, Society, Identity, and the Making of the Jim Crow South: Travel and Segregation on Tennessee Railroads, 1875–1905," *Law and Social Inquiry* 24 (Spring 1999): 377–409.

29. Kathryn Page, "A First Born Child of Liberty: The Constitution of 1864," in Billings and Haas, ed., *In Search of Fundamental Law,* 52–53.

30. Ibid., 53–54; Shugg, *Origins of Class Struggle,* 200.

31. General Order No. 23, Dept. of the Gulf, 3 Feb. 1864, in Ira Berlin, Thavolia Glymph, Steven F. Miller, Joseph P. Reidy, Leslie S. Rowland, and Julie Saville, eds., *Freedom: A Documentary History of Emancipation, 1861–1867,*

ser. I, vol. III, *The Wartime Genesis of Free Labor: The Lower South* (Cambridge: Cambridge University Press, 1990), 512–517.

32. *Debates in the Convention for the Revision and Amendment of the Constitution of Louisiana,* Assembled at Liberty Hall, New Orleans, April 6, 1864 (New Orleans: W. R. Fish, Printer, 1864), 143.

33. Ibid., 140.

34. Ibid., 143.

35. Ibid., 546; Ted Tunnel, *Crucible of Reconstruction: War Radicalism and Race in Louisiana, 1862–1877* (Baton Rouge: Louisiana State University Press, 1984), 56.

36. Ibid., 158.

37. Ibid., 492.

38. Ibid., 546.

39. Priscilla Ferguson Clement, *Growing Pains: Children in the Industrial Age, 1850–1890* (New York: Twayne, 1997), 97–99.

40. Donald E. DeVore and Joseph Logsdon, *Crescent City Schools: Public Education in New Orleans, 1841–1991* (Lafayette, LA: Center for Louisiana Studies, 1991), 17–24; Elisabeth Joan Doyle, "Nurseries of Treason: Schools in Occupied New Orleans," *Journal of Southern History* 26 (May 1960): 161–179.

41. W. E. B. Du Bois, *Black Reconstruction in America, 1860–1880* (New York, Atheneum, 1992 [1935]), 638; Eric Foner, *Reconstruction: America's Unfinished Revolution, 1863–1877* (New York: Harper and Row, 1988), 96–102. Because of freedpeople's desire for education, and black legislators' work to ensure a system of public education for the benefit of *all* children in the South, by 1870 every southern state constitution had a provision for state-funded public education. Anderson, *The Education of Blacks in the South,* 19.

42. Du Bois, *Black Reconstruction in America,* 641.

43. Shugg, *Origins of Class Struggle,* 74–75.

44. Anderson, *Education of Blacks in the South,* 26; Shelley Sallee, *The Whiteness of Child Labor Reform in the New South* (Athens: University of Georgia Press, 2004), 106–107.

45. U.S. Bureau of the Census, *Eighth Census of the United States, 1860* (Washington, DC: National Archives and Record Administration), Ward 7, Lafourche, LA, M653_413, image 82, accessed through Ancestry.com, *1860 United States Federal Census* [online database] (Provo, UT: The Generations Network, 2005); *Debates in the Convention . . . 1864,* 197–198.

46. *Debates in the Convention . . . 1864,* 161; Du Bois, *Black Reconstruction in America,* 647.

47. *Debates in the Convention . . . 1864,* 161.

48. Ibid., 476.

49. *Constitution of the State of Louisiana* (1864), art. 141; Page, "A First Born Child of Liberty," 59; Shugg, *Origins of Class Struggle,* 207.

50. Petition endorsed by A. Baird, 28 Nov. 1865, C-636 pt. 1 LA, Dept. of the Gulf, Letters Received, Box 2, F 307, RG 393, BRFAL, FSSP [A-1757].

51. A. Baird to E. R. S. Canby, 15 Nov. 1865, Letters Received, C-636 Pt. 1, Dept. of the Gulf, New Orleans, LA, RG 393, BRFAL

52. James C. Tucker to Capt. H. R. Pease, 3 Dec. 1865, Unregistered Letters Received, ser. 1333, LA Supt. of Education, RG 105, BRFAL, FSSP [A-8768].

53. White, *The Freedmen's Bureau in Louisiana,* 17–22, 166–200; DeVore and Logsdon, *Crescent City Schools,* 66; Anderson, *The Education of Blacks in the South,* 9–10.

54. Du Bois, *Black Reconstruction in America,* chap. 15; Robert C. Morris, *Reading, 'Riting, and Reconstruction: The Education of Freedmen in the South 1861–1870* (Chicago: University of Chicago Press, 1976); Leon F. Litwack, *Been in the Storm So Long: The Aftermath of Slavery* (New York: Vintage Books, 1979), 472–501; Foner, *Reconstruction,* 96–102; Tera W. Hunter, *To 'Joy My Freedom: Black Women's Lives and Labors after the Civil War* (Cambridge, MA: Harvard University Press, 1997), 40–43.

55. Herbert G. Gutman, "Afro-American Kinship before and after Emancipation in North America," in Hans Medick and David Warren Sabean, eds., *Interest and Emotion: Essays on the Study of Family and Kinship* (Cambridge: Cambridge University Press, 1984), 253–255; on freedpeople's communal political activism, see also Julie Saville, *The Work of Reconstruction: From Slave to Wage Labor in South Carolina 1860–1870* (Cambridge: Cambridge University Press, 1994), esp. 160–170.

56. Lt. John Brough to Capt. A. F. Hayden, 18 May 1866, vol. 261/2, p. 7, Letters Sent, ser. 1577, Donaldsonville, LA, Asst. Subasst. Comr., RG 105, BRFAL, FSSP [A-8518].

57. The freedpeople of Plaquemines Parish lodged such complaints to the local bureau agent. Bvt. Charles E. Merrill to Bvt. Capt. H. H. Pierce, Genl. Supt. of Education, 3 Sept. 1868, Letters Sent, ser. 1842, vol. 425, n.p., Plaquemine, LA, Asst. Subasst. Comr., RG 105, BRFAL.

58. John Richard Dennett, *The South as It Is, 1865–1868,* ed. Henry M. Christman (New York: Viking, 1965), 322, quoted in Litwack, *Been in the Storm So Long,* 473.

59. Allen W. Trelease, *White Terror: The Ku Klux Klan Conspiracy and Southern Reconstruction* (Baton Rouge: Louisiana State University Press, 1971); George C. Rable, *But There Was No Peace: The Role of Violence in the Politics of Reconstruction* (Athens: University of Georgia Press, 1984).

60. Interview with Mrs. Elizabeth Ross Hite, Federal Writers' Project Papers, Northwestern State University of Louisiana, Watson Memorial Library,

Cammie G. Henry Research Center, folder 19. After 1869, the Klan was not strong in Louisiana, in comparison to the White League and other groups. Trelease, *White Terror*, 136.

61. Du Bois, *Black Reconstruction in America*, chaps. 1–2.

62. Opposition to schools for freedchildren could also have been an opportunity for poor whites, as well as elites, to practice white supremacy. On later examples of this, see Hale, *Making Whiteness*, passim.

63. Testimony of Thomas W. Conway, in U.S. Congress, Joint Committee on Reconstruction, *Report of Joint Committee on Reconstruction, at the First Session, Thirty-ninth Congress* (Washington, DC: Government Printing Office, 1866), pt. 4, p. 82. See also the testimony of Rev. Joseph E. Roy, agent of the American Home Missionary Society, p. 63. On the Joint Committee, see Foner, *Reconstruction*, 246–247.

64. Edmonia Highgate to Rev. George Whipple, 17 Dec. 1866, American Missionary Association Archives, Amistad Research Center, Tulane University (hereafter AMA), microfilm, Reel 1 [45702]. See also T. W. Conway's account of violence to schools and teachers along the Red River in western Louisiana. *Report of Joint Committee on Reconstruction*, pt. 4, p. 79. Though most occurred in the years just after the war, schoolhouse burnings continued to occur throughout Reconstruction. See, for instance, *New Orleans Republican*, September 9, 1876, p. 1 col. 4, Marcus Christian Collection, Works Progress Administration Newspaper Transcriptions (hereafter WPA), Earl K. Long Library Special Collections, University of New Orleans (hereafter UNO).

65. *New Orleans Republican*, February 26, 1873, p. 8, col. 2, WPA, UNO; *New Orleans Daily Crescent*, October 3, 1868, p .4, col. 4, cited in Marcus B. Christian, "A Black History," chap. 32, p. 9, Marcus Christian Collection, UNO.

66. There were many days of correspondence concerning this incident in the records of the Freedmen's Bureau. 1st Lt. James DeGrey to Capt. Hayden, 3–7 July 1866, vol. 234, pp. 121–128, Letters Sent, ser. 1546, Clinton, LA, Agent Asst. Subasst. Comr., RG 105, BRFAL, FSSP [A-8662].

67. *New Orleans Tribune*, December 29, 1865.

68. Agency Aid E. J. Barkdull to Special Agent of Treasury Dept. B. F. Flanders, 14 June 1864, Incoming Correspondence, New Orleans, LA, 3rd Special Agency, RG 366, BRFAL, FSSP [Q-222].

69. Proceedings of Provost Court, n.d., 1863, ser. 1683, vol. 241, p. 410, New Orleans, LA, RG 393, Pt. 4, Dept. of the Gulf, BRFAL.

70. Lt. John Brough to Capt. A. F. Hayden, 7 June 1866, vol. 26, p. 7, Letters Sent, ser. 1577, Donaldsonville, LA, Agent Asst. Subasst. Comr., RG 105, BRFAL, FSSP [A-8518]. On harassment of children and teachers: Journal of Business Transacted, 26 April 1867, vol. 199, ser. 1469, p. 9, Algiers, LA, Asst. Subasst. Comr., RG 105; R. Folles to Capt. Wm. H. Sterling Pro. Mar. Genl., 20

Oct. 1866, Letters Sent, ser. 1447 vol. 187, p. 69, Algiers, LA, Agent Asst. Subasst. Comr., RG 105; E. M. Wheelock to Capt. Wade Pro. Mar., 18 Feb. 1865, Letters Received, ser. 1482, Carrolton, LA, Pro. Mar., RG 393, Pt. 4; E. M. Wheelock to Capt. Edward Bigelow Pro. Mar., 18 Jan. 1865, Letters Received, ser. 1488, Lafourche, LA, Pro. Mar., RG 393, Pt. 4; Bvt. Capt. Richard Folles to Asst. Comr., 20 April 1867, Letters Received, Algiers, LA, Asst. Comr., microfilm, M-1027, Reel 15 [0365]; W. H. Van Ornum to Thomas W. Conway, 4 Sept. 1865, Letters Received, St. Charles Parish, LA, Asst. Comr., microfilm, M-1027, Reel 13 [307–310]. On refusal to board teachers: Lt. James DeGrey to Capt. Wm H. Sterling, 30 April 1867, Letters Received, Clinton, LA, Asst. Comr., microfilm, M-1027, Reel 14 [861]. All in BRFAL. Marcus Christian, "A Black History," chap. 32, Marcus Christian Collection, UNO.

71. Prof. Bennett Puryear, *The Public School in Its Relation to the Negro* (Richmond, 1877), 11, quoted in Litwack, *Been in the Storm So Long*, 486.

72. Translation from *Lettres Annuelles 1863–1866*, Society of the Sacred Heart, in Louise Callan, A.M., Ph.D., Religious of the Sacred Heart, *The Society of the Sacred Heart in North America* (New York: Longmans, Green, 1937), 524–525.

73. Foner, *Reconstruction*, 140.

74. William Woods ASAC to Capt. L. H. Warren AAAG, 10 Feb. 1868, Letters Sent, ser. 1634, vol. 294, p. 71, Houma, LA, Agent Asst. Subasst. Comr., RG 105, BRFAL.

75. Bvt. Charles Merrill ASAC to Bvt. Capt. H. H. Pierce Genl. Supt. of Ed., 3 Sept. 1868, Letters Sent, ser. 1842, vol. 425, Plaquemines Parish, LA, Asst. Subasst. Comr., RG 105, BRFAL.

76. H. E. Barton ASAC to Bvt. Capt. H. H. Pierce, Genl. Supt. of Ed., 15 Sept. 1868, Letters Sent, p. 20, vol. 248, ser. 1546, Clinton, LA, Asst. Subasst. Comr., RG 105, BRFAL.

77. Charges and specifications against Robert C. Moore, Dec. 1865, Wm. Wright to Capt. H. R. Pease, 21 Oct. 1865, C-579 Pt. 1, Dept. of the Gulf, 1756 Letters Received, Box 14 M4 (1865) Suppl. Terrebonne Parish, Oct.–Nov. 1865, RG 393, BRFAL. For other examples of planters and managers who obstructed the education of freedchildren, see Alex. Morales to E. T. Lewis, Esq., Subagent, 1 July 1867, Unregistered Letters Received, ser. 1516, box 7, Bayou Sara, LA [West Feliciana Parish], Asst. Subasst. Comr., RG 105, BRFAL; Charles Otill SAC to Bvt. Maj. B. J. Hutchins AAAG, 30 Sept. 1868, Letters Sent, pp. 149–150, vol. 216, ser. 1486, Baton Rouge, LA, Asst. Subasst. Comr., RG 105, BRFAL; Chaplain L. L. Moss Agt. B. to Capt. H. R. Pease, Bd. of Educ., 18 Aug. 1865, Letters Received, Ascension Parish, LA, Asst. Comr., RG 105, BRFAL, microfilm, M-1027, Reel 8 [736]; Bvt. Maj. Thomas H. Hopwood to Bvt. Maj. J. H. Mahuken Capt. & Asst. Inspector Genl., 30 April 1866, Narrative Trimonthly Reports of Operations from Subordinate Officers, ser. 1310,

New Roads, LA, Asst. Comr., RG 105, BRFAL, FSSP [A-8529]; F. A. Clover ASAC to Lt. J. M. Lee Winnsborough, AAAG, 10 Feb. 1868, A1-D89, Letters Received, ser. 4575, 5th Military Dist, RG 393 pt. 1 [SS-2051] BRFAL.

78. Litwack, *Been in the Storm So Long,* 488.

79. *National Antislavery Standard,* June 6, 1863.

80. Elizabeth Hyde Botume, *First Days amongst the Contrabands* (New York: Arno Press, 1968 [1893]), 257–258.

81. Sending their children to a white-only school, like making enough money so that their wives did not have to work in the field, may have been a claim to higher status for formerly nonslaveholding white men. On the antebellum history of this class and its racial politics, see Stephanie McCurry, *Masters of Small Worlds: Yeoman Households, Gender Relations, and the Political Culture of the Antebellum South Carolina Low Country* (New York: Oxford University Press, 1995).

82. T. A. McMasters to Rev. George Whipple, 2 May 1864, Port Hudson, LA, AMA, microfilm, Reel 1 [45429]; C. Tambling to Rev. Charles Jocelyn, 22 April 1864, New Orleans, LA, AMA, microfilm, Reel 1 [45415]; *American Missionary,* May 1865, 103; *American Missionary,* June 1864, 189. This pattern was true for other southern states as well. See Litwack, *Been in the Storm So Long,* 489.

83. J. H. Merrifield to Rev. George Whipple, 7 June 1864, Baton Rouge, LA, AMA, microfilm, Reel 1 [45470H].

84. J. H. Merrifield to Rev. George Whipple, 26 July 1864, Baton Rouge, LA, AMA, microfilm, Reel 1 [45532].

85. *Report of the Superintendent of Public Education to the General Assembly of the State of Louisiana* (New Orleans: J. O. Nixon, State Printer, 1867), 10–11.

86. Circular No. 3, Office of the State Superintendent of Public Education, June 2, 1866, in *Report of the Superintendent of Public Education* (1867), 16.

87. *Report of the Superintendent of Public Education* (1867), 10.

88. Circular No. 4, Office of the State Superintendent of Public Education, July 2, 1866, in *Report of the Superintendent of Public Education* (1867), 17–18.

89. For summary and analysis of the historiographical debate over the origins of segregation, see John W. Cell, *The Highest Stage of White Supremacy: The Origins of Segregation in South Africa and the American South* (Cambridge: Cambridge University Press, 1982), chap. 4.

90. Harlan, "Desegregation in New Orleans Public Schools," 673–675.

91. Everett, "Demands of the New Orleans Free Colored Population," 55–56. On the composition of black leadership in New Orleans, see Rankin, "The Origins of Black Leadership in New Orleans during Reconstruction," 420–422.

92. *New Orleans Tribune,* December 6, 1864.

93. *New Orleans Tribune,* December 27, 29, 1864.

94. Cossé Bell, " '*Une Chimère,*' " 148; Cossé Bell, *Revolution, Romanticism, and the Afro-Creole Protest Tradition, 1718–1868* (Baton Rouge: Louisiana State University Press, 1997), 278. Similar land reform was proposed later by the short-lived Unification movement in Louisiana, a platform built on biracial political compromise that aimed to return the state government to "home rule" (ejecting the Republican "carpetbagger" legislature) while supporting the rights of blacks. T. Harry Williams, "The Louisiana Unification Movement of 1873," *Journal of Southern History* 11 (August 1945): 350–353.

95. *Acts of Louisiana,* 1865, sec. 18.

96. Houzeau, *My Passage at the New Orleans Tribune,* 71–72; Cossé Bell, *Revolution, Romanticism, and the Afro-Creole Protest Tradition in Louisiana,* 252–258; Cossé Bell, " '*Une Chimère,*' " 143. On Trévigne's many accomplishments, see R. L. Desdunes, *Nos hommes et notre histoire: Notices biographiques accompagneés de reflexions et de souvenirs personnels, hommage à la population créole, en souvenir des grands hommes qu'elle a produits et des bonnes choses qu'elle a accomplies* (Montreal: Arbour and Dupont, 1911), 90–93, published in translation as Rodolphe Lucien Desdunes, *Our People and Our History,* trans. Sister Dorothea Olga McCants (Baton Rouge: Louisiana State University Press, 1973), 66–68; subsequent citations will give page numbers for both editions.

97. *New Orleans Tribune,* February 17, 1865.

98. Ibid.

99. *New Orleans Tribune,* March 5, 1865.

100. On the riots in Memphis and New Orleans, see Rable, *But There Was No Peace,* chaps. 3–4; Cossé Bell, *Revolution, Romanticism, and the Afro-Creole Protest Tradition in Louisiana,* 261–264; Foner, *Reconstruction,* 261–264, 271–291.

101. Vincent, "Black Constitution Makers," 73–79; *Constitution Adopted by the State Constitutional Convention of the State of Louisiana March 7, 1868* (New Orleans: New Orleans Republican, 1868).

102. Vincent, "Black Constitution Makers," 74; Cossé Bell, " '*Une Chimère,*' " 143; Cossé Bell, *Revolution, Romanticism, and the Afro-Creole Protest Tradition in Louisiana,* chap. 7.

103. *Constitution Adopted by the State Constitutional Convention of the State of Louisiana March 7, 1868,* art. 135.

104. *Official Journal of the Proceeding of the Convention for Framing a Constitution for the State of Louisiana* (New Orleans: J.B. Roudanez & Co. Printers to the Convention, 1867–1868), 201.

105. *Official Journal of the Proceeding of the Convention,* 289; Vincent, "Black Constitution Makers," 78–79.

106. Roger Fischer, *The Segregation Struggle in Louisiana, 1862–1877*

(Urbana: University of Illinois Press, 1974), 30–41; Olsen, *The Thin Disguise,* 31–36.

107. Valentine to J. R. Slawson, Esq., Memphis, Ten., February 14, 1861, Catholic Institution Letterbook II, AANO, p. 174.

108. "Two Tests," *New Orleans Tribune,* July 31, 1867.

109. *New Orleans Tribune,* July 31, 1867.

110. Ibid.

111. *New Orleans Tribune,* October 24, 1867.

112. *New Orleans Daily Picayune,* August 13, 1868.

113. "Report of the Committee on Colored Schools," Minutes of the New Orleans School Board, September 16, 1867, vol. 7, pp. 203–236, Special Collections, Earl K. Long Library, University of New Orleans (hereafter UNO); DeVore and Logsdon, *Crescent City Schools,* 66.

114. DeVore and Logsdon, *Crescent City Schools,* 67.

115. "Report of the Committee on Colored Schools," Minutes of the New Orleans School Board, September 16, 1867, vol. 7, p. 205, UNO.

116. Ibid. Historian Howard Rabinowitz has argued that freedpeople suffered segregation in public services in order to avoid total exclusion. See Rabinowitz, *Race Relations in the Urban South,* passim.

117. *New York Times,* December 15, 1867, 5.

118. Louisiana Educational Association, "The Question of Mixed Schools," September/October 1867, AMA, microfilm, Reel 1 [45720]. Edmonia Highgate taught in Vermillionville, Louisiana, the previous year. She was recommended to the local agent as a teacher whose "whole soul is in the cause of her race." 1st Lt. & Genl. Supt. of Education Frank R. Chase to Capt. S. W. Purchase, 13 Sept. 1866, Registered Letters Received, ser. 1919, vol. 485, box 31, Vermillionville, LA, Asst. Subasst. Comr., RG 105, BRFAL. She seems to have been supported by the AMA, however. It was to Rev. Whipple at the AMA that she reported having been shot at twice "in my room" but wrote that despite this opposition to her school, "God has wondrously spared me." Edmonia G. Highgate to Rev. George Whipple, 17 Dec. 1866, Vermillionville, LA, AMA, microfilm, Reel 1 [45702].

119. *Constitution of the State of Louisiana* (1868), art. 135; *Official Journal* (1867–1868), 306. The same convention also provided for equal accommodation in public facilities. Cossé Bell, *Revolution, Romanticism, and the Afro-Creole Protest Traditions in Louisiana,* 272; Fischer, *The Segregation Struggle in Louisiana,* 53–60.

120. Wm. O. Rogers, Supt. to Madame S. Bigot, Principal of Bayou Road School, 7 May 1868, Minutes of the New Orleans School Board, vol. 7, p. 322., UNO; Mdme S. Bigot to Wm. O. Rogers, 21 May 1868, Minutes of the New Orleans School Board, vol. 7, pp. 322–323, UNO.

121. "Resolution Preventing Colored Children to Enter the White Schools," Minutes of the New Orleans School Board, vol. 7, p. 327, 21 May 1868, UNO, emphasis added.

122. Circular, 23 May 1868, Minutes of the New Orleans School Board, vol. 5a, p. 298, UNO.

123. Wm. O. Rogers to Mr. Dauphine, 8 June 1868, Minutes of the New Orleans School Board, vol. 5a, pp. 308–309, UNO; Wm. O. Rogers to Mr. Edmunds, 8 June 1868, Minutes of the New Orleans School Board, vol. 5a, p. 308, UNO. A common means of discerning someone's race in the antebellum South was according to the testimony of neighbors, though this, of course, was a process fraught with bias and inconsistency. See Hodes, *White Women, Black Men*, chap. 5. Historically, documentation of a person's race in Louisiana has been an intricate and even dangerous process. If the children were baptized in the Catholic Church, their baptismal records would not have provided sure evidence of their race. On the complexities of racial categorization in Louisiana, see Virginia R. Domínguez, *White by Definition: Social Classification in Creole Louisiana* (New Brunswick, NJ: Rutgers University Press, 1994), esp. chap. 2.

124. *New Orleans Tribune*, February 14, 1869.

125. DeVore and Logsdon, *Crescent City Schools*, 69–70.

126. *New Orleans Daily Picayune*, January 12, 1871; DeVore and Logsdon, *Crescent City Schools*, 354–355.

127. *New Orleans Daily Picayune*, November 24, 1870.

128. *New Orleans Daily Picayune*, January 4, 1872.

129. *New Orleans Daily Picayune*, October 19, 1872.

130. Cell, *The Highest State of White Supremacy*, chap. 6.

131. The Republican-controlled school board did not designate the city's schools by racial composition in the years 1870 to 1877, so exact numbers are difficult to figure. DeVore and Logsdon, *Crescent City Schools*, 70.

132. Ibid.

133. George W. Cable, *The Negro Question*, ed. Arlin Turner (New York: Doubleday, 1958), 9. Cable's essay "My Politics" was published in 1889. Cable became a strong supporter of integrated schools and wrote letters to the editors of the New Orleans Democratic papers in the vain hope of convincing white Democrats of their shortsightedness. See Cable, *The Negro Question*, 26–33.

134. Conway to the editor of the *Washington National Republican*, in *Washington New National Era*, June 4, 1874, quoted in Harlan, "Desegregation in New Orleans Public Schools," 664.

135. *Congressional Globe*, 40th Cong., 1st sess. (March 16, 1867), 381.

136. Clement, *Growing Pains*, 106.

137. *Congressional Globe*, 40th Cong., 2nd sess. (May 13, 1868), 2449.

138. *Congressional Globe*, 42nd Cong., 2nd sess. (February 5, 1872), 819.

139. Ibid.

140. On the joint development of white fears of black sexual predation and Jim Crow, see Hodes, *White Women, Black Men,* pt. 2.

141. *Congressional Globe,* 42nd Cong., 2nd sess. (February 6, 1872), 856.

142. Ibid., 858.

143. Ibid.

144. *Congressional Record,* 43rd Cong., 1st sess. (May 22, 1874), 4144.

145. Ibid., 4173.

146. Alfred H. Kelly, "The Congressional Controversy over School Segregation, 1867–1875," *American Historical Review* 64 (April 1959): 561.

147. George W. Cable, *Strange True Stories of Louisiana* (New York: Scribner's, 1890), 224–226; DeVore and Logsdon, *Crescent City Schools,* 76.

148. *New Orleans Republican,* December 18, 1874. See also Christian, "A Black History of Louisiana," 23–28, Marcus Christian Collection, UNO.

149. *New Orleans Republican,* December 18, 1874; Marcus Christian, "A Black History," chap. 32, pp. 23–28, Marcus Christian Collection, UNO.

150. *Annual Report of the State Superintendent of Public Education . . . to the General Assembly of Louisiana for the Year 1875* (Baton Rouge: State Superintendent of Public Education Printed at the Republican Office, 1876), 161; Christian, "A Black History," chap. 32, p. 28, Marcus Christian Collection, UNO.

151. "Color in the New Orleans Schools," *Harper's Weekly,* February 13, 1875, 147–148.

152. *New Orleans Times,* January 12, 1875, p. 2, cols. 3–4, WPA, UNO.

153. *New Orleans Bulletin,* December 15, 1874, in *The Annual Report of the State Superintendent of Education, 1875.*

154. *New Orleans Weekly Times,* November 11, 1875, p. 4, cols. 1–2; Christian, "A Black History," chap. 32, p. 28, Marcus Christian Collection, UNO.

155. Harlan, "Desegregation in New Orleans Public Schools during Reconstruction," 666.

156. *Annual Report of the State Superintendent of Public Education . . . to the General Assembly for the Year 1877* (New Orleans: Office of the Democrat, 1878), 303.

157. Foner, *Reconstruction,* chap. 12.

158. DeVore and Logsdon, *Crescent City Schools,* 81.

159. Wm. O. Rogers, Superintendent New Orleans Public Schools to J. T. Leath, Esq., Superintendent, Memphis, Tenn., 23 July 1877, Minutes of the New Orleans School Board, vol. 5a, pp. 402–403, UNO.

160. *Annual Report of the State Superintendent of Public Education . . . 1877,* iv–v.

161. According to Rodolphe Desdunes, this led to the decline of the Catholic Institution for several years until it was revived in the 1880s, in the aftermath of the segregation struggle. Rodolphe Desdunes, *Nos hommes et notre histoire,* 192; *Our People and Our History,* 107.

162. *Annual Report of the State Superintendent of Public Education . . . for the Year 1877.*

163. DeVore and Logsdon, *Crescent City Schools,* 87–88; Cossé Bell, *Revolution, Romanticism, and the Afro-Creole Protest Tradition in Louisiana,* 280.

164. *New Orleans Tribune,* February 14, 1869.

165. Brief of Appellant, Paul Trévigne versus School Board et al., No. 6832, Supreme Court of Louisiana, filed 12 December 1878, Supreme Court of Louisiana Collection, UNO.

166. Paul Trévigne vs. School Board and Wm O. Rogers, No. 9545, 6th District Court, Orleans Parish, State of Louisiana, filed 22 November 1877, Supreme Court of Louisiana Collection, UNO.

167. Paul Trévigne v. School Board and W. O. Rogers, New Orleans (1879) 31, La. Ann. 105, Docket No. 6832, *Reports of Cases Argued and Determined in the Supreme Court of Louisiana and in the Superior Court of the Territory of Louisiana,* annotated ed., Book 38, vol. 31 (St. Paul, MN: West Publishing, 1908), 70–71; DeVore and Logsdon, *Crescent City Schools,* 88–89.

168. Arnold Bertonneau v. The Board of Directors of City Schools, et al., U.S. District Court (5th District), November 1878, *Cases Argued and Determined before the Circuit Courts of the United States for the Fifth Judicial District* [1870–1883].

169. State ex rel. Ursin Dellande v. New Orleans School Board, No. 7500, Supreme Court of the State of Louisiana, Supreme Court of Louisiana Collection, UNO.

170. Ex Rel Ursin Dellande v. City School Board, No. 9784, 6th District Court, Orleans Parish, State of Louisiana, Supreme Court of Louisiana Collection, UNO.

171. For similar kinds of imaginings in the late nineteenth century, see Hale, *Making Whiteness,* passim.

172. Desdunes, *Nos hommes et notre histoire,* 179; *Our People and Our History,* 135.

173. Desdunes, *Nos hommes et notre histoire,* 181; *Our People Our History,* 137–138.

174. State ex rel. Ursin Dellande v. New Orleans School Board, No. 7500, Supreme Court of the State of Louisiana, Supreme Court of Louisiana Collection, UNO.

175. See Barbara Jeanne Fields, "Slavery, Race, and Ideology in the United States of America," *New Left Review* 181 (May/June 1990): 95–118.

176. Sundquist, *To Wake the Nations*, 398.

177. Louis R. Harlan, *Separate and Unequal: Public School Campaigns and Racism in the Southern Seaboard States, 1901–1915* (New York: Atheneum, 1968), 11–13.

178. On the complicated legacy of the *Brown* decision, see "Round Table: Brown v. Board of Education, Fifty Years After," *Journal of American History* 91 (June 2004): 19–118.

179. Brief of Homer Plessy, *Files Copies of Briefs 1895*, VIII (October term, 1895), in Olsen, *A Thin Disguise*, 85.

180. Desdunes was six years younger than Grégoire, entering the Catholic Institution in 1855, at the age of six. *Journal des Séances de la direction de l'institution Catholique pour l'instruction des Orphelins dans l'indigence*, 5 Septembre 1855, p. 1, AANO. See also Joseph Logsdon and Lawrence Powell, "Rodolphe Lucien Desdunes: Forgotten Organizer of the *Plessy* Protest," in Sam Hyde, ed., *Sunbelt Revolution: The Historical Progression of the Civil Rights Struggle in the Gulf South, 1866–2000* (Gainesville: University Press of Florida, 2003), 42–70; and Lester Sullivan, "The Unknown Rodolphe Desdunes: Writings in the New Orleans *Crusader*," *Xavier Review* 10 (1990): 1–17.

181. Desdunes, *Nos hommes et notre histoire*, 90–91; *Our People and Our History*, 66–68. On the *Crusader*, see Sullivan, "The Unknown Rodolphe Desdunes," and Rebecca J. Scott, *Degrees of Freedom: Louisiana and Cuba after Slavery* (Cambridge, MA: Belknap/Harvard University Press, 2005), 3.

182. 30 Decembre 1869, *Journal des Séances de la Société Catholique pour l'Instruction des Orphelins dans l'Indigence commence le 23 de avril 1859*, AANO: "Nous avons visité l'école et l'avons trouvée dans un état de misère pitoyable, sans livres, sans [illg] enfin manquant de tout. La sale des classes des desmoiselles, sans vitres aux chassis, le tout coulant affreusement durant les pluies continuelles, les plafonds crevasses partout."

183. Petition of Francis C. Levray, Archbishop, to the Honorable Judges of the Civil District Court of the Parish of Orleans, 1885(?), AANO.

184. Roger Baudier, Sr., "The Story of St. Louis School of Holy Redeemer Parish, New Orleans, LA., Formerly St. Louis School for the Colored, l'Institution Catholique pour l'Instruction des Orphelins dans l'Indigence, Widow Couvent's School, 1847–1956," unpublished ms., AANO.

185. 2 Novembre 1854 and 4 Mai 1853, *Séance Extraordinaire, Journal des Séances de la Société Catholique pour l'Instruction des Orphelins dans l'Indigence commence le 26 de Avril, 1851*, AANO.

186. Desdunes, *Nos hommes et notre histoire*, 185, 192; *Our People and Our History*, 147.

NOTES TO THE CONCLUSION

1. James D. Anderson, *The Education of Blacks in the South, 1860–1935* (Chapel Hill: University of North Carolina Press, 1988), chaps. 2–3; Michele Mitchell, *Righteous Propagation: African Americans and the Politics of Racial Destiny after Reconstruction* (Chapel Hill: University of North Carolina Press, 2004), passim.

2. Anderson, *The Education of Blacks in the South*, 92; Shelley Sallee, *The Whiteness of Child Labor Reform in the New South* (Athens: University of Georgia Press, 2004), 1, 5–10.

3. According to historian Heather Richardson, in the imaginations of many northerners, freedpeople became emblematic of late nineteenth-century political corruption and fears of Populism, socialism, and communism. See Heather Cox Richardson, *The Death of Reconstruction: Race, Labor, and Politics in the Post–Civil War North, 1865–1901* (Cambridge, MA: Harvard University Press, 2001), xv and chap. 6.

4. Rodolphe Lucien Desdunes, *A Few Words to Dr. Du Bois with Malice toward None* (New Orleans, 1907), Tulane University, Amistad Research Center, Alexander Pierre Tureaud Papers, 1909–1972, Roll 57, folder 38, No. 1063. See also Joseph Logsdon, "Rodolphe Lucien Desdunes: The Franco-American Ideology of a New Orleans Creole," unpublished paper, Ethel and Herman Midlo Center for New Orleans Studies, University of New Orleans. Du Bois later wrote about the long tradition of Creole protest in his landmark book *Black Reconstruction in America, 1860–1880* (1935), but he made no mention of Desdunes's history of the Afro-Creoles, published in 1911, in his bibliography. In the journal the *Crisis*, in 1934, he did praise the Afro-Creoles as having "the longest history in modern culture of any group of Negro descent in the United States." W. E. B. Du Bois, "A Journey to Texas and New Orleans," *Crisis* (April 1934), quoted in Logsdon, "Rodolphe Lucien Desdunes," 5.

5. W. E. B. Du Bois, *The Souls of Black Folk* (New York: Bantam Books, 1989 [1903]), 150. There is no doubt that the history of race relations in the United States has become more complicated since the late nineteenth century, after generations of global immigration to this country. The struggle for racial equality, nationally, has long ceased to be simply black versus white. But in much of the South, and most certainly in New Orleans, Du Bois's words remain relevant.

Index

Abell, Edmund, 195, 196, 198

abolitionism: civilizing the South, 99–100, 108; conventional symbols, assumptions, 261n10; fear of ex-slave rebellion, 96; free families compared to and slave families, 155; freedpeople, 207; gradual emancipation, 261n12; *The Greek Slave,* 76–77; labor contracts, 154; middle-class domesticity, 67; middle class origins, 250n19; photographs of freedpeople, 58, 72; photographs of white-looking children, 72; racial equality, 207; relationships between black and white childhood, 69–70; sexuality of southern slaveholders, 81; *Uncle Tom's Cabin,* 21; white-skinned slave girls, 55, 56, 74–75, 91; white slavery (enslavement of whites), 60

ACS. *See* American Colonization Society

Adam (freedchild), 160

Africa: American Missionary Association in, 111; American readers' fascination with, 111; emigration to, 23–24, 25; European imperialism in, 94; mission schools, 105–106

African colonization, 23–24

Afro-Creoles, 190–193, 206–209; aspirations for equality, 12; Catholic Institution, 18, 223, 229; Civil War, 43, 209; definition, 9; Du Bois and, 232; education and, 190–192, 206–207; emigration movement, 26; emigration to Haiti, 12–13, 36–41, 44–45; emigration to Mexico, 12, 29–36; freedpeople, alliance with, 206–207; identification with broader Atlantic community, 12; integrated schools, 206–207; intellectual accomplishments, 9; legal challenges to

postbellum segregation of the South, 193, 226, 228; in Louisiana state legislature, 208–209; on New Orleans school board, 216, 224; *New Orleans Tribune,* 206; *Plessy v. Ferguson,* 10, 192–193; political activism, 9, 18; public schools, 190–192, 229; during Reconstruction, 191; representativeness of, 9; Republican Party, 206; three-tiered school system, 223–224; and transAtlantic community, 12; vision of the future, 228, 230

Agassiz, Louis, 66

Alabama, 161, 196

Alden, E. H., 132–133, 273n148

Alger, Horatio, *Ragged Dick,* 116

Alonzo (freedchild), 177

Alphonse (freedman), 164

Alvord, John W., 139

AMA. *See* American Missionary Association

American Colonization Society (ACS), 24–25, 58

American Freedman's Aid Commission, 101

American Freedmen's Inquiry Commission, 103

American Home Missionary Society, 189

American Missionary Association (AMA): abilities of mulatto and black children, 131–132; in Africa, 111; and civilizing, 129, 132–133; education of freedpeople, 101, 102; in Louisiana, 129; Louisiana Educational Association, 214; northern tour of freedpeople, 52; official organ of, 69

American Missionary (magazine): appearance of freedchildren in schools, 130;

About the Author

Mary Niall Mitchell is Assistant Professor of History at the University of New Orleans.